KA KI
SHOJO!!

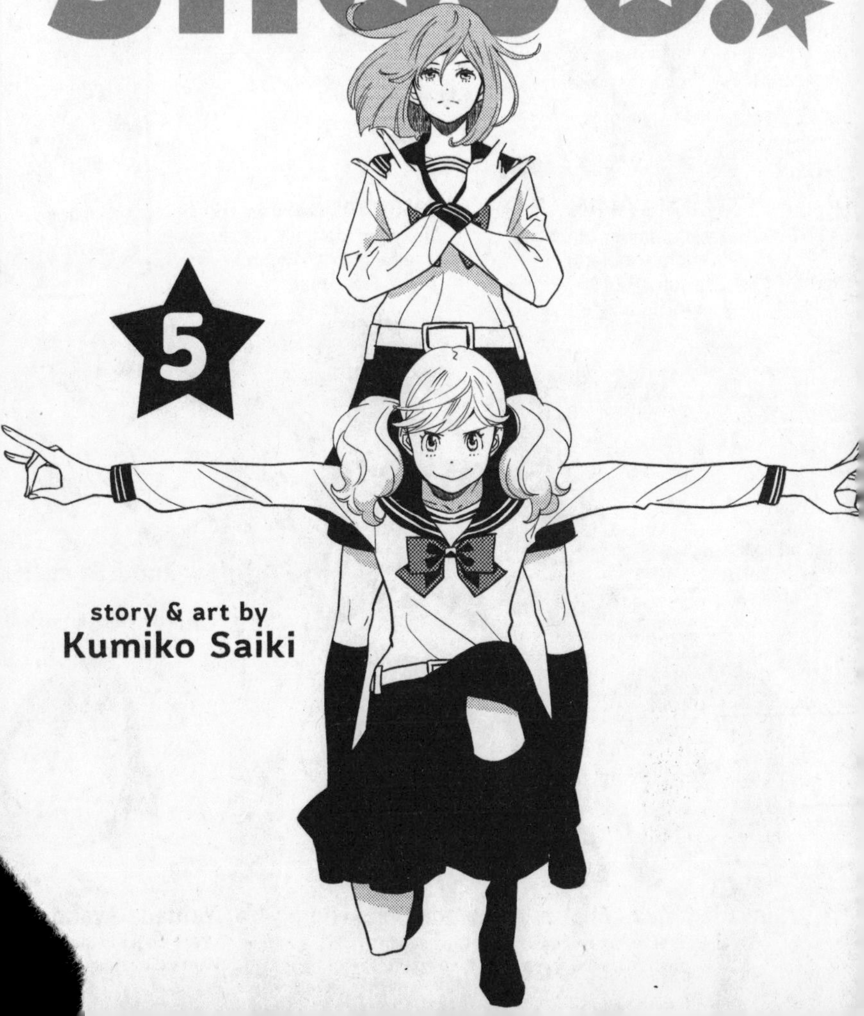

5

story & art by
Kumiko Saiki

Characters

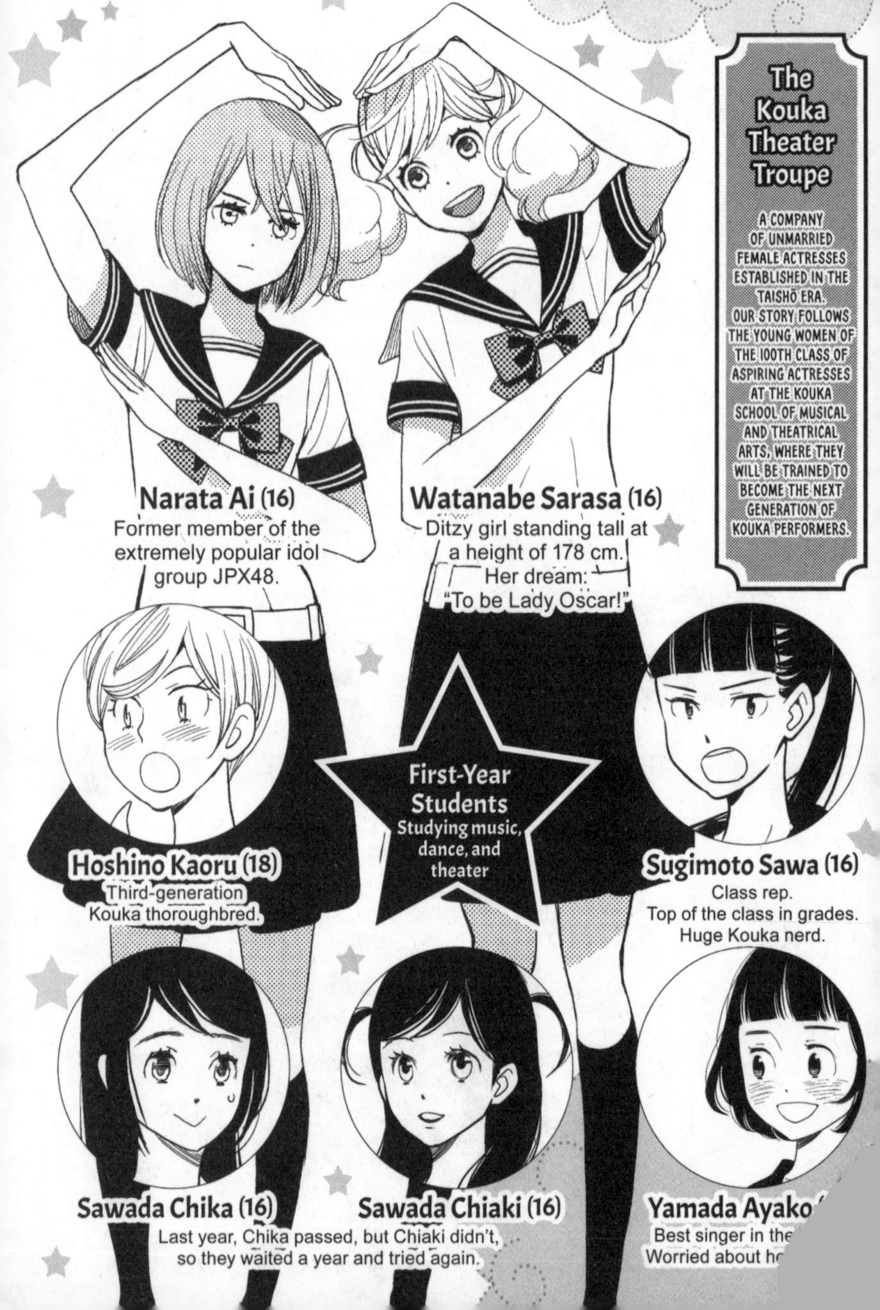
The Kouka Theater Troupe
A COMPANY OF UNMARRIED FEMALE ACTRESSES ESTABLISHED IN THE TAISHO ERA. OUR STORY FOLLOWS THE YOUNG WOMEN OF THE 100TH CLASS OF ASPIRING ACTRESSES AT THE KOUKA SCHOOL OF MUSICAL AND THEATRICAL ARTS, WHERE THEY WILL BE TRAINED TO BECOME THE NEXT GENERATION OF KOUKA PERFORMERS.
Watanabe Sarasa (16)
Ditzy girl standing tall at a height of 178 cm. Her dream: "To be Lady Oscar!"
Narata Ai (16)
Former member of the extremely popular idol group JPX48.
Sugimoto Sawa (16)
Class rep. Top of the class in grades. Huge Kouka nerd.
First-Year Students
Studying music, dance, and theater
Hoshino Kaoru (18)
Third-generation Kouka thoroughbred.
Yamada Ayako
Best singer in the
Worried about h
Sawada Chiaki (16)
Sawada Chika (16)
Last year, Chika passed, but Chiaki didn't, so they waited a year and tried again.

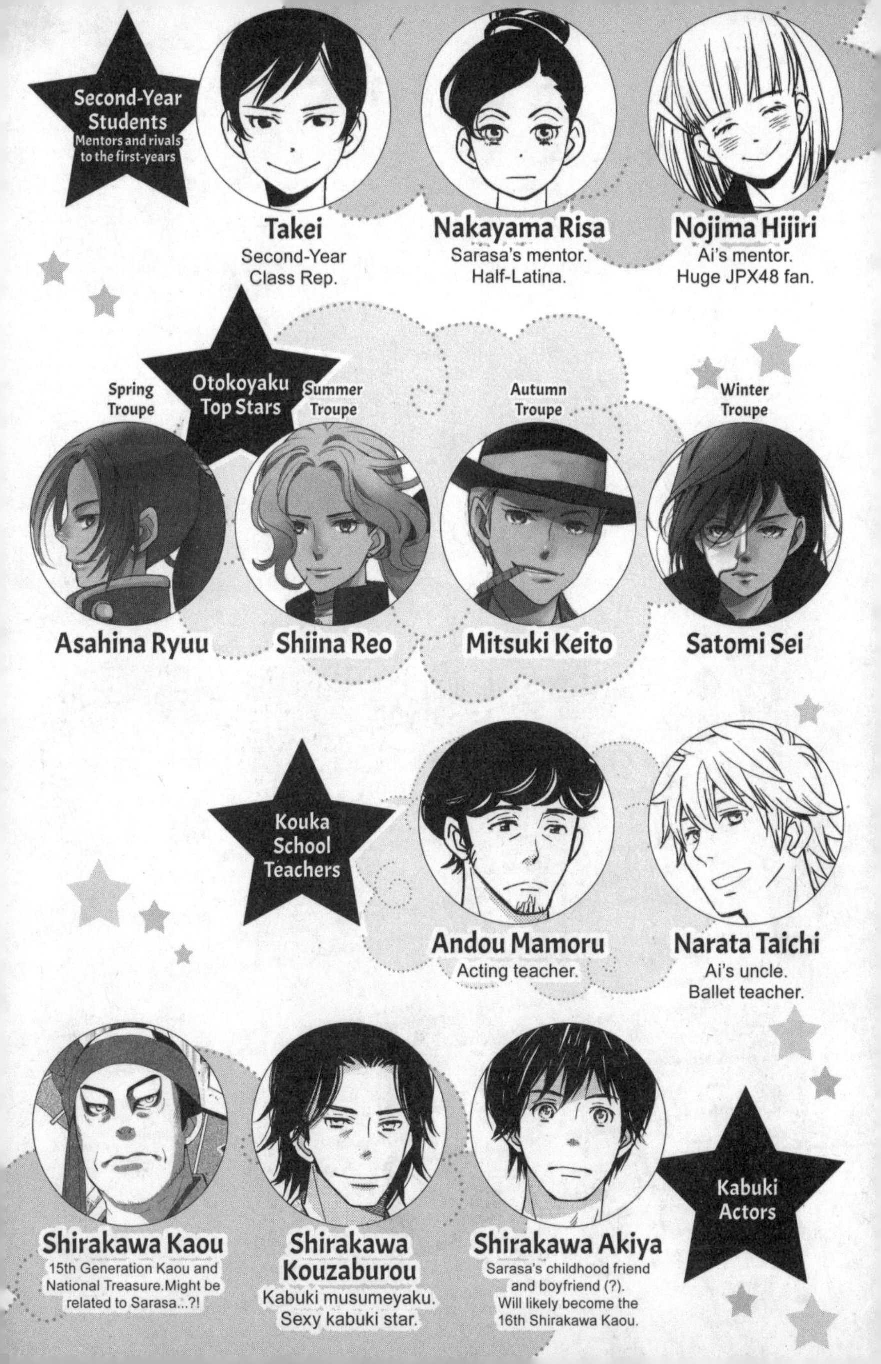
Second-Year Students
Mentors and rivals to the first-years
Takei
Second-Year Class Rep.
Nakayama Risa
Sarasa's mentor. Half-Latina.
Nojima Hijiri
Ai's mentor. Huge JPX48 fan.
Otokoyaku Top Stars
Spring Troupe
Summer Troupe
Autumn Troupe
Winter Troupe
Asahina Ryuu
Shiina Reo
Mitsuki Keito
Satomi Sei
Kouka School Teachers
Andou Mamoru
Acting teacher.
Narata Taichi
Ai's uncle. Ballet teacher.
Kabuki Actors
Shirakawa Kaou
15th Generation Kaou and National Treasure.Might be related to Sarasa...?!
Shirakawa Kouzaburou
Kabuki musumeyaku. Sexy kabuki star.
Shirakawa Akiya
Sarasa's childhood friend and boyfriend (?). Will likely become the 16th Shirakawa Kaou.

CONTENTS

No.

Date

Kouka Troupe Terms to Know! ★

Kouka Theater Troupe
Founded a hundred years ago as a theater troupe comprised of young, unmarried women. Split into four troupes (Spring/Summer/Autumn/Winter). Main theater is in Kobe.

Otokoyaku / Musumeyaku
Designated roles for the gender of characters actresses play. Otokoyaku actresses play male or masculine characters, while musumeyaku actresses play female or feminine characters.

Top Star
The actress who heads her troupe. Each troupe has an otokoyaku top star and musumeyaku top star. Top stars appear in every major production.

Kouka School of Musical and Theatrical Arts
Two-year prep school where the next stars of the Kouka Troupe are forged. Girls can apply anytime between 9th and 12th grade!

First-Year Students vs. Second-Year Students
While first-year students primarily focus on their studies, second-year students are tasked both with their studies and mentoring the first-year students, as well as managing their cleaning schedule and helping them with lifestyle adjustments.

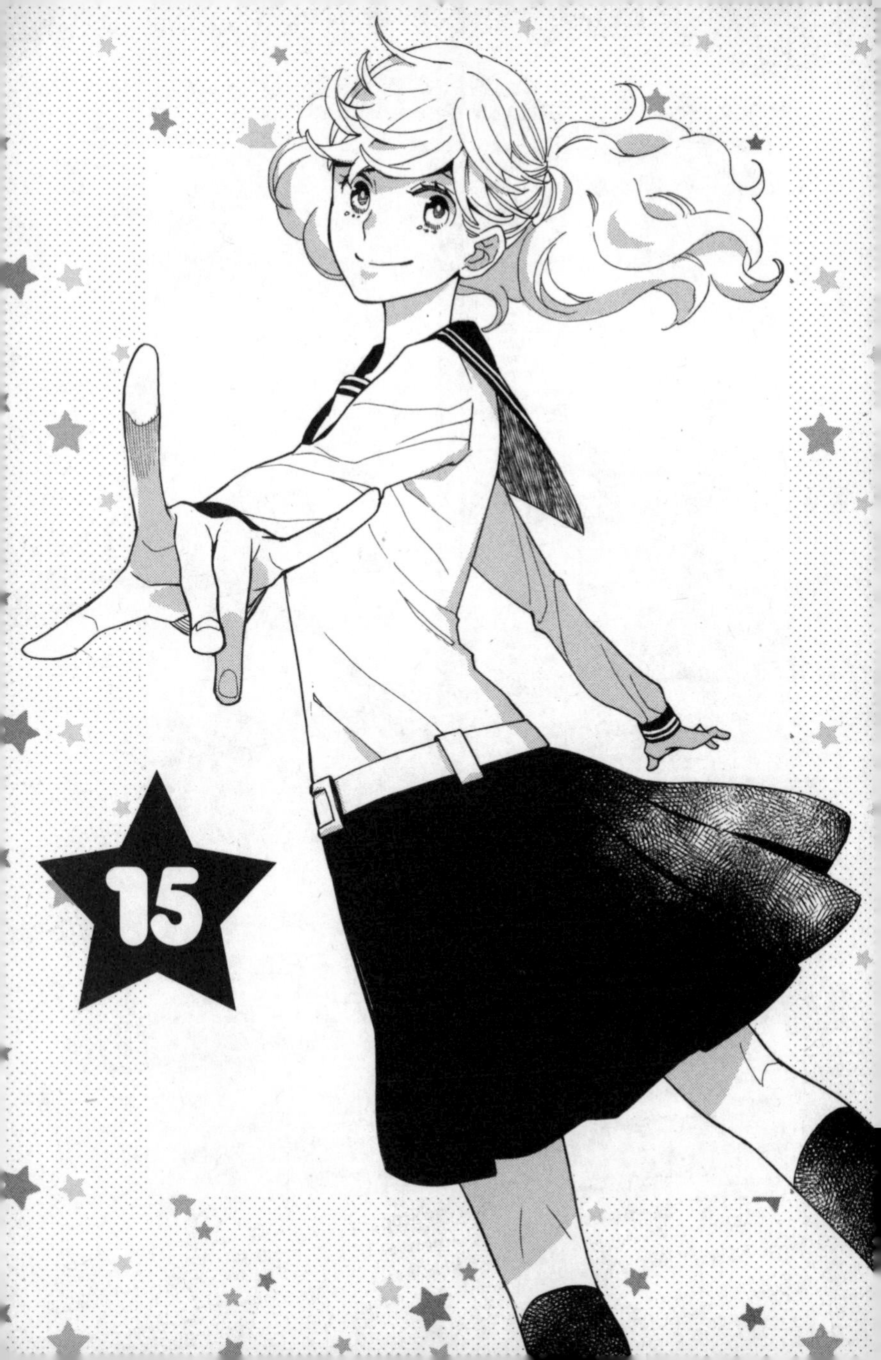
15

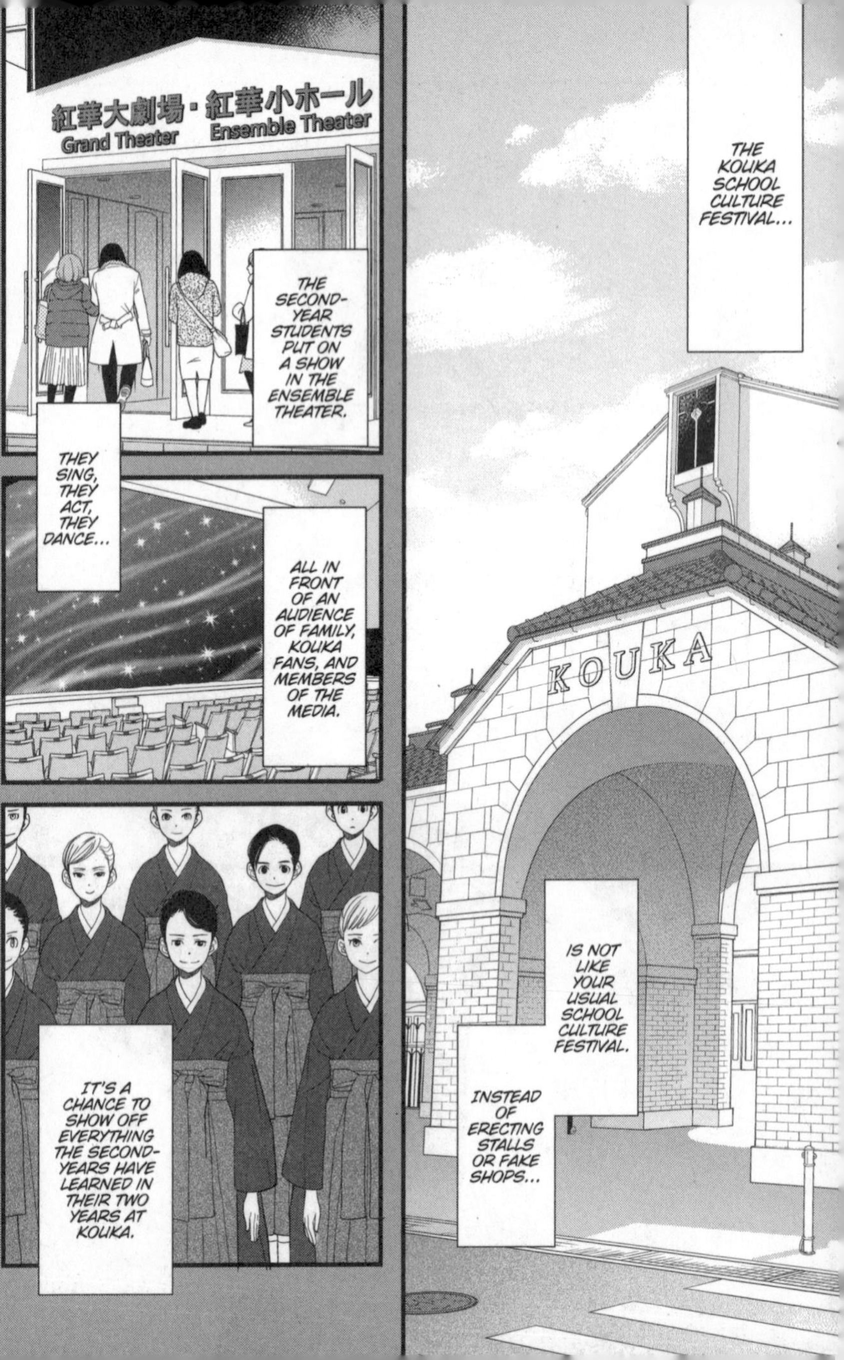
THE KOUKA SCHOOL CULTURE FESTIVAL...
KOUKA
IS NOT LIKE YOUR USUAL SCHOOL CULTURE FESTIVAL.
INSTEAD OF ERECTING STALLS OR FAKE SHOPS...
紅華大劇場・紅華小ホール
Grand Theater
Ensemble Theater
THE SECOND-YEAR STUDENTS PUT ON A SHOW IN THE ENSEMBLE THEATER.
THEY SING, THEY ACT, THEY DANCE...
ALL IN FRONT OF AN AUDIENCE OF FAMILY, KOUKA FANS, AND MEMBERS OF THE MEDIA.
IT'S A CHANCE TO SHOW OFF EVERYTHING THE SECOND-YEARS HAVE LEARNED IN THEIR TWO YEARS AT KOUKA.

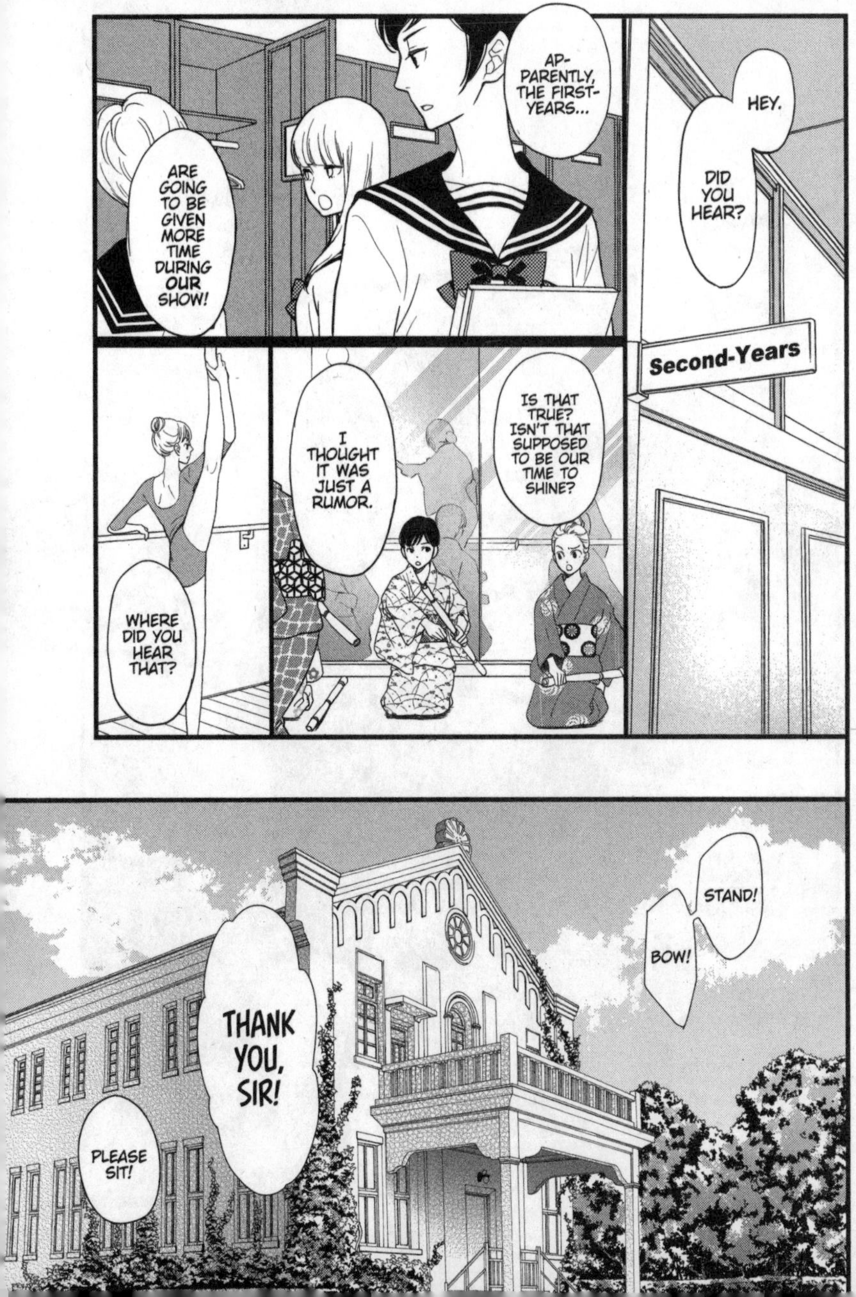
HEY.
DID YOU HEAR?
Second-Years
AP-PARENTLY, THE FIRST-YEARS...
ARE GOING TO BE GIVEN MORE TIME DURING OUR SHOW!
IS THAT TRUE? ISN'T THAT SUPPOSED TO BE OUR TIME TO SHINE?
I THOUGHT IT WAS JUST A RUMOR.
WHERE DID YOU HEAR THAT?
STAND!
BOW!
THANK YOU, SIR!
PLEASE SIT!

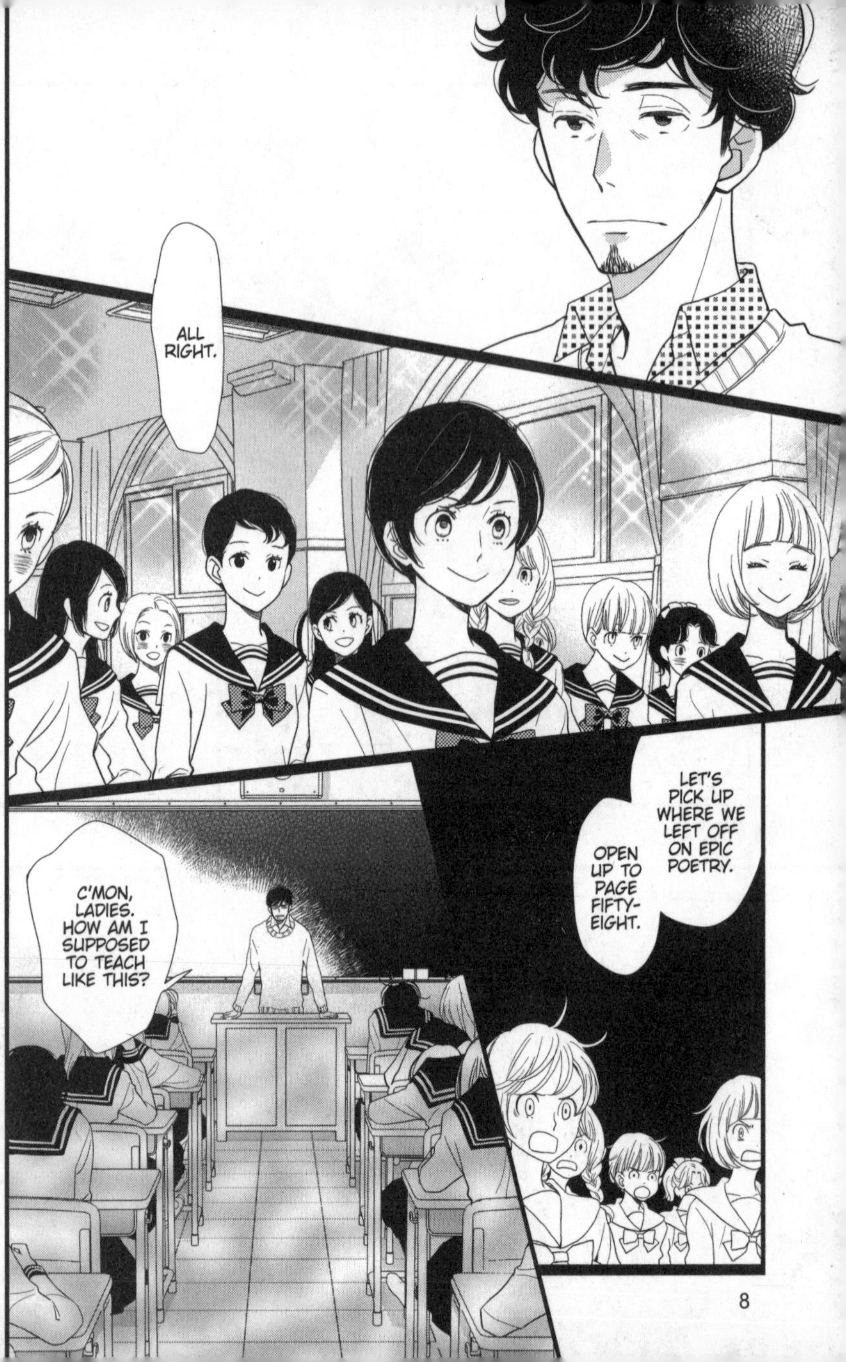
ALL RIGHT.
LET'S PICK UP WHERE WE LEFT OFF ON EPIC POETRY.
OPEN UP TO PAGE FIFTY-EIGHT.
C'MON, LADIES. HOW AM I SUPPOSED TO TEACH LIKE THIS?

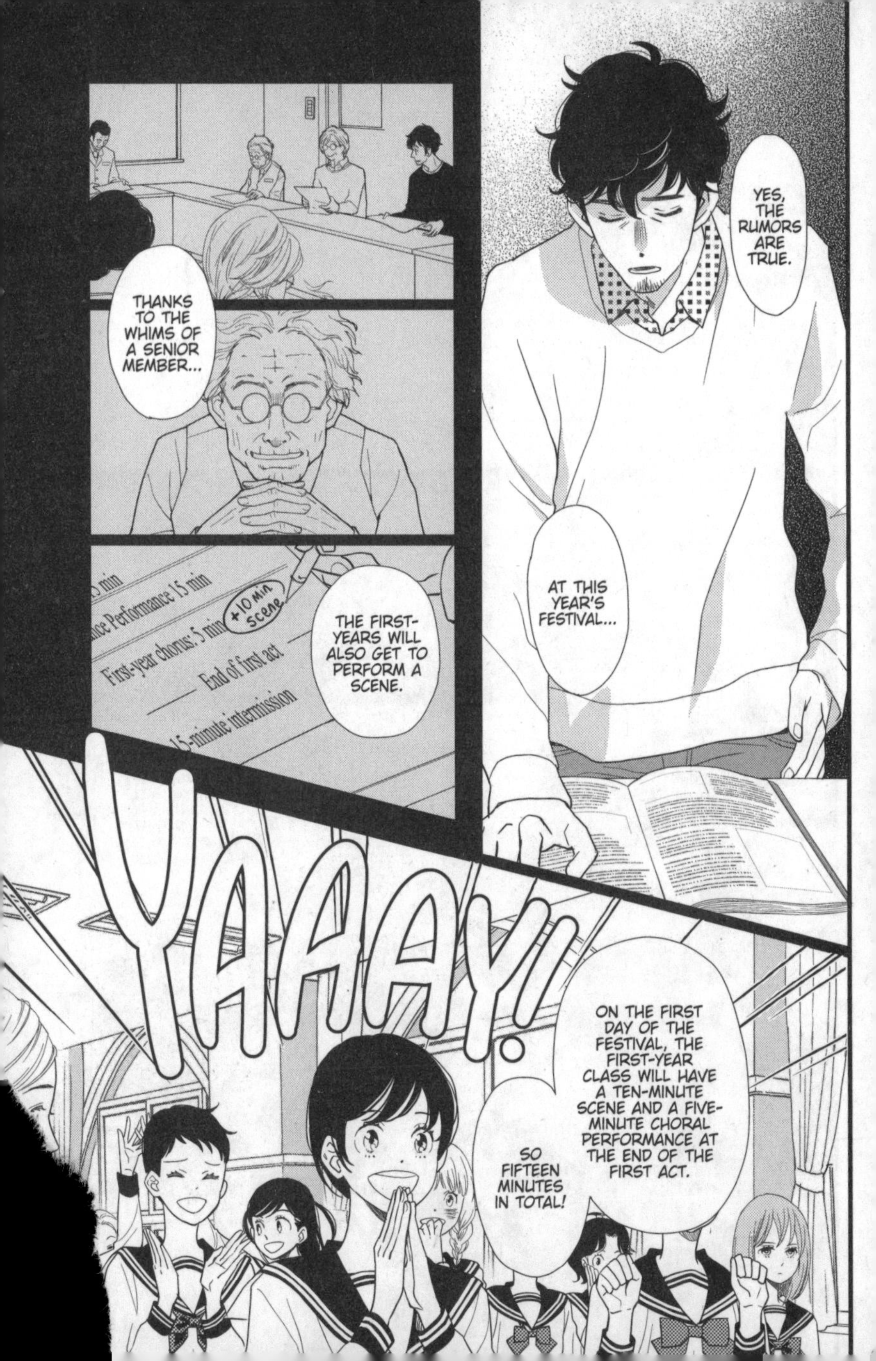
YES, THE RUMORS ARE TRUE.
AT THIS YEAR'S FESTIVAL...
THANKS TO THE WHIMS OF A SENIOR MEMBER...
ce Performance 15 min
First-year chorus: 5 min
+10 min scene
End of first act
15-minute intermission
THE FIRST-YEARS WILL ALSO GET TO PERFORM A SCENE.
YAAAY!
ON THE FIRST DAY OF THE FESTIVAL, THE FIRST-YEAR CLASS WILL HAVE A TEN-MINUTE SCENE AND A FIVE-MINUTE CHORAL PERFORMANCE AT THE END OF THE FIRST ACT.
SO FIFTEEN MINUTES IN TOTAL!

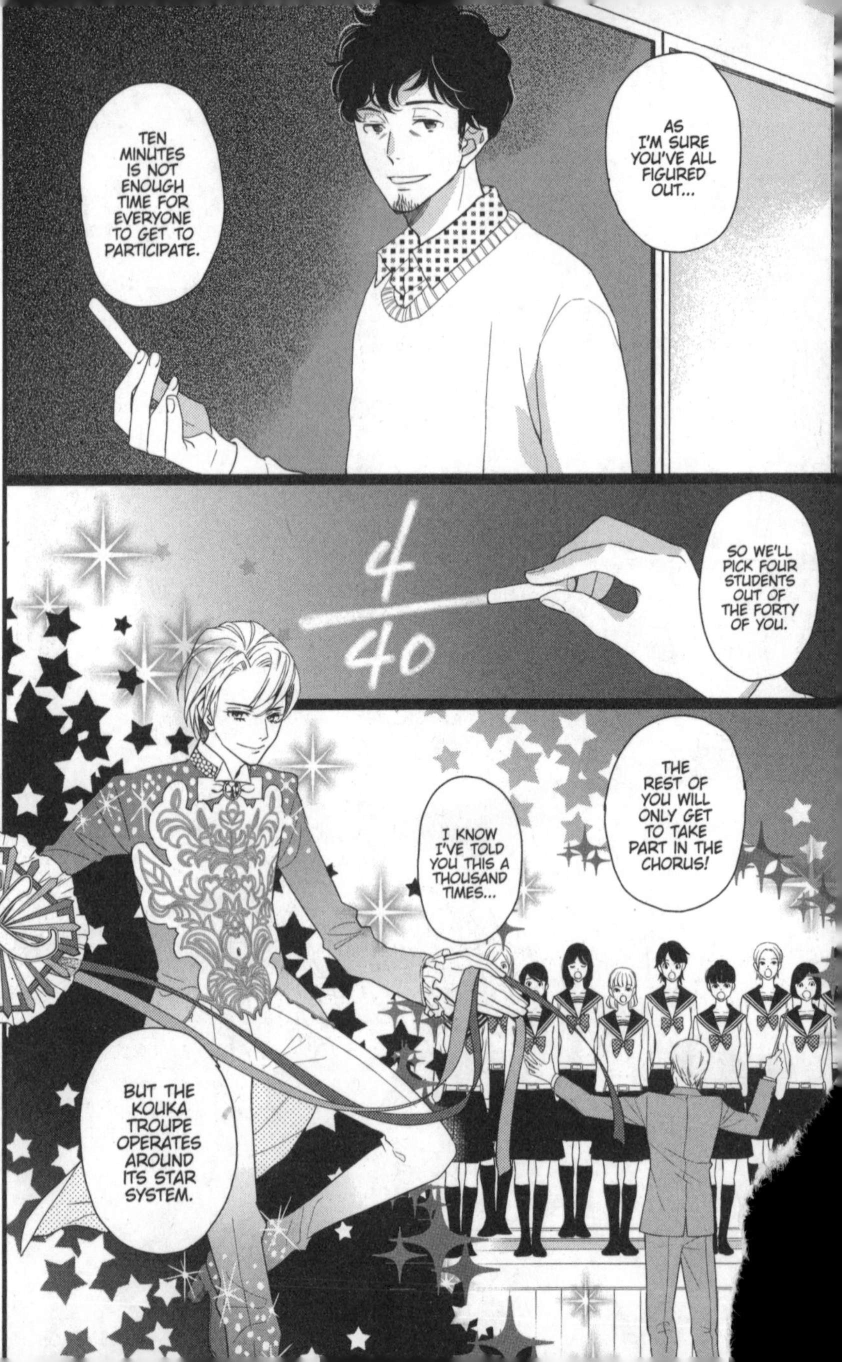
AS I'M SURE YOU'VE ALL FIGURED OUT...
TEN MINUTES IS NOT ENOUGH TIME FOR EVERYONE TO GET TO PARTICIPATE.
4
40
SO WE'LL PICK FOUR STUDENTS OUT OF THE FORTY OF YOU.
THE REST OF YOU WILL ONLY GET TO TAKE PART IN THE CHORUS!
I KNOW I'VE TOLD YOU THIS A THOUSAND TIMES...
BUT THE KOUKA TROUPE OPERATES AROUND ITS STAR SYSTEM.

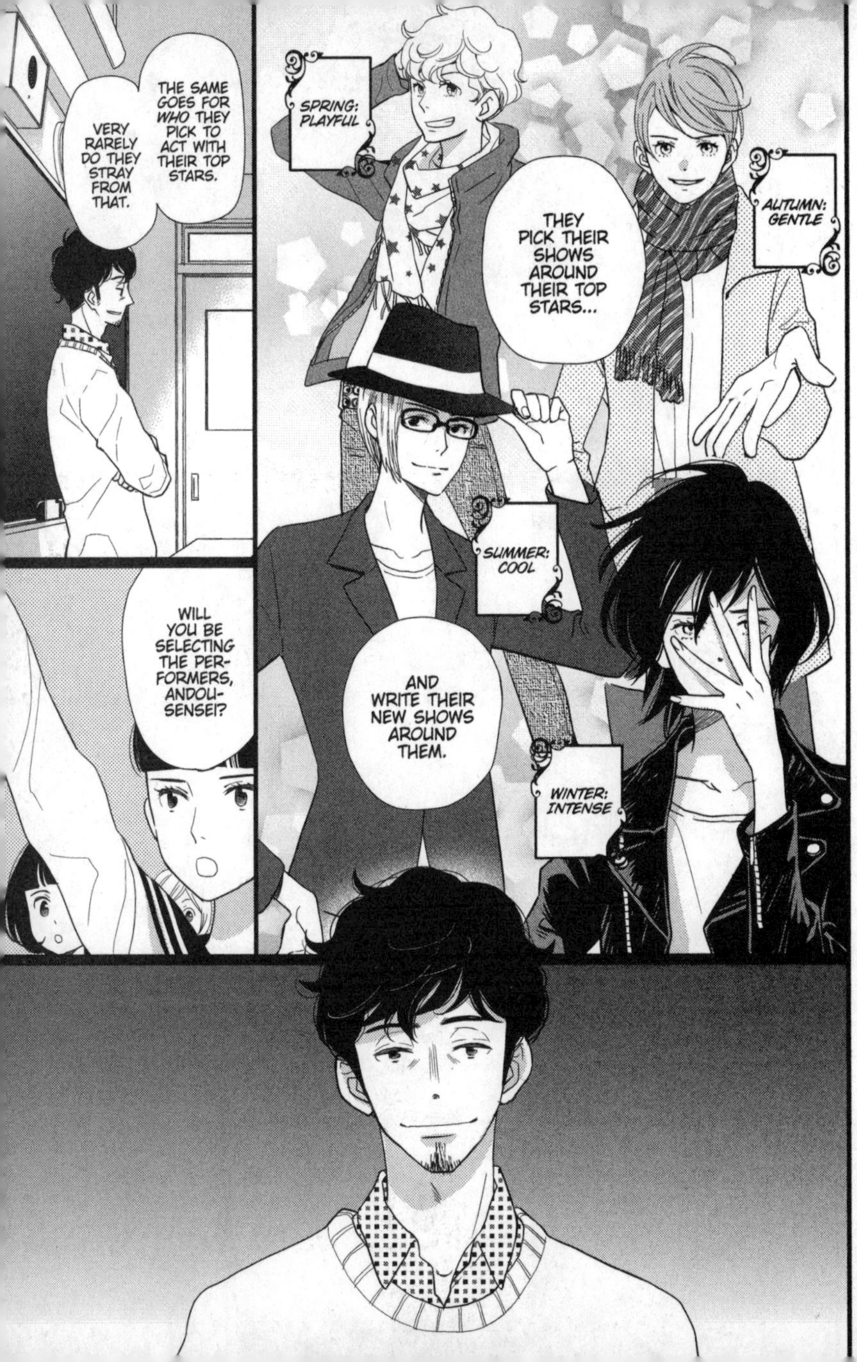
SPRING: PLAYFUL
AUTUMN: GENTLE
THEY PICK THEIR SHOWS AROUND THEIR TOP STARS...
SUMMER: COOL
AND WRITE THEIR NEW SHOWS AROUND THEM.
WINTER: INTENSE
THE SAME GOES FOR WHO THEY PICK TO ACT WITH THEIR TOP STARS.
VERY RARELY DO THEY STRAY FROM THAT.
WILL YOU BE SELECTING THE PER-FORMERS, ANDOU-SENSEI?

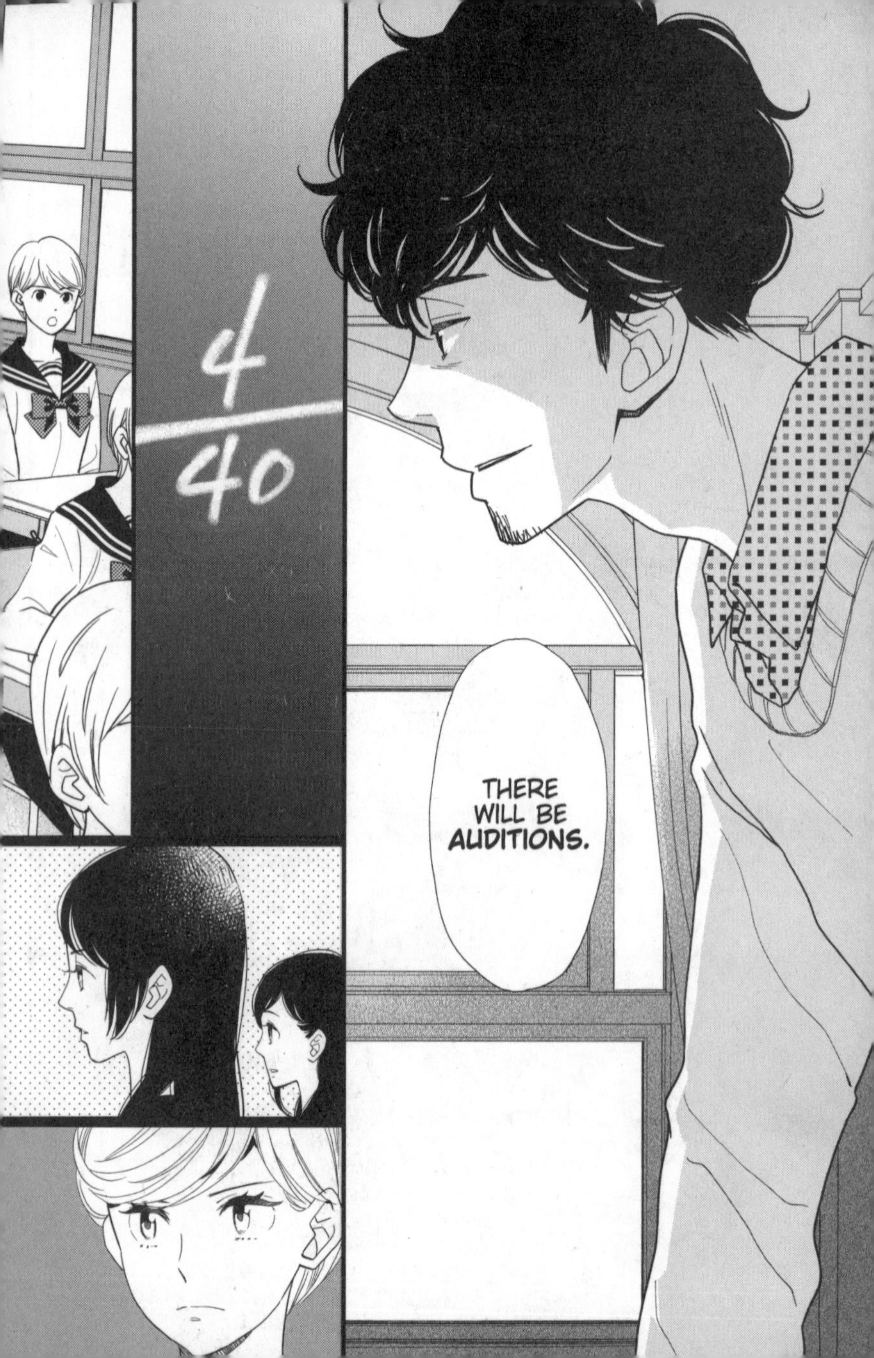
4/40
THERE WILL BE AUDITIONS.

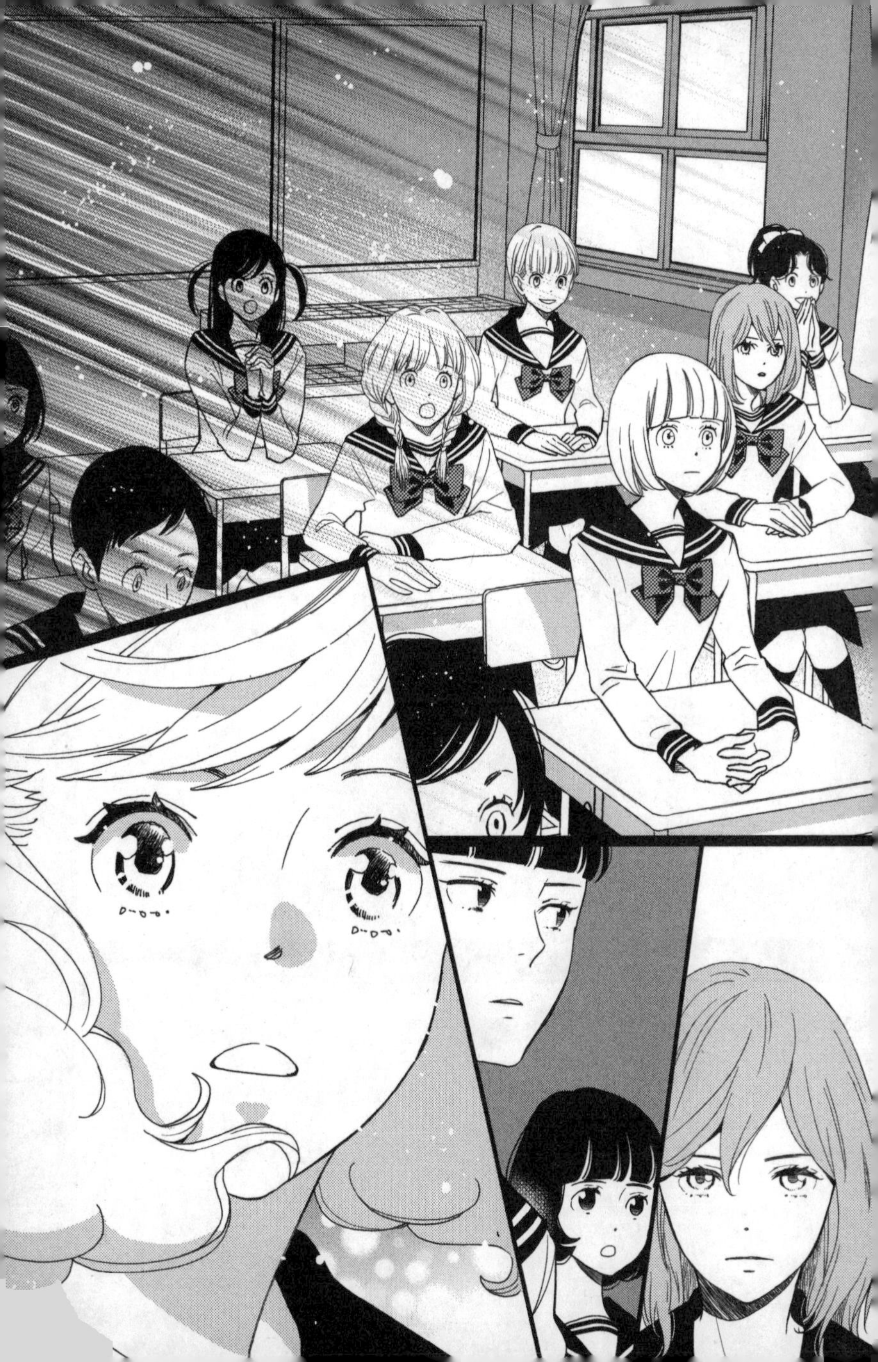

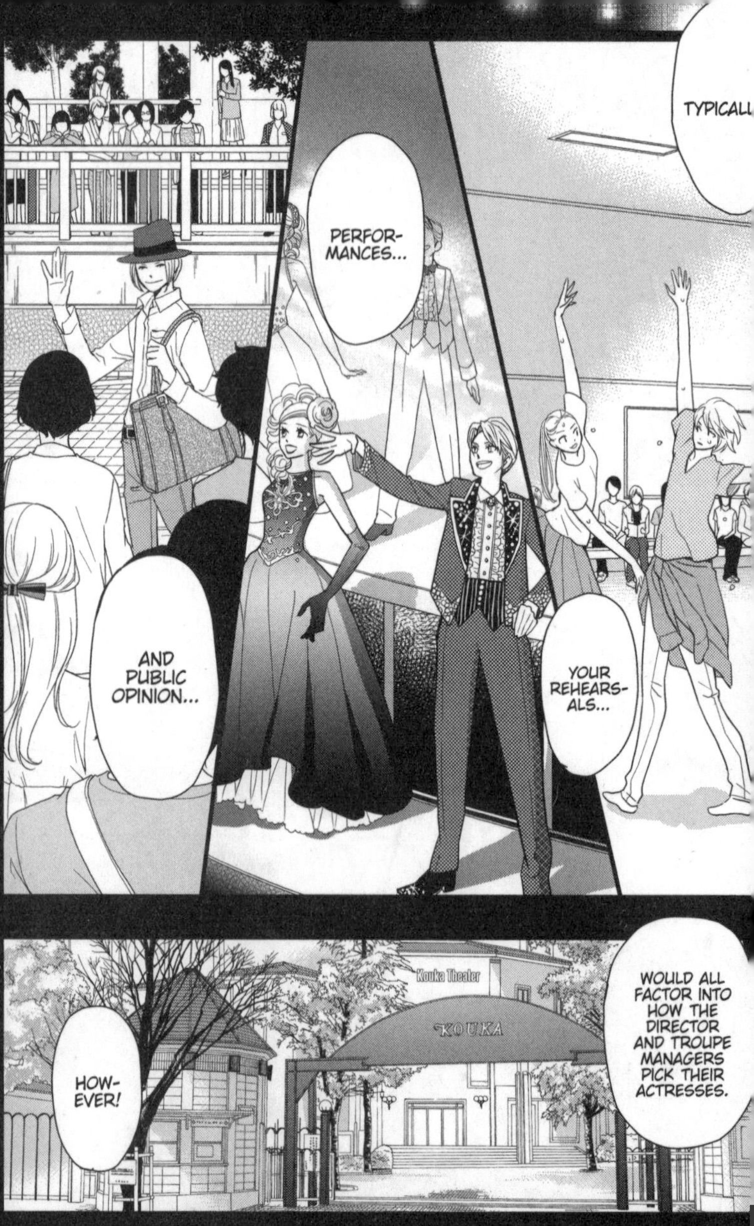
TYPICALL
YOUR REHEARS-ALS...
PERFOR-MANCES...
AND PUBLIC OPINION...
WOULD ALL FACTOR INTO HOW THE DIRECTOR AND TROUPE MANAGERS PICK THEIR ACTRESSES.
Kouka Theater
KOUKA
HOW-EVER!

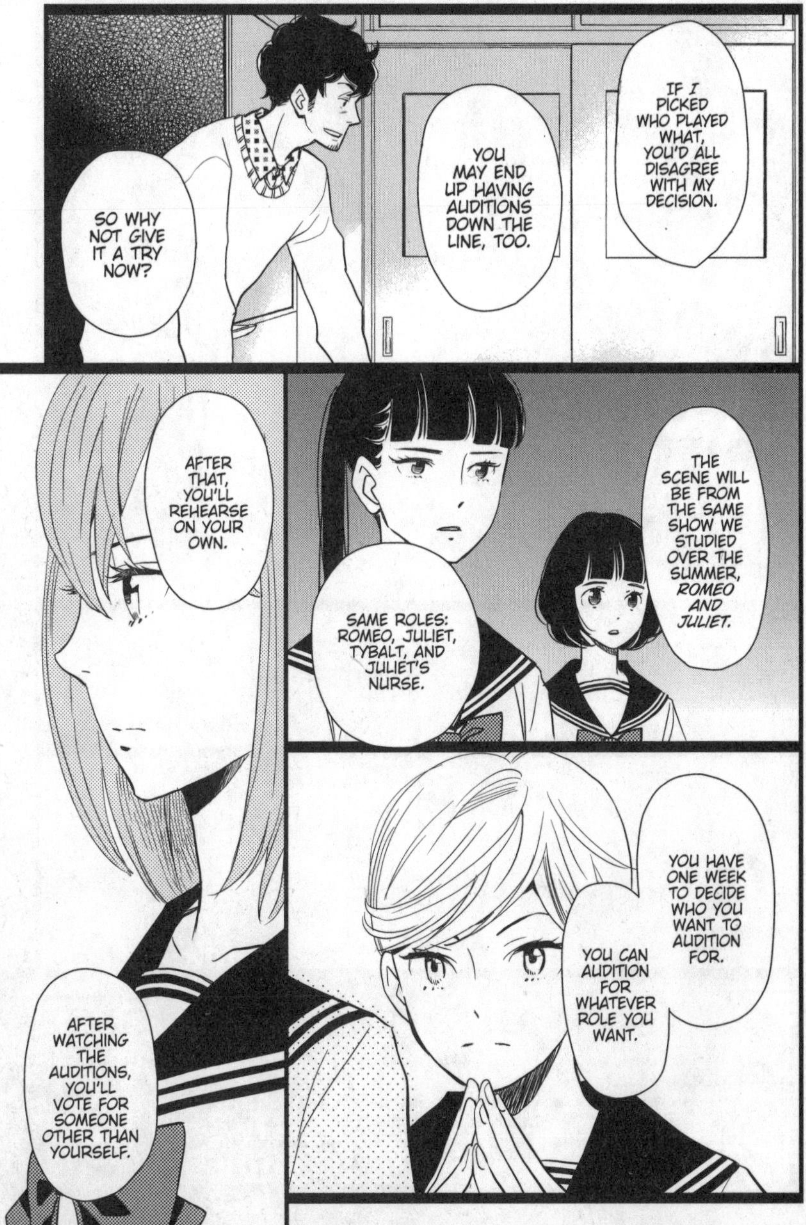
IF I PICKED WHO PLAYED WHAT, YOU'D ALL DISAGREE WITH MY DECISION.
YOU MAY END UP HAVING AUDITIONS DOWN THE LINE, TOO.
SO WHY NOT GIVE IT A TRY NOW?
THE SCENE WILL BE FROM THE SAME SHOW WE STUDIED OVER THE SUMMER, *ROMEO AND JULIET.*
SAME ROLES: ROMEO, JULIET, TYBALT, AND JULIET'S NURSE.
YOU HAVE ONE WEEK TO DECIDE WHO YOU WANT TO AUDITION FOR.
YOU CAN AUDITION FOR WHATEVER ROLE YOU WANT.
AFTER THAT, YOU'LL REHEARSE ON YOUR OWN.
AFTER WATCHING THE AUDITIONS, YOU'LL VOTE FOR SOMEONE OTHER THAN YOURSELF.

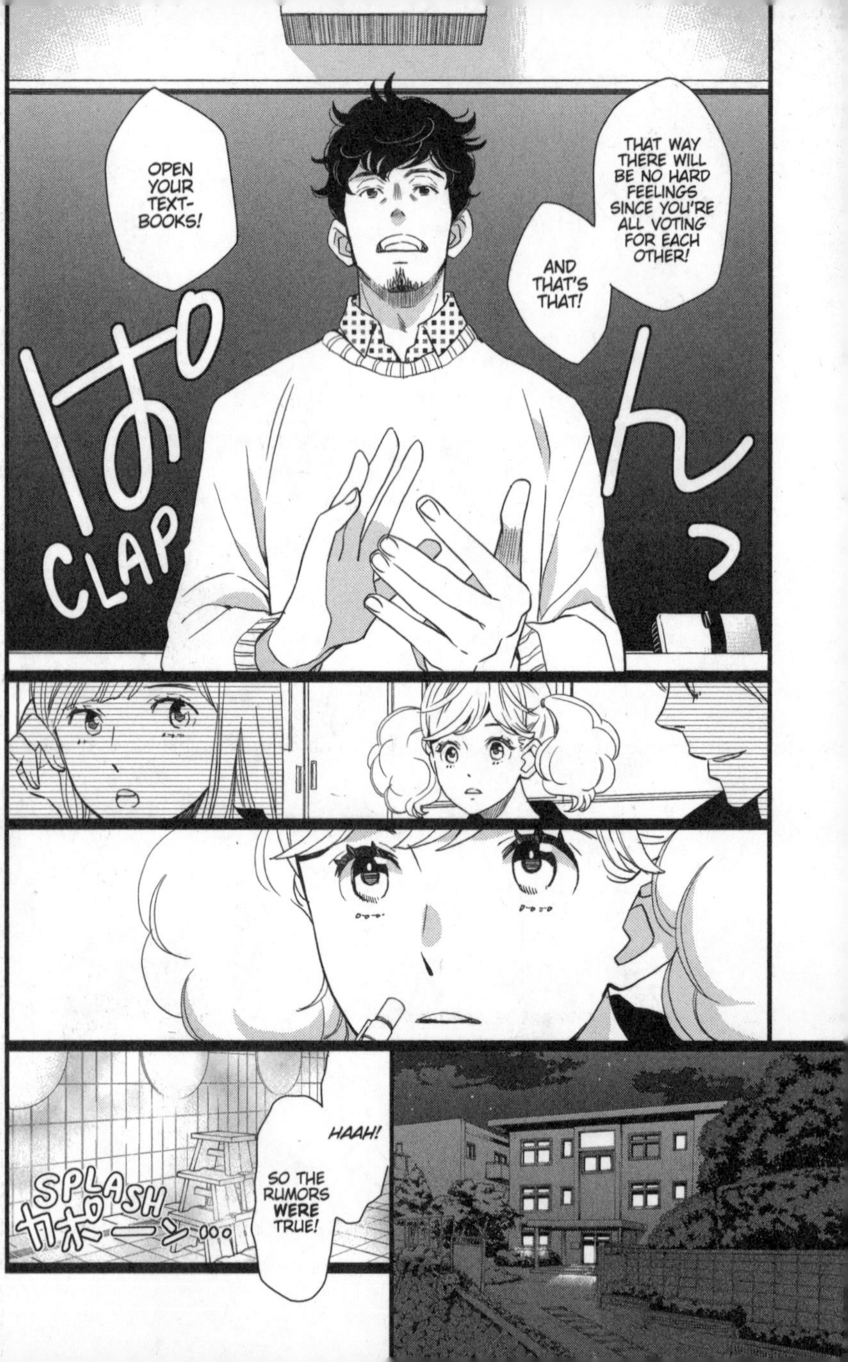
THAT WAY THERE WILL BE NO HARD FEELINGS SINCE YOU'RE ALL VOTING FOR EACH OTHER!
AND THAT'S THAT!
OPEN YOUR TEXT-BOOKS!
ぱんっ
CLAP
HAAH!
SO THE RUMORS WERE TRUE!
SPLASH
カポーン

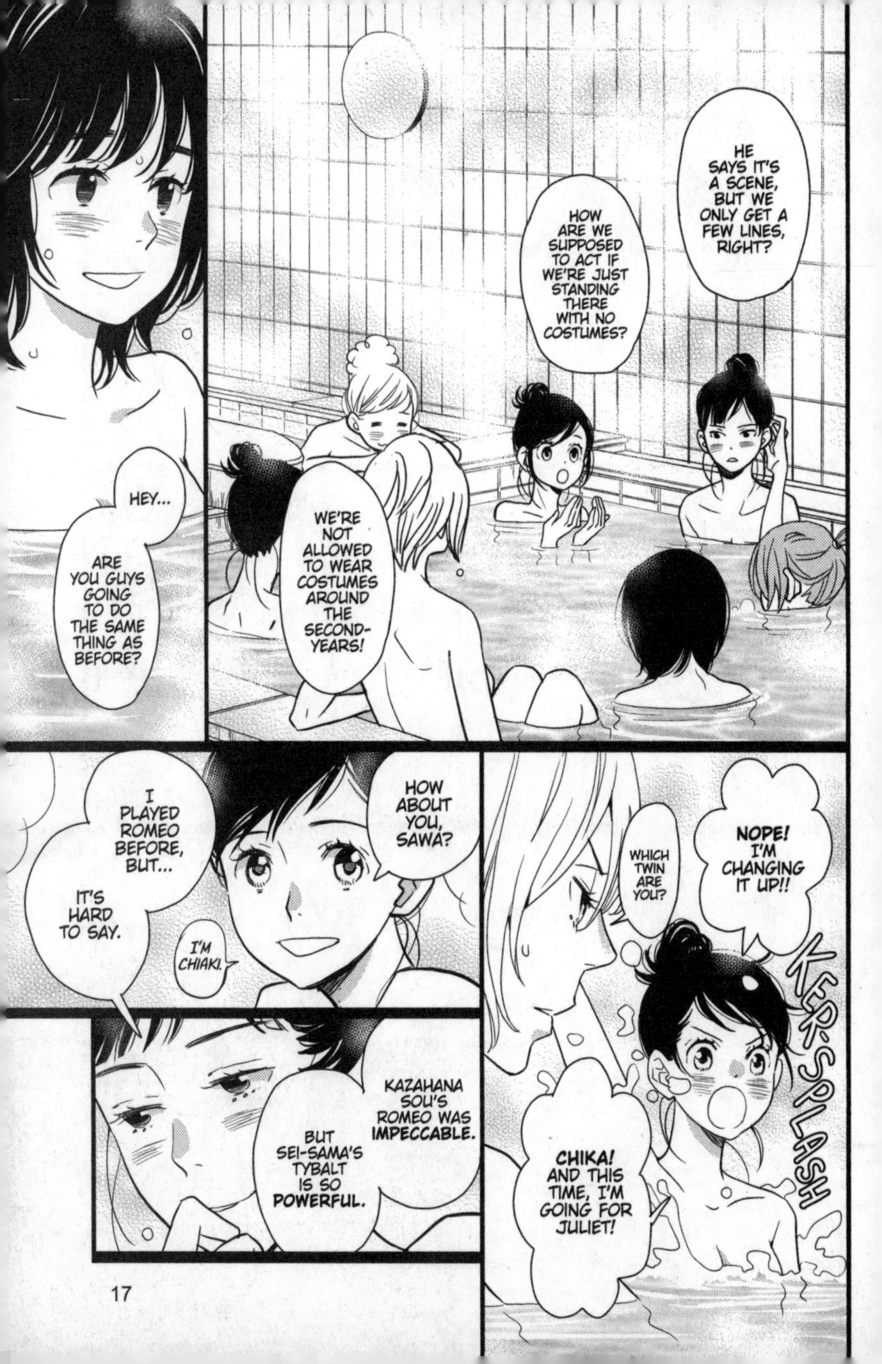
HE SAYS IT'S A SCENE, BUT WE ONLY GET A FEW LINES, RIGHT?
HOW ARE WE SUPPOSED TO ACT IF WE'RE JUST STANDING THERE WITH NO COSTUMES?
WE'RE NOT ALLOWED TO WEAR COSTUMES AROUND THE SECOND-YEARS!
HEY...
ARE YOU GUYS GOING TO DO THE SAME THING AS BEFORE?
NOPE! I'M CHANGING IT UP!!
WHICH TWIN ARE YOU?
KER-SPLASH
CHIKA! AND THIS TIME, I'M GOING FOR JULIET!
HOW ABOUT YOU, SAWA?
I'M CHIAKI.
I PLAYED ROMEO BEFORE, BUT...
IT'S HARD TO SAY.
KAZAHANA SOU'S ROMEO WAS IMPECCABLE.
BUT SEI-SAMA'S TYBALT IS SO POWERFUL.

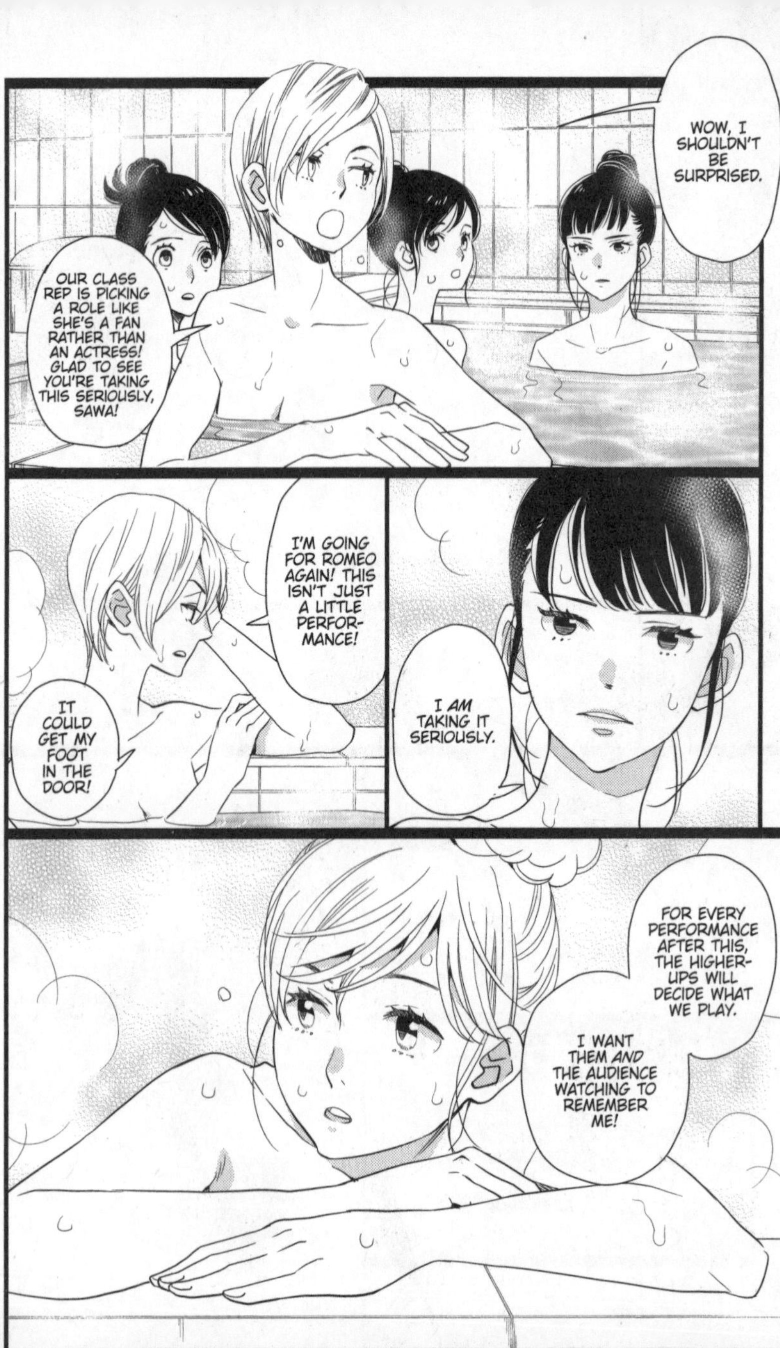
WOW, I SHOULDN'T BE SURPRISED.
OUR CLASS REP IS PICKING A ROLE LIKE SHE'S A FAN RATHER THAN AN ACTRESS! GLAD TO SEE YOU'RE TAKING THIS SERIOUSLY, SAWA!
I *AM* TAKING IT SERIOUSLY.
I'M GOING FOR ROMEO AGAIN! THIS ISN'T JUST A LITTLE PERFORMANCE!
IT COULD GET MY FOOT IN THE DOOR!
FOR EVERY PERFORMANCE AFTER THIS, THE HIGHER-UPS WILL DECIDE WHAT WE PLAY.
I WANT THEM *AND* THE AUDIENCE WATCHING TO REMEMBER ME!

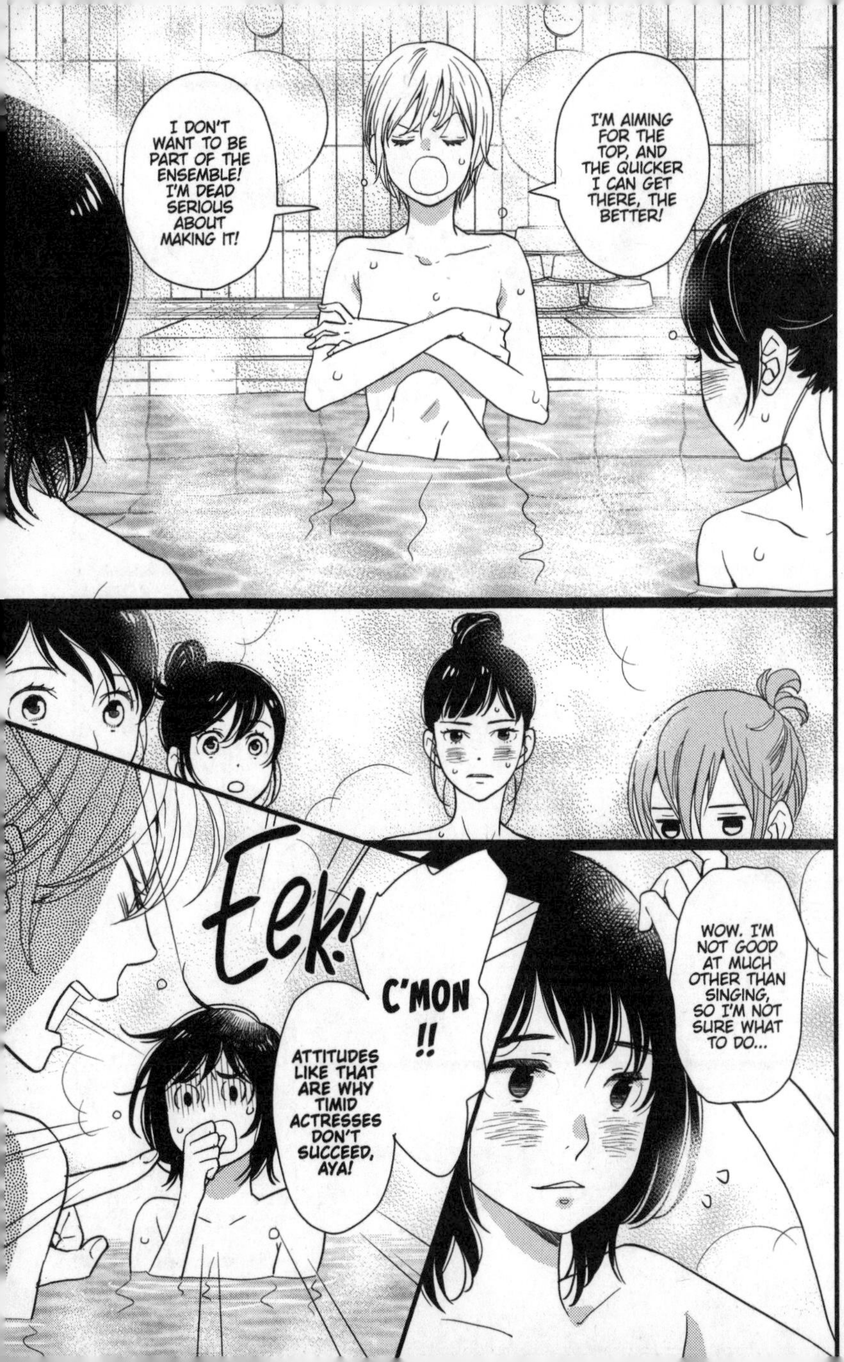
I'M AIMING FOR THE TOP, AND THE QUICKER I CAN GET THERE, THE BETTER!
I DON'T WANT TO BE PART OF THE ENSEMBLE! I'M DEAD SERIOUS ABOUT MAKING IT!
WOW. I'M NOT GOOD AT MUCH OTHER THAN SINGING, SO I'M NOT SURE WHAT TO DO...
C'MON !!
Eek!
ATTITUDES LIKE THAT ARE WHY TIMID ACTRESSES DON'T SUCCEED, AYA!

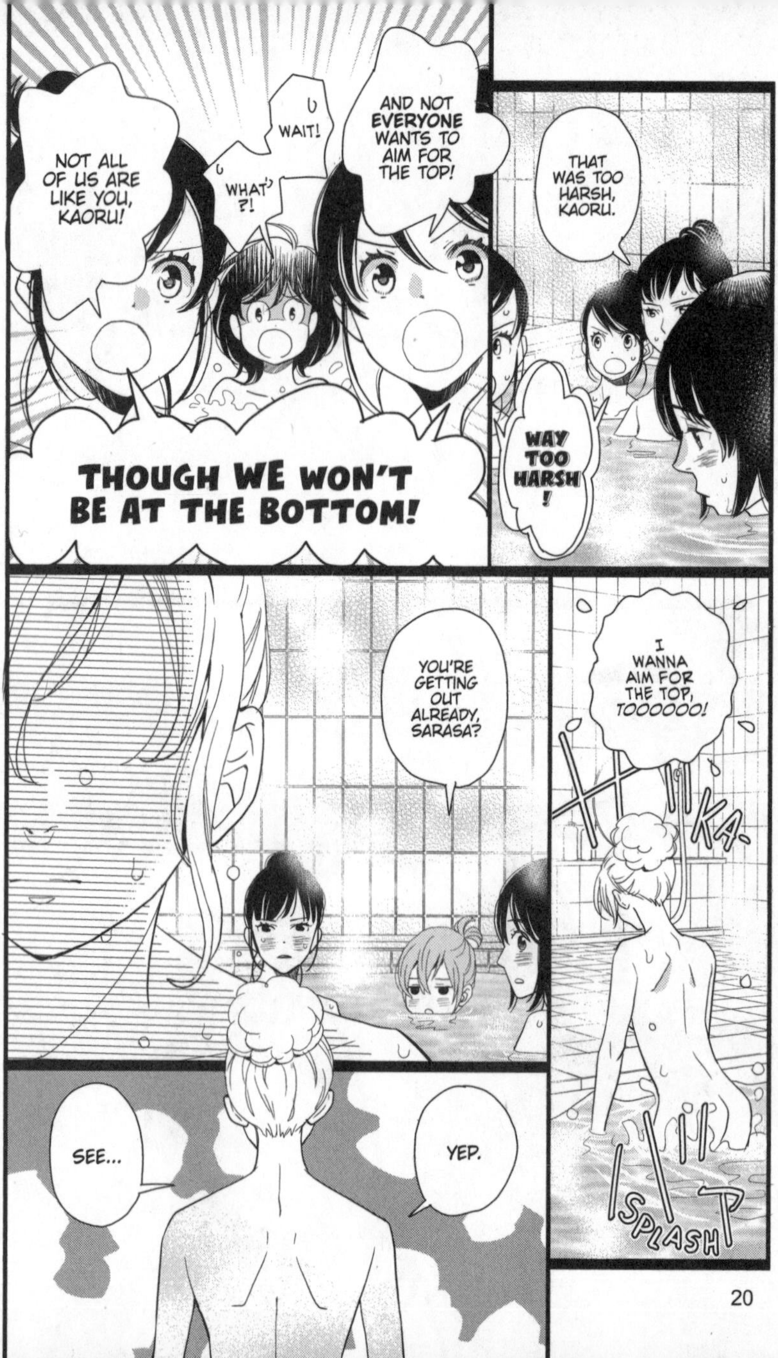
THAT WAS TOO HARSH, KAORU.
WAY TOO HARSH!
AND NOT EVERYONE WANTS TO AIM FOR THE TOP!
WAIT!
WHAT?!
NOT ALL OF US ARE LIKE YOU, KAORU!
THOUGH WE WON'T BE AT THE BOTTOM!
I WANNA AIM FOR THE TOP, TOOOOOO!
KA-
SPLASH
YOU'RE GETTING OUT ALREADY, SARASA?
YEP.
SEE...

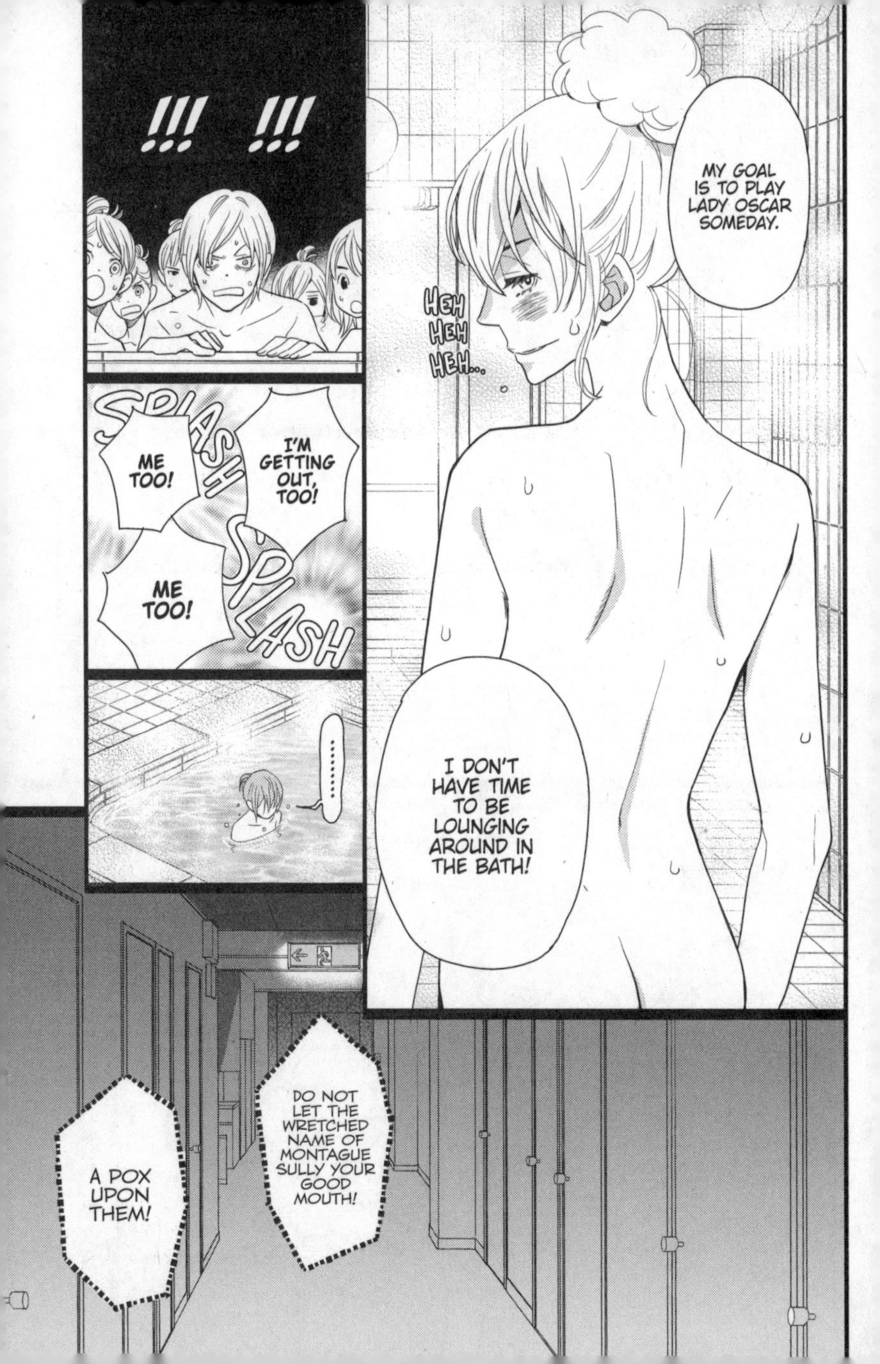
MY GOAL IS TO PLAY LADY OSCAR SOMEDAY.
HEH HEH HEH...
I DON'T HAVE TIME TO BE LOUNGING AROUND IN THE BATH!
!!! !!!
I'M GETTING OUT, TOO!
SPLASH
ME TOO!
SPLASH
ME TOO!
......
DO NOT LET THE WRETCHED NAME OF MONTAGUE SULLY YOUR GOOD MOUTH!
A POX UPON THEM!

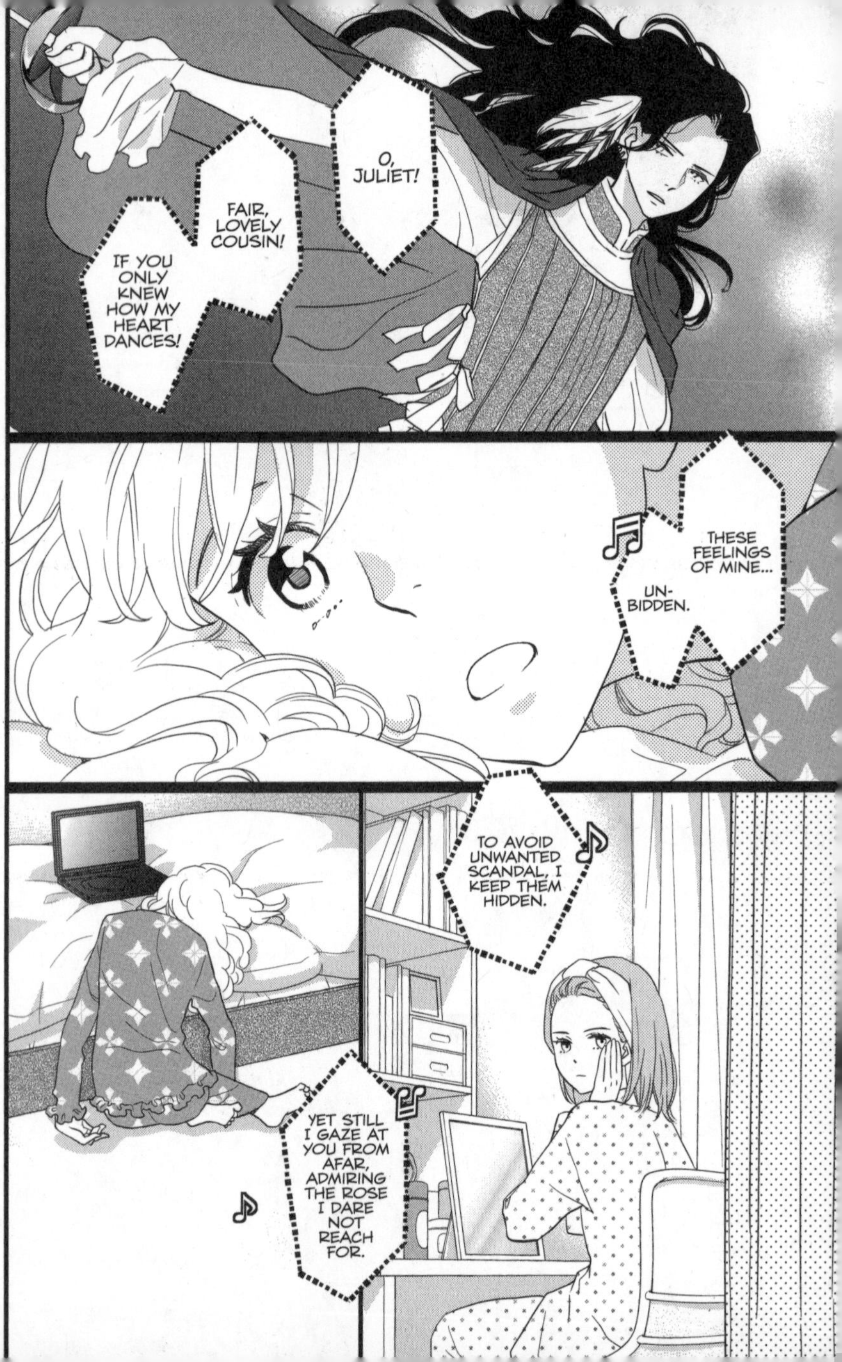
O, JULIET!
FAIR, LOVELY COUSIN!
IF YOU ONLY KNEW HOW MY HEART DANCES!
THESE FEELINGS OF MINE...
UN-BIDDEN.
TO AVOID UNWANTED SCANDAL, I KEEP THEM HIDDEN.
YET STILL I GAZE AT YOU FROM AFAR, ADMIRING THE ROSE I DARE NOT REACH FOR.

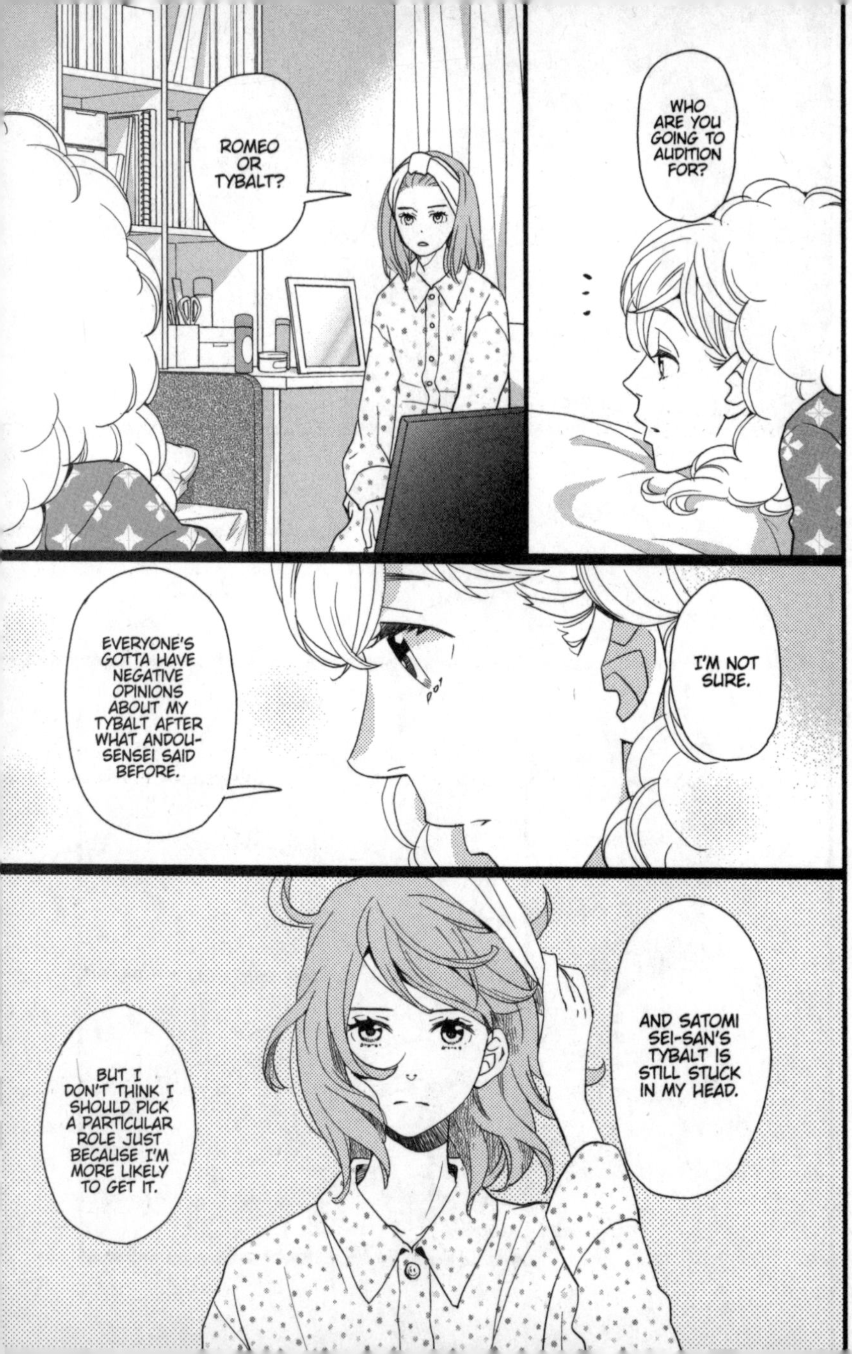
WHO ARE YOU GOING TO AUDITION FOR?
...
ROMEO OR TYBALT?
I'M NOT SURE.
EVERYONE'S GOTTA HAVE NEGATIVE OPINIONS ABOUT MY TYBALT AFTER WHAT ANDOU-SENSEI SAID BEFORE.
AND SATOMI SEI-SAN'S TYBALT IS STILL STUCK IN MY HEAD.
BUT I DON'T THINK I SHOULD PICK A PARTICULAR ROLE JUST BECAUSE I'M MORE LIKELY TO GET IT.

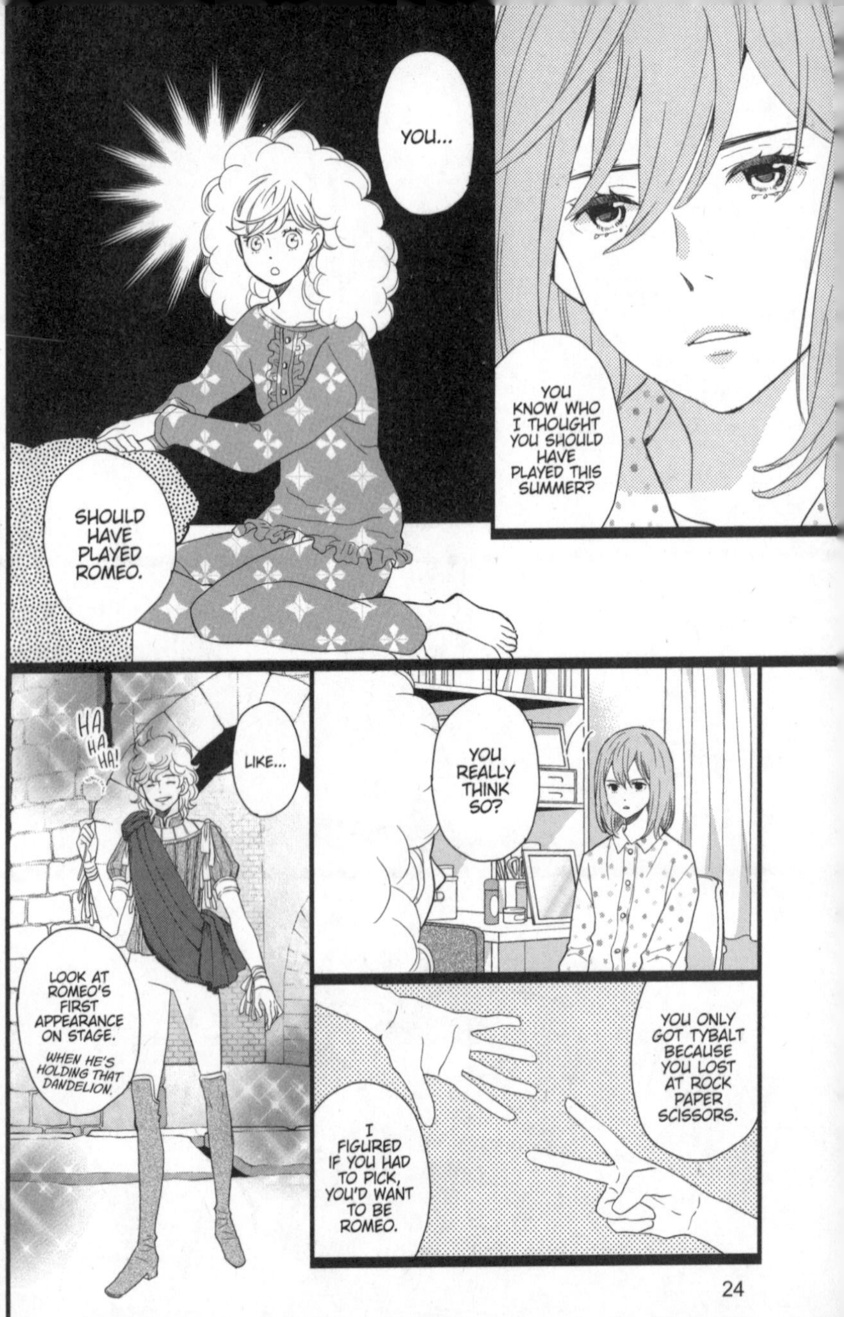
YOU KNOW WHO I THOUGHT YOU SHOULD HAVE PLAYED THIS SUMMER?
YOU...
SHOULD HAVE PLAYED ROMEO.
YOU REALLY THINK SO?
YOU ONLY GOT TYBALT BECAUSE YOU LOST AT ROCK PAPER SCISSORS.
I FIGURED IF YOU HAD TO PICK, YOU'D WANT TO BE ROMEO.
LIKE...
HA HA HA!
LOOK AT ROMEO'S FIRST APPEARANCE ON STAGE.
WHEN HE'S HOLDING THAT DANDELION.

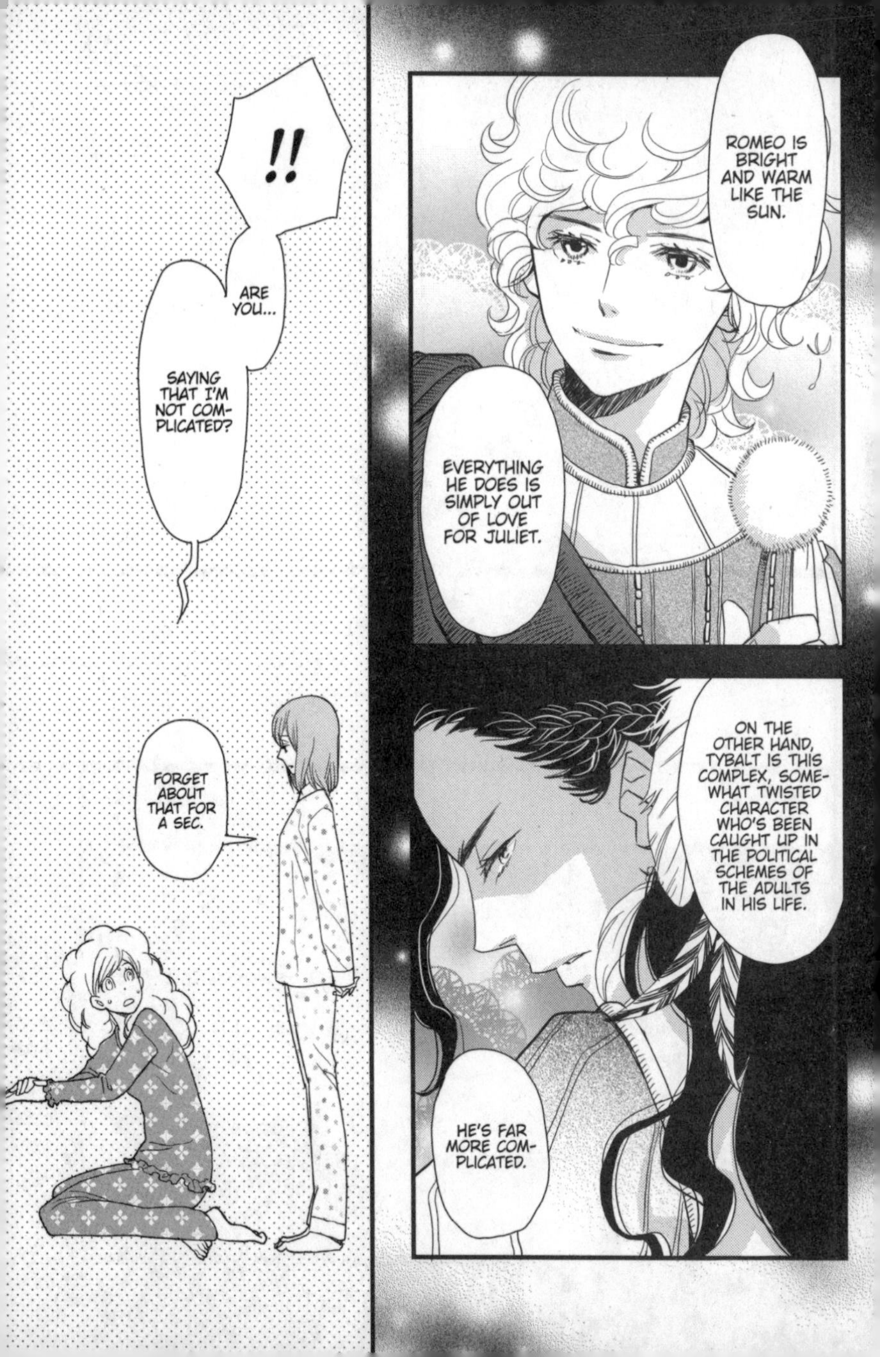
ROMEO IS BRIGHT AND WARM LIKE THE SUN.
EVERYTHING HE DOES IS SIMPLY OUT OF LOVE FOR JULIET.
ON THE OTHER HAND, TYBALT IS THIS COMPLEX, SOME-WHAT TWISTED CHARACTER WHO'S BEEN CAUGHT UP IN THE POLITICAL SCHEMES OF THE ADULTS IN HIS LIFE.
HE'S FAR MORE COM-PLICATED.
!!
ARE YOU...
SAYING THAT I'M NOT COM-PLICATED?
FORGET ABOUT THAT FOR A SEC.

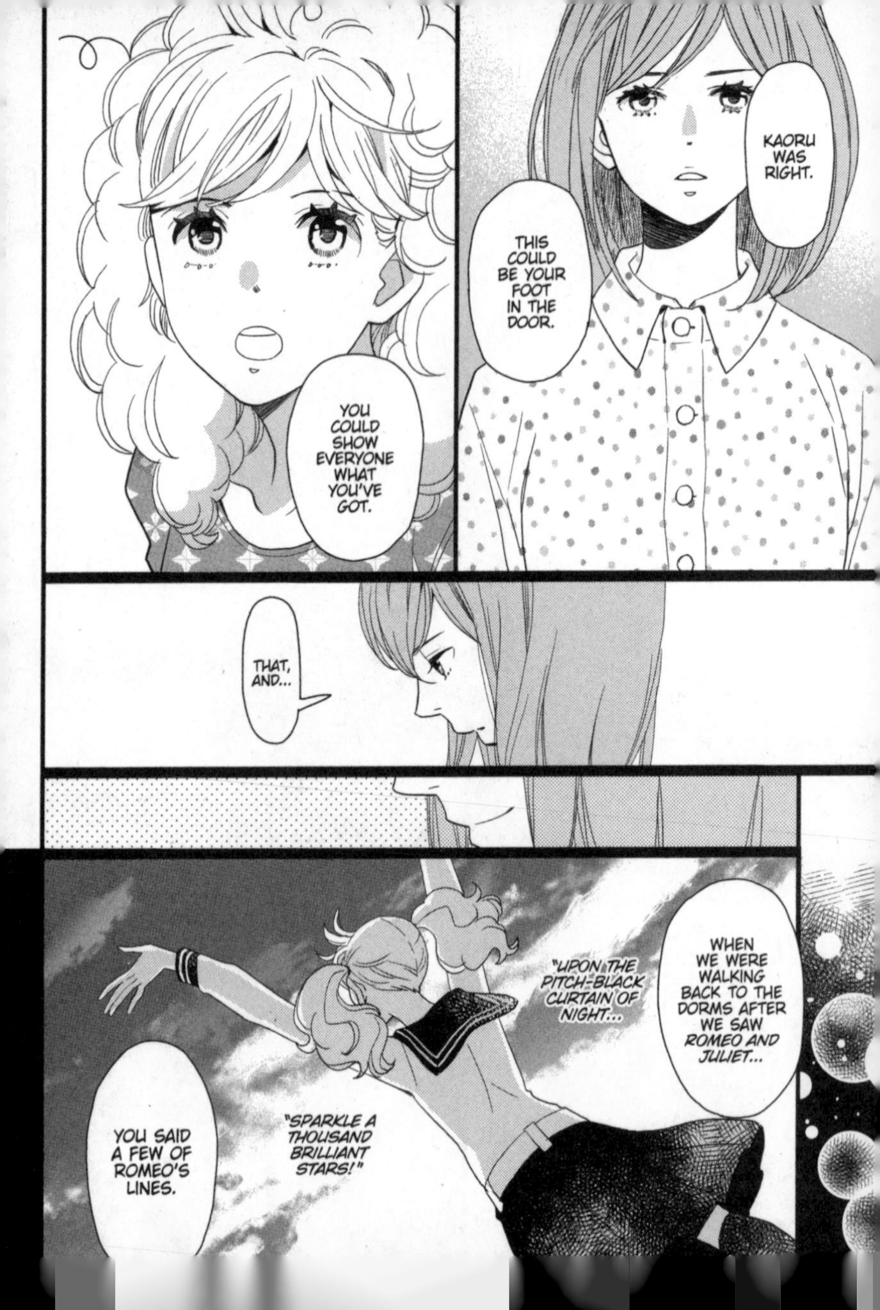
KAORU WAS RIGHT.
THIS COULD BE YOUR FOOT IN THE DOOR.
YOU COULD SHOW EVERYONE WHAT YOU'VE GOT.
THAT, AND...
WHEN WE WERE WALKING BACK TO THE DORMS AFTER WE SAW *ROMEO AND JULIET*...
"UPON THE PITCH-BLACK CURTAIN OF NIGHT...
"SPARKLE A THOUSAND BRILLIANT STARS!"
YOU SAID A FEW OF ROMEO'S LINES.

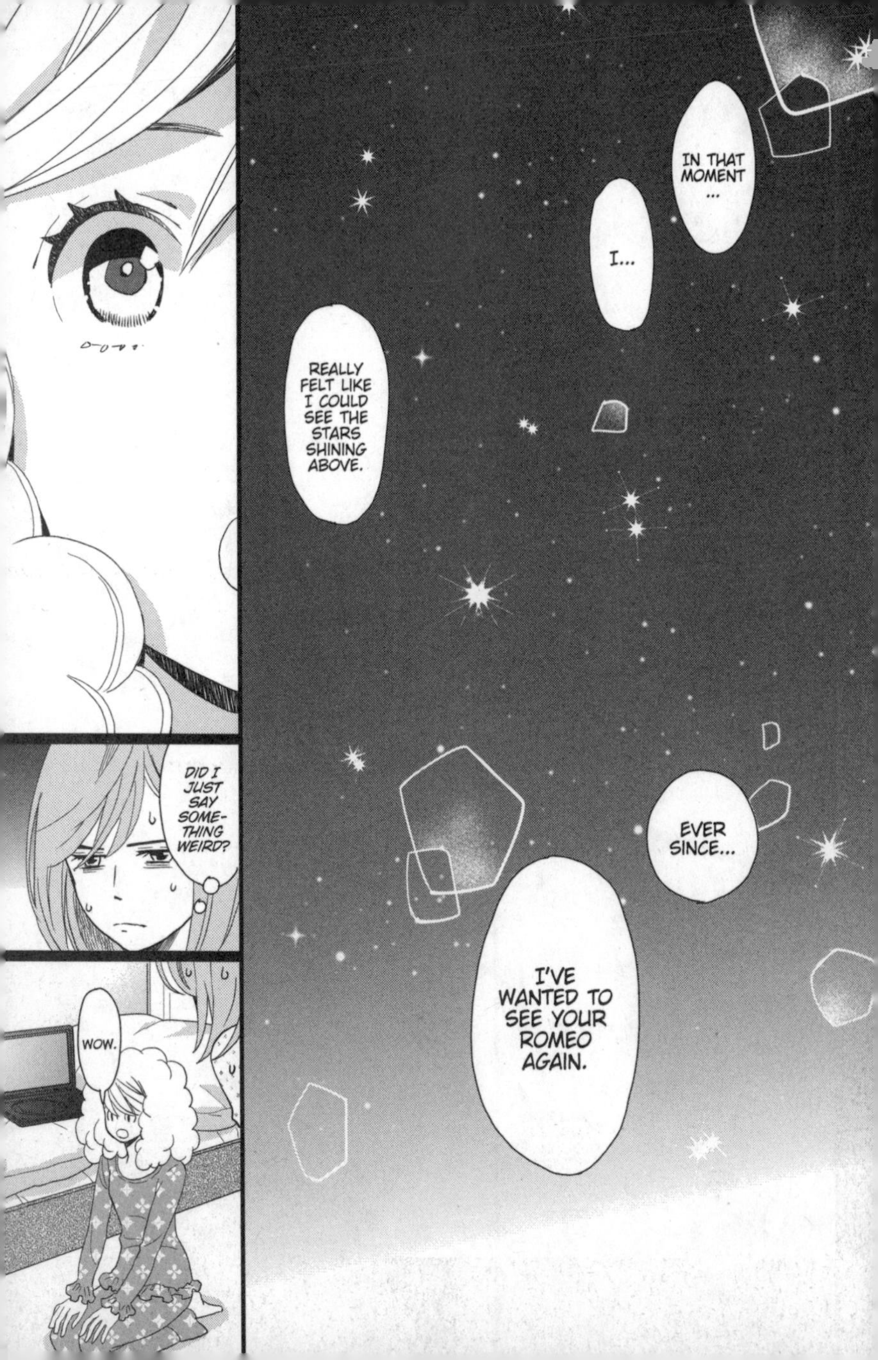
IN THAT MOMENT ...
I...
REALLY FELT LIKE I COULD SEE THE STARS SHINING ABOVE.
EVER SINCE...
I'VE WANTED TO SEE YOUR ROMEO AGAIN.
DID I JUST SAY SOME-THING WEIRD?
WOW.

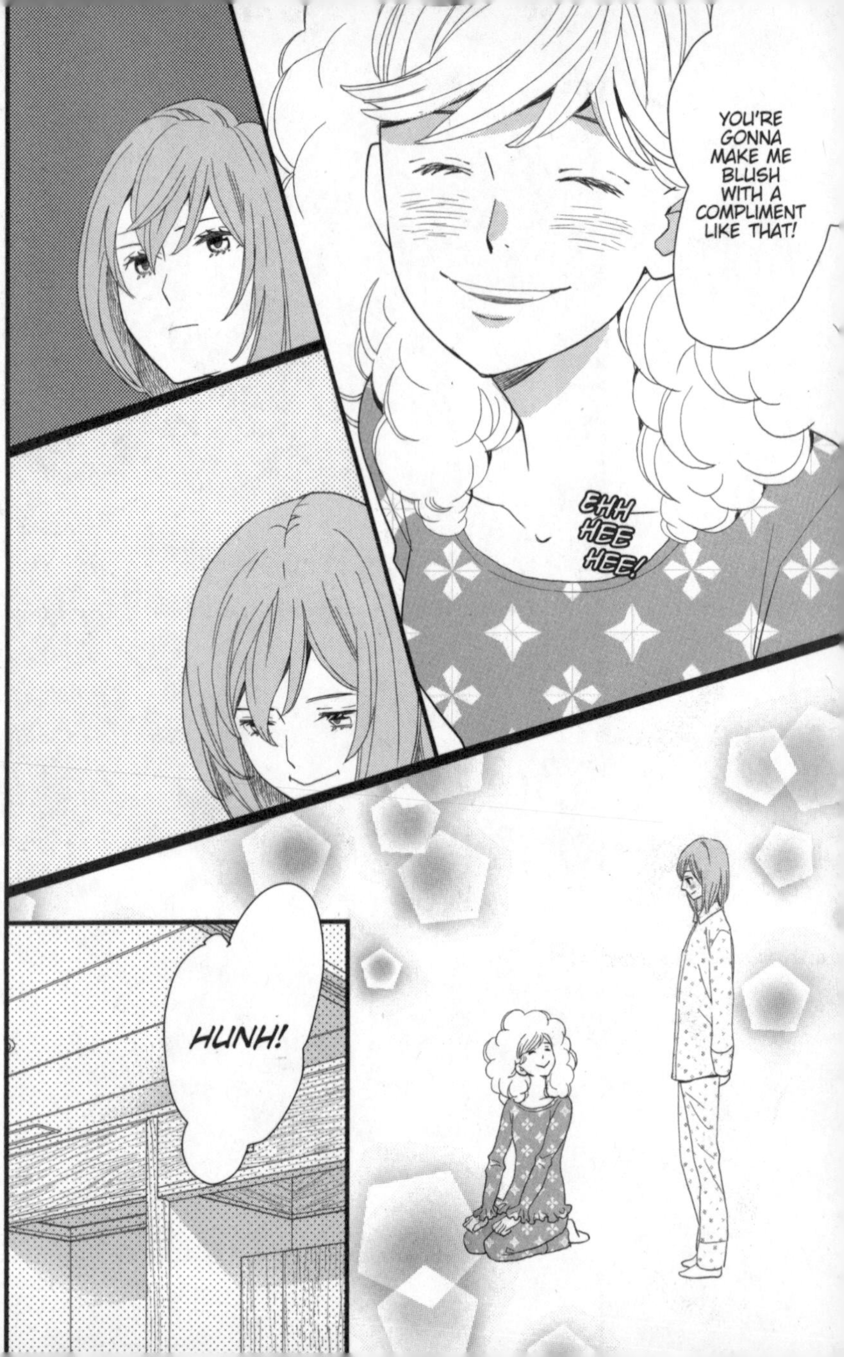
YOU'RE GONNA MAKE ME BLUSH WITH A COMPLIMENT LIKE THAT!
EHH HEE HEE!
HUNH!

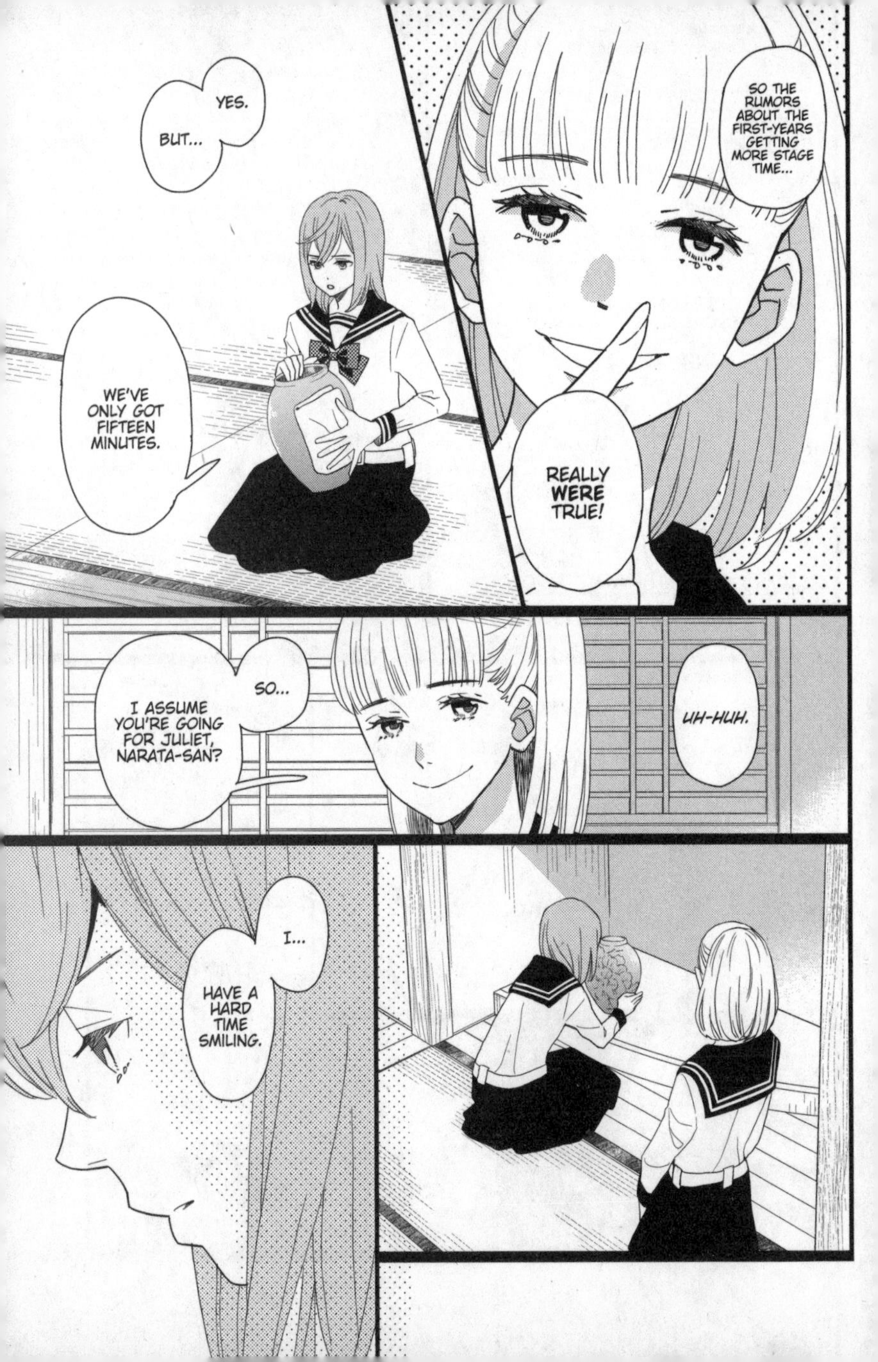
SO THE RUMORS ABOUT THE FIRST-YEARS GETTING MORE STAGE TIME...
REALLY WERE TRUE!
YES.
BUT...
WE'VE ONLY GOT FIFTEEN MINUTES.
UH-HUH.
SO...
I ASSUME YOU'RE GOING FOR JULIET, NARATA-SAN?
I...
HAVE A HARD TIME SMILING.

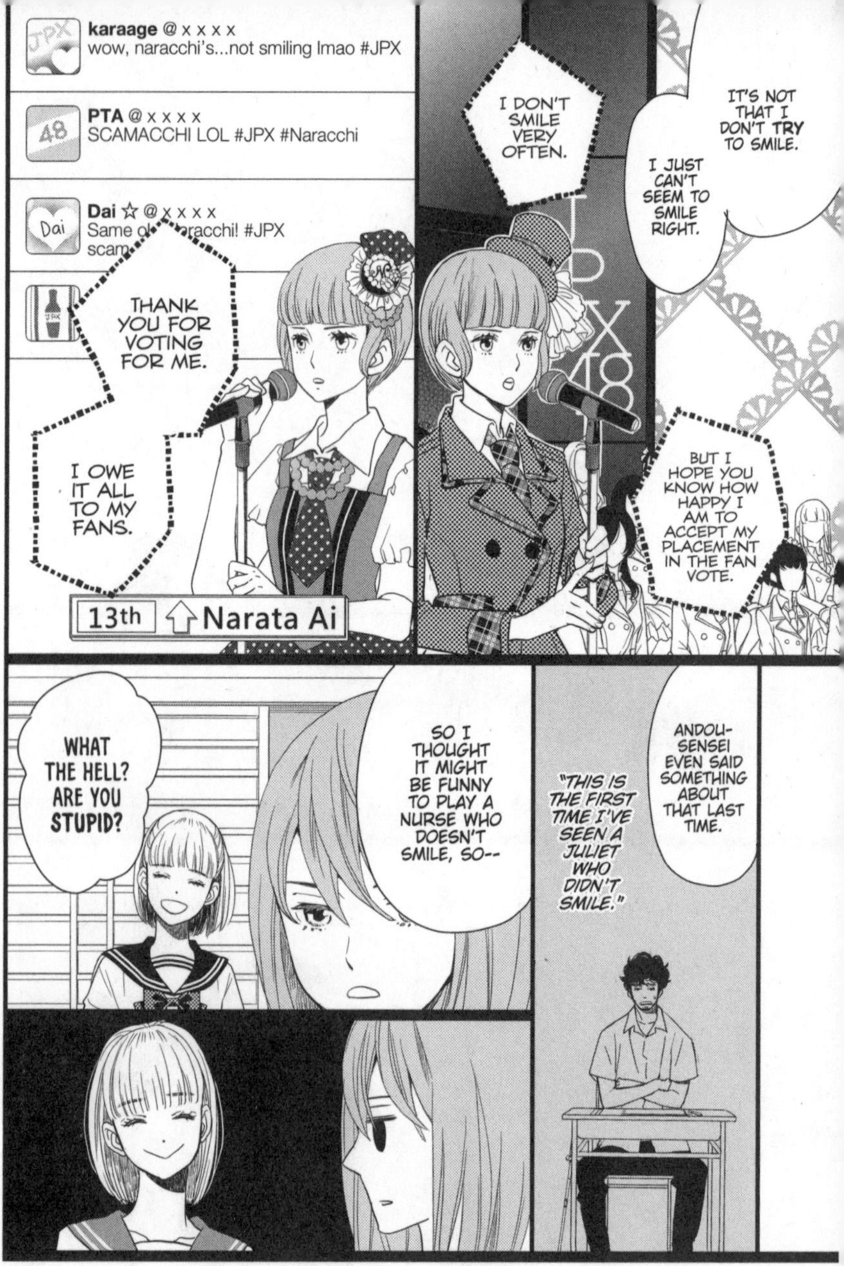
I DON'T SMILE VERY OFTEN.
IT'S NOT THAT I DON'T **TRY** TO SMILE.
I JUST CAN'T SEEM TO SMILE RIGHT.
BUT I HOPE YOU KNOW HOW HAPPY I AM TO ACCEPT MY PLACEMENT IN THE FAN VOTE.
JPX 48
karaage @ x x x x
wow, naracchi's...not smiling lmao #JPX
PTA @ x x x x
SCAMACCHI LOL #JPX #Naracchi
Dai ☆ @ x x x x
Same o aracchi! #JPX
scam
THANK YOU FOR VOTING FOR ME.
I OWE IT ALL TO MY FANS.
13th ⇧ Narata Ai
ANDOU-SENSEI EVEN SAID SOMETHING ABOUT THAT LAST TIME.
"THIS IS THE FIRST TIME I'VE SEEN A JULIET WHO DIDN'T SMILE."
SO I THOUGHT IT MIGHT BE FUNNY TO PLAY A NURSE WHO DOESN'T SMILE, SO--
WHAT THE HELL? ARE YOU STUPID?

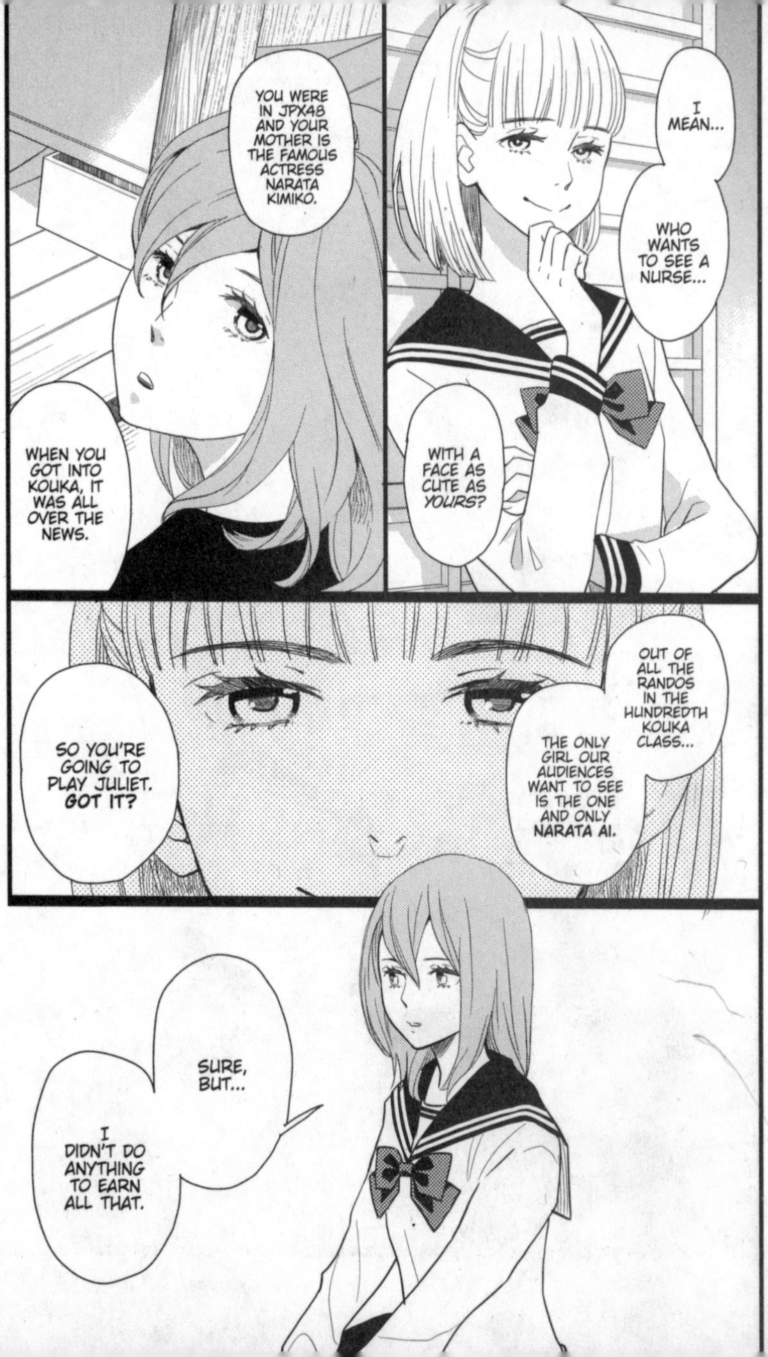
I MEAN...
WHO WANTS TO SEE A NURSE...
WITH A FACE AS CUTE AS *YOURS?*
YOU WERE IN JPX48 AND YOUR MOTHER IS THE FAMOUS ACTRESS NARATA KIMIKO.
WHEN YOU GOT INTO KOUKA, IT WAS ALL OVER THE NEWS.
OUT OF ALL THE RANDOS IN THE HUNDREDTH KOUKA CLASS...
THE ONLY GIRL OUR AUDIENCES WANT TO SEE IS THE ONE AND ONLY **NARATA AI.**
SO YOU'RE GOING TO PLAY JULIET. **GOT IT?**
SURE, BUT...
I DIDN'T DO ANYTHING TO EARN ALL THAT.

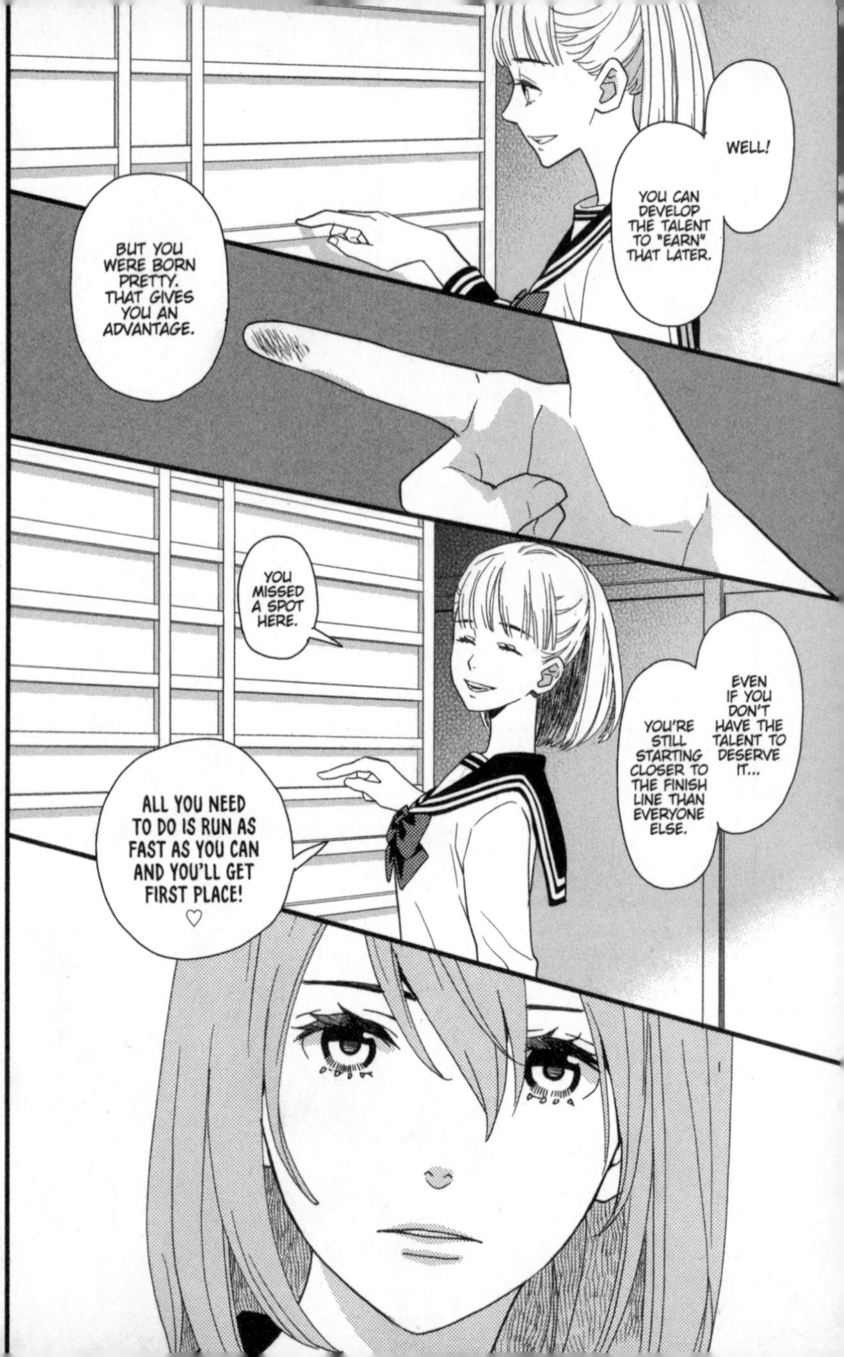
WELL!
YOU CAN DEVELOP THE TALENT TO "EARN" THAT LATER.
BUT YOU WERE BORN PRETTY. THAT GIVES YOU AN ADVANTAGE.
YOU MISSED A SPOT HERE.
EVEN IF YOU DON'T HAVE THE TALENT TO DESERVE IT...
YOU'RE STILL STARTING CLOSER TO THE FINISH LINE THAN EVERYONE ELSE.
ALL YOU NEED TO DO IS RUN AS FAST AS YOU CAN AND YOU'LL GET FIRST PLACE! ♡

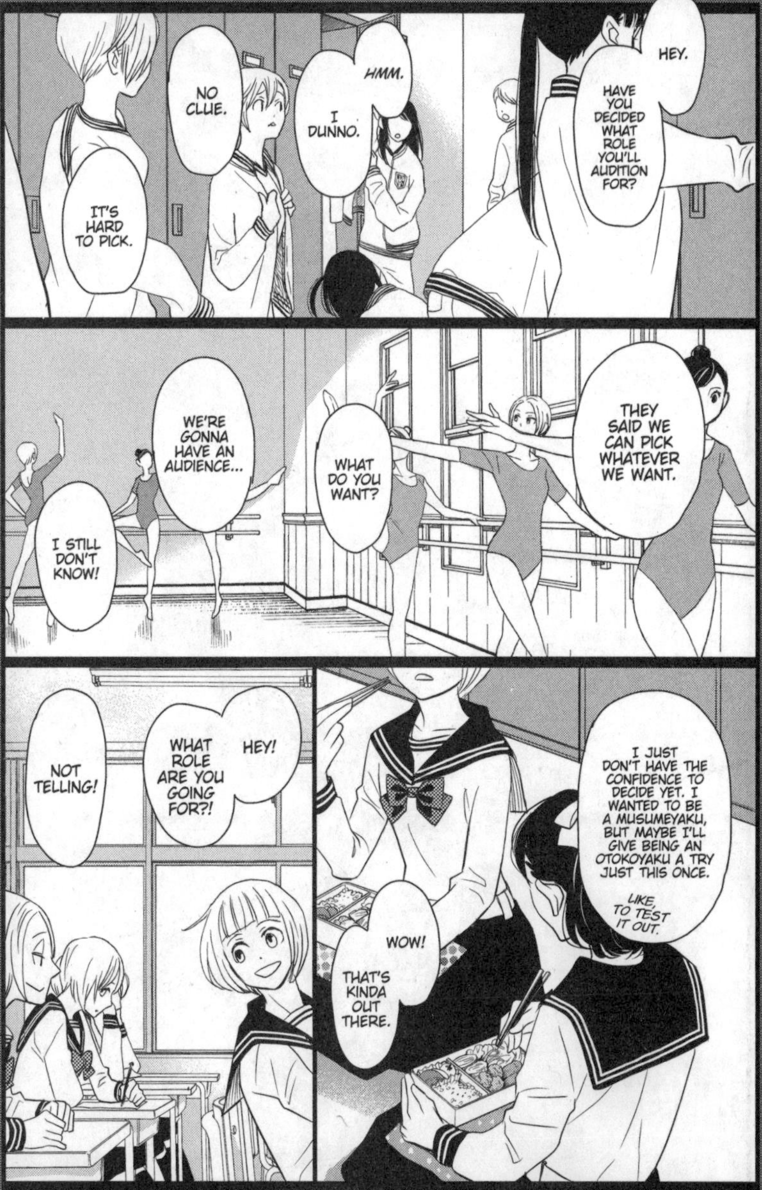
HEY.
HAVE YOU DECIDED WHAT ROLE YOU'LL AUDITION FOR?
HMM.
I DUNNO.
NO CLUE.
IT'S HARD TO PICK.
THEY SAID WE CAN PICK WHATEVER WE WANT.
WHAT DO YOU WANT?
WE'RE GONNA HAVE AN AUDIENCE...
I STILL DON'T KNOW!
I JUST DON'T HAVE THE CONFIDENCE TO DECIDE YET. I WANTED TO BE A MUSUMEYAKU, BUT MAYBE I'LL GIVE BEING AN OTOKOYAKU A TRY JUST THIS ONCE.
LIKE, TO TEST IT OUT.
WOW!
THAT'S KINDA OUT THERE.
HEY!
WHAT ROLE ARE YOU GOING FOR?!
NOT TELLING!

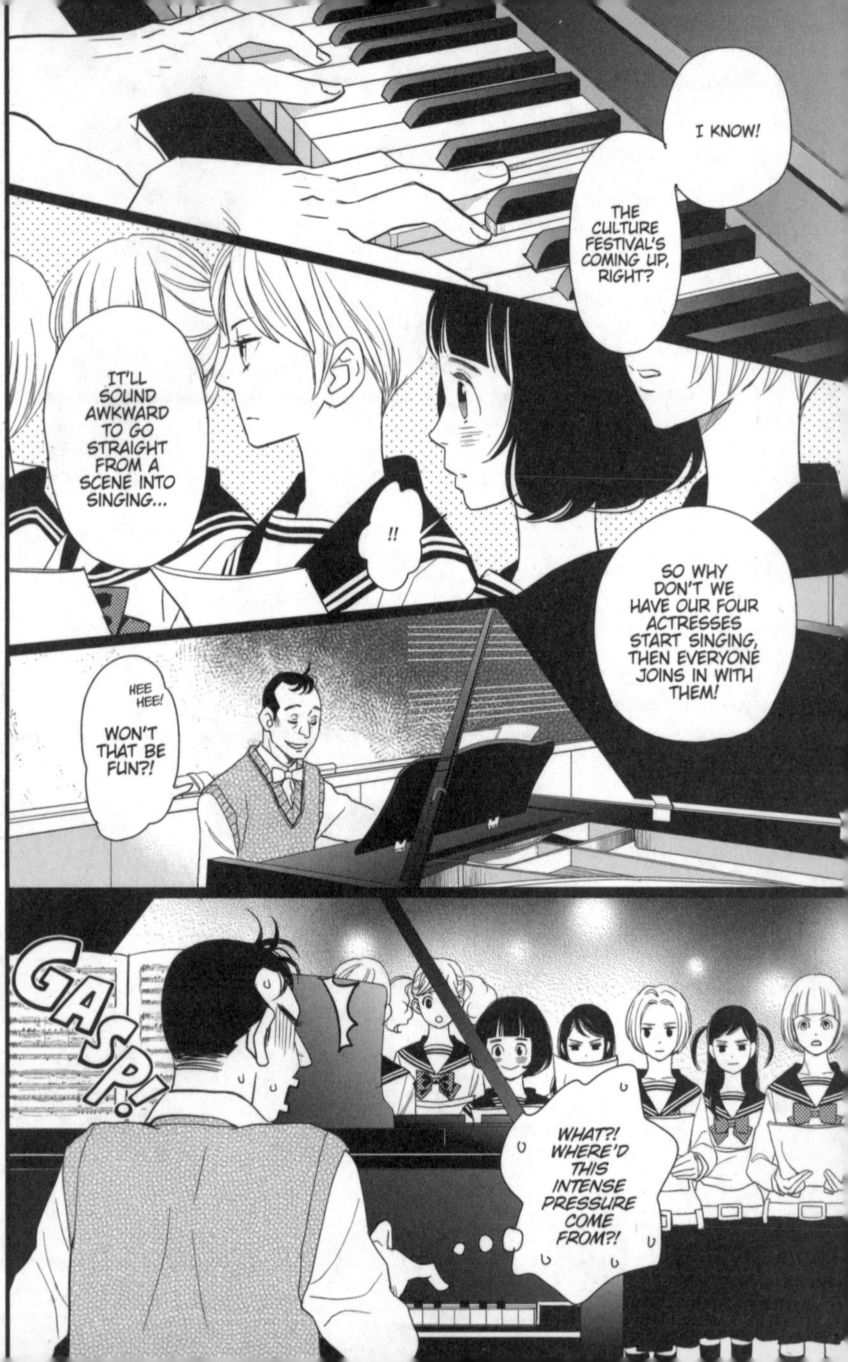
I KNOW!
THE CULTURE FESTIVAL'S COMING UP, RIGHT?
IT'LL SOUND AWKWARD TO GO STRAIGHT FROM A SCENE INTO SINGING...
!!
SO WHY DON'T WE HAVE OUR FOUR ACTRESSES START SINGING, THEN EVERYONE JOINS IN WITH THEM!
HEE HEE!
WON'T THAT BE FUN?!
GASP!
WHAT?! WHERE'D THIS INTENSE PRESSURE COME FROM?!
...

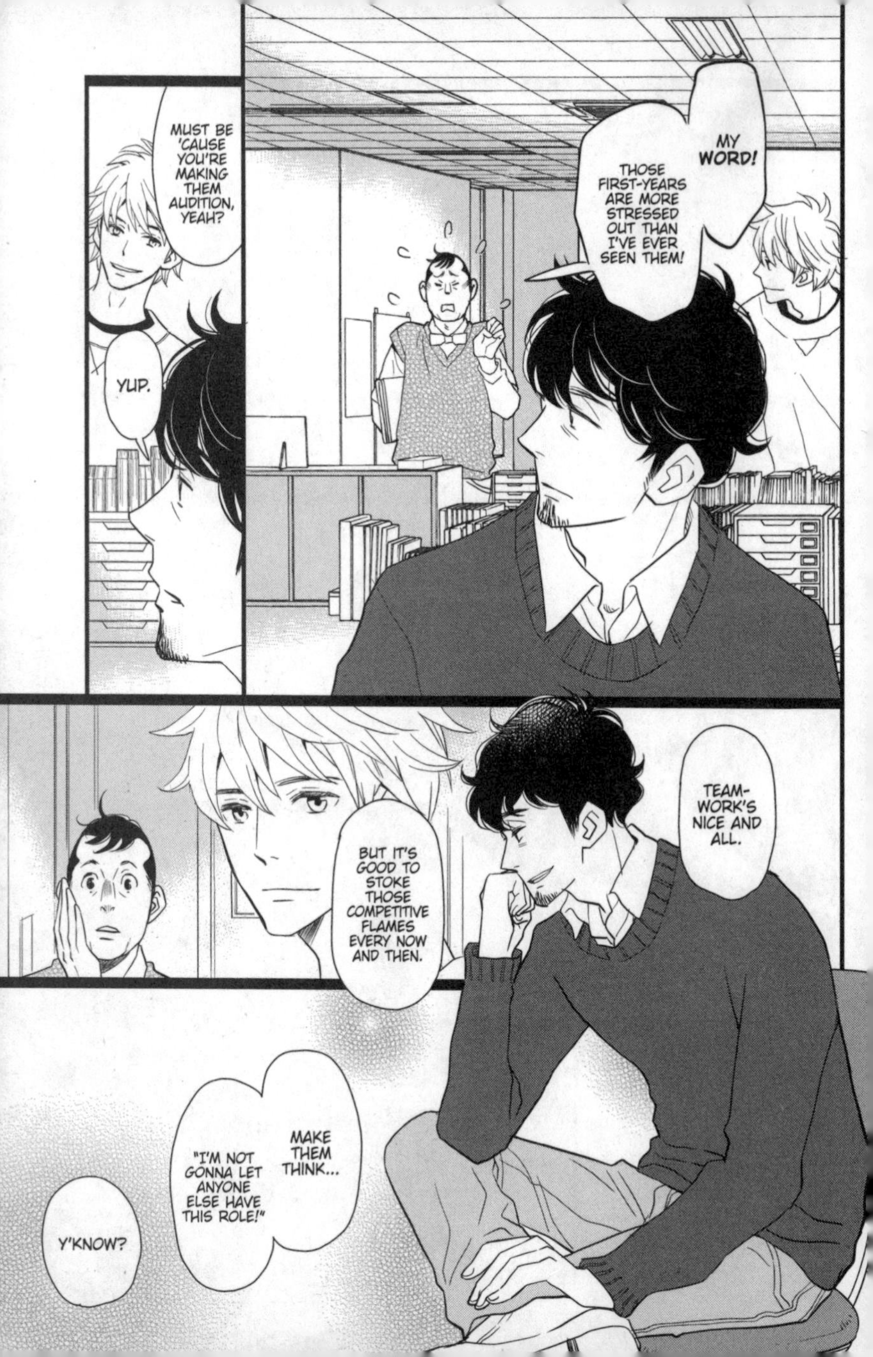
MY WORD! THOSE FIRST-YEARS ARE MORE STRESSED OUT THAN I'VE EVER SEEN THEM!
MUST BE 'CAUSE YOU'RE MAKING THEM AUDITION, YEAH?
YUP.
TEAM-WORK'S NICE AND ALL.
BUT IT'S GOOD TO STOKE THOSE COMPETITIVE FLAMES EVERY NOW AND THEN.
MAKE THEM THINK...
"I'M NOT GONNA LET ANYONE ELSE HAVE THIS ROLE!"
Y'KNOW?

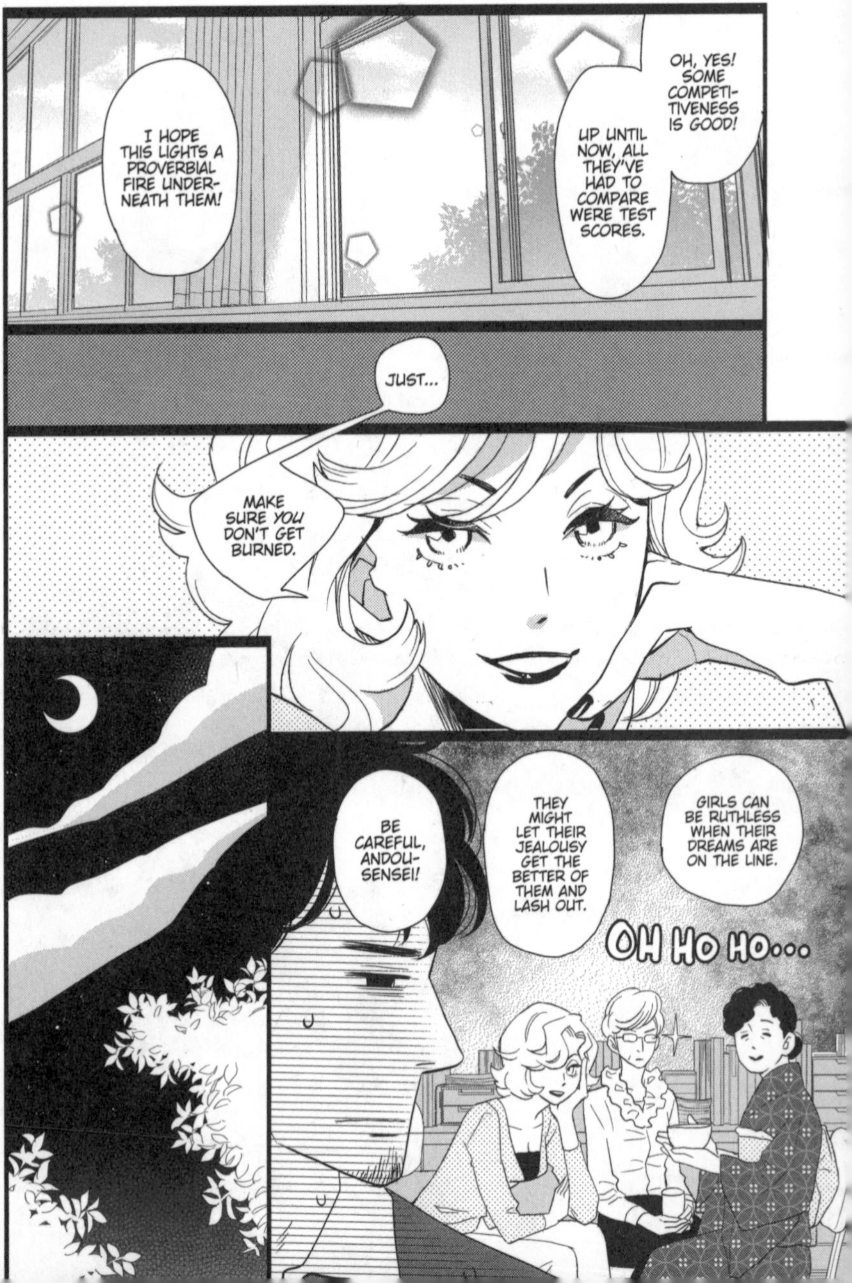
OH, YES! SOME COMPETITI- TIVENESS IS GOOD!
UP UNTIL NOW, ALL THEY'VE HAD TO COMPARE WERE TEST SCORES.
I HOPE THIS LIGHTS A PROVERBIAL FIRE UNDER- NEATH THEM!
JUST...
MAKE SURE *YOU* DON'T GET BURNED.
GIRLS CAN BE RUTHLESS WHEN THEIR DREAMS ARE ON THE LINE.
THEY MIGHT LET THEIR JEALOUSY GET THE BETTER OF THEM AND LASH OUT.
BE CAREFUL, ANDOU- SENSEI!
OH HO HO...

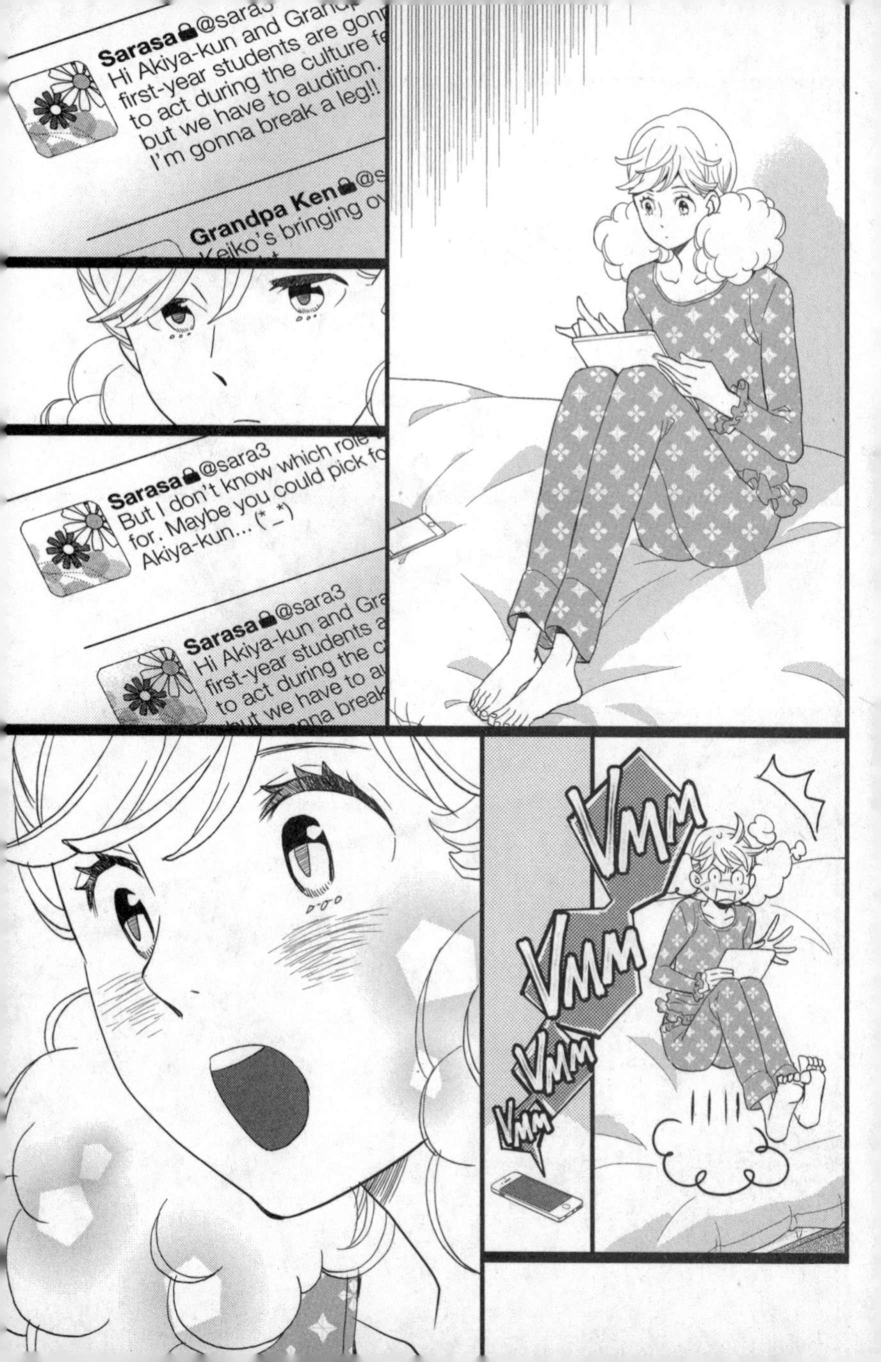
Sarasa @sara3
Hi Akiya-kun and Grand
first-year students are gon
to act during the culture fe
but we have to audition.
I'm gonna break a leg!!
Grandpa Ken @s
Keiko's bringing ov
Sarasa @sara3
But I don't know which role
for. Maybe you could pick fo
Akiya-kun... (*_*)
Sarasa @sara3
Hi Akiya-kun and Gra
first-year students a
to act during the c
to act we have to a
VMM
VMM
VMM
VMM

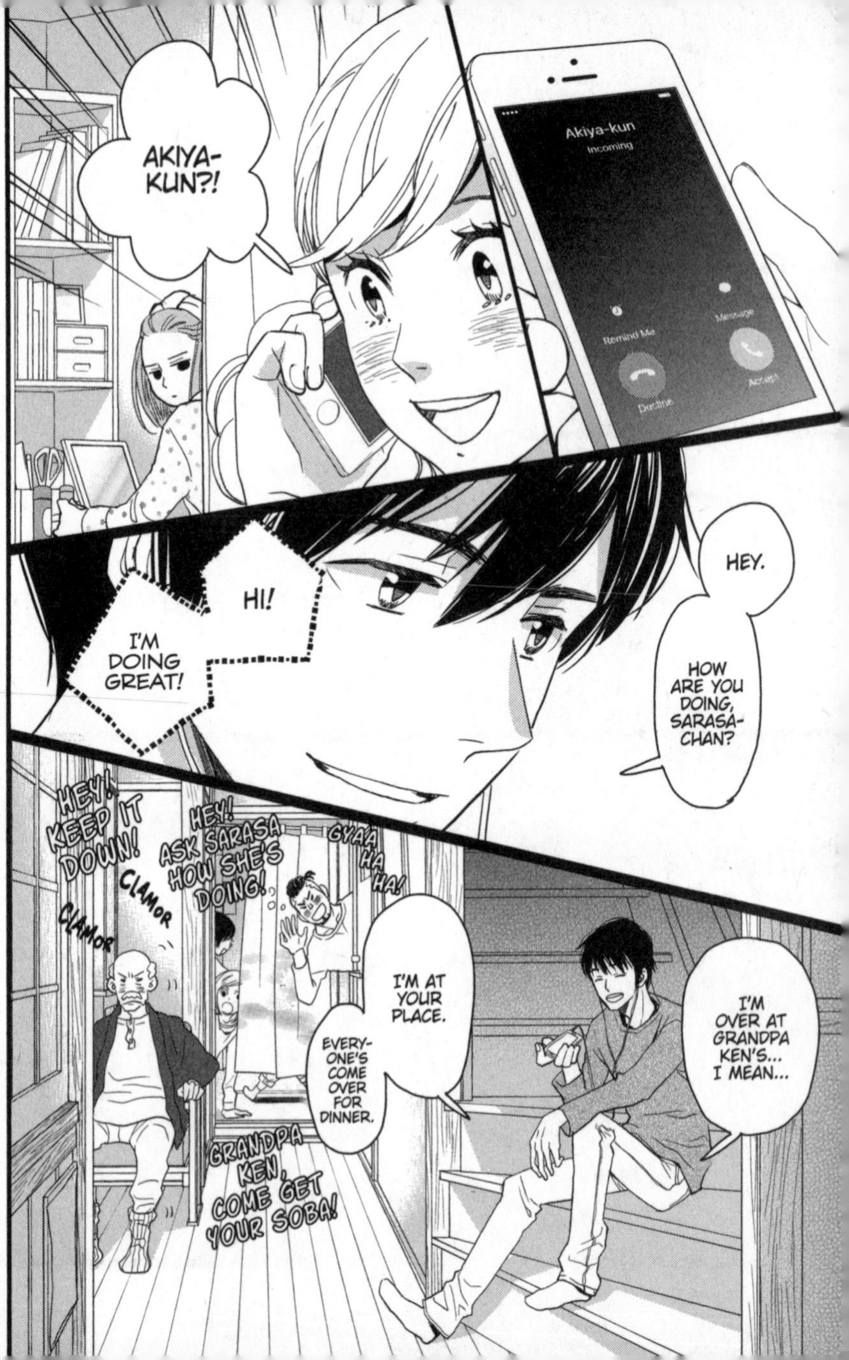
Akiya-kun
Incoming
Message
Remind Me
Accept
Decline
AKIYA-KUN?!
HEY.
HOW ARE YOU DOING, SARASA-CHAN?
HI!
I'M DOING GREAT!
I'M OVER AT GRANDPA KEN'S... I MEAN...
I'M AT YOUR PLACE.
EVERY-ONE'S COME OVER FOR DINNER.
GYAA HA HA!
HEY! ASK SARASA HOW SHE'S DOING!
HEY! KEEP IT DOWN!
CLAMOR
CLAMOR
GRANDPA KEN, COME GET YOUR SOBA!

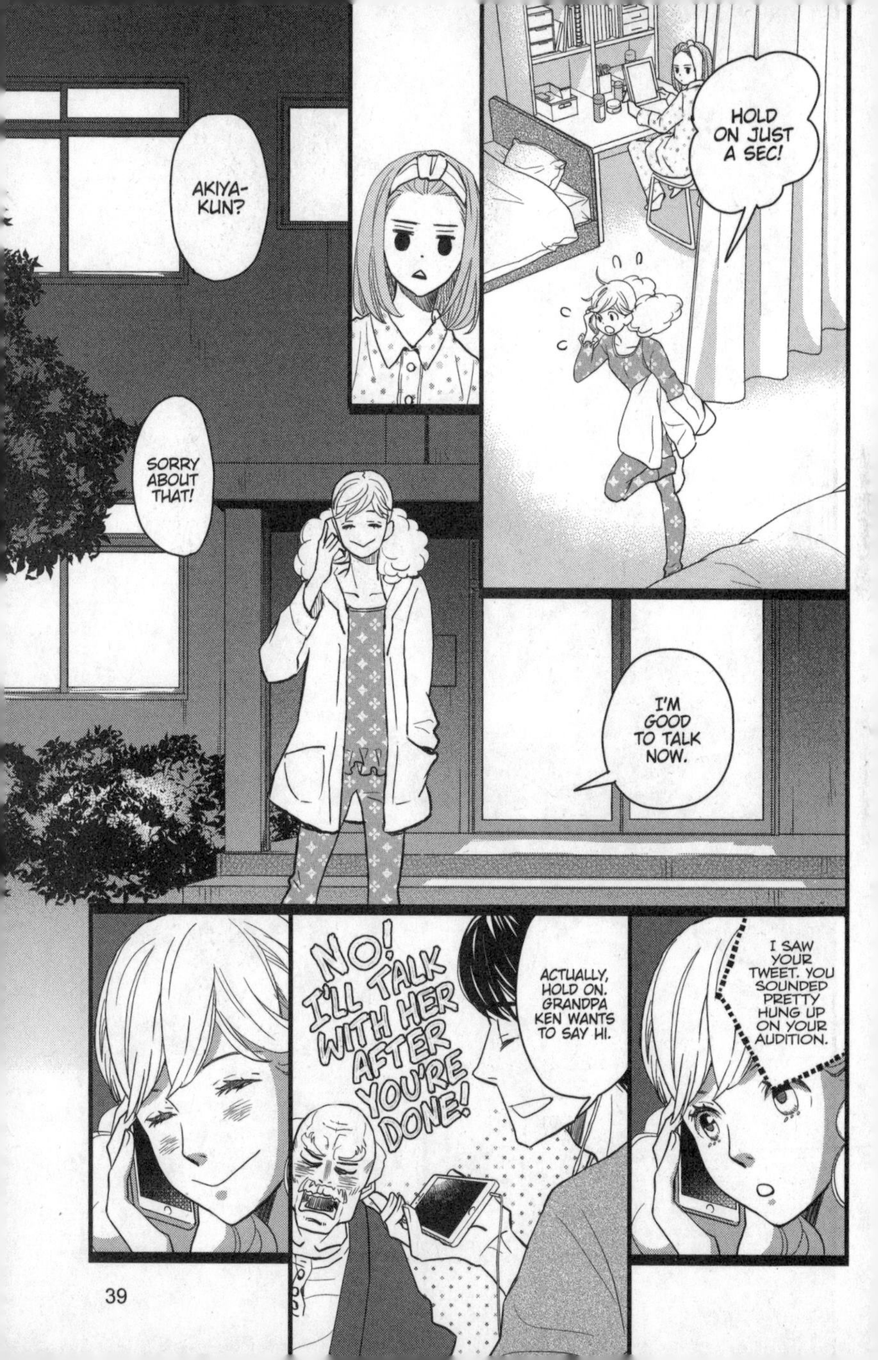
HOLD ON JUST A SEC!
AKIYA-KUN?
SORRY ABOUT THAT!
I'M GOOD TO TALK NOW.
I SAW YOUR TWEET. YOU SOUNDED PRETTY HUNG UP ON YOUR AUDITION.
ACTUALLY, HOLD ON. GRANDPA KEN WANTS TO SAY HI.
NO! I'LL TALK WITH HER AFTER YOU'RE DONE!

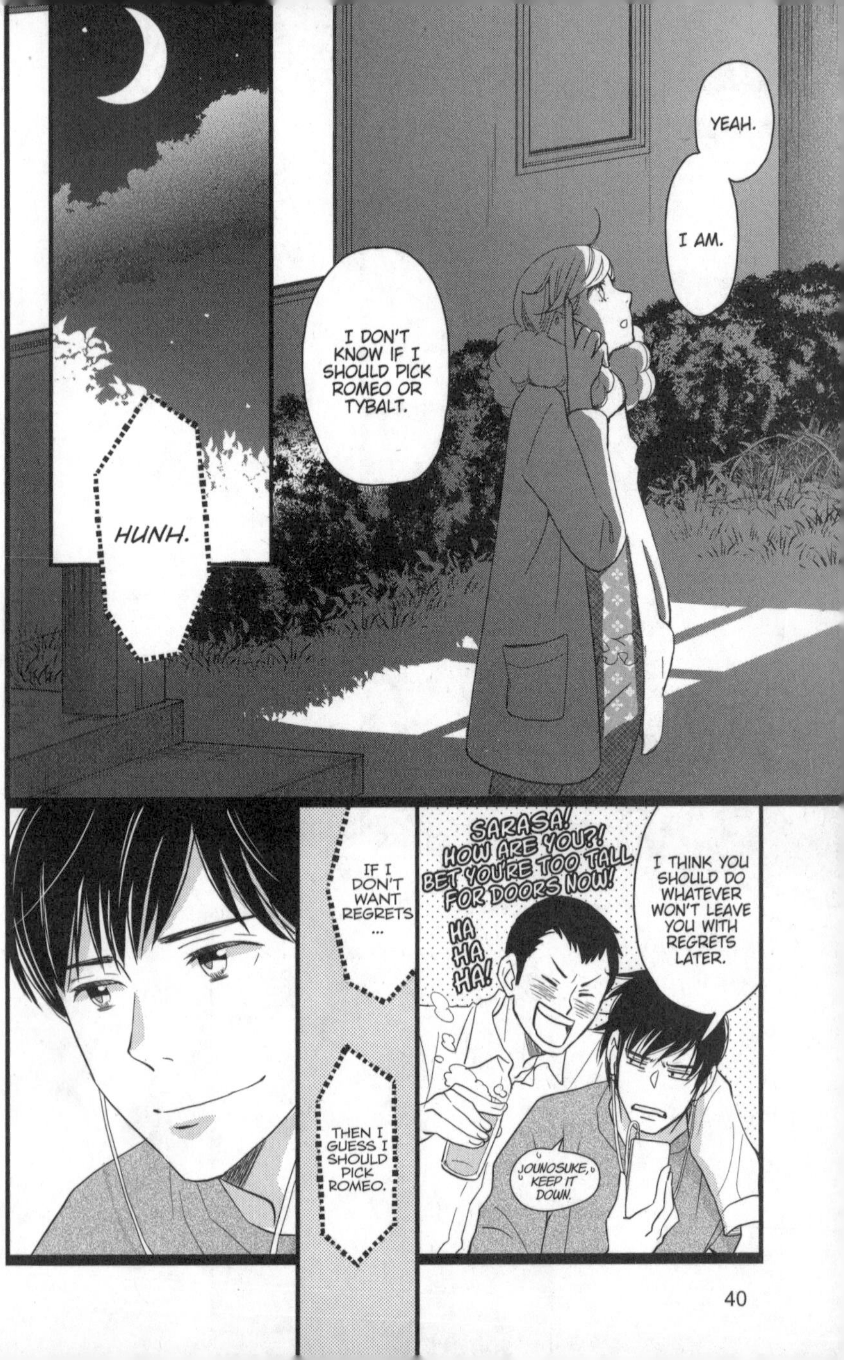
YEAH.
I AM.
I DON'T KNOW IF I SHOULD PICK ROMEO OR TYBALT.
HUNH.
I THINK YOU SHOULD DO WHATEVER WON'T LEAVE YOU WITH REGRETS LATER.
SARASA! HOW ARE YOU?! BET YOU'RE TOO TALL FOR DOORS NOW!
HA HA HA!
JOUNOSUKE, KEEP IT DOWN.
IF I DON'T WANT REGRETS ...
THEN I GUESS I SHOULD PICK ROMEO.

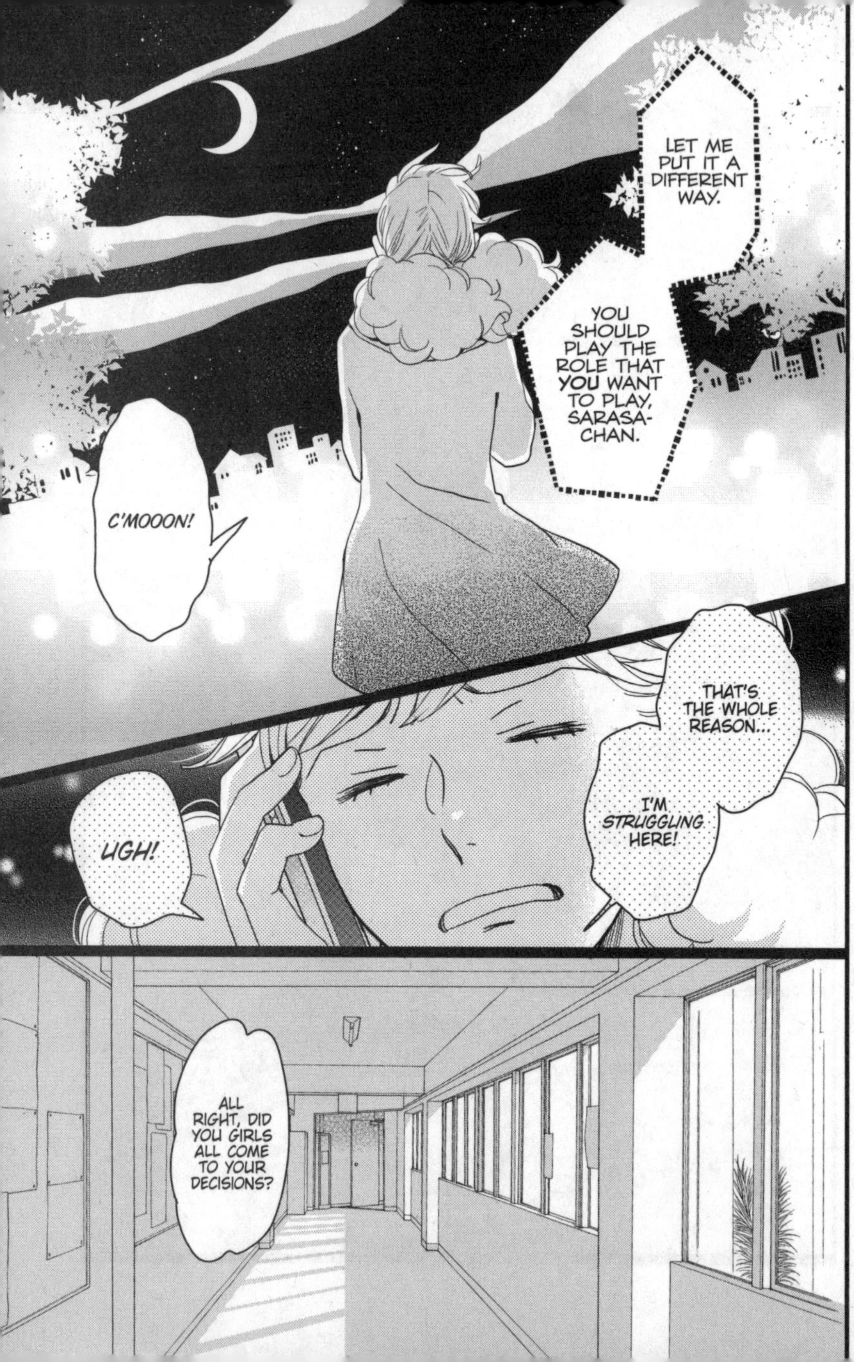

LET ME PUT IT A DIFFERENT WAY.
YOU SHOULD PLAY THE ROLE THAT **YOU** WANT TO PLAY, SARASA-CHAN.
C'MOOON!
THAT'S THE WHOLE REASON...
I'M *STRUGGLING* HERE!
UGH!
ALL RIGHT, DID YOU GIRLS ALL COME TO YOUR DECISIONS?

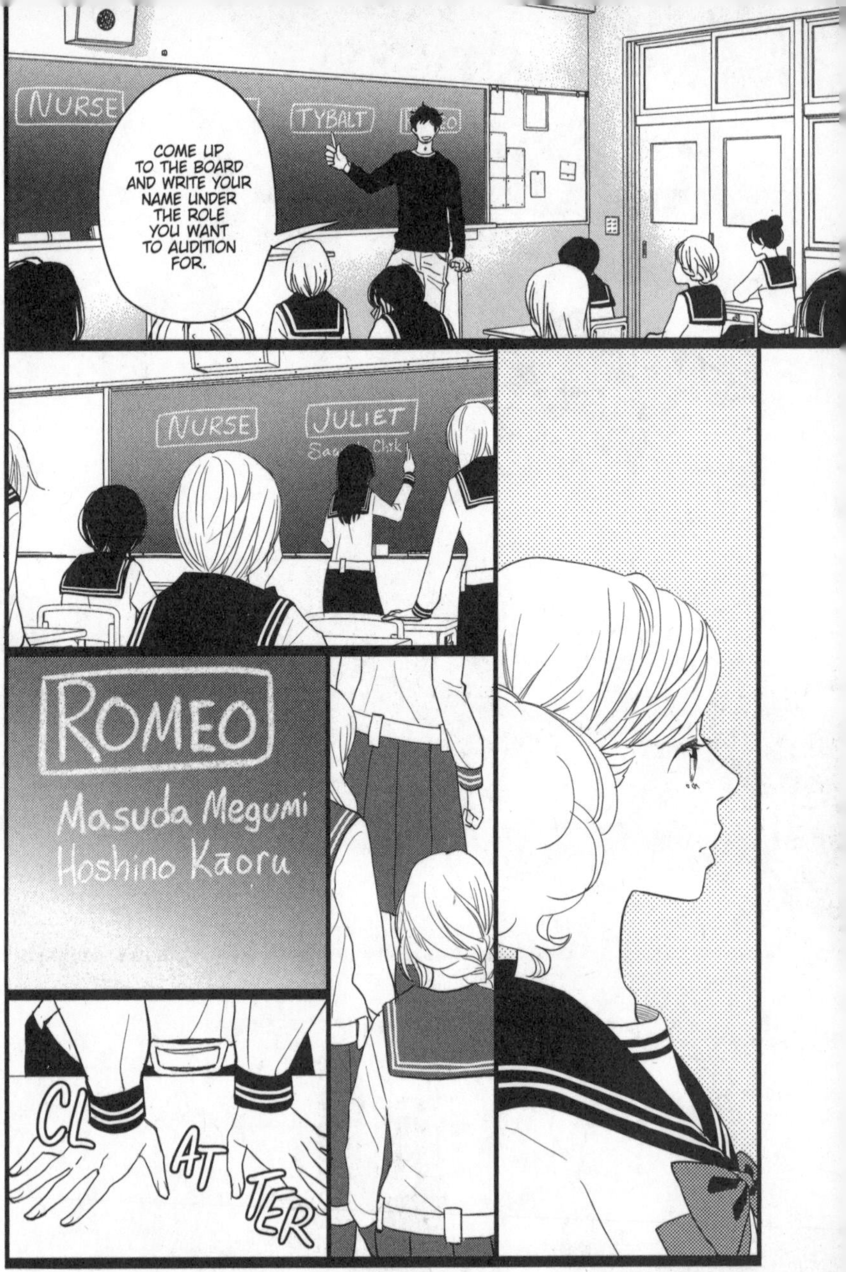
NURSE
TYBALT
COME UP TO THE BOARD AND WRITE YOUR NAME UNDER THE ROLE YOU WANT TO AUDITION FOR.
NURSE
JULIET
ROMEO
Masuda Megumi
Hoshino Kaoru
CLATTER

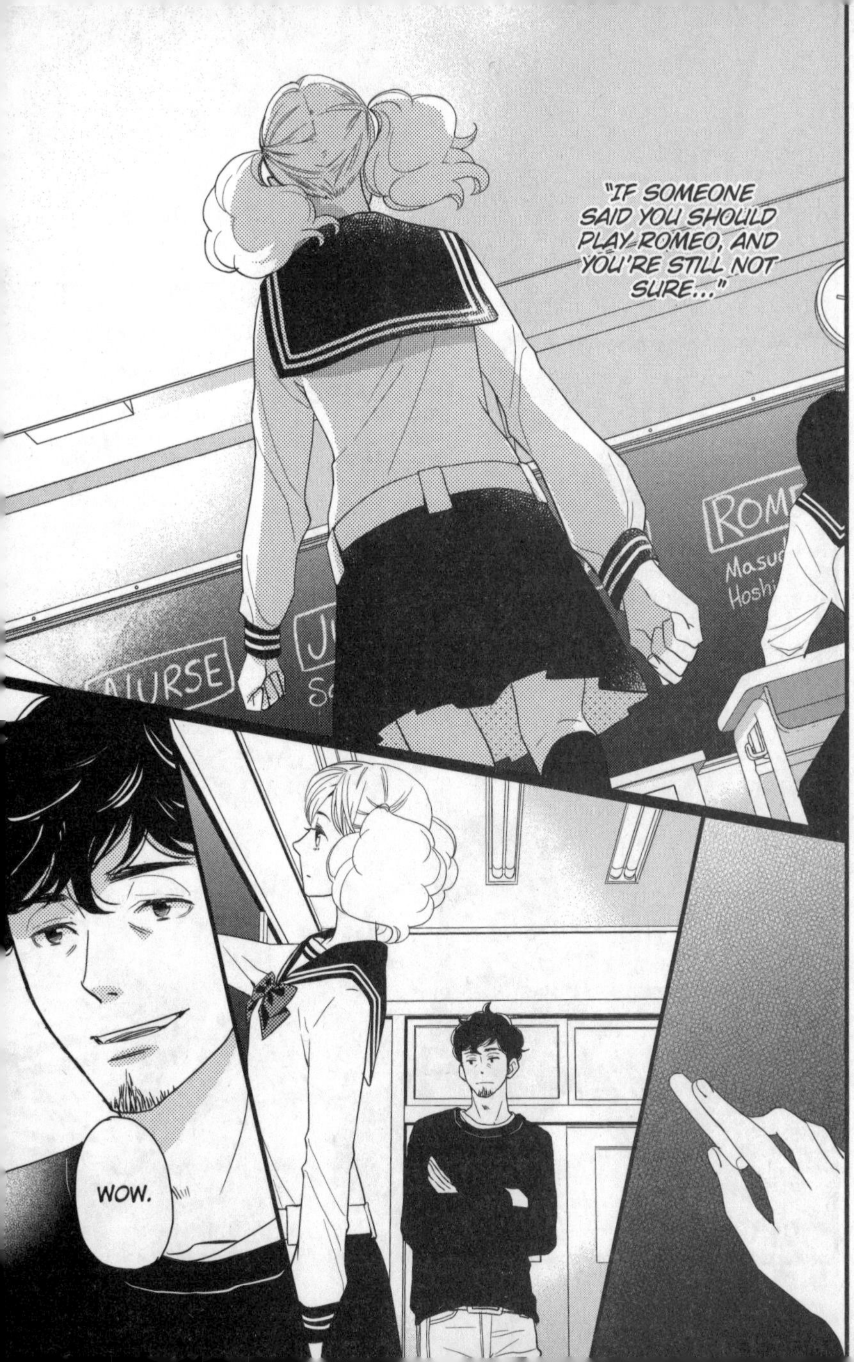
"IF SOMEONE SAID YOU SHOULD PLAY ROMEO, AND YOU'RE STILL NOT SURE..."
ROM
Masu
Hoshi
JU
So
NURSE
WOW.

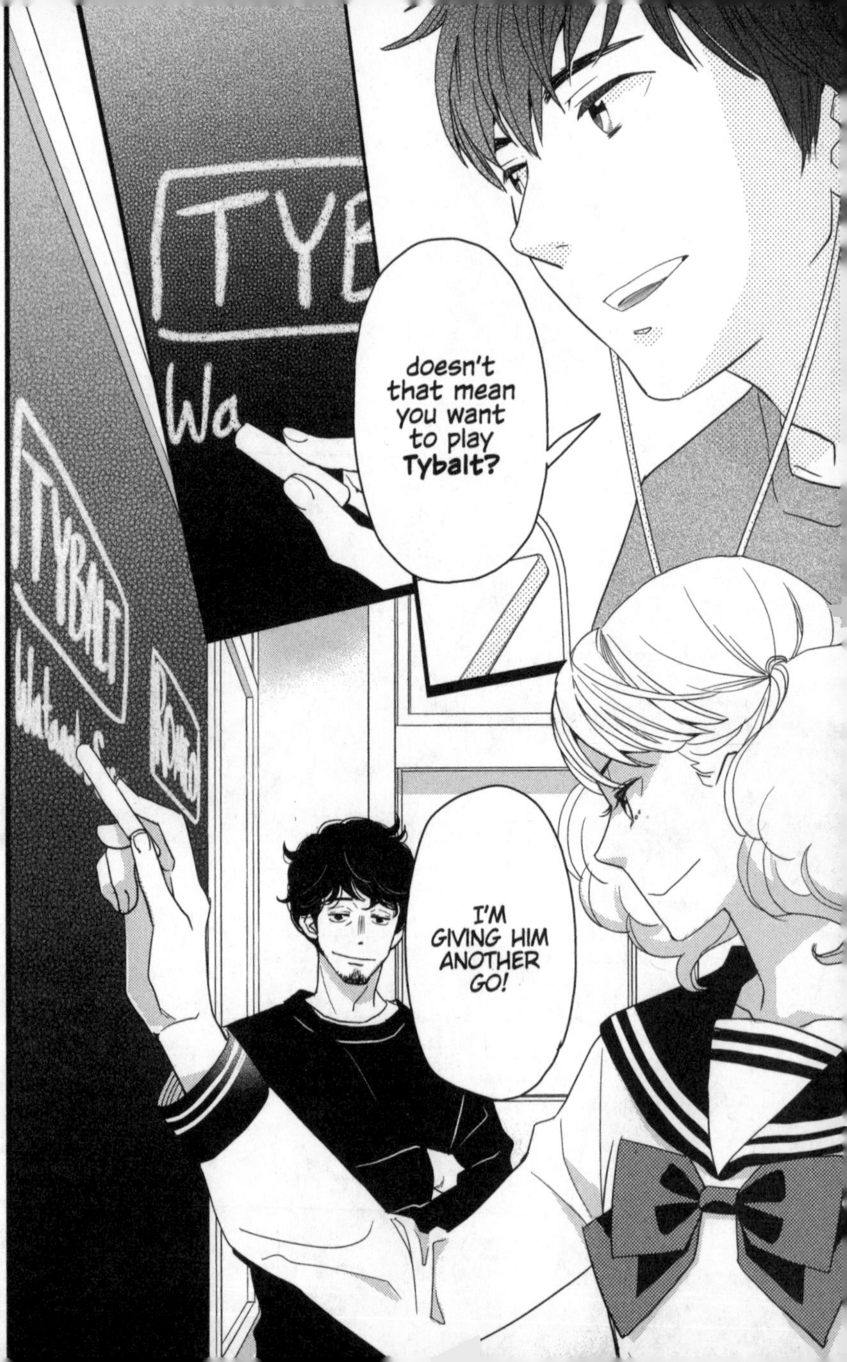
doesn't that mean you want to play **Tybalt?**
I'M GIVING HIM ANOTHER GO!
TYBALT
ROMEO

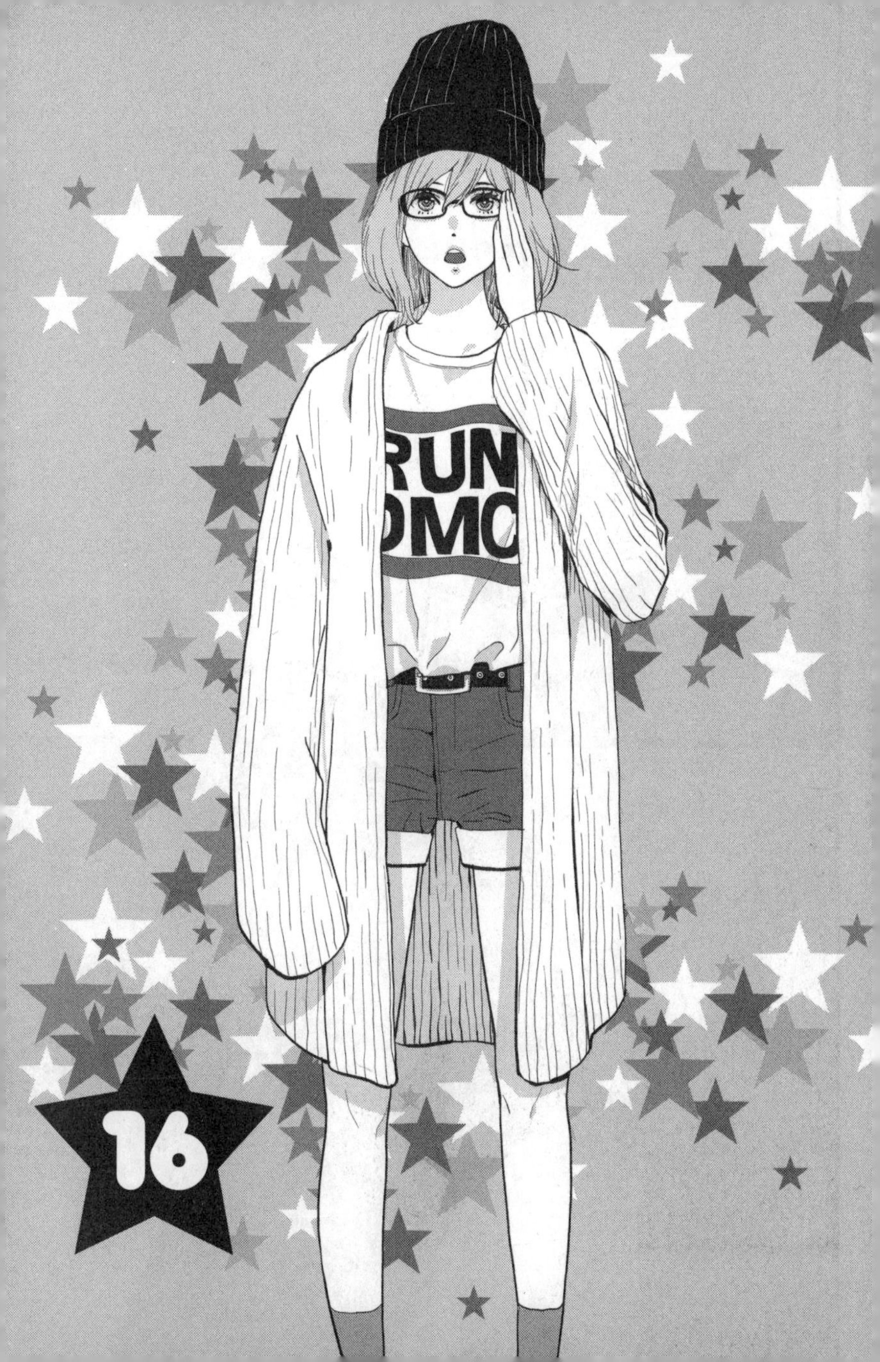
16

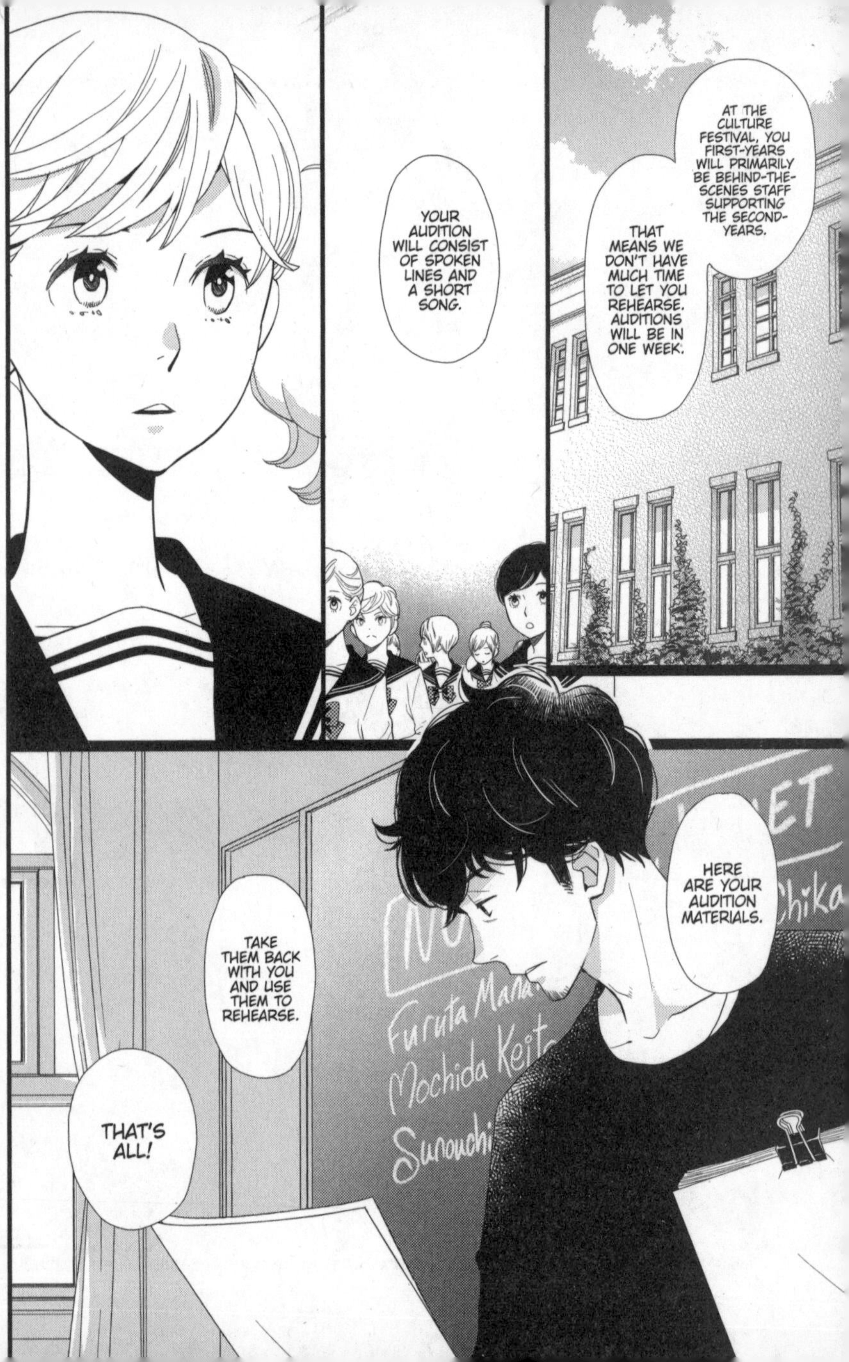
AT THE CULTURE FESTIVAL, YOU FIRST-YEARS WILL PRIMARILY BE BEHIND-THE-SCENES STAFF SUPPORTING THE SECOND-YEARS.
THAT MEANS WE DON'T HAVE MUCH TIME TO LET YOU REHEARSE. AUDITIONS WILL BE IN ONE WEEK.
YOUR AUDITION WILL CONSIST OF SPOKEN LINES AND A SHORT SONG.
HERE ARE YOUR AUDITION MATERIALS.
TAKE THEM BACK WITH YOU AND USE THEM TO REHEARSE.
THAT'S ALL!

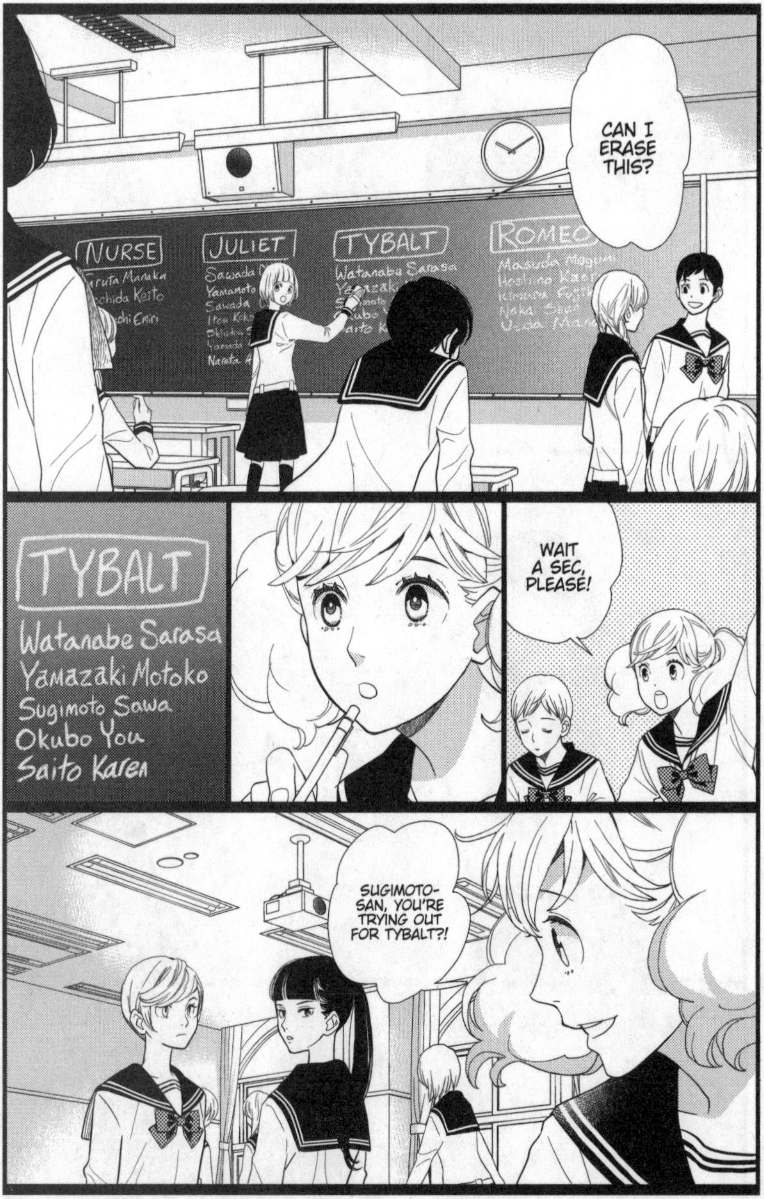
CAN I ERASE THIS?
NURSE
JULIET
TYBALT
ROMEO
WAIT A SEC, PLEASE!
TYBALT
Watanabe Sarasa
Yamazaki Motoko
Sugimoto Sawa
Okubo You
Saito Karen
SUGIMOTO-SAN, YOU'RE TRYING OUT FOR TYBALT?!

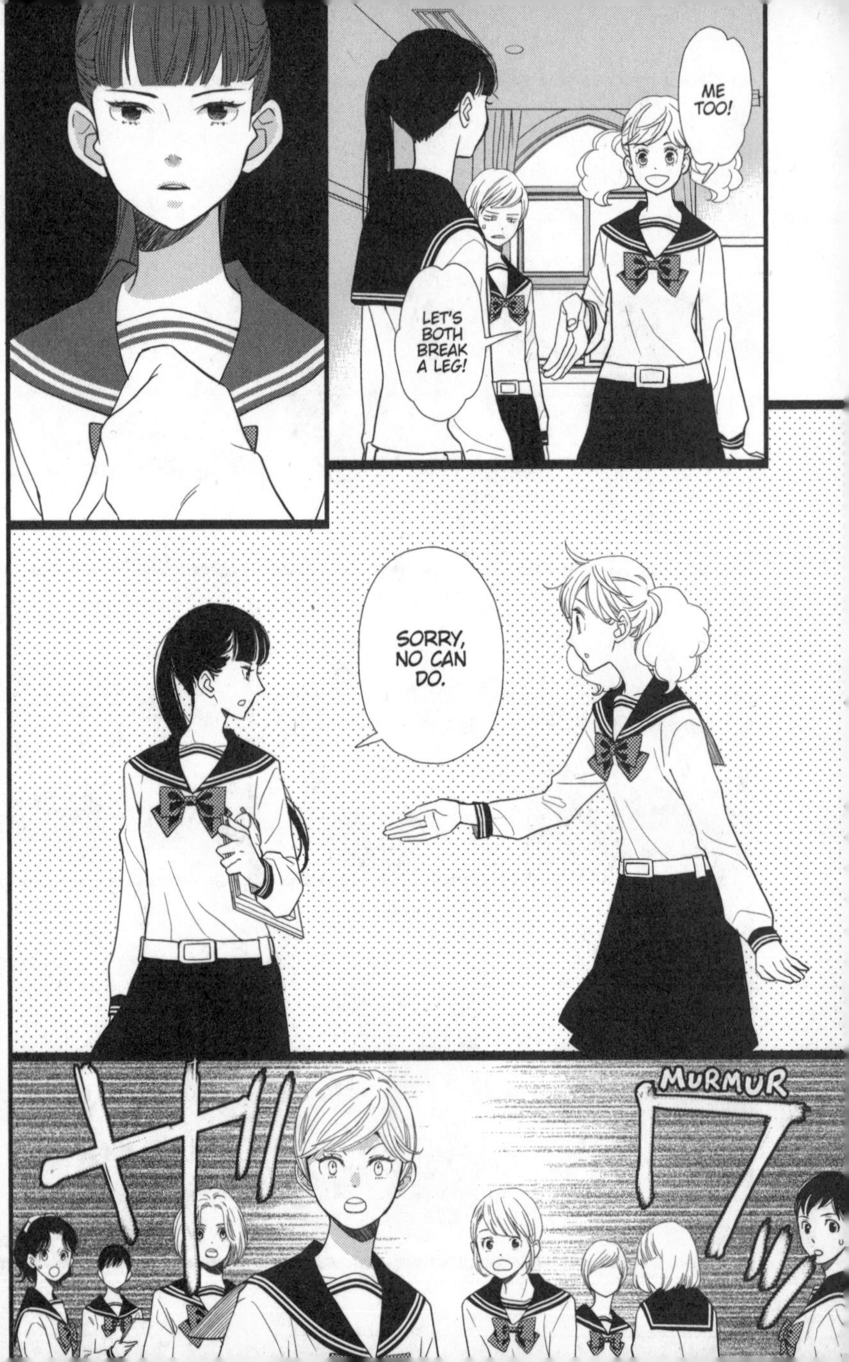

ME TOO!
LET'S BOTH BREAK A LEG!
SORRY, NO CAN DO.
MURMUR

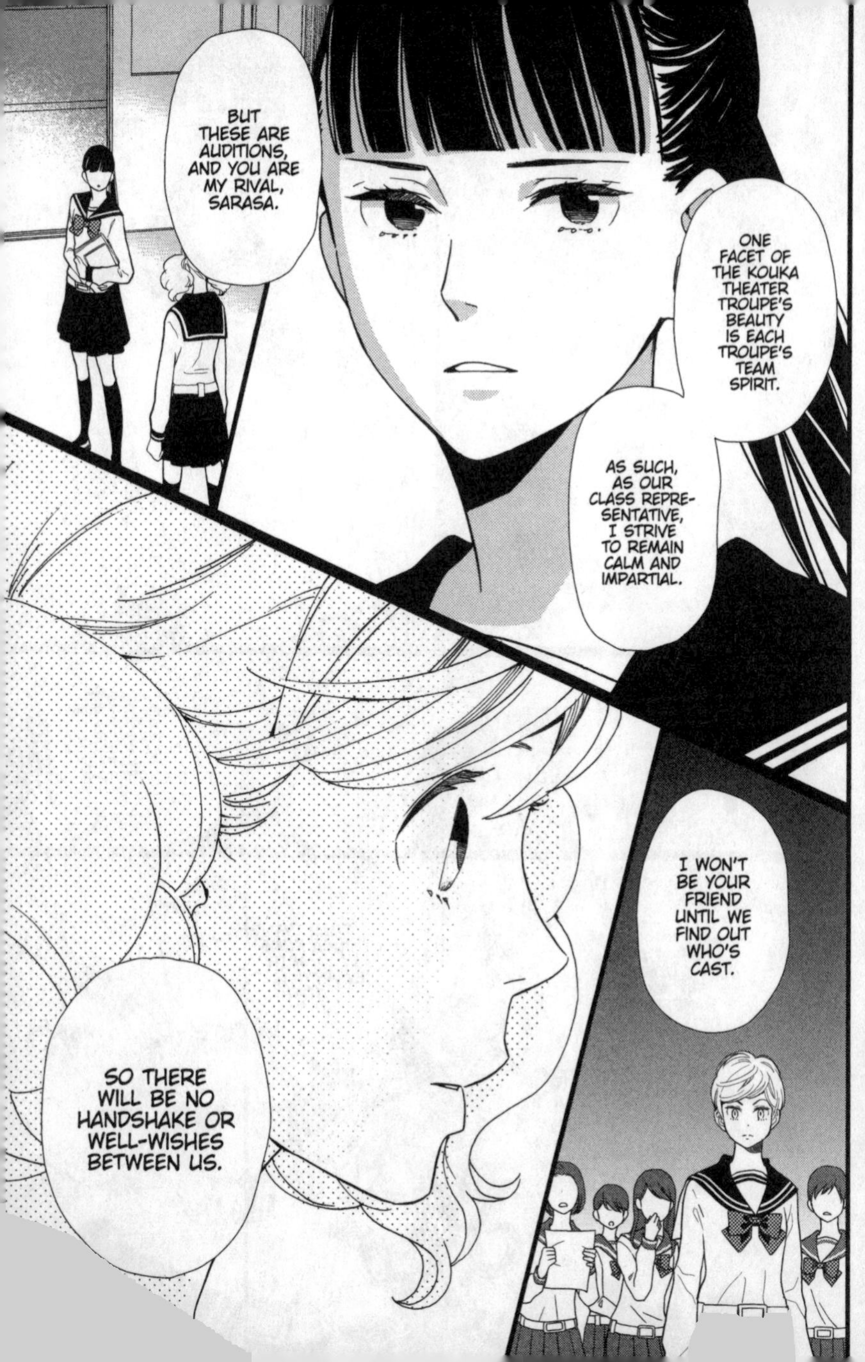
ONE FACET OF THE KOUKA THEATER TROUPE'S BEAUTY IS EACH TROUPE'S TEAM SPIRIT.
AS SUCH, AS OUR CLASS REPRE-SENTATIVE, I STRIVE TO REMAIN CALM AND IMPARTIAL.
BUT THESE ARE AUDITIONS, AND YOU ARE MY RIVAL, SARASA.
I WON'T BE YOUR FRIEND UNTIL WE FIND OUT WHO'S CAST.
SO THERE WILL BE NO HANDSHAKE OR WELL-WISHES BETWEEN US.

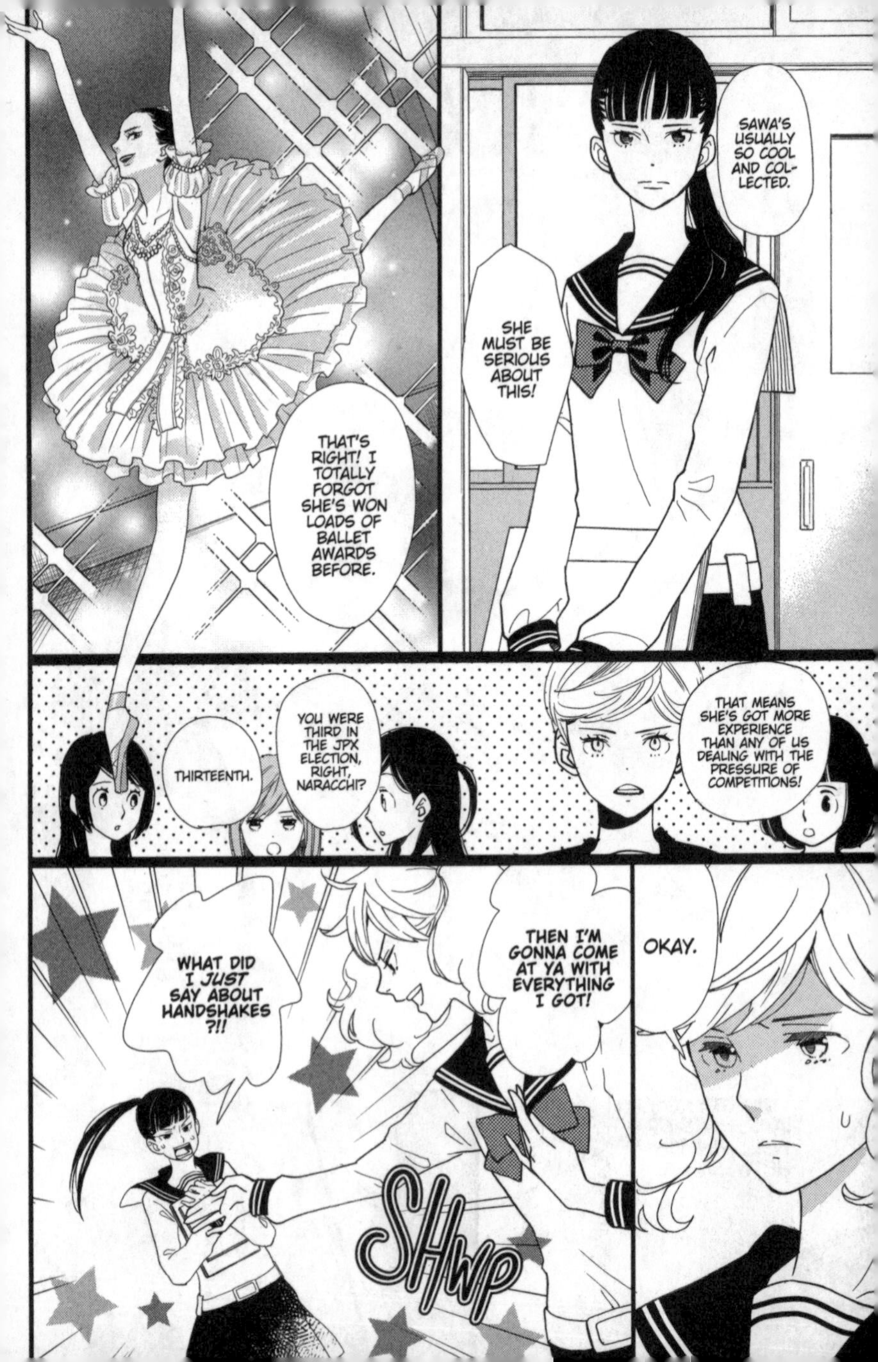
SAWA'S USUALLY SO COOL AND COL-LECTED.
SHE MUST BE SERIOUS ABOUT THIS!
THAT'S RIGHT! I TOTALLY FORGOT SHE'S WON LOADS OF BALLET AWARDS BEFORE.
THAT MEANS SHE'S GOT MORE EXPERIENCE THAN ANY OF US DEALING WITH THE PRESSURE OF COMPETITIONS!
YOU WERE THIRD IN THE JPX ELECTION, RIGHT, NARACCHI?
THIRTEENTH.
OKAY.
THEN I'M GONNA COME AT YA WITH EVERYTHING I GOT!
WHAT DID I JUST SAY ABOUT HANDSHAKES?!!
SHWP

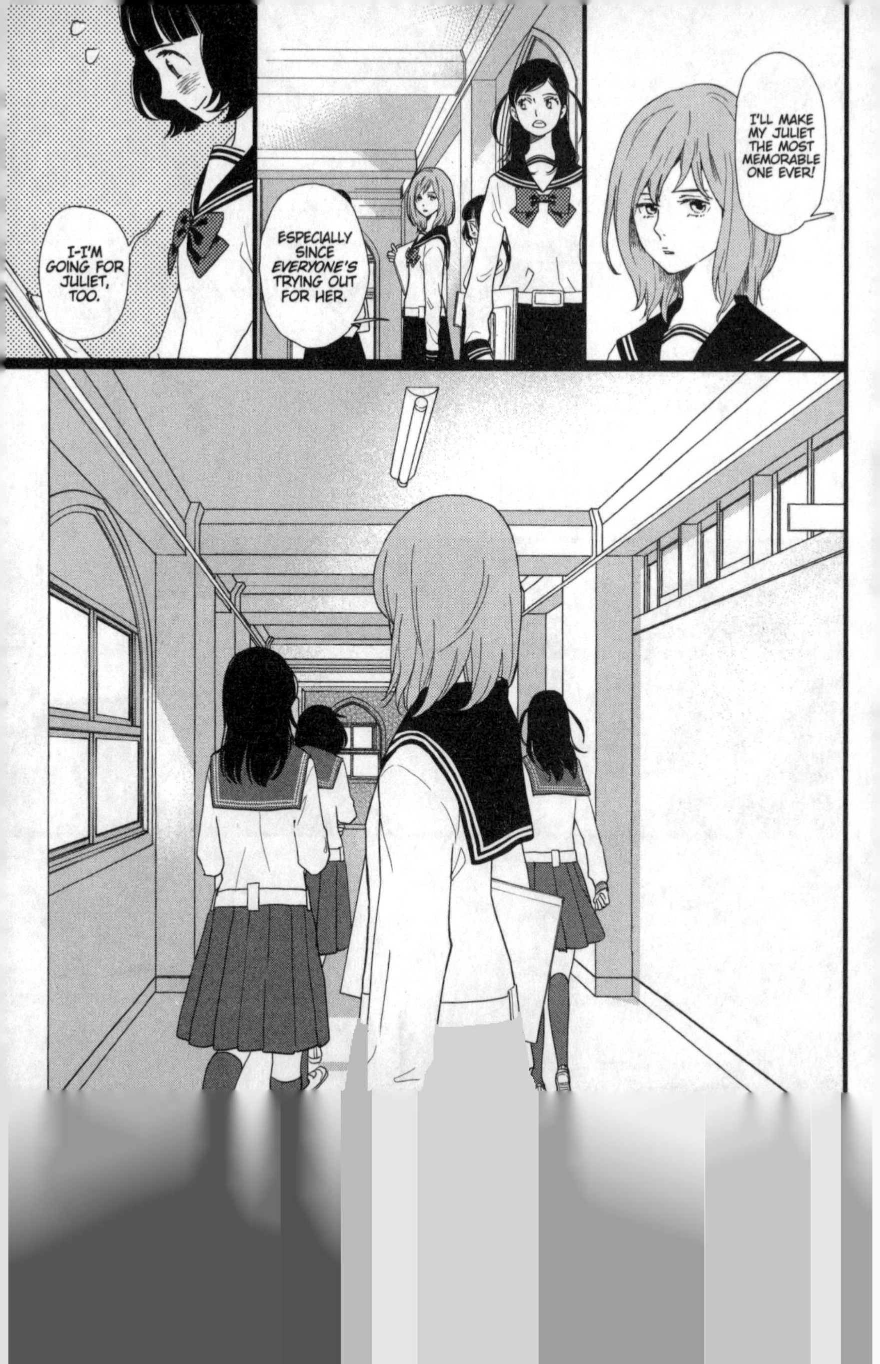
I'LL MAKE MY JULIET THE MOST MEMORABLE ONE EVER!
ESPECIALLY SINCE *EVERYONE'S* TRYING OUT FOR HER.
I-I'M GOING FOR JULIET, TOO.

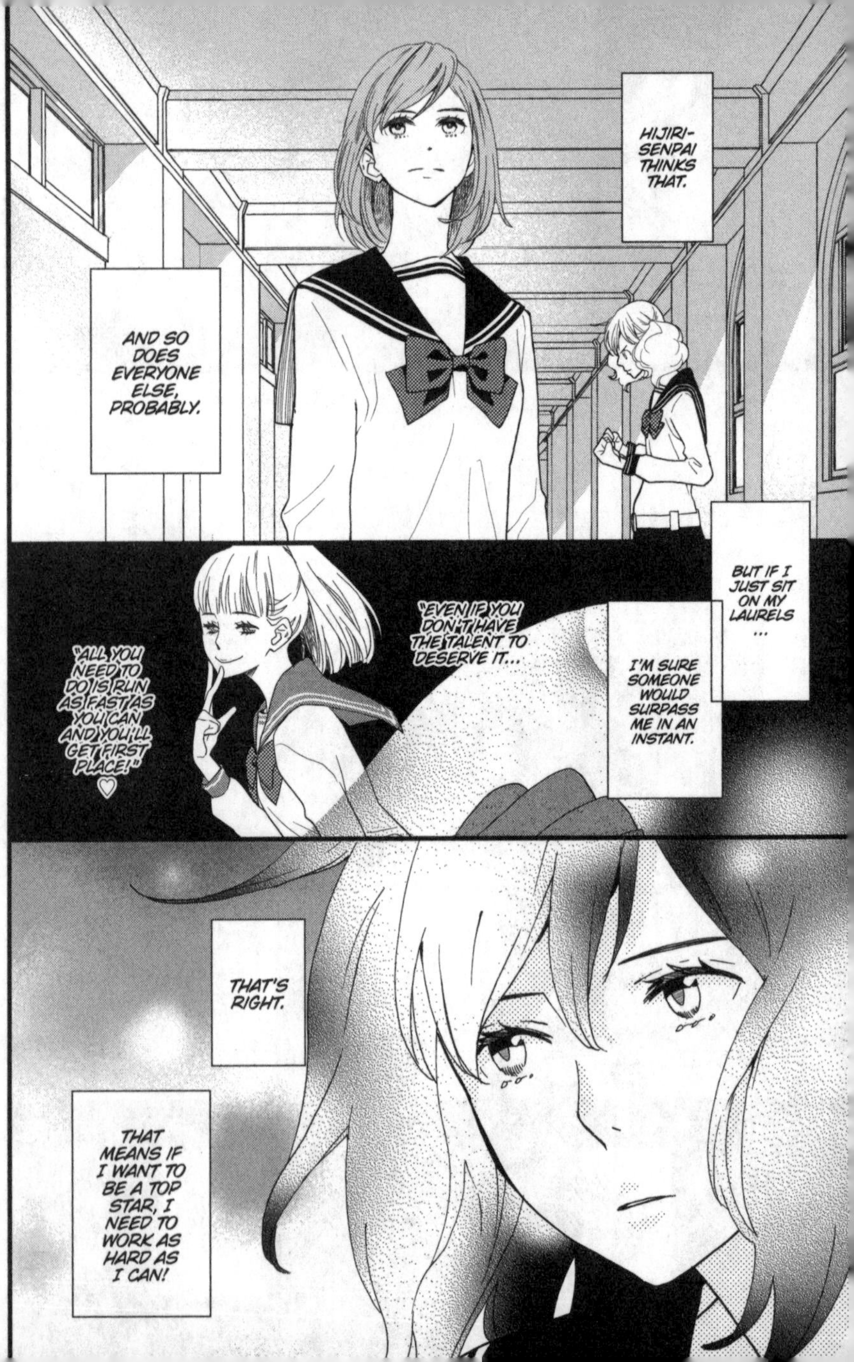
HIJIRI-SENPAI THINKS THAT.
AND SO DOES EVERYONE ELSE, PROBABLY.
BUT IF I JUST SIT ON MY LAURELS ...
I'M SURE SOMEONE WOULD SURPASS ME IN AN INSTANT.
"EVEN IF YOU DON'T HAVE THE TALENT TO DESERVE IT...
ALL YOU NEED TO DO IS RUN AS FAST AS YOU CAN AND YOU'LL GET FIRST PLACE!" ♡
THAT'S RIGHT.
THAT MEANS IF I WANT TO BE A TOP STAR, I NEED TO WORK AS HARD AS I CAN!

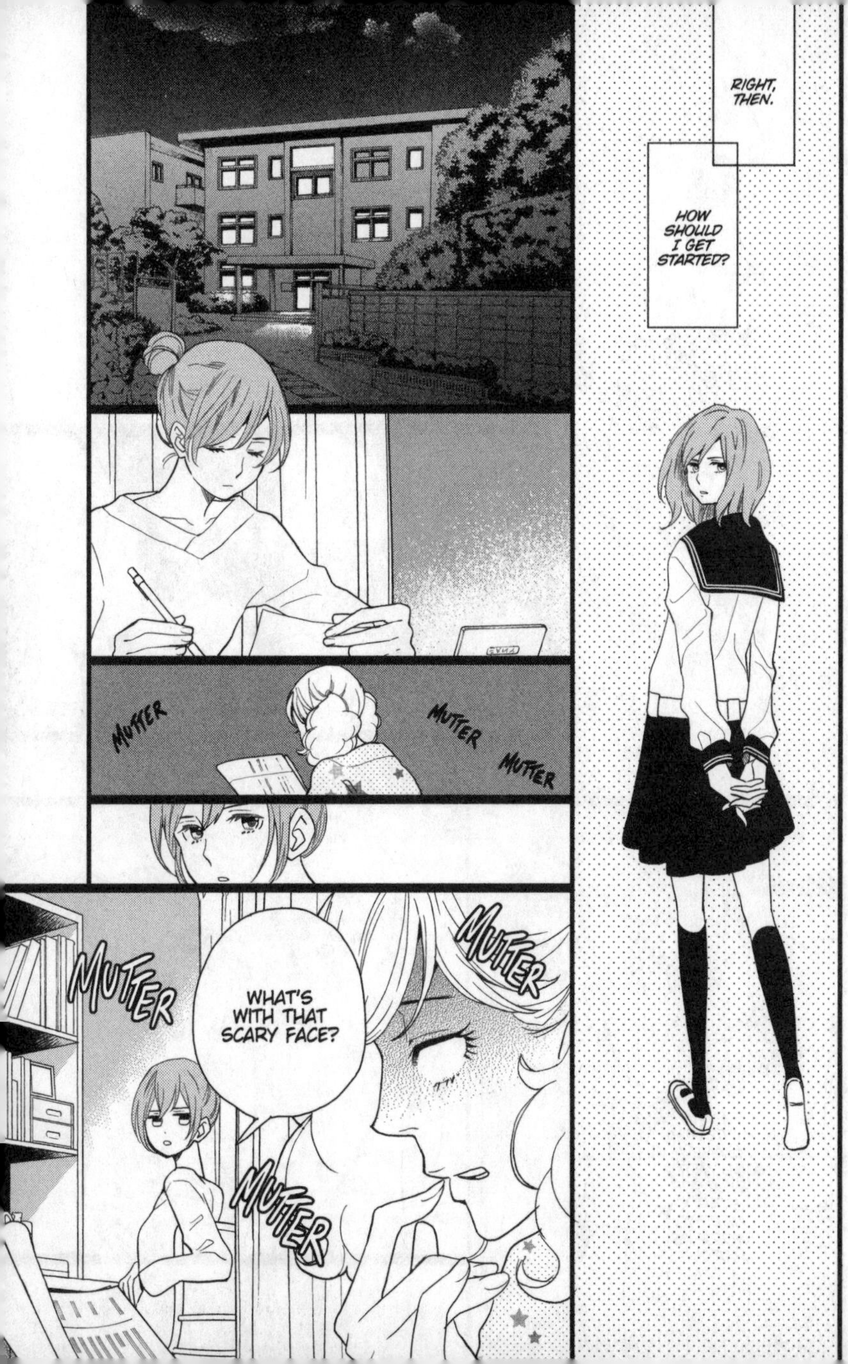
RIGHT, THEN.
HOW SHOULD I GET STARTED?
MUTTER
MUTTER
MUTTER
MUTTER
WHAT'S WITH THAT SCARY FACE?
MUTTER
MUTTER

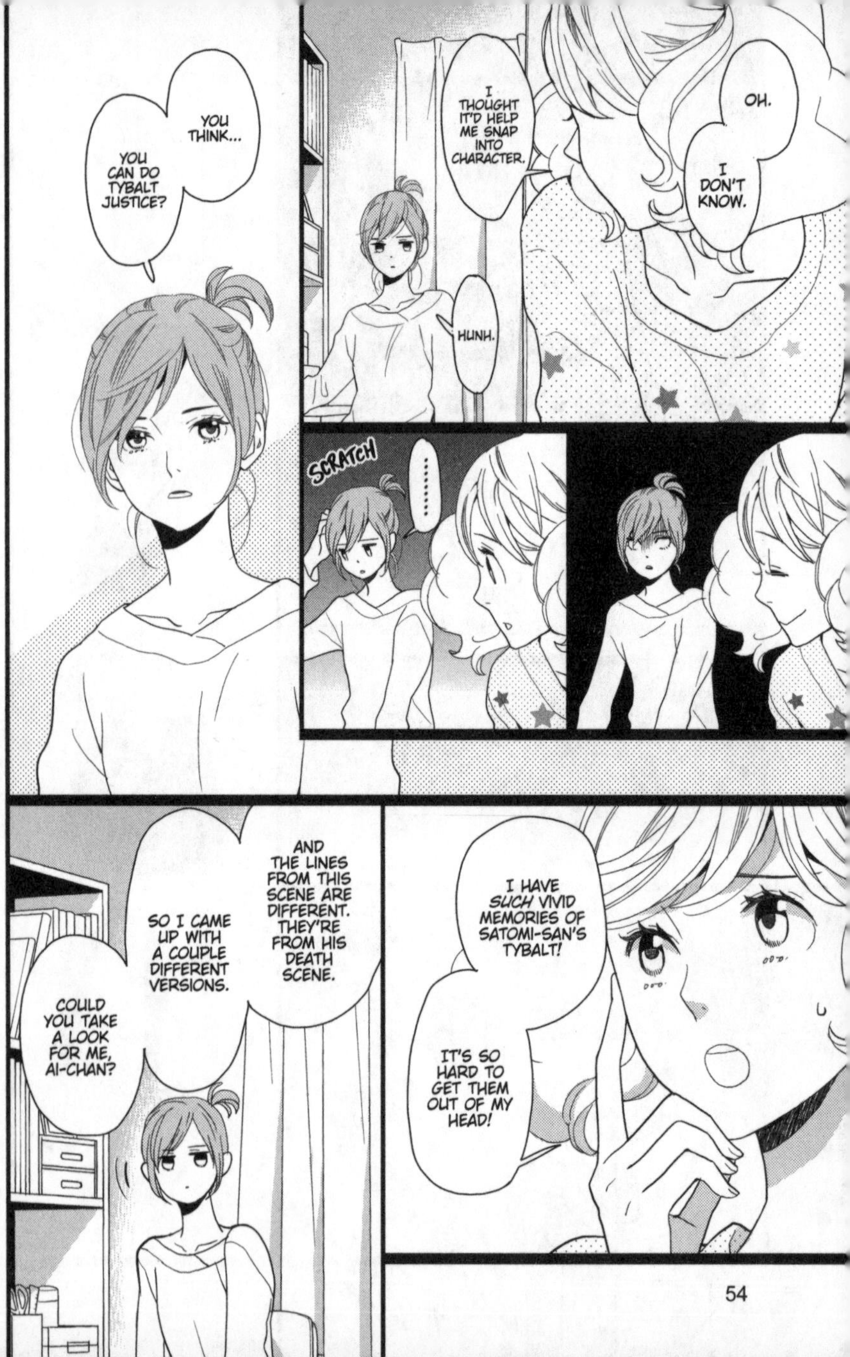
OH.
I DON'T KNOW.
I THOUGHT IT'D HELP ME SNAP INTO CHARACTER.
HUNH.
SCRATCH
......
YOU THINK...
YOU CAN DO TYBALT JUSTICE?
I HAVE *SUCH* VIVID MEMORIES OF SATOMI-SAN'S TYBALT!
IT'S SO HARD TO GET THEM OUT OF MY HEAD!
AND THE LINES FROM THIS SCENE ARE DIFFERENT. THEY'RE FROM HIS DEATH SCENE.
SO I CAME UP WITH A COUPLE DIFFERENT VERSIONS.
COULD YOU TAKE A LOOK FOR ME, AI-CHAN?

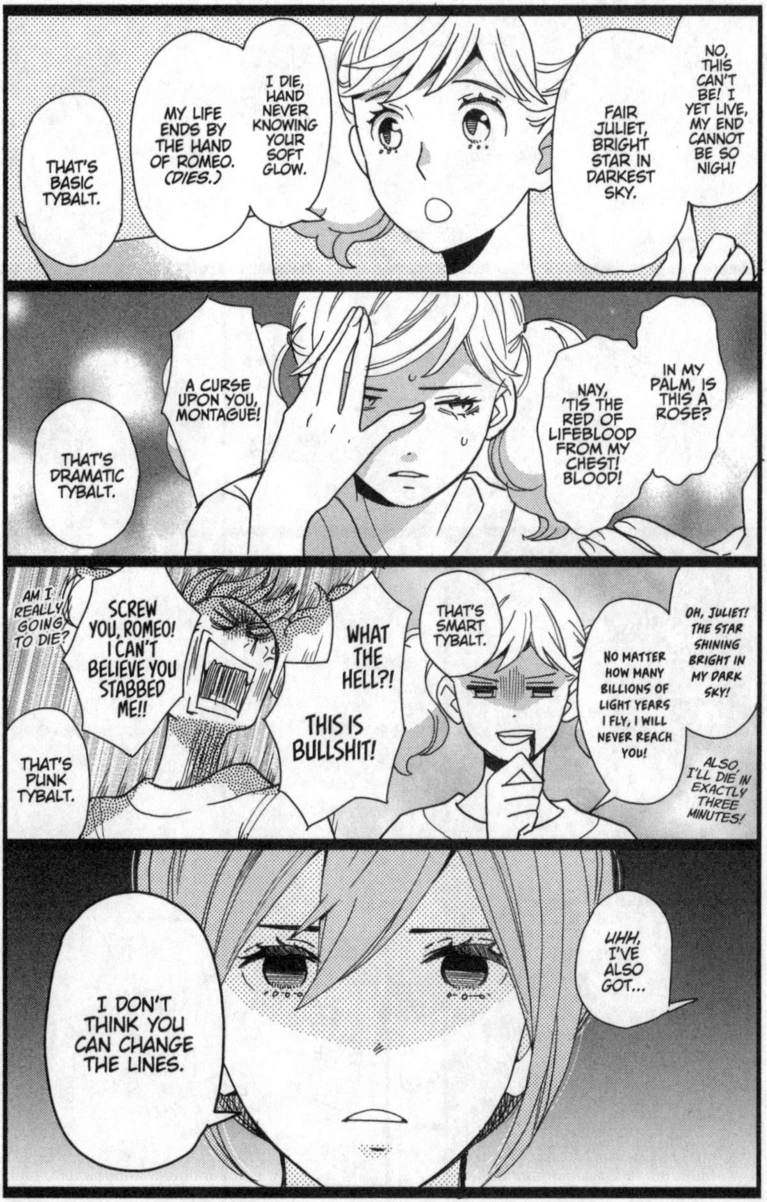
NO, THIS CAN'T BE! I YET LIVE, MY END CANNOT BE SO NIGH!
FAIR JULIET, BRIGHT STAR IN DARKEST SKY.
I DIE, HAND NEVER KNOWING YOUR SOFT GLOW.
MY LIFE ENDS BY THE HAND OF ROMEO. (DIES.)
THAT'S BASIC TYBALT.
IN MY PALM, IS THIS A ROSE?
NAY, 'TIS THE RED OF LIFEBLOOD FROM MY CHEST! BLOOD!
A CURSE UPON YOU, MONTAGUE!
THAT'S DRAMATIC TYBALT.
OH, JULIET! THE STAR SHINING BRIGHT IN MY DARK SKY!
NO MATTER HOW MANY BILLIONS OF LIGHT YEARS I FLY, I WILL NEVER REACH YOU!
ALSO, I'LL DIE IN EXACTLY THREE MINUTES!
THAT'S SMART TYBALT.
WHAT THE HELL?!
THIS IS BULLSHIT!
SCREW YOU, ROMEO! I CAN'T BELIEVE YOU STABBED ME!!
AM I REALLY GOING TO DIE?
THAT'S PUNK TYBALT.
UHH, I'VE ALSO GOT...
I DON'T THINK YOU CAN CHANGE THE LINES.

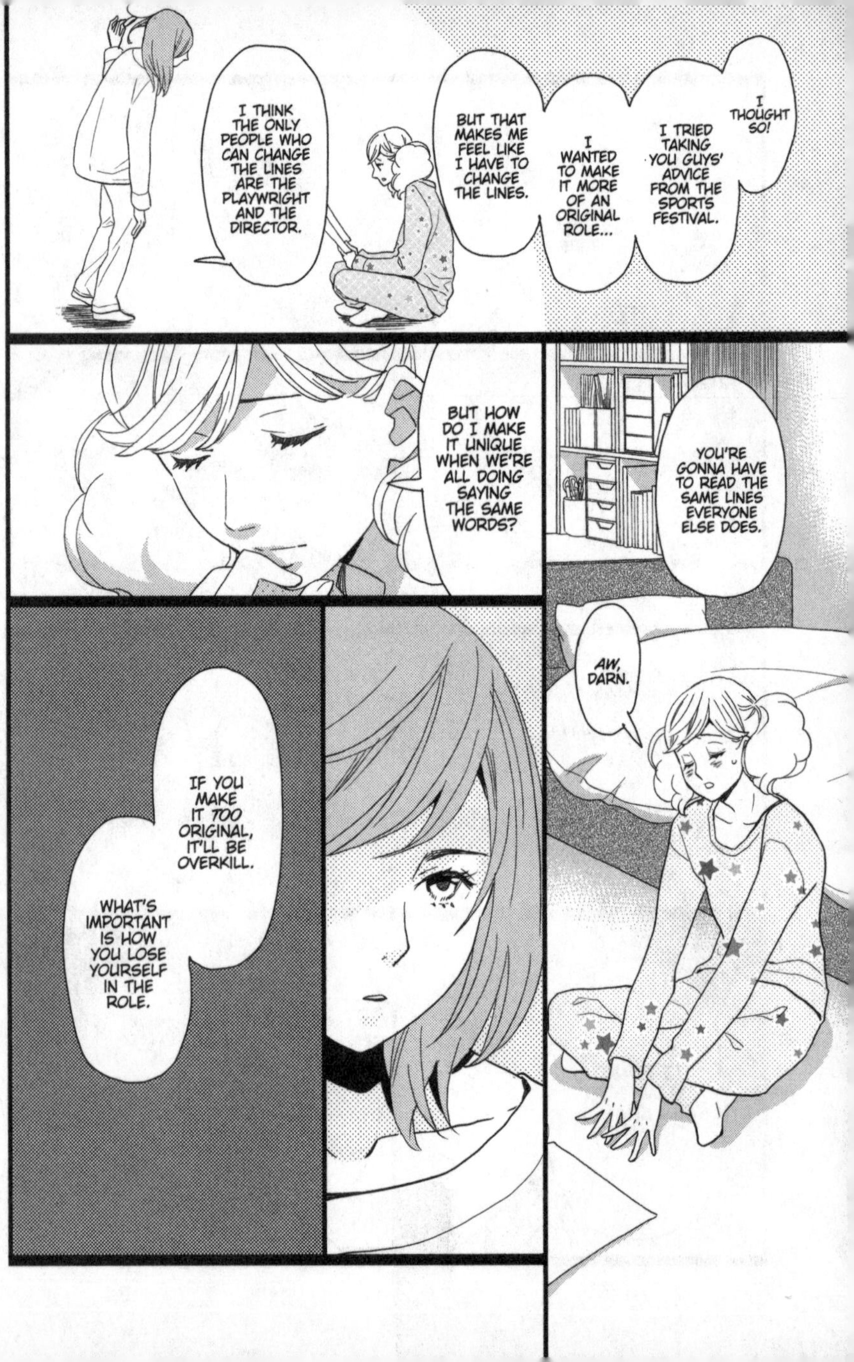
I THOUGHT SO!
I TRIED TAKING YOU GUYS' ADVICE FROM THE SPORTS FESTIVAL.
I WANTED TO MAKE IT MORE OF AN ORIGINAL ROLE...
BUT THAT MAKES ME FEEL LIKE I HAVE TO CHANGE THE LINES.
I THINK THE ONLY PEOPLE WHO CAN CHANGE THE LINES ARE THE PLAYWRIGHT AND THE DIRECTOR.
YOU'RE GONNA HAVE TO READ THE SAME LINES EVERYONE ELSE DOES.
AW, DARN.
BUT HOW DO I MAKE IT UNIQUE WHEN WE'RE ALL DOING SAYING THE SAME WORDS?
IF YOU MAKE IT *TOO* ORIGINAL, IT'LL BE OVERKILL.
WHAT'S IMPORTANT IS HOW YOU LOSE YOURSELF IN THE ROLE.

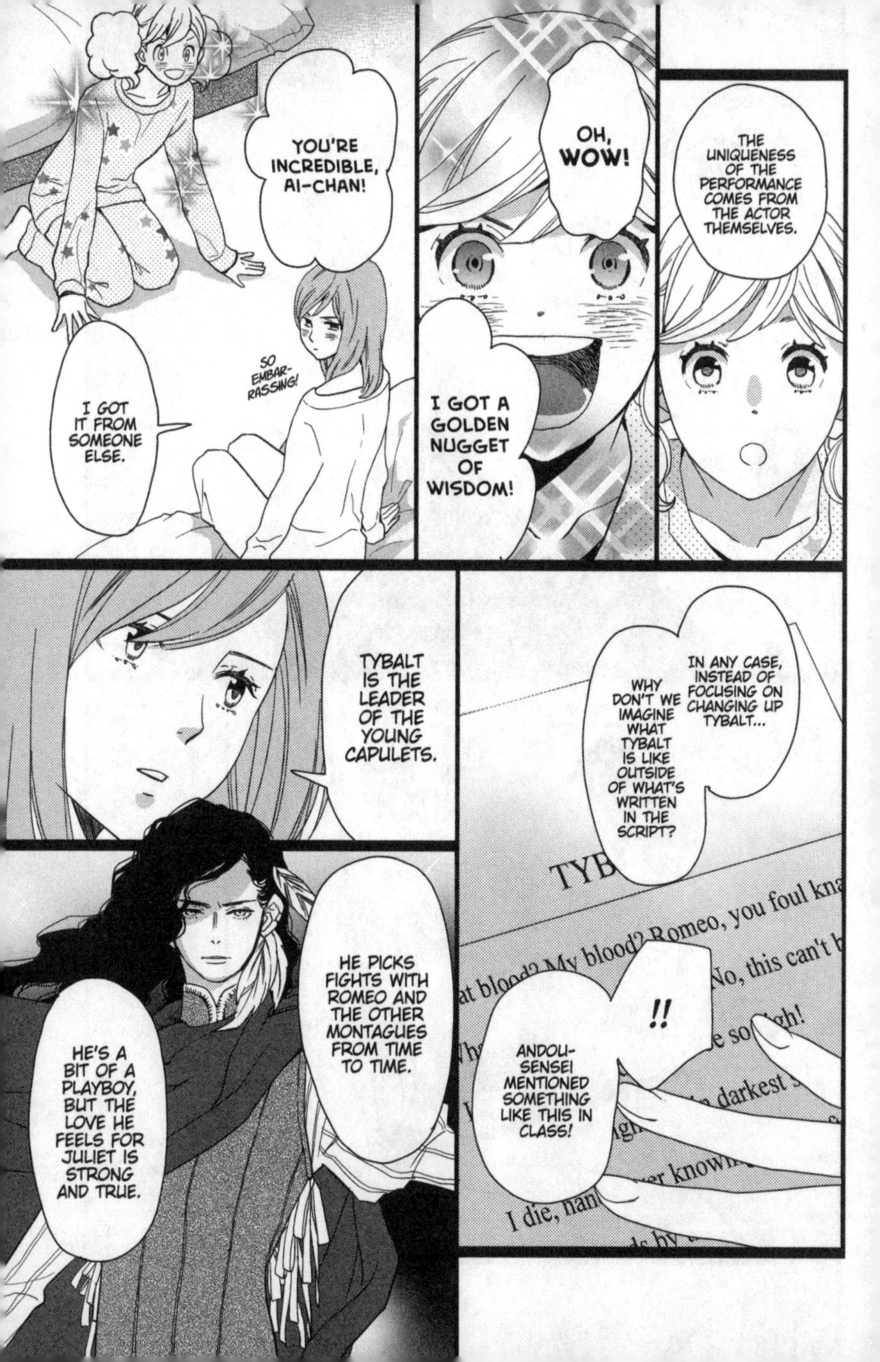
THE UNIQUENESS OF THE PERFORMANCE COMES FROM THE ACTOR THEMSELVES.
OH, WOW!
I GOT A GOLDEN NUGGET OF WISDOM!
YOU'RE INCREDIBLE, AI-CHAN!
SO EMBARRASSING!
I GOT IT FROM SOMEONE ELSE.
IN ANY CASE, INSTEAD OF FOCUSING ON CHANGING UP TYBALT...
WHY DON'T WE IMAGINE WHAT TYBALT IS LIKE OUTSIDE OF WHAT'S WRITTEN IN THE SCRIPT?
!!
ANDOU-SENSEI MENTIONED SOMETHING LIKE THIS IN CLASS!
TYBALT IS THE LEADER OF THE YOUNG CAPULETS.
HE PICKS FIGHTS WITH ROMEO AND THE OTHER MONTAGUES FROM TIME TO TIME.
HE'S A BIT OF A PLAYBOY, BUT THE LOVE HE FEELS FOR JULIET IS STRONG AND TRUE.

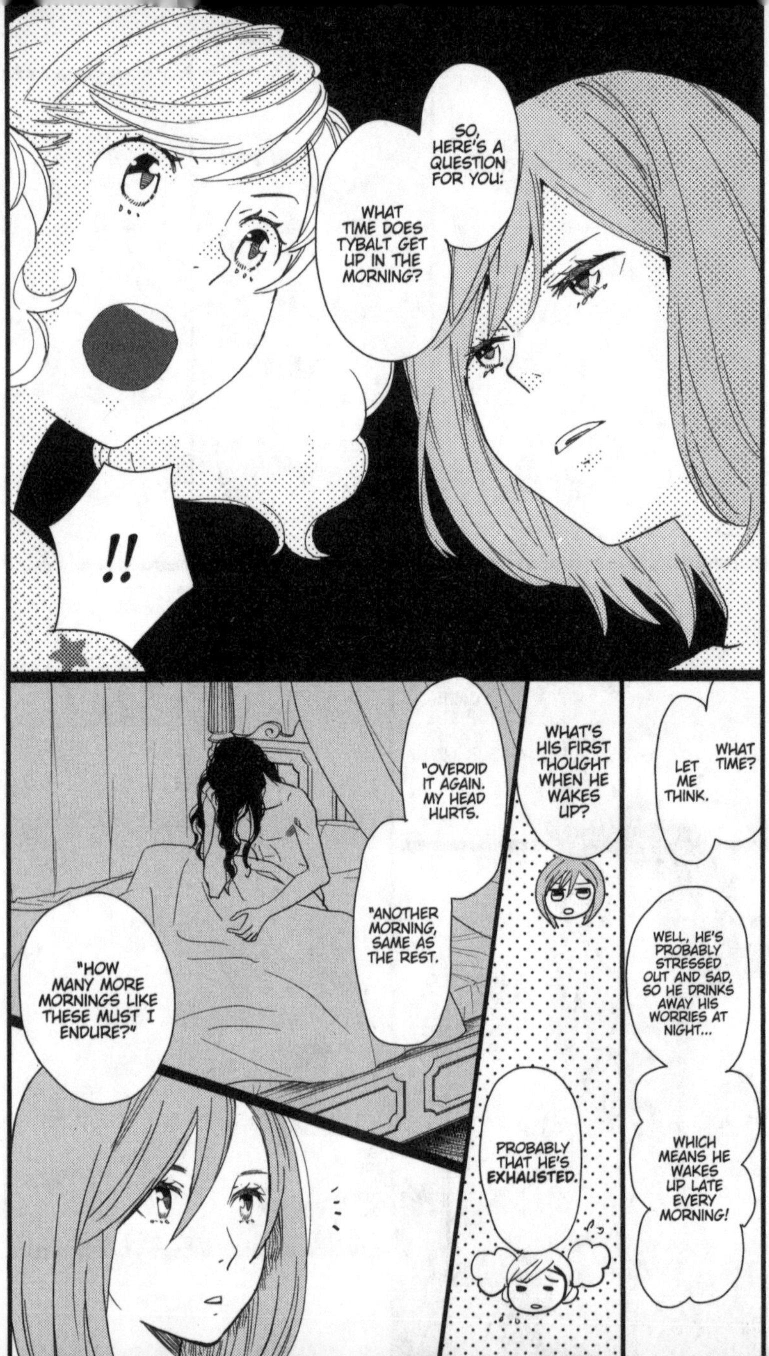
SO, HERE'S A QUESTION FOR YOU:
WHAT TIME DOES TYBALT GET UP IN THE MORNING?
!!
WHAT TIME?
LET ME THINK.
WELL, HE'S PROBABLY STRESSED OUT AND SAD, SO HE DRINKS AWAY HIS WORRIES AT NIGHT...
WHICH MEANS HE WAKES UP LATE EVERY MORNING!
WHAT'S HIS FIRST THOUGHT WHEN HE WAKES UP?
PROBABLY THAT HE'S **EXHAUSTED**.
"OVERDID IT AGAIN. MY HEAD HURTS.
"ANOTHER MORNING, SAME AS THE REST.
"HOW MANY MORE MORNINGS LIKE THESE MUST I ENDURE?"

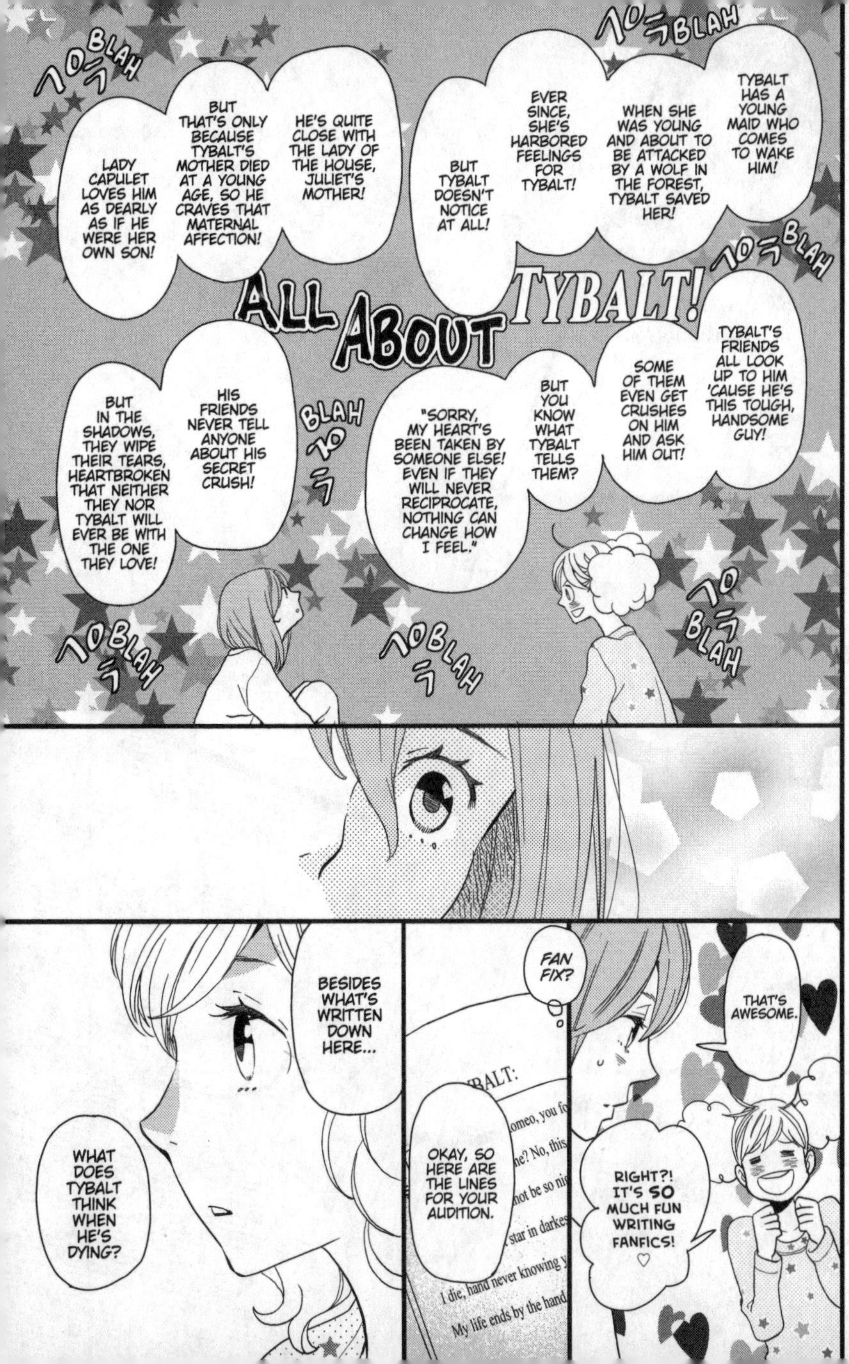
ヘロヘラ BLAH
TYBALT HAS A YOUNG MAID WHO COMES TO WAKE HIM!
WHEN SHE WAS YOUNG AND ABOUT TO BE ATTACKED BY A WOLF IN THE FOREST, TYBALT SAVED HER!
EVER SINCE, SHE'S HARBORED FEELINGS FOR TYBALT!
BUT TYBALT DOESN'T NOTICE AT ALL!
ヘロヘラ BLAH
HE'S QUITE CLOSE WITH THE LADY OF THE HOUSE, JULIET'S MOTHER!
BUT THAT'S ONLY BECAUSE TYBALT'S MOTHER DIED AT A YOUNG AGE, SO HE CRAVES THAT MATERNAL AFFECTION!
LADY CAPULET LOVES HIM AS DEARLY AS IF HE WERE HER OWN SON!
ヘロヘラ BLAH
ALL ABOUT TYBALT!
TYBALT'S FRIENDS ALL LOOK UP TO HIM 'CAUSE HE'S THIS TOUGH, HANDSOME GUY!
SOME OF THEM EVEN GET CRUSHES ON HIM AND ASK HIM OUT!
BUT YOU KNOW WHAT TYBALT TELLS THEM?
"SORRY, MY HEART'S BEEN TAKEN BY SOMEONE ELSE! EVEN IF THEY WILL NEVER RECIPROCATE, NOTHING CAN CHANGE HOW I FEEL."
BLAH ヘロヘラ
HIS FRIENDS NEVER TELL ANYONE ABOUT HIS SECRET CRUSH!
BUT IN THE SHADOWS, THEY WIPE THEIR TEARS, HEARTBROKEN THAT NEITHER THEY NOR TYBALT WILL EVER BE WITH THE ONE THEY LOVE!
ヘロヘラ BLAH
ヘロヘラ BLAH
ヘロヘラ BLAH
THAT'S AWESOME.
FAN FIX?
RIGHT?! IT'S SO MUCH FUN WRITING FANFICS! ♡
OKAY, SO HERE ARE THE LINES FOR YOUR AUDITION.
BESIDES WHAT'S WRITTEN DOWN HERE...
WHAT DOES TYBALT THINK WHEN HE'S DYING?

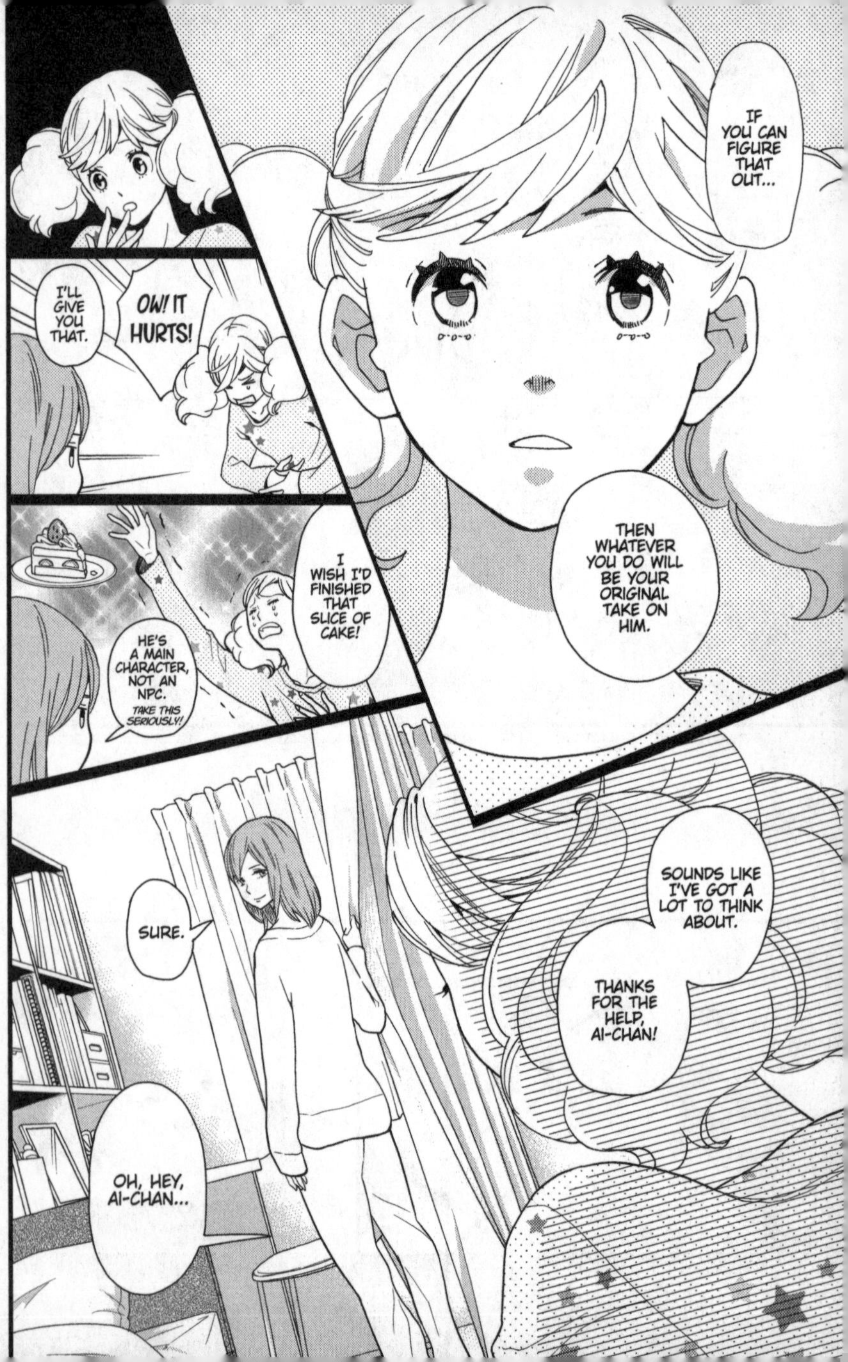
IF YOU CAN FIGURE THAT OUT...
THEN WHATEVER YOU DO WILL BE YOUR ORIGINAL TAKE ON HIM.
OW! IT HURTS!
I'LL GIVE YOU THAT.
I WISH I'D FINISHED THAT SLICE OF CAKE!
HE'S A MAIN CHARACTER, NOT AN NPC. TAKE THIS SERIOUSLY!
SOUNDS LIKE I'VE GOT A LOT TO THINK ABOUT.
THANKS FOR THE HELP, AI-CHAN!
SURE.
OH, HEY, AI-CHAN...

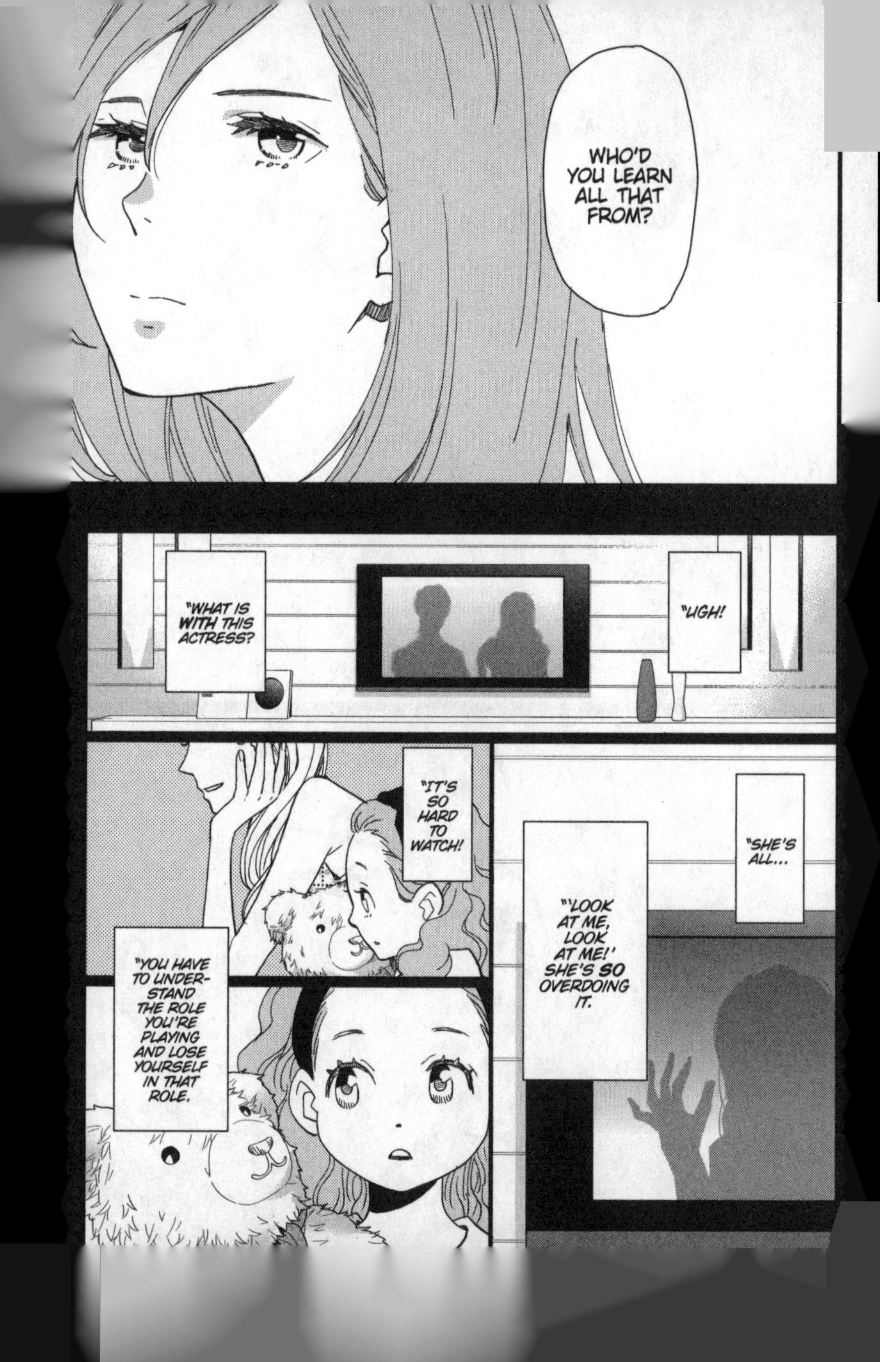
WHO'D YOU LEARN ALL THAT FROM?
"UGH!
"WHAT IS WITH THIS ACTRESS?
"SHE'S ALL...
"'LOOK AT ME, LOOK AT ME!' SHE'S SO OVERDOING IT.
"IT'S SO HARD TO WATCH!
"YOU HAVE TO UNDER-STAND THE ROLE YOU'RE PLAYING AND LOSE YOURSELF IN THAT ROLE.

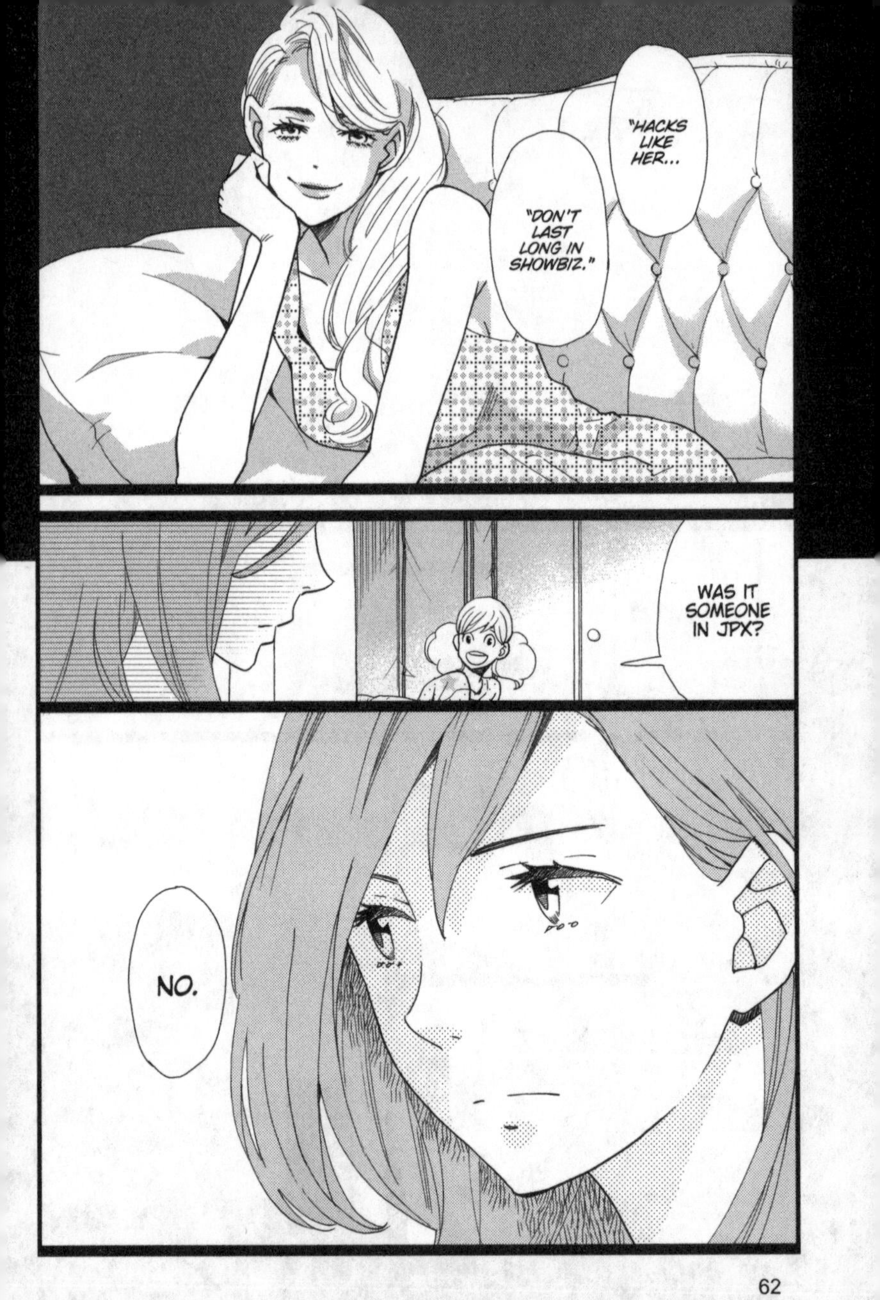
"HACKS LIKE HER...
"DON'T LAST LONG IN SHOWBIZ."
WAS IT SOMEONE IN JPX?
NO.

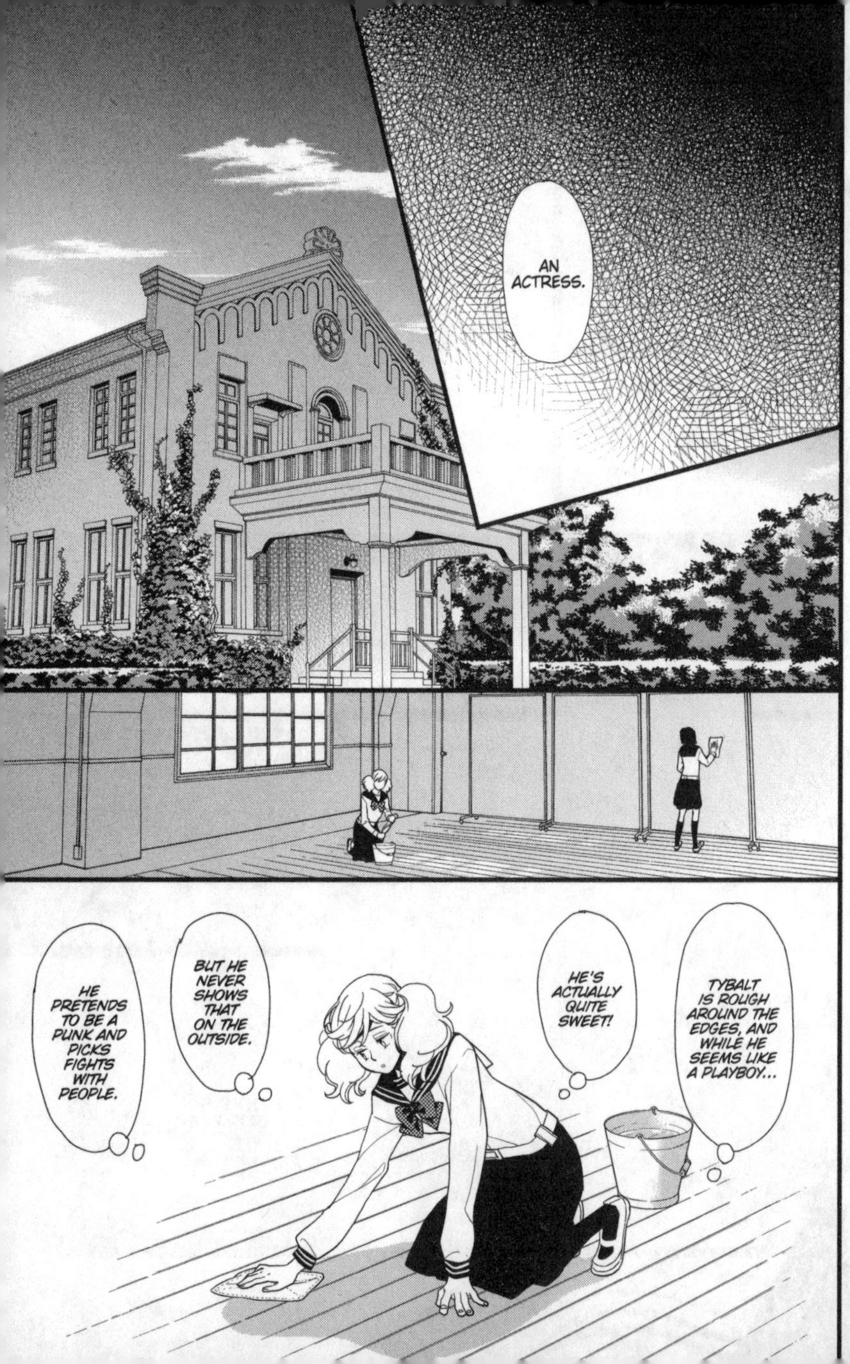
AN ACTRESS.
TYBALT IS ROUGH AROUND THE EDGES, AND WHILE HE SEEMS LIKE A PLAYBOY...
HE'S ACTUALLY QUITE SWEET!
BUT HE NEVER SHOWS THAT ON THE OUTSIDE.
HE PRETENDS TO BE A PUNK AND PICKS FIGHTS WITH PEOPLE.

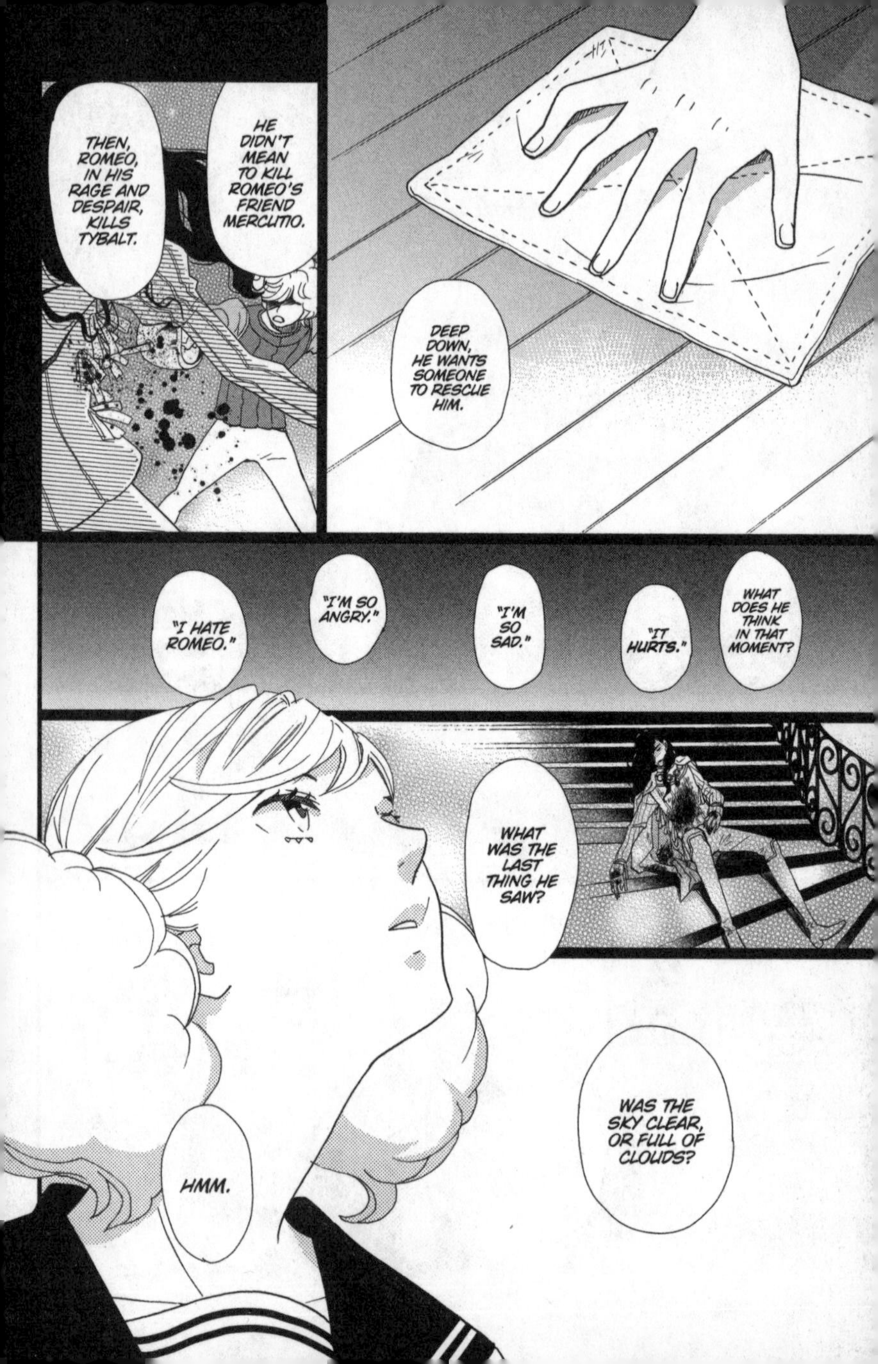
DEEP DOWN, HE WANTS SOMEONE TO RESCUE HIM.
HE DIDN'T MEAN TO KILL ROMEO'S FRIEND MERCUTIO.
THEN, ROMEO, IN HIS RAGE AND DESPAIR, KILLS TYBALT.
WHAT DOES HE THINK IN THAT MOMENT?
"IT HURTS."
"I'M SO SAD."
"I'M SO ANGRY."
"I HATE ROMEO."
WHAT WAS THE LAST THING HE SAW?
WAS THE SKY CLEAR, OR FULL OF CLOUDS?
HMM.

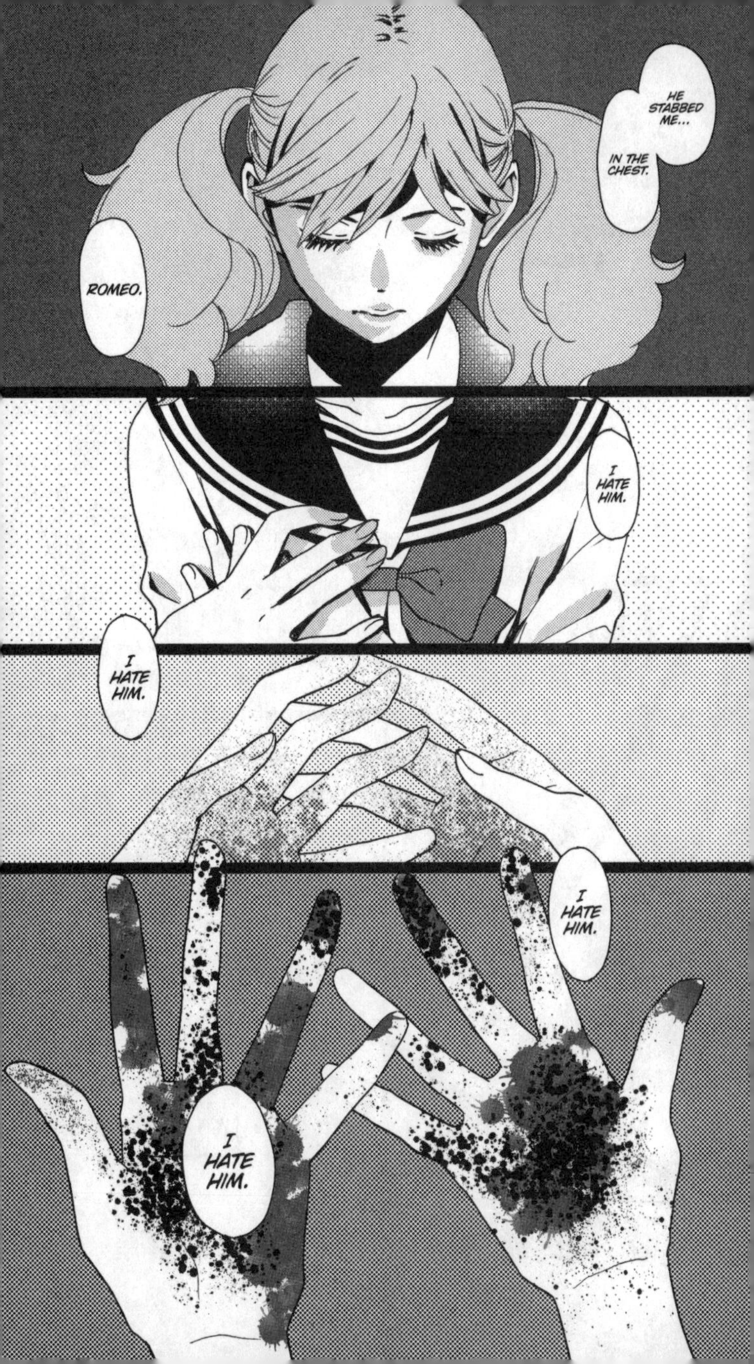
HE STABBED ME...
IN THE CHEST.
ROMEO.
I HATE HIM.
I HATE HIM.
I HATE HIM.
I HATE HIM.

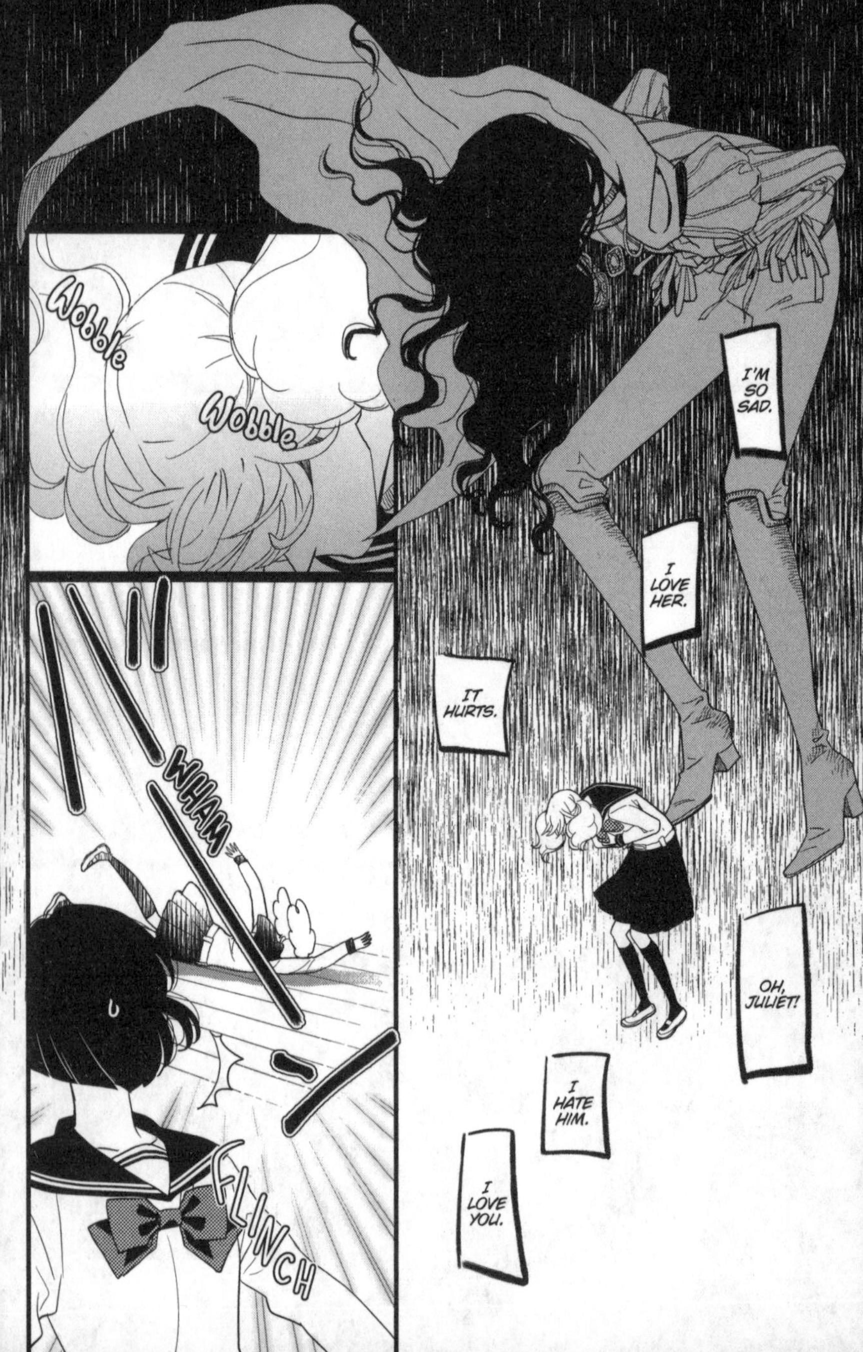
I'M SO SAD.
I LOVE HER.
IT HURTS.
OH, JULIET!
I HATE HIM.
I LOVE YOU.
Wobble
Wobble
WHAM
FLINCH

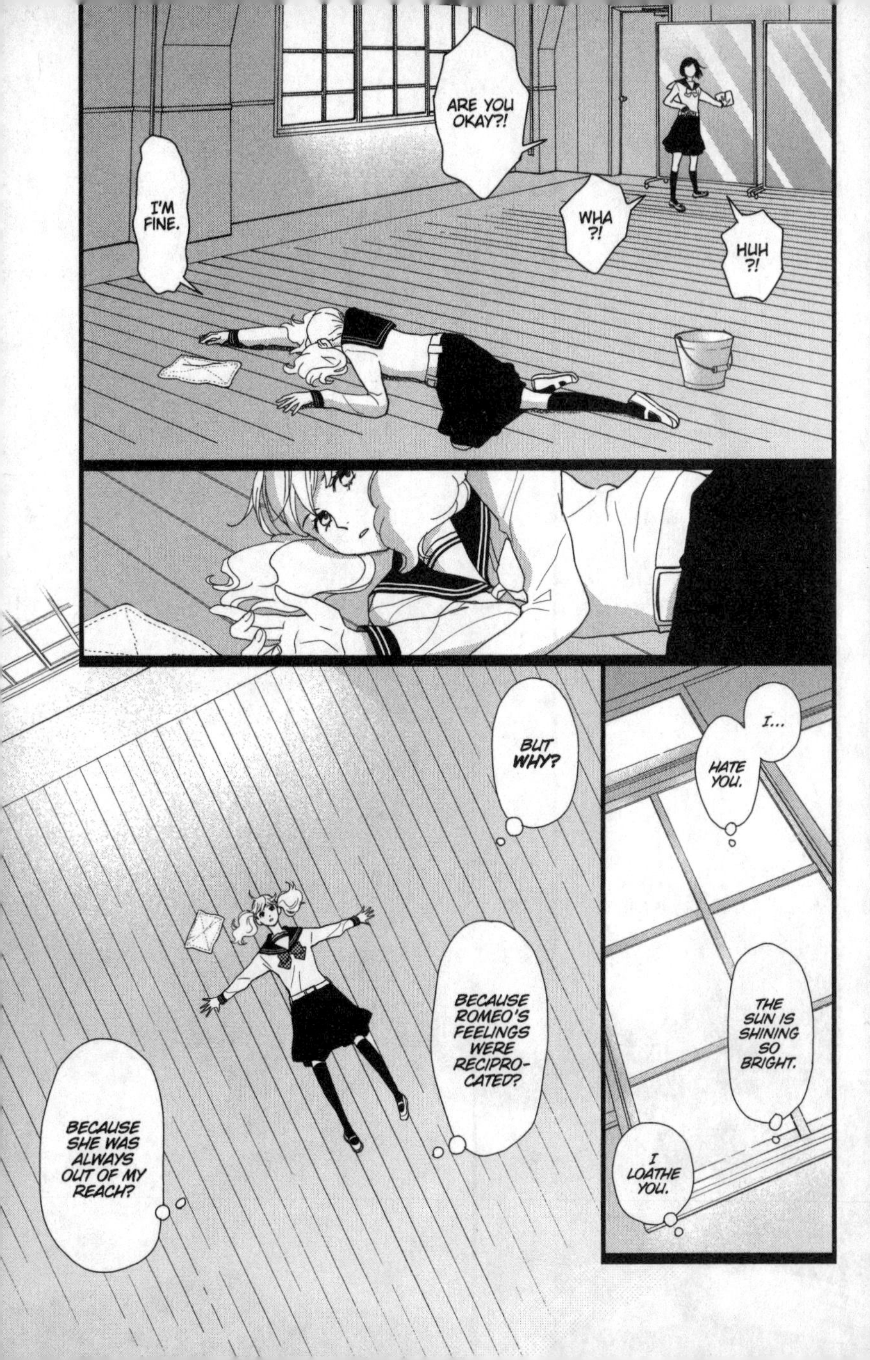
ARE YOU OKAY?!
HUH ?!
WHA ?!
I'M FINE.
I...
HATE YOU.
THE SUN IS SHINING SO BRIGHT.
I LOATHE YOU.
BUT WHY?
BECAUSE ROMEO'S FEELINGS WERE RECIPRO- CATED?
BECAUSE SHE WAS ALWAYS OUT OF MY REACH?

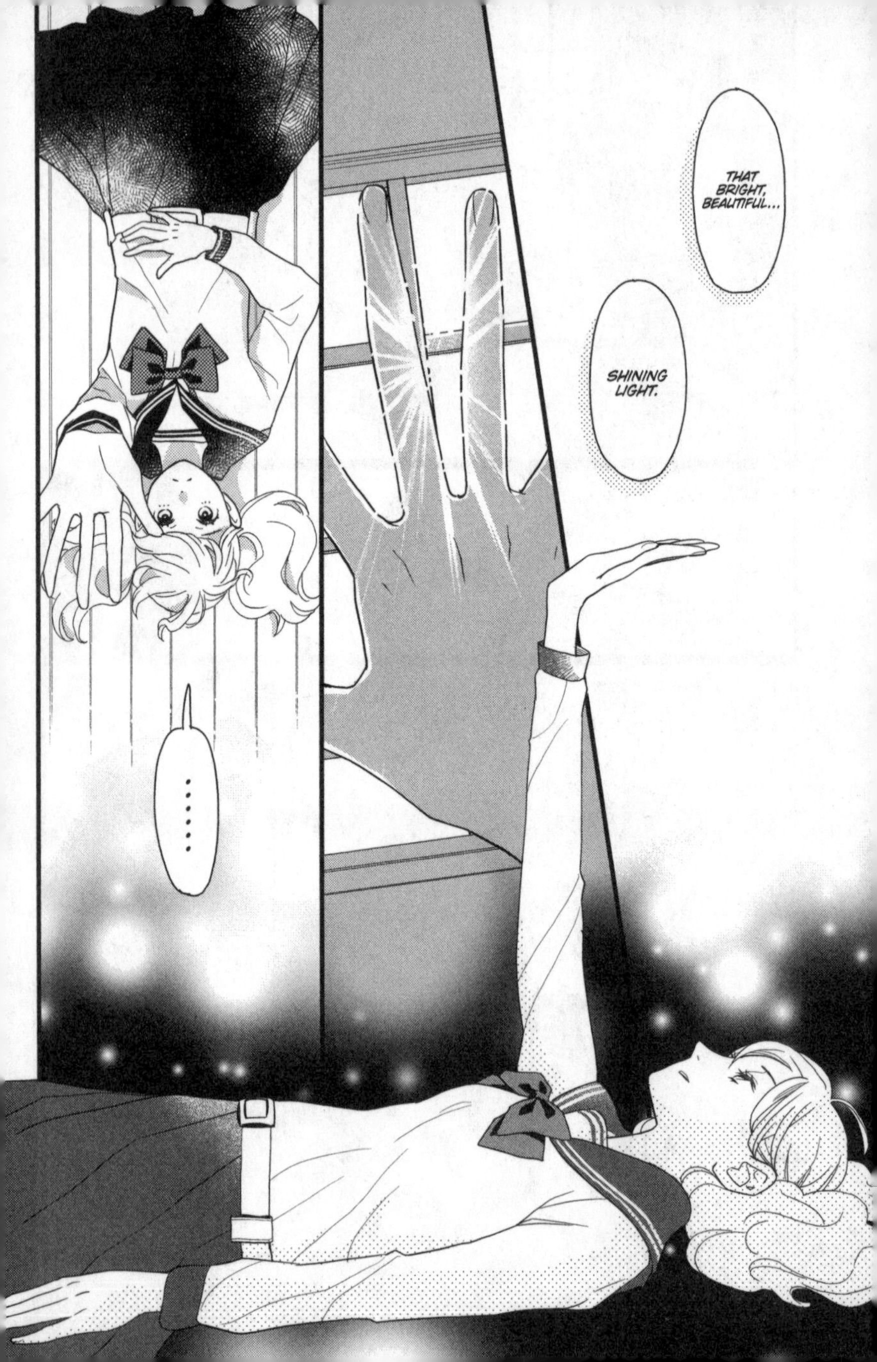
THAT BRIGHT, BEAUTIFUL...
SHINING LIGHT.
......

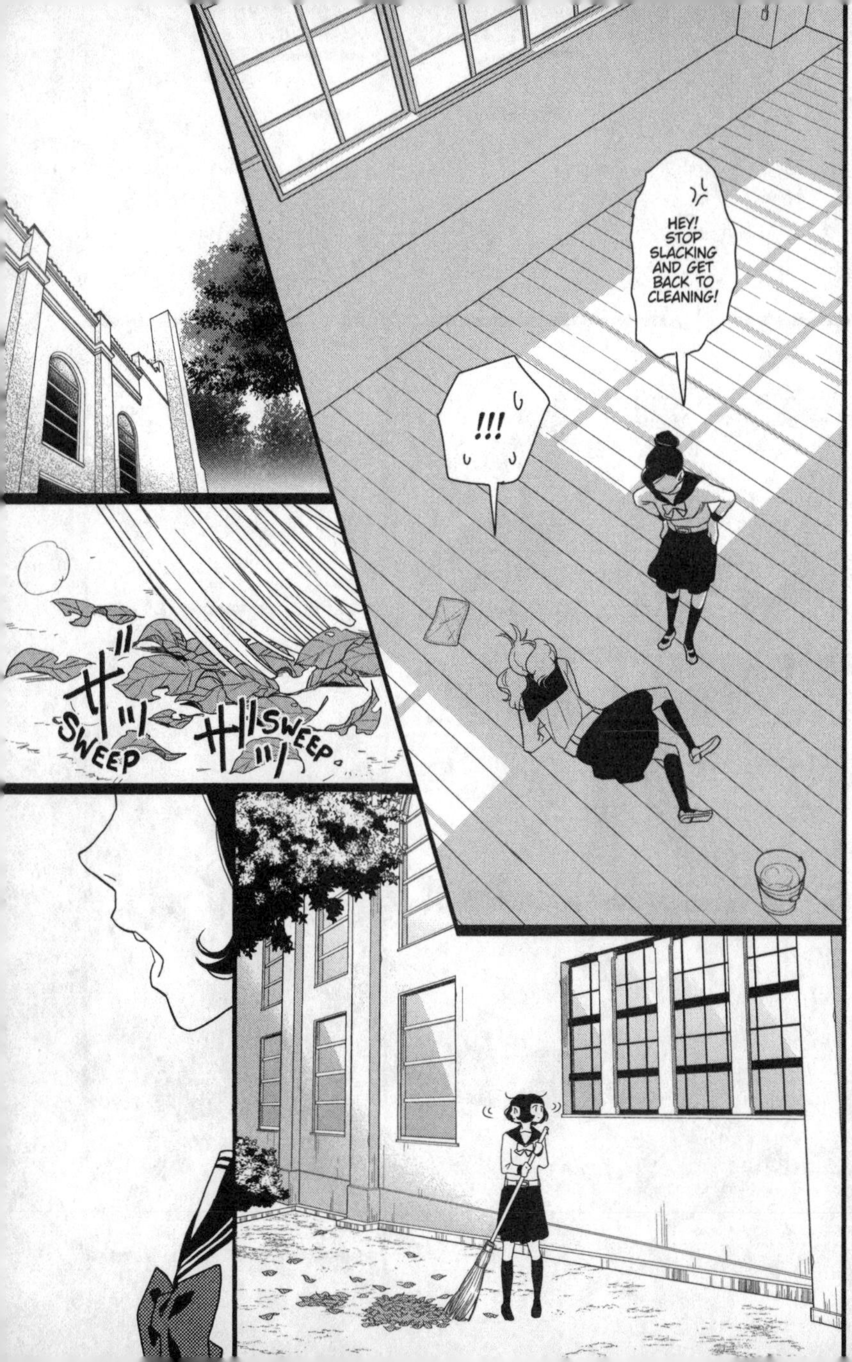

HEY! STOP SLACKING AND GET BACK TO CLEANING!
!!!
ザッ SWEEP
ザッ SWEEP

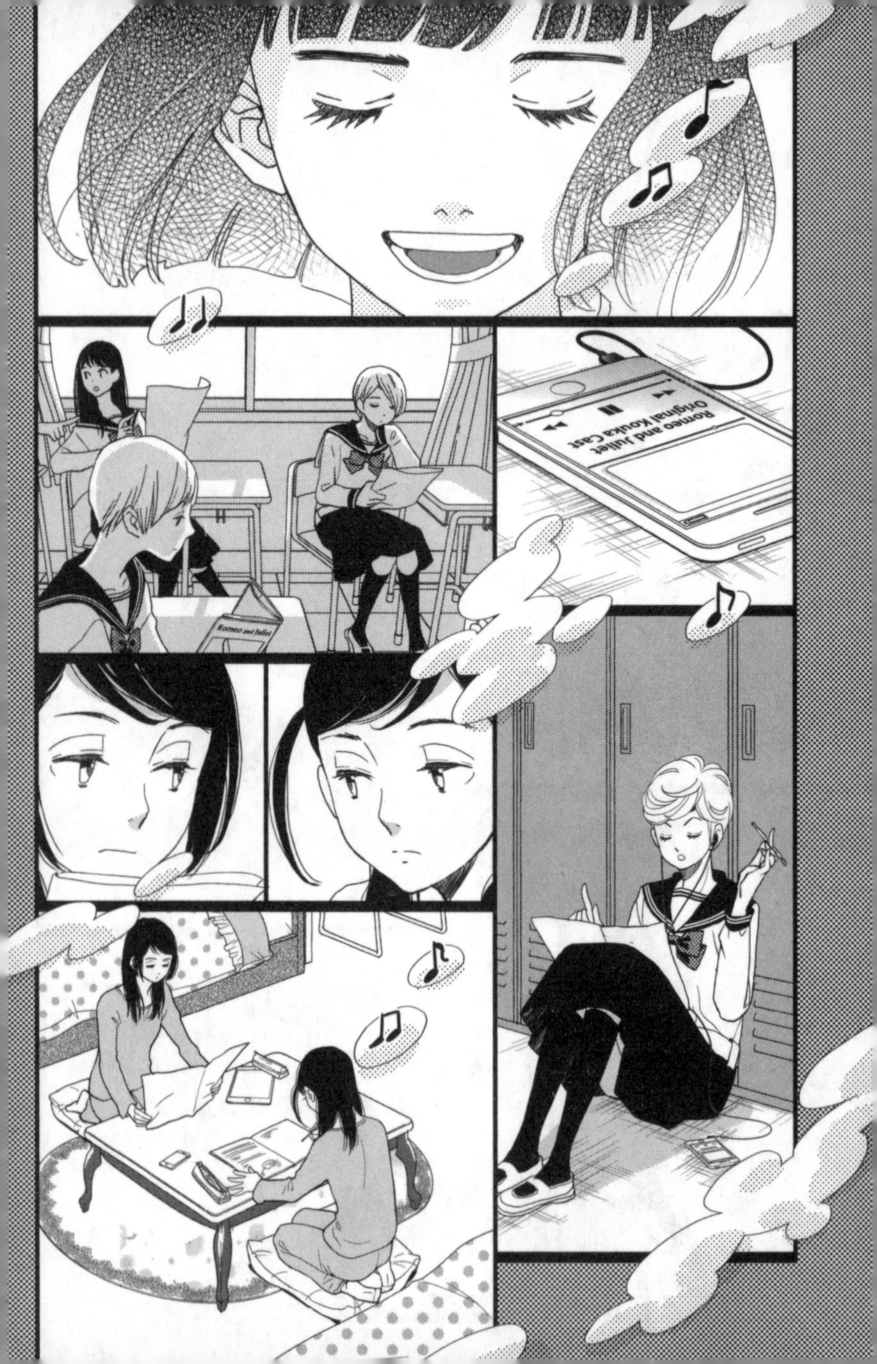
Romeo and Juliet
Original Kouka Cast
Romeo and Juliet

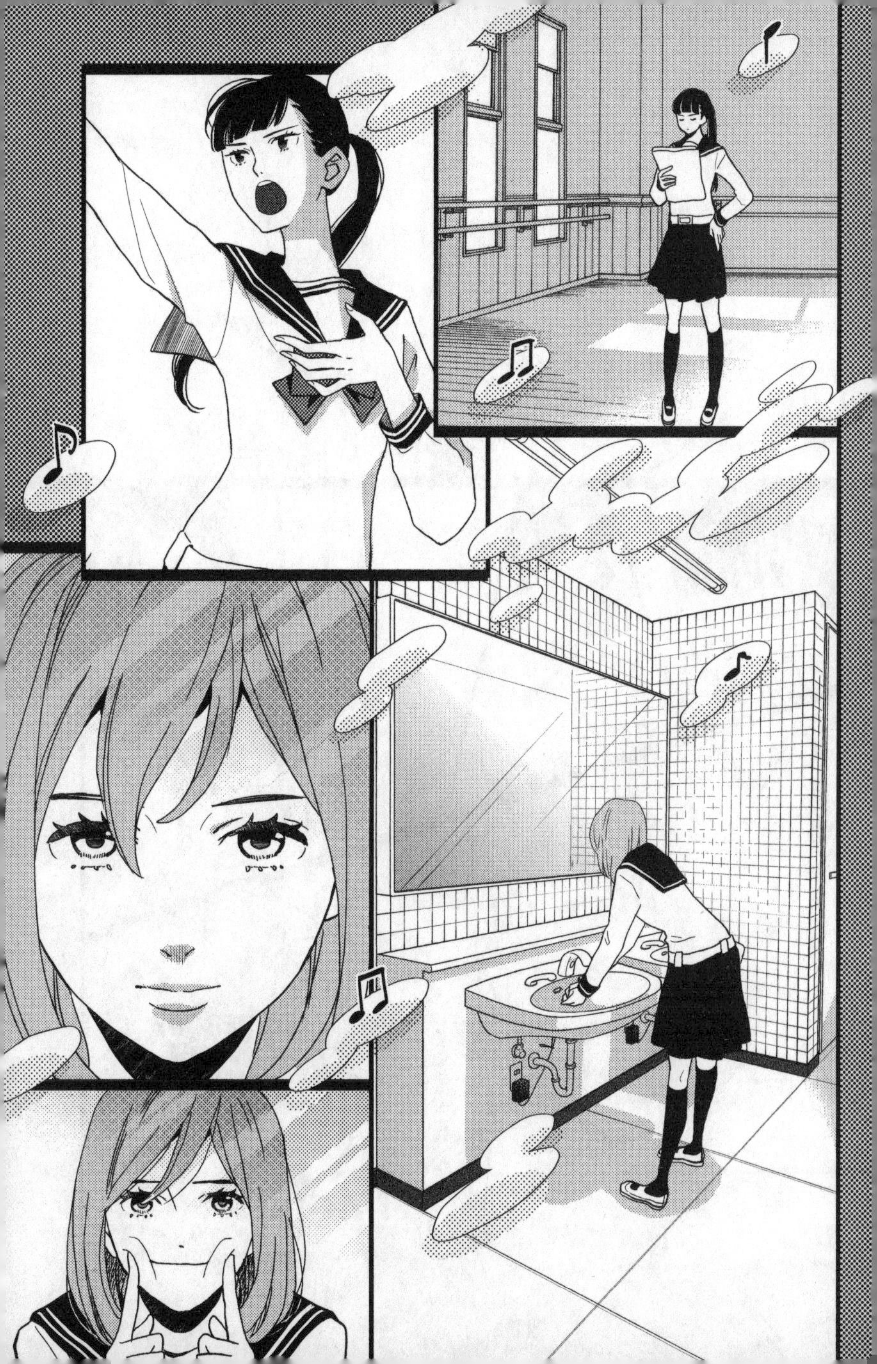

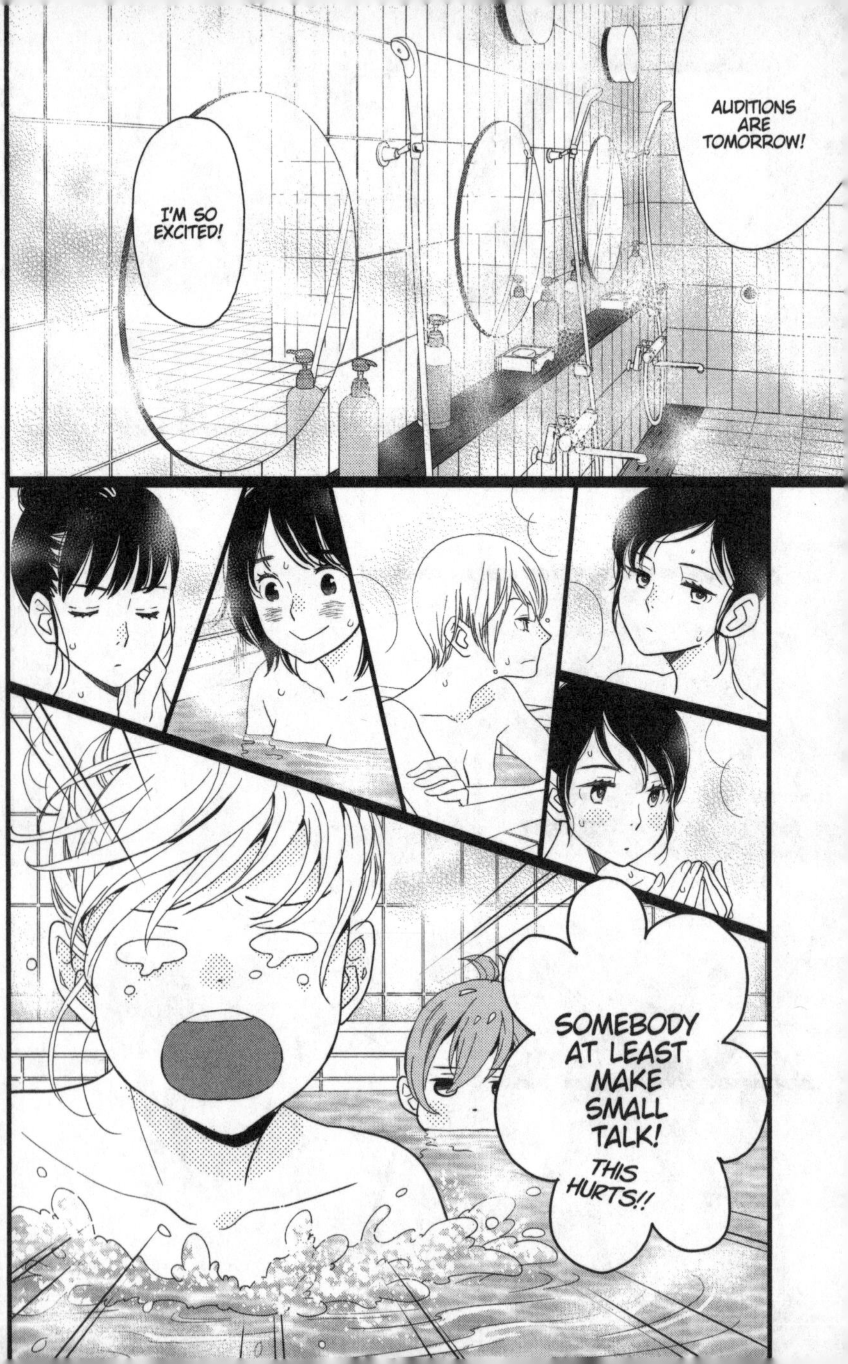
AUDITIONS ARE TOMORROW!
I'M SO EXCITED!
SOMEBODY AT LEAST MAKE SMALL TALK!
THIS HURTS!!

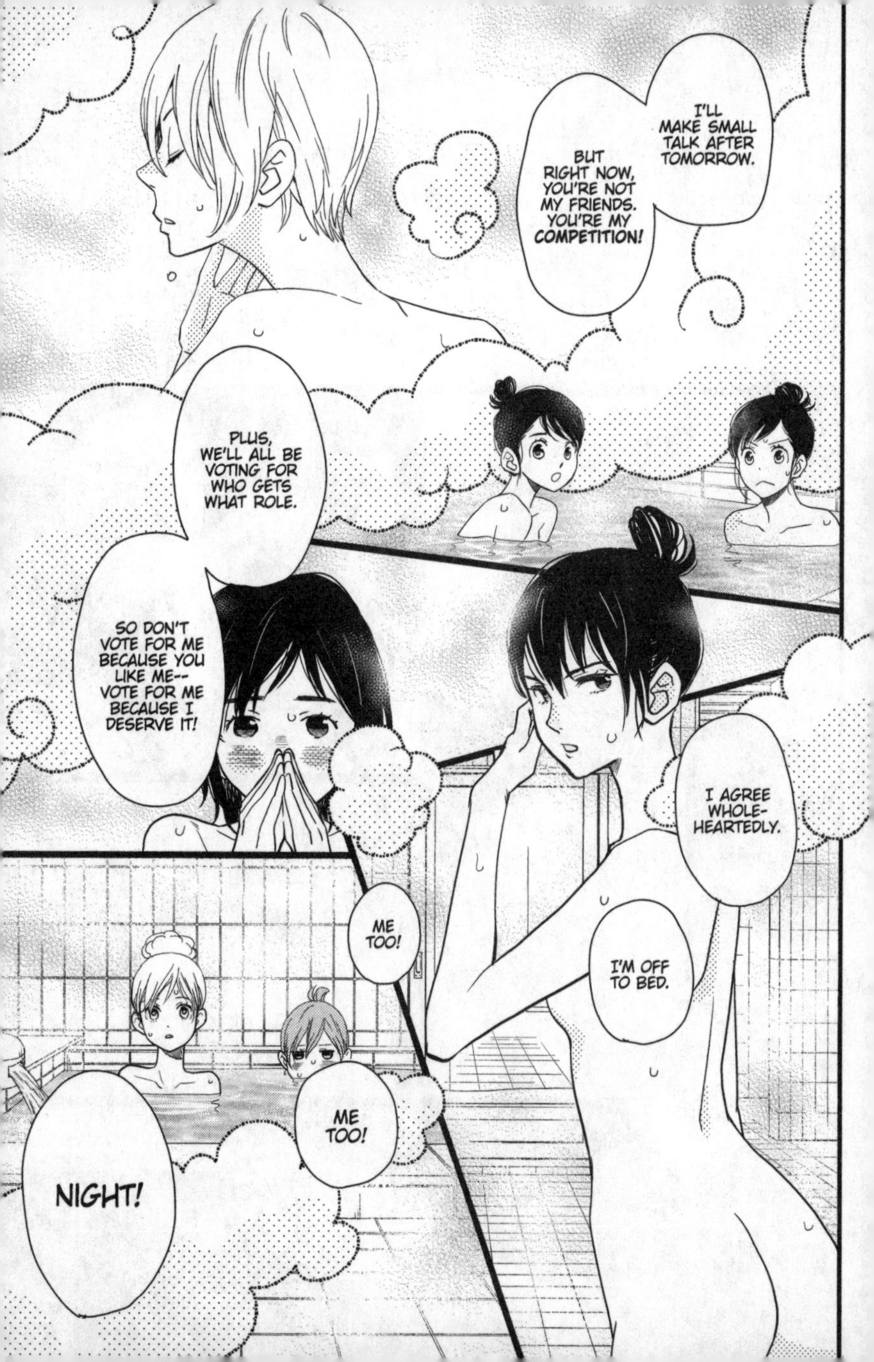
I'LL MAKE SMALL TALK AFTER TOMORROW.
BUT RIGHT NOW, YOU'RE NOT MY FRIENDS. YOU'RE MY COMPETITION!
PLUS, WE'LL ALL BE VOTING FOR WHO GETS WHAT ROLE.
SO DON'T VOTE FOR ME BECAUSE YOU LIKE ME-- VOTE FOR ME BECAUSE I DESERVE IT!
I AGREE WHOLE-HEARTEDLY.
I'M OFF TO BED.
ME TOO!
ME TOO!
NIGHT!

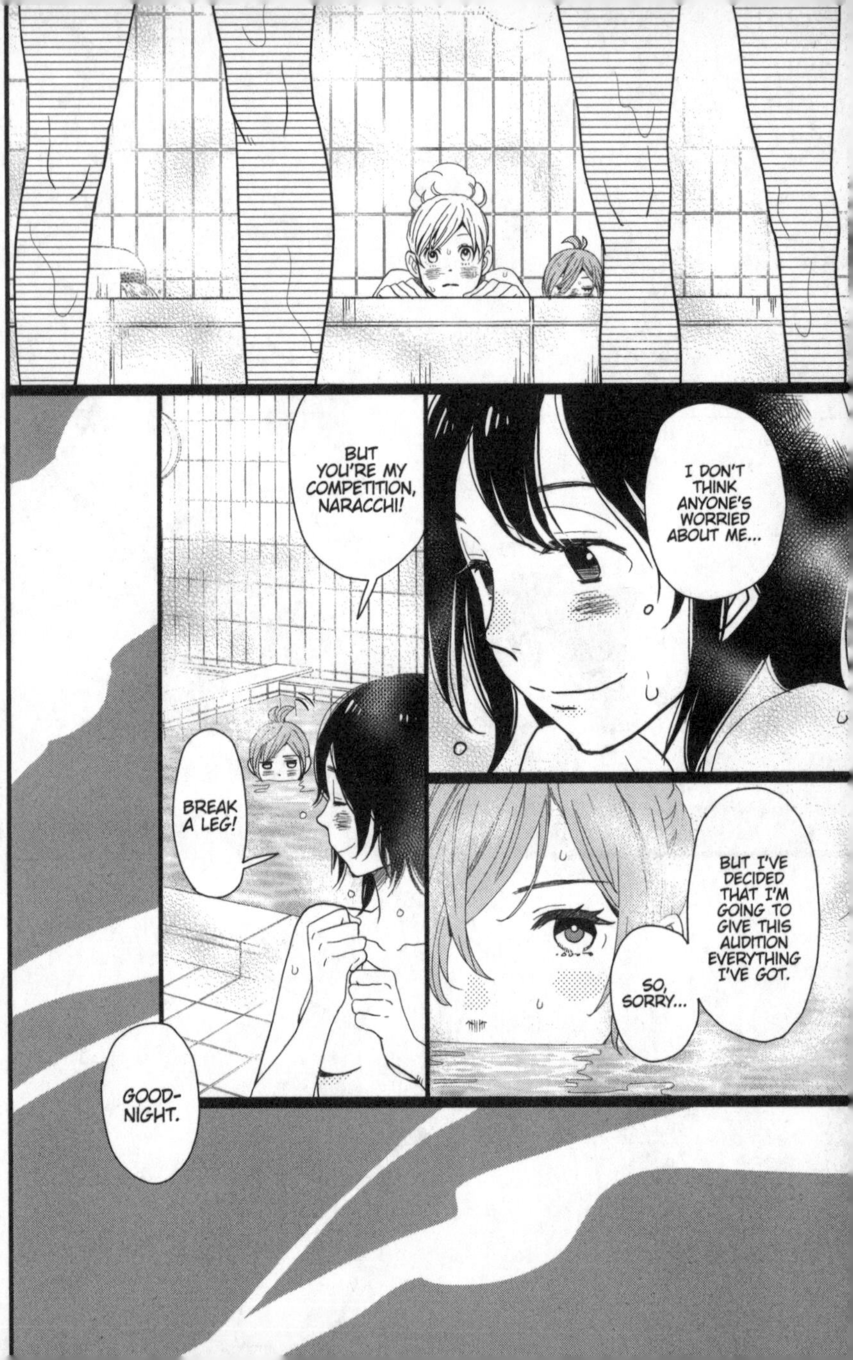
I DON'T THINK ANYONE'S WORRIED ABOUT ME...
BUT I'VE DECIDED THAT I'M GOING TO GIVE THIS AUDITION EVERYTHING I'VE GOT.
SO, SORRY...
BUT YOU'RE MY COMPETITION, NARACCHI!
BREAK A LEG!
GOOD-NIGHT.

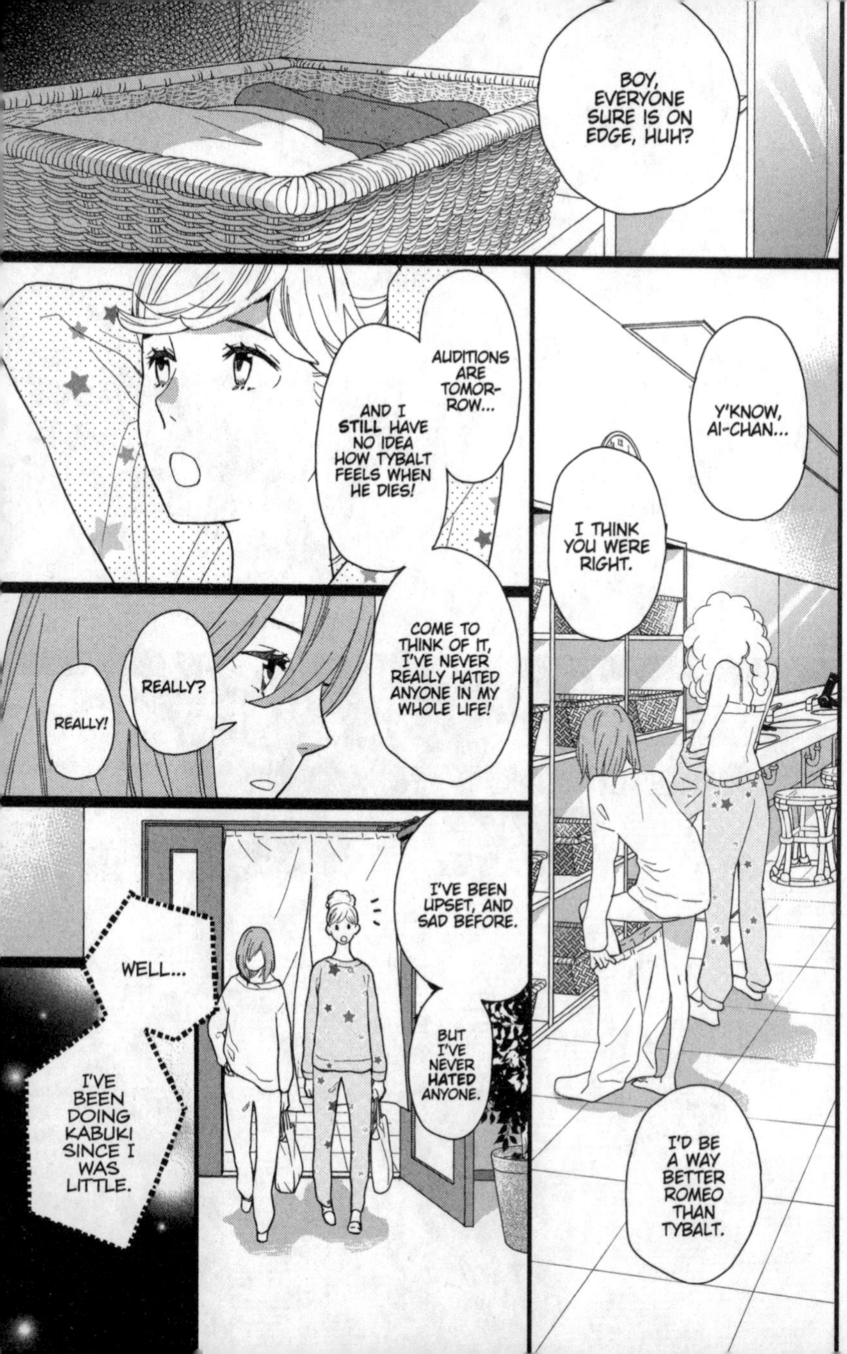
BOY, EVERYONE SURE IS ON EDGE, HUH?
Y'KNOW, AI-CHAN...
I THINK YOU WERE RIGHT.
I'D BE A WAY BETTER ROMEO THAN TYBALT.
AUDITIONS ARE TOMORROW...
AND I STILL HAVE NO IDEA HOW TYBALT FEELS WHEN HE DIES!
COME TO THINK OF IT, I'VE NEVER REALLY HATED ANYONE IN MY WHOLE LIFE!
REALLY?
REALLY!
I'VE BEEN UPSET, AND SAD BEFORE.
BUT I'VE NEVER HATED ANYONE.
WELL...
I'VE BEEN DOING KABUKI SINCE I WAS LITTLE.

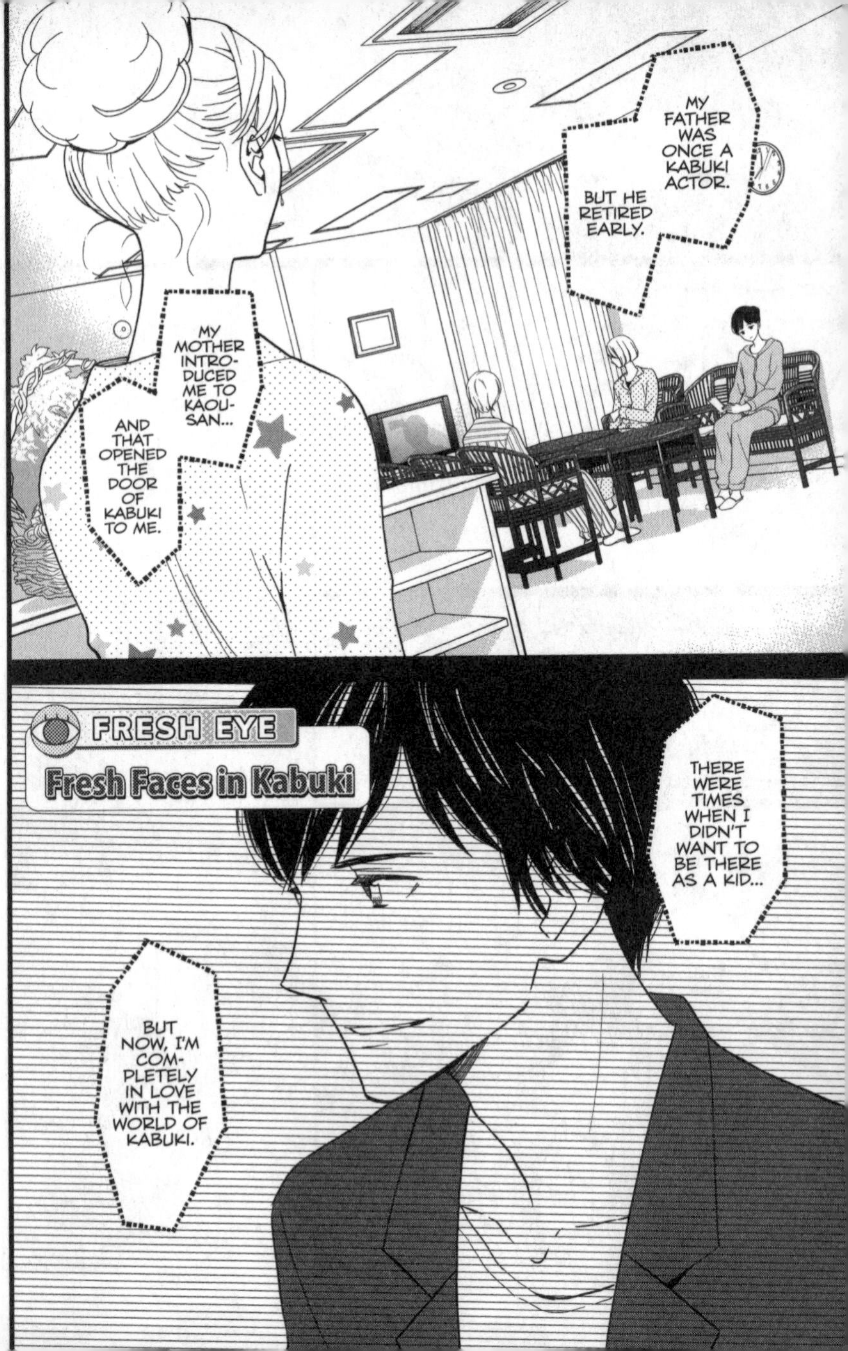
MY FATHER WAS ONCE A KABUKI ACTOR.
BUT HE RETIRED EARLY.
MY MOTHER INTRODUCED ME TO KAOU-SAN...
AND THAT OPENED THE DOOR OF KABUKI TO ME.
THERE WERE TIMES WHEN I DIDN'T WANT TO BE THERE AS A KID...
FRESH EYE
Fresh Faces in Kabuki
BUT NOW, I'M COMPLETELY IN LOVE WITH THE WORLD OF KABUKI.

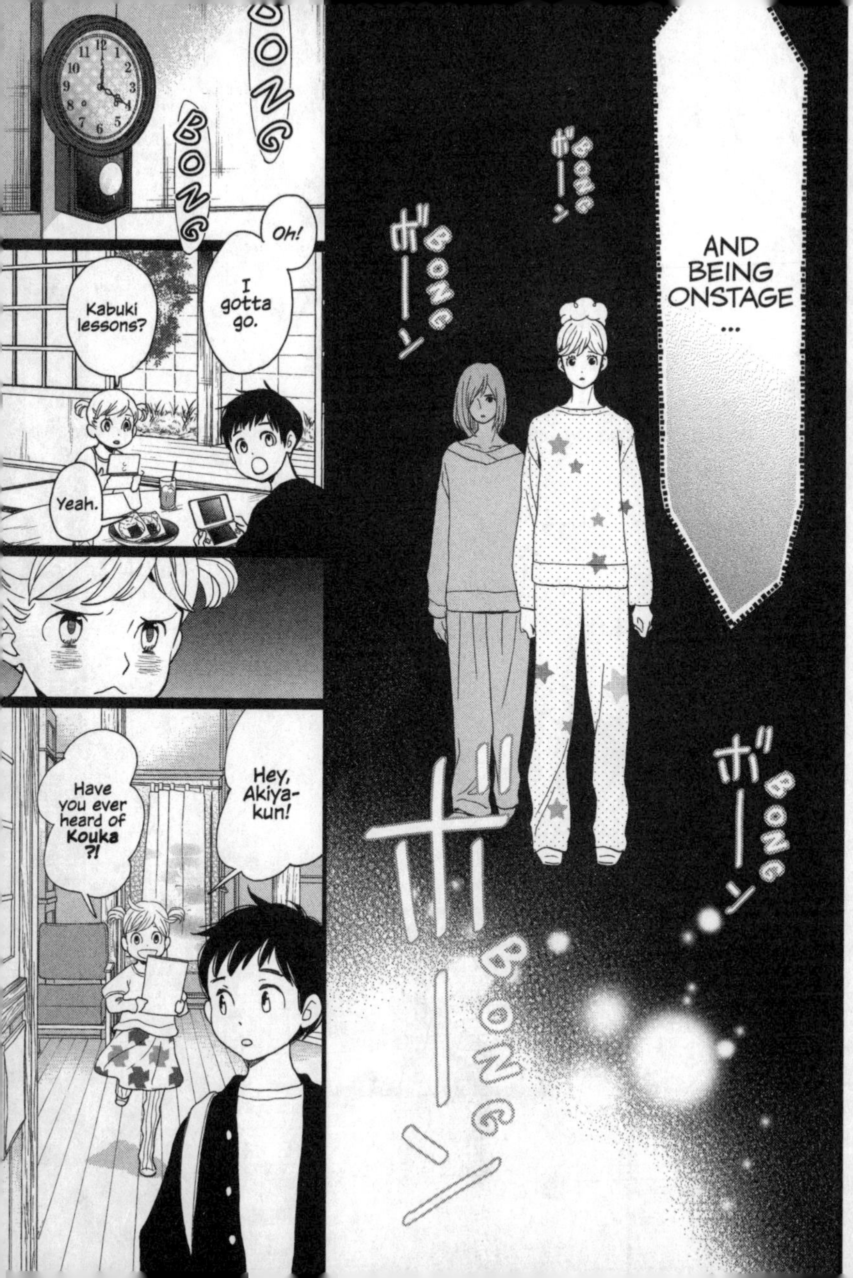
AND BEING ONSTAGE ...
ボーン BONG
ボーン BONG
ボーン BONG
ボーン BONG
DONG
BONG
Oh!
I gotta go.
Kabuki lessons?
Yeah.
Hey, Akiya-kun!
Have you ever heard of Kouka ?!

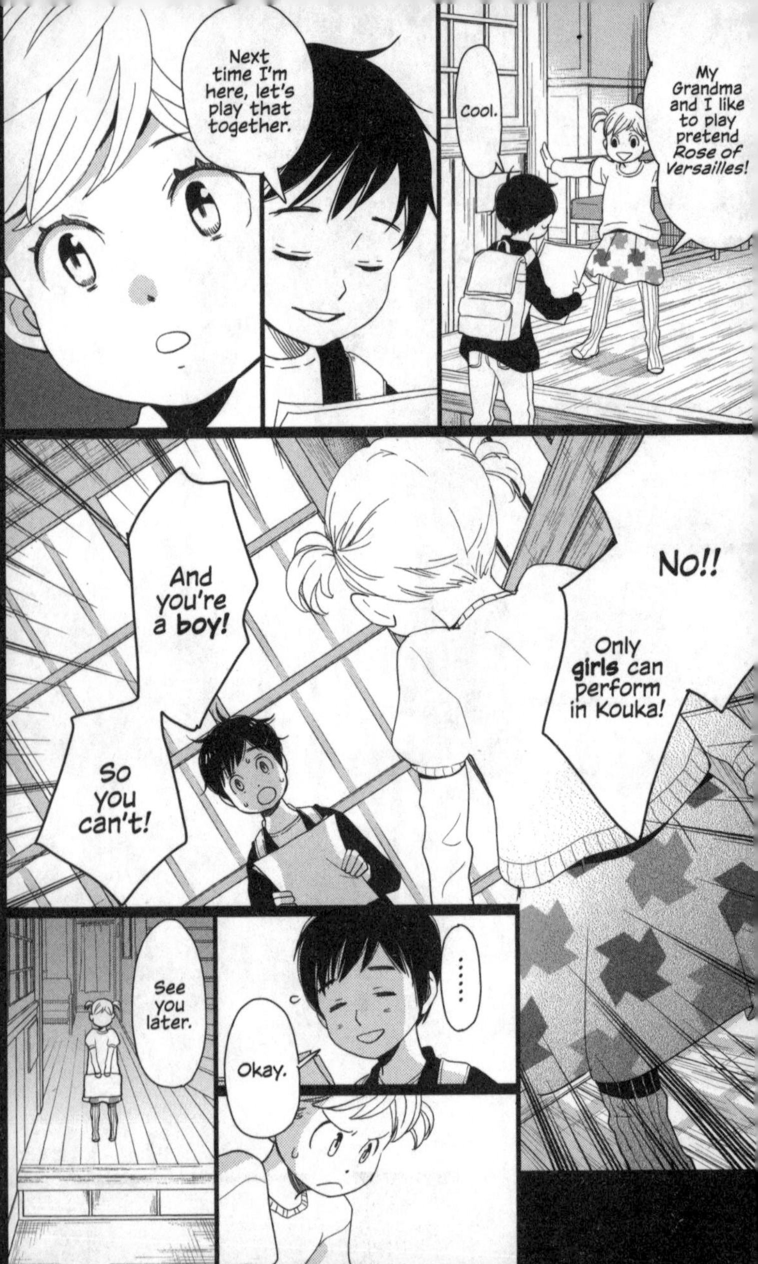
My Grandma and I like to play pretend *Rose of Versailles!*
Cool.
Next time I'm here, let's play that together.
NO!!
Only **girls** can perform in Kouka!
And you're a **boy!**
So you can't!
......
Okay.
See you later.

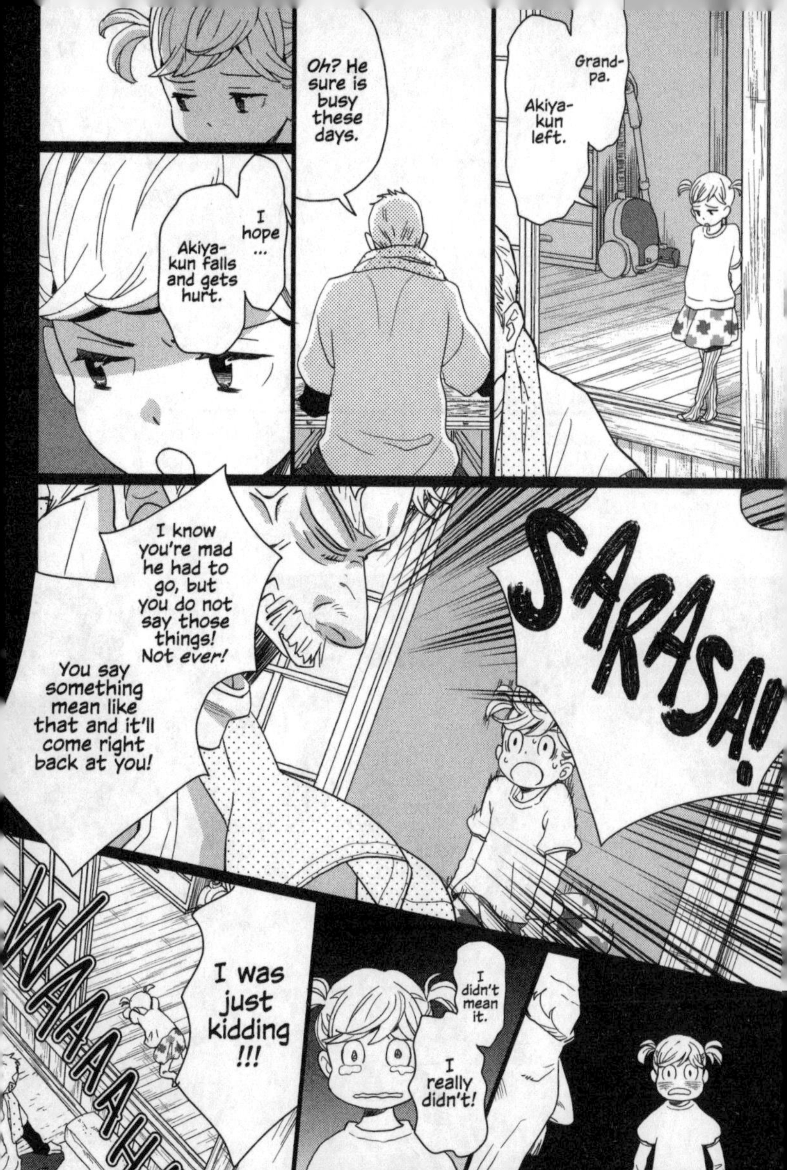
Grand-pa.
Akiya-kun left.
Oh? He sure is busy these days.
I hope ... Akiya-kun falls and gets hurt.
SARASA!
I know you're mad he had to go, but you do not say those things! Not *ever*!
You say something mean like that and it'll come right back at you!
I didn't mean it.
I really didn't!
I was just kidding!!!
WAAAAH

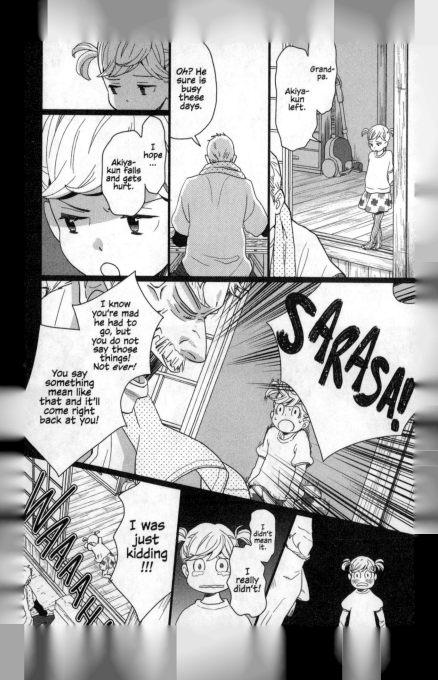

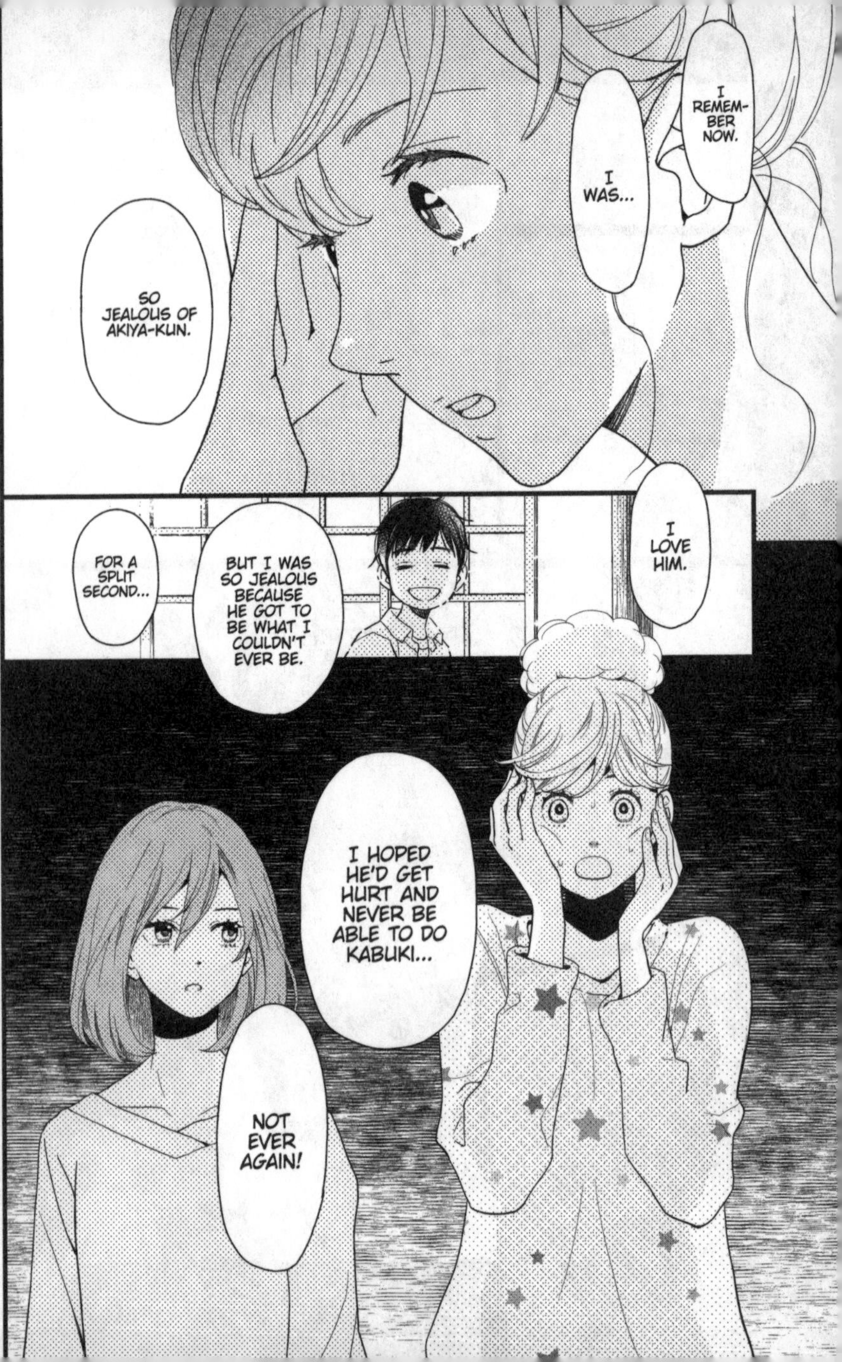
I REMEMBER NOW.
I WAS...
SO JEALOUS OF AKIYA-KUN.
I LOVE HIM.
BUT I WAS SO JEALOUS BECAUSE HE GOT TO BE WHAT I COULDN'T EVER BE.
FOR A SPLIT SECOND...
I HOPED HE'D GET HURT AND NEVER BE ABLE TO DO KABUKI...
NOT EVER AGAIN!

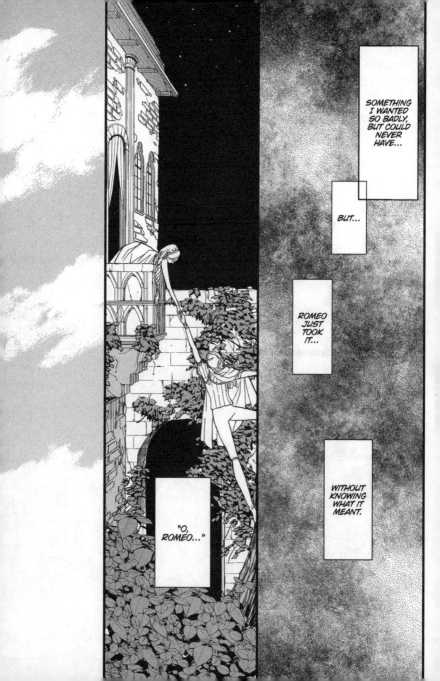

SOMETHING I WANTED SO BADLY, BUT COULD NEVER HAVE...

BUT...

ROMEO JUST TOOK IT...

WITHOUT KNOWING WHAT IT MEANT.

"O, ROMEO..."

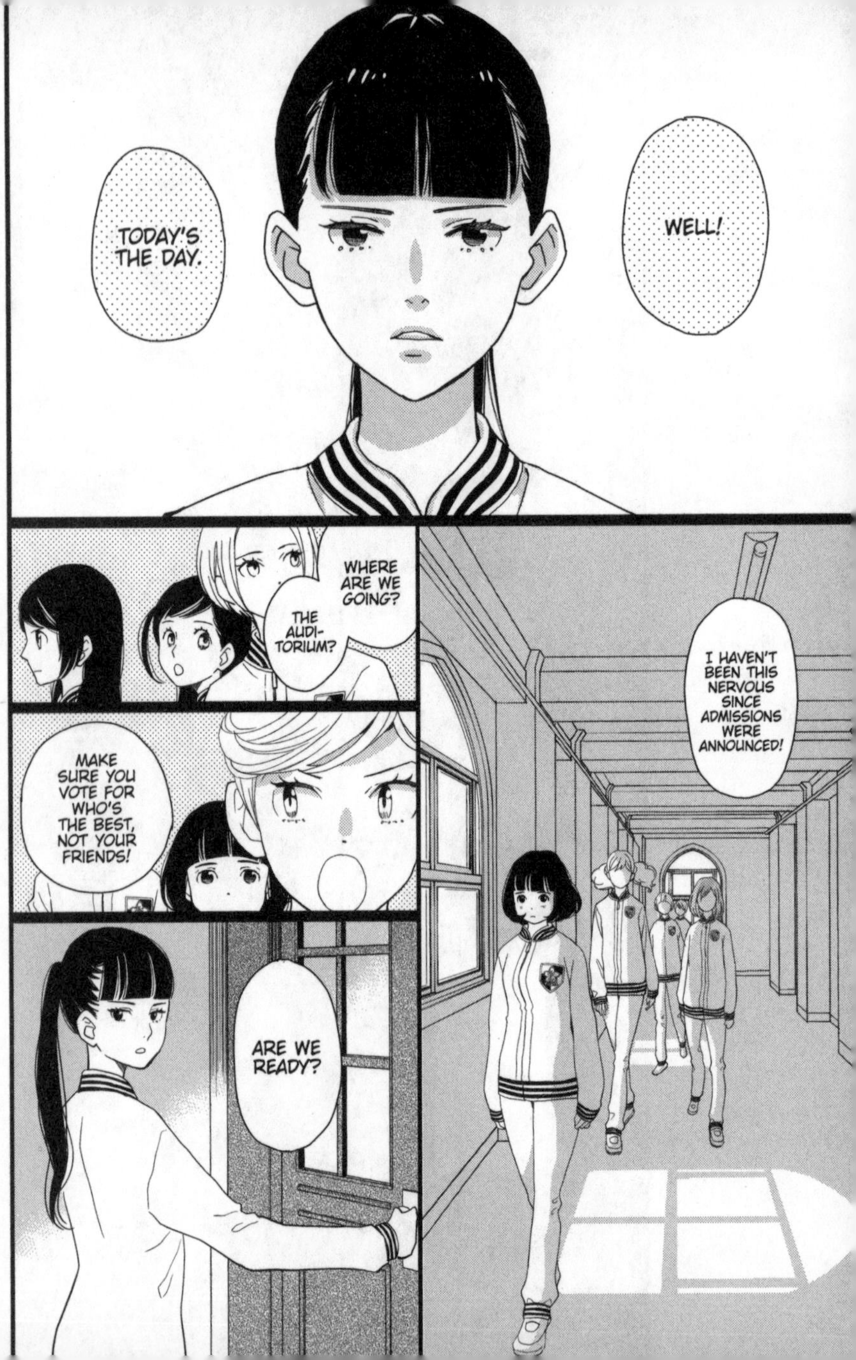
WELL!
TODAY'S THE DAY.
I HAVEN'T BEEN THIS NERVOUS SINCE ADMISSIONS WERE ANNOUNCED!
WHERE ARE WE GOING?
THE AUDITORIUM?
MAKE SURE YOU VOTE FOR WHO'S THE BEST, NOT YOUR FRIENDS!
ARE WE READY?

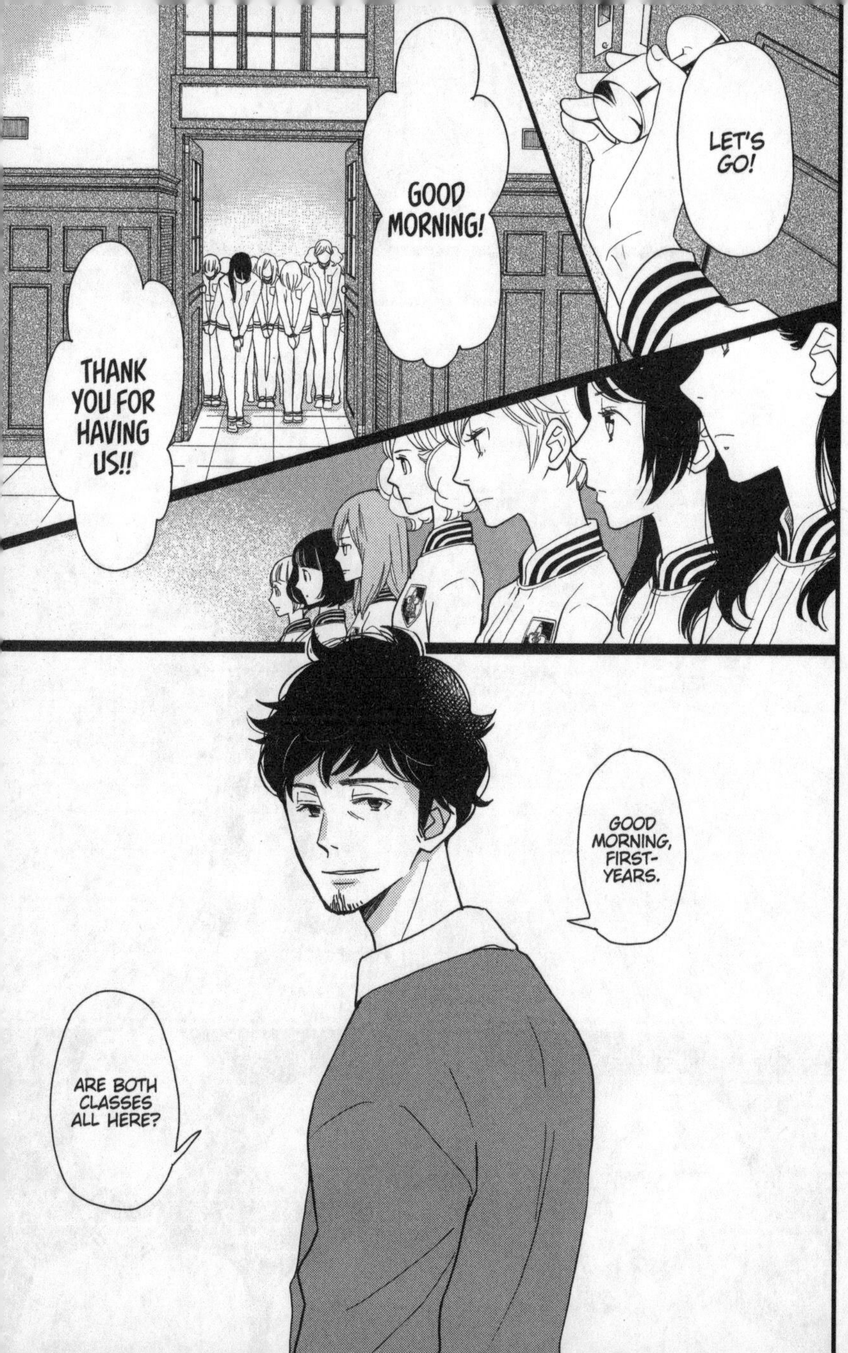
LET'S GO!
GOOD MORNING!
THANK YOU FOR HAVING US!!
GOOD MORNING, FIRST-YEARS.
ARE BOTH CLASSES ALL HERE?

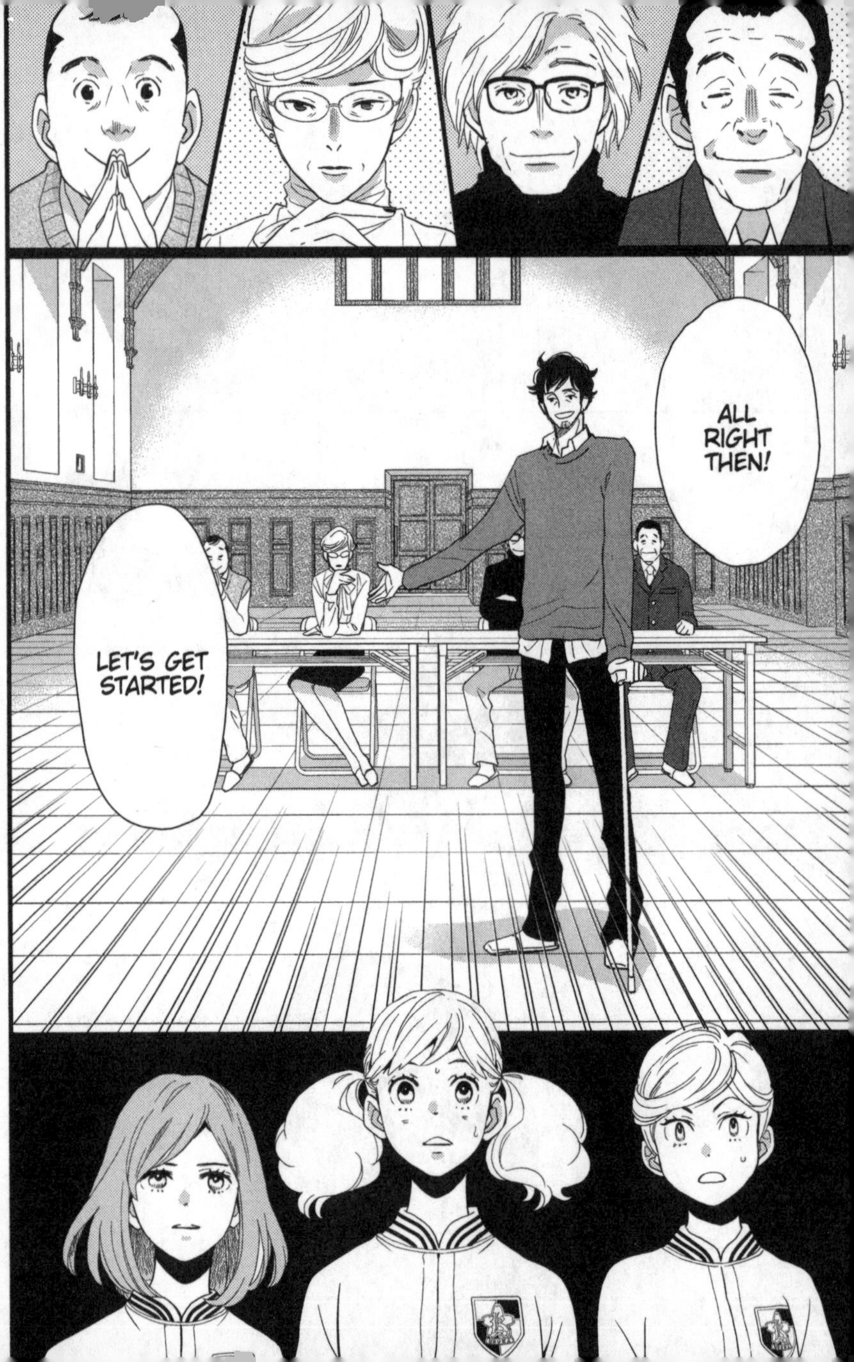
ALL RIGHT THEN!
LET'S GET STARTED!

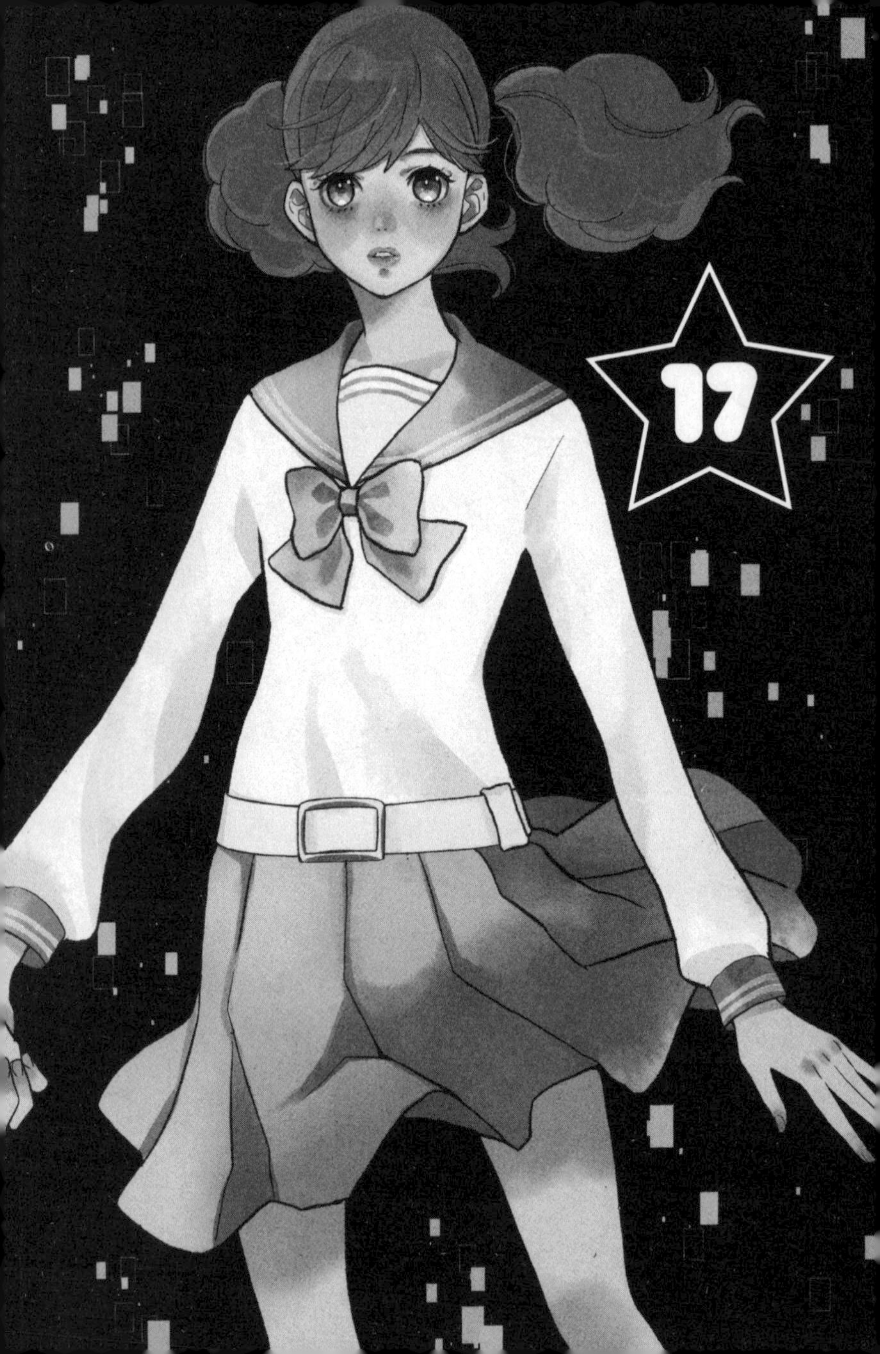
17

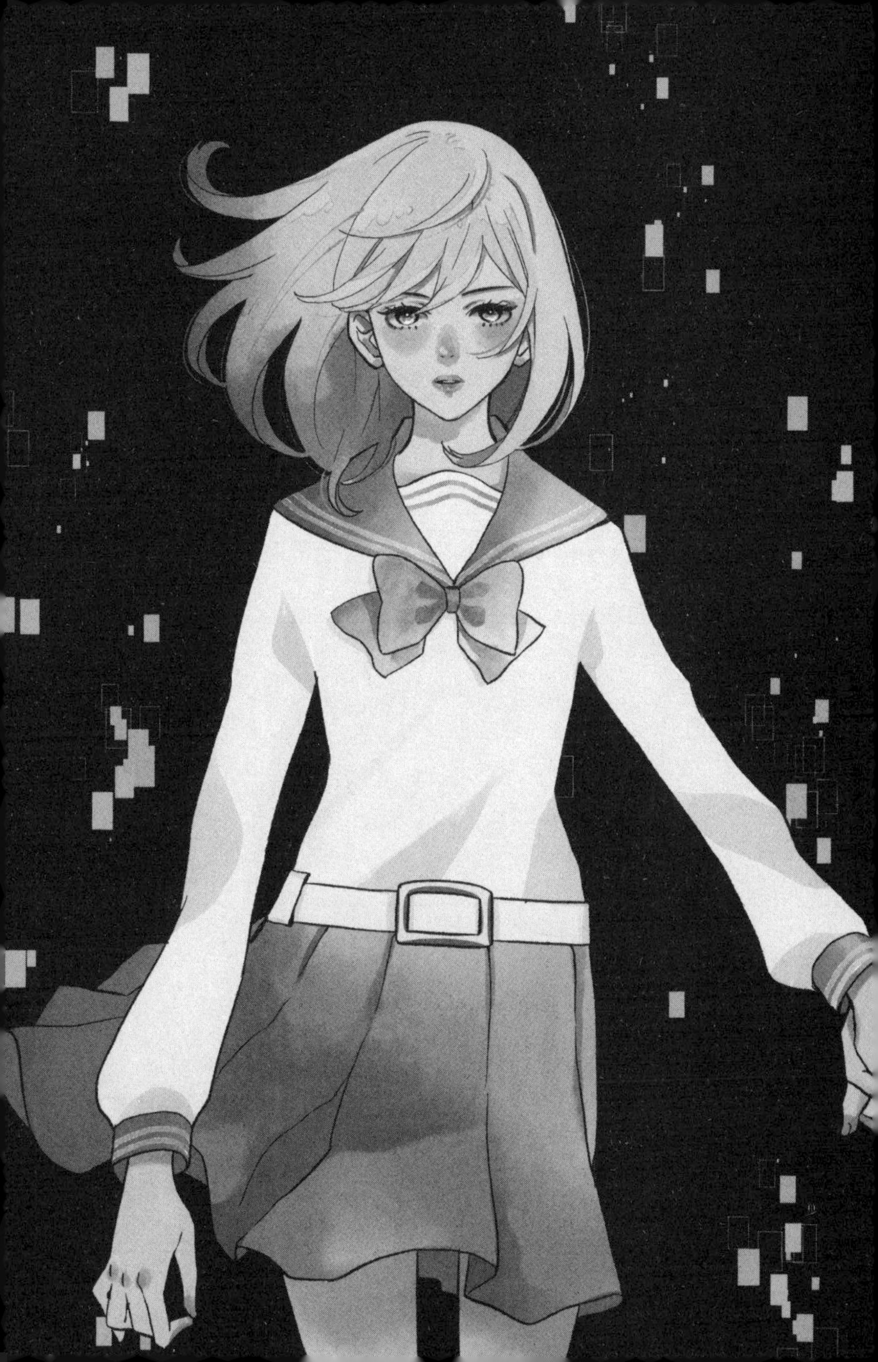

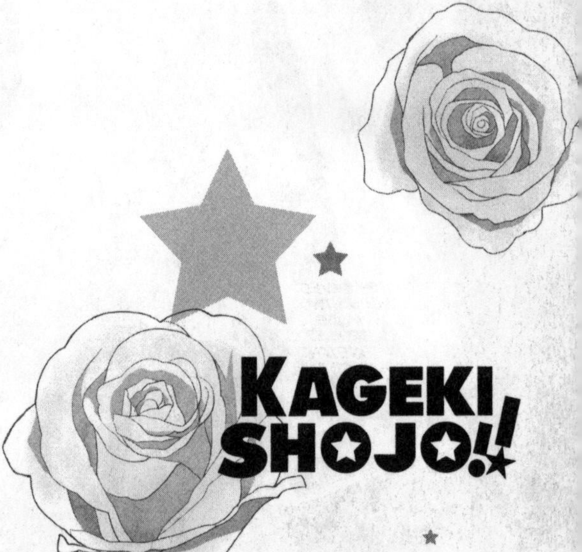
KAGEKI SHOJO!!

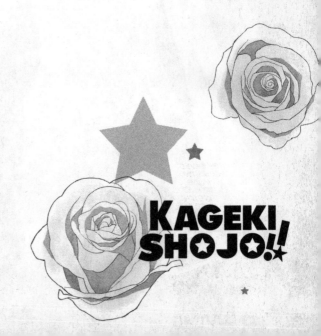

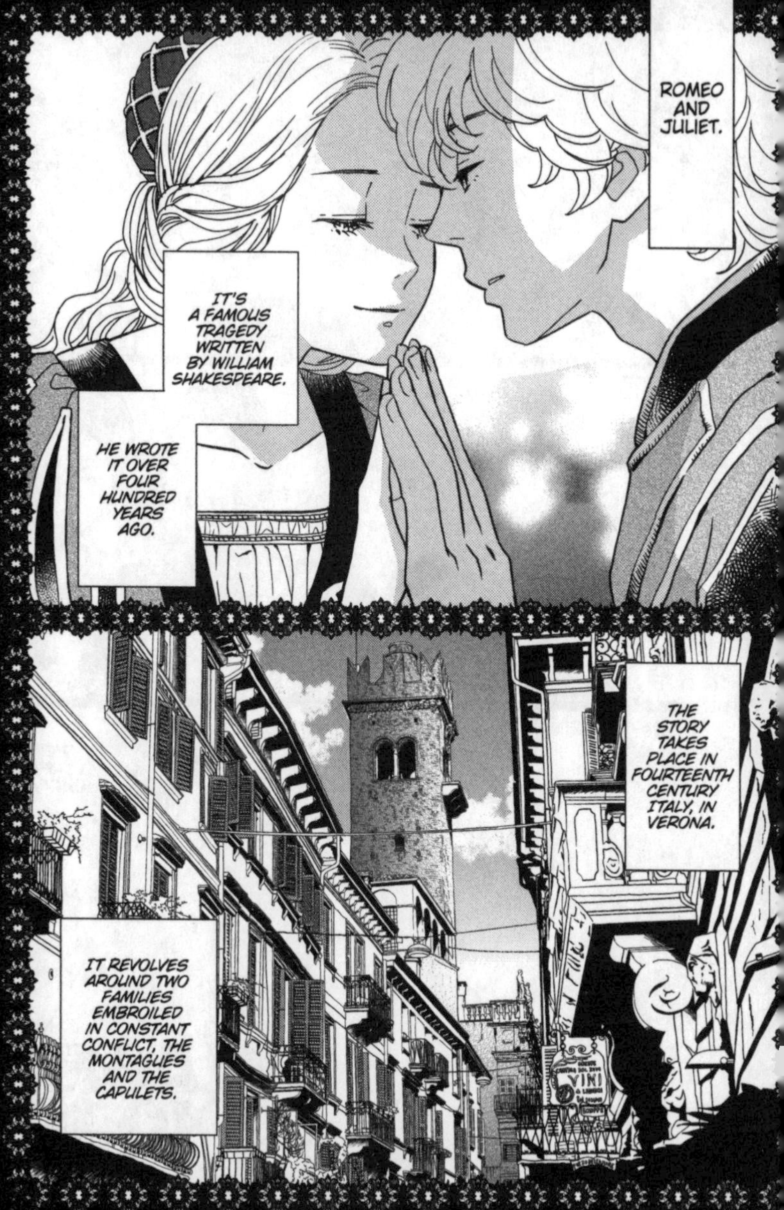
ROMEO AND JULIET.
IT'S A FAMOUS TRAGEDY WRITTEN BY WILLIAM SHAKESPEARE.
HE WROTE IT OVER FOUR HUNDRED YEARS AGO.
THE STORY TAKES PLACE IN FOURTEENTH CENTURY ITALY, IN VERONA.
IT REVOLVES AROUND TWO FAMILIES EMBROILED IN CONSTANT CONFLICT, THE MONTAGUES AND THE CAPULETS.
VINI

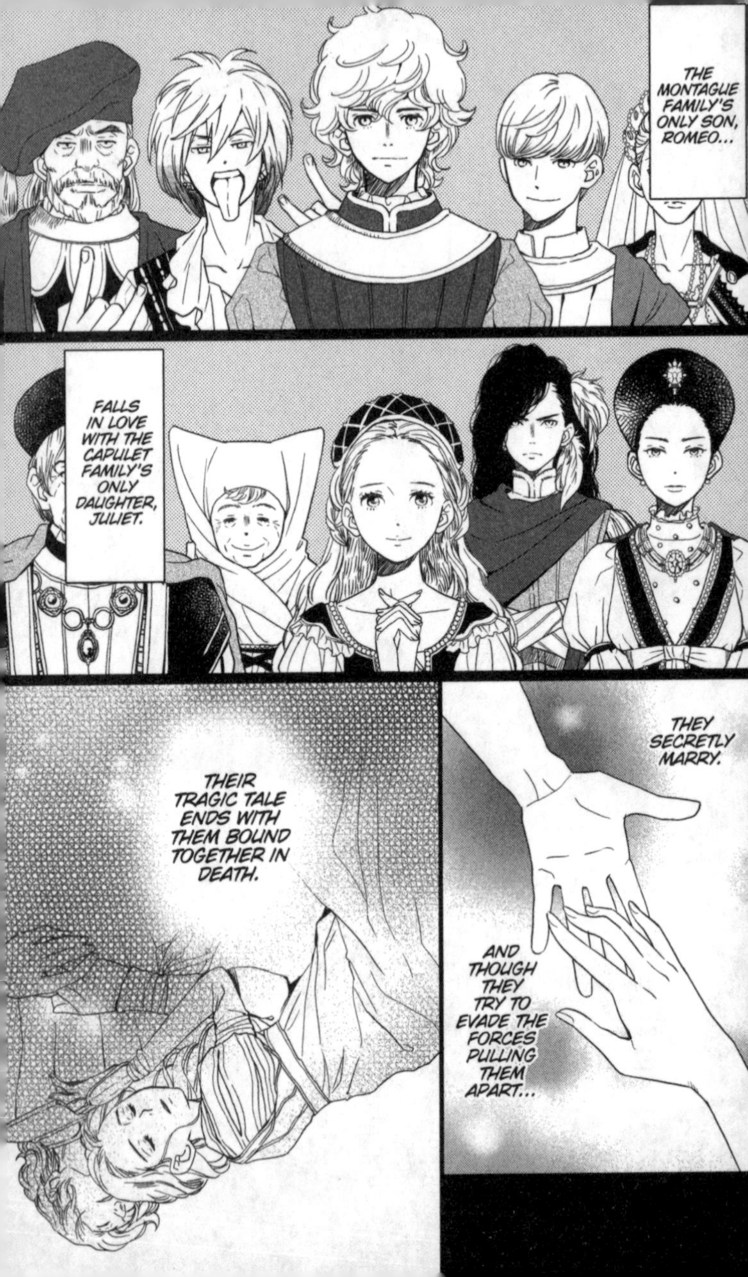
THE MONTAGUE FAMILY'S ONLY SON, ROMEO...
FALLS IN LOVE WITH THE CAPULET FAMILY'S ONLY DAUGHTER, JULIET.
THEY SECRETLY MARRY.
AND THOUGH THEY TRY TO EVADE THE FORCES PULLING THEM APART...
THEIR TRAGIC TALE ENDS WITH THEM BOUND TOGETHER IN DEATH.

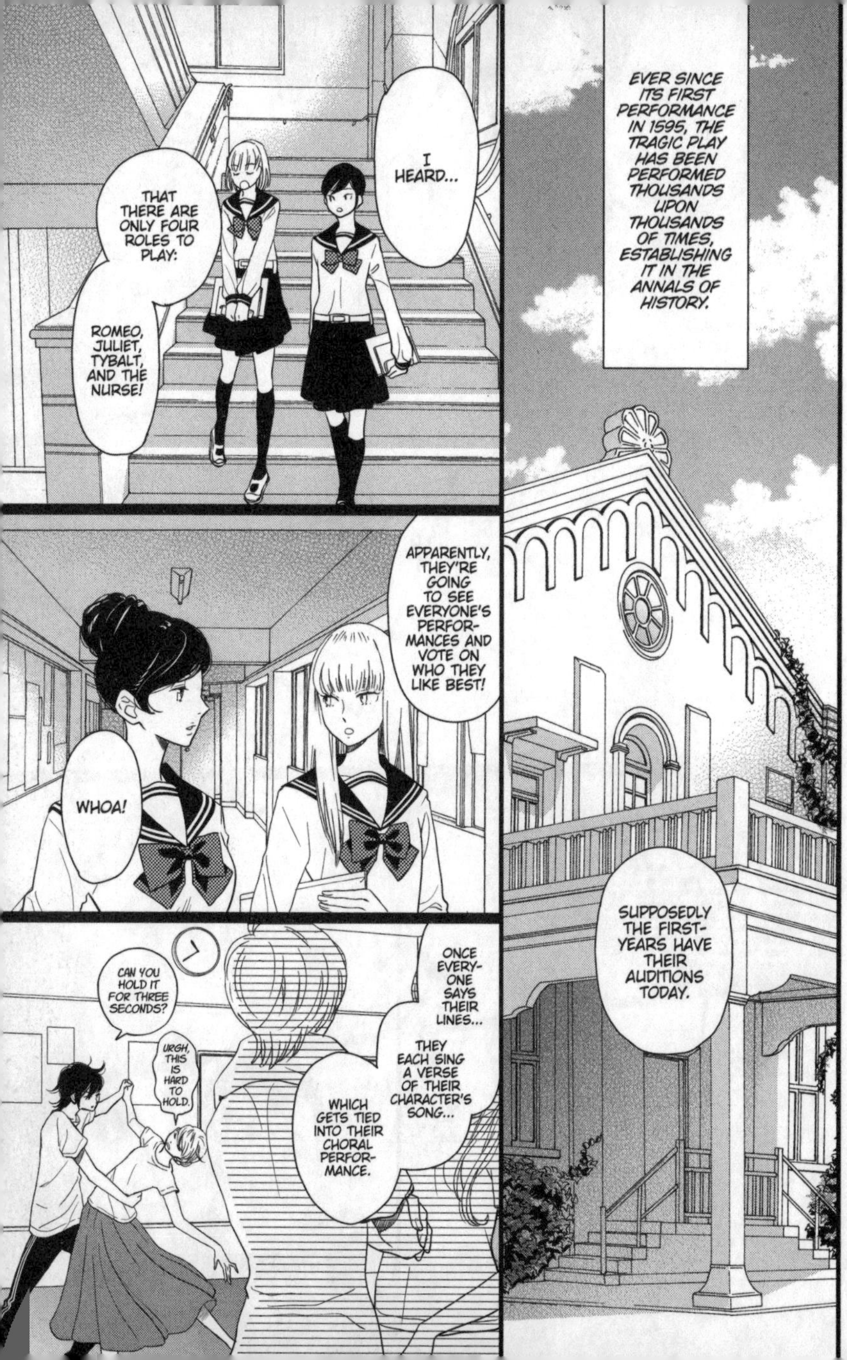
EVER SINCE ITS FIRST PERFORMANCE IN 1595, THE TRAGIC PLAY HAS BEEN PERFORMED THOUSANDS UPON THOUSANDS OF TIMES, ESTABLISHING IT IN THE ANNALS OF HISTORY.
SUPPOSEDLY THE FIRST-YEARS HAVE THEIR AUDITIONS TODAY.
I HEARD...
THAT THERE ARE ONLY FOUR ROLES TO PLAY:
ROMEO, JULIET, TYBALT, AND THE NURSE!
APPARENTLY, THEY'RE GOING TO SEE EVERYONE'S PERFORMANCES AND VOTE ON WHO THEY LIKE BEST!
WHOA!
ONCE EVERYONE SAYS THEIR LINES...
THEY EACH SING A VERSE OF THEIR CHARACTER'S SONG...
WHICH GETS TIED INTO THEIR CHORAL PERFORMANCE.
CAN YOU HOLD IT FOR THREE SECONDS?
URGH, THIS IS HARD TO HOLD.

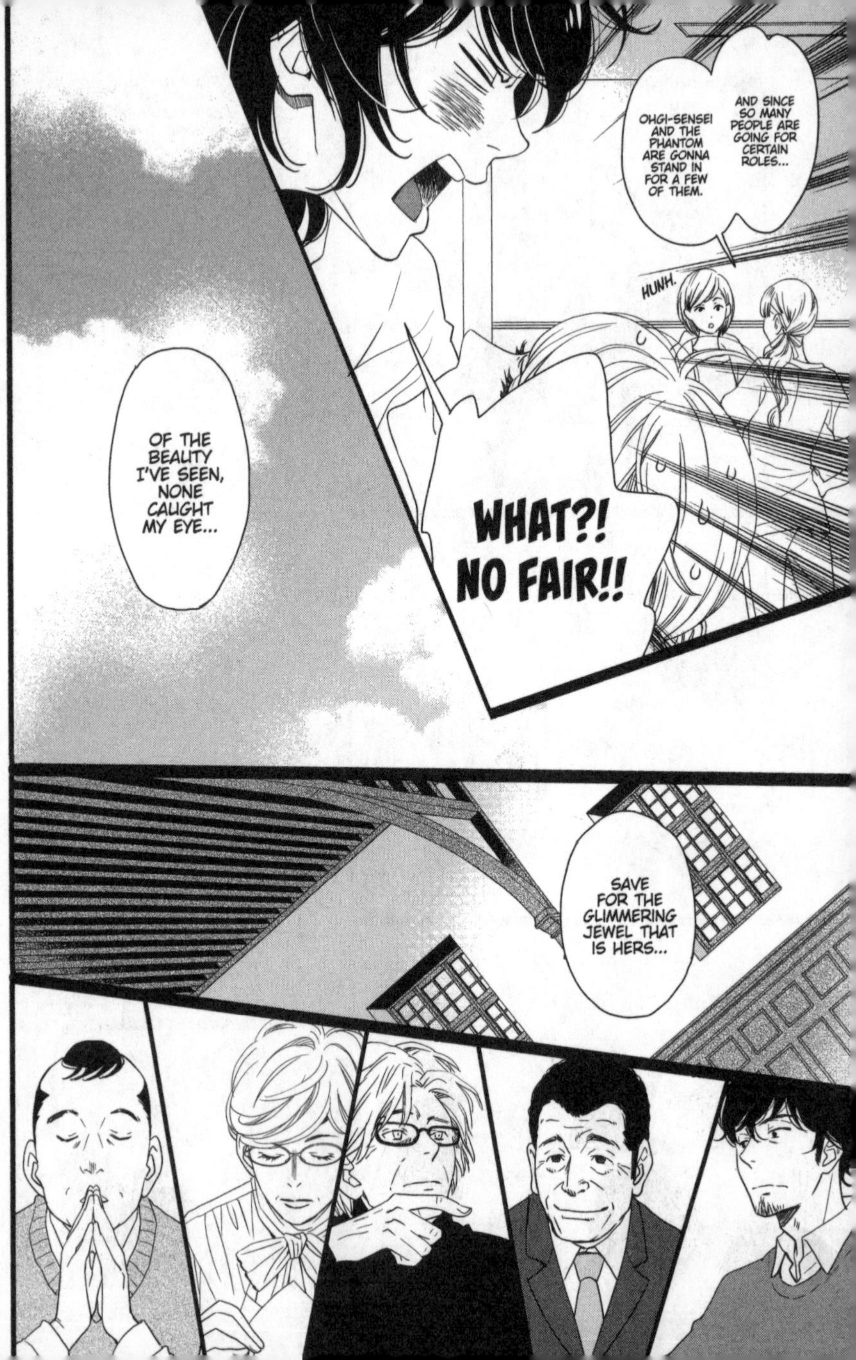
AND SINCE SO MANY PEOPLE ARE GOING FOR CERTAIN ROLES...
OHGI-SENSEI AND THE PHANTOM ARE GONNA STAND IN FOR A FEW OF THEM.
HUNH.
WHAT?! NO FAIR!!
OF THE BEAUTY I'VE SEEN, NONE CAUGHT MY EYE...
SAVE FOR THE GLIMMERING JEWEL THAT IS HERS...

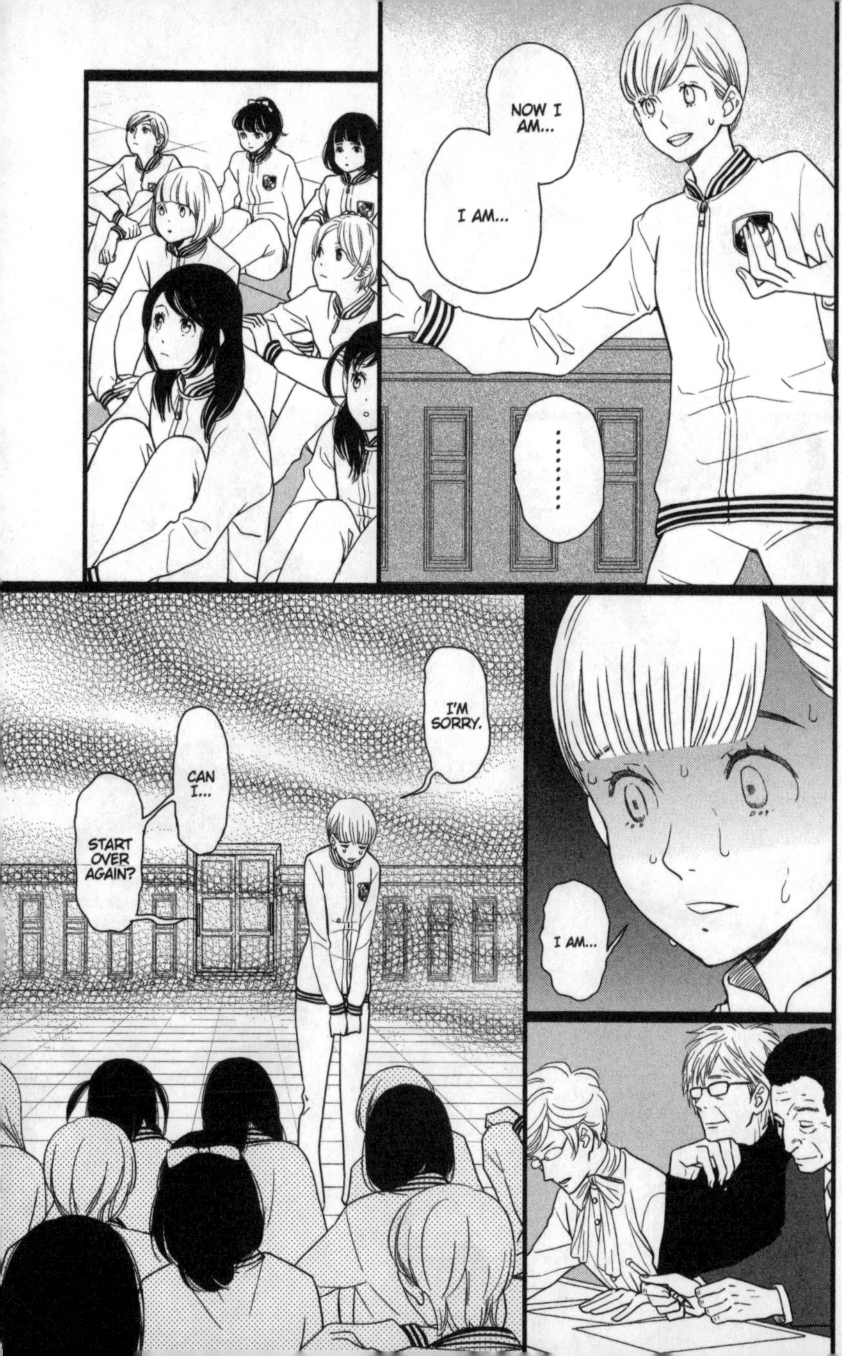
NOW I AM...
I AM...
......
I AM...
I'M SORRY.
CAN I...
START OVER AGAIN?

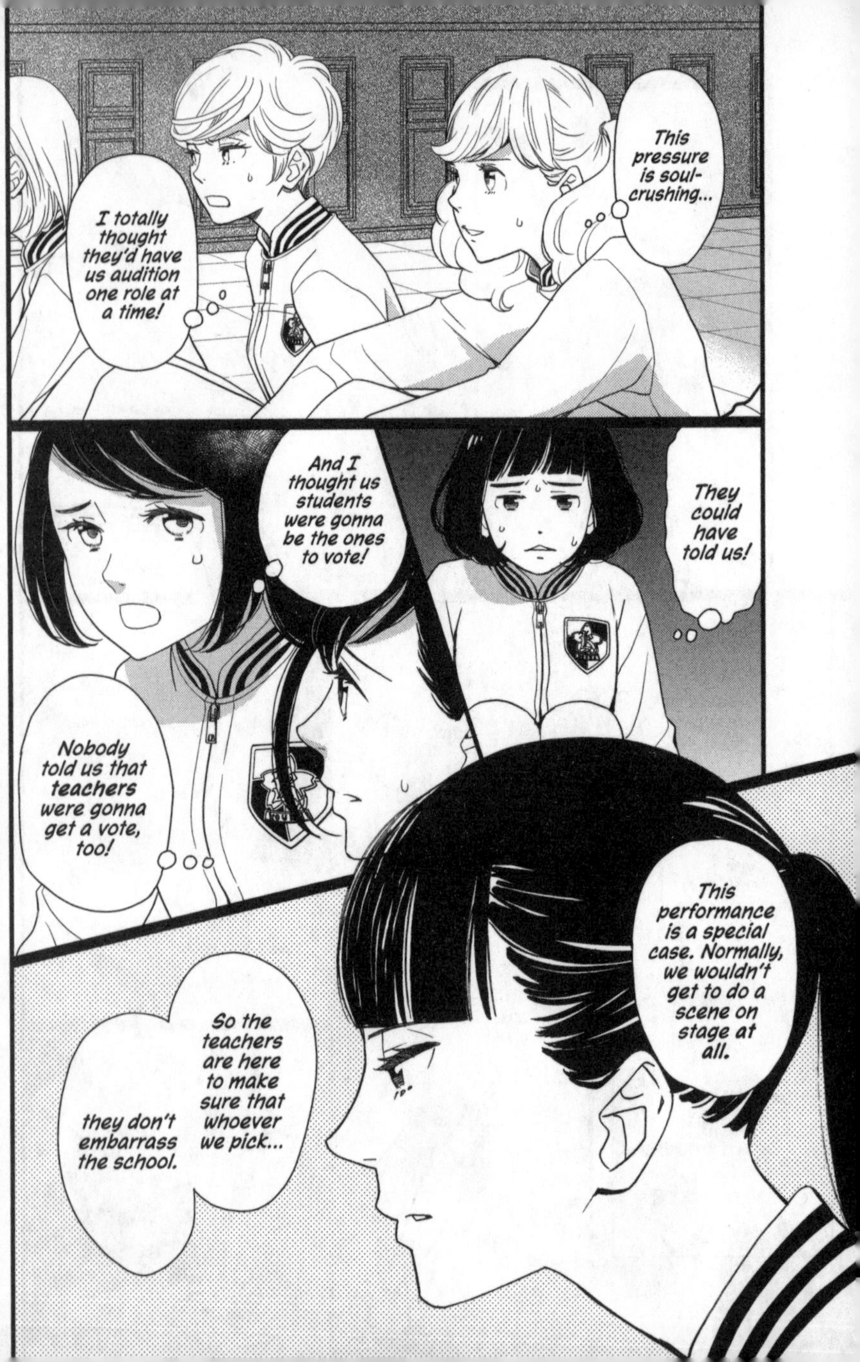
This pressure is soul-crushing...
I totally thought they'd have us audition one role at a time!
They could have told us!
And I thought us students were gonna be the ones to vote!
Nobody told us that teachers were gonna get a vote, too!
This performance is a special case. Normally, we wouldn't get to do a scene on stage at all.
So the teachers are here to make sure that whoever we pick...
they don't embarrass the school.

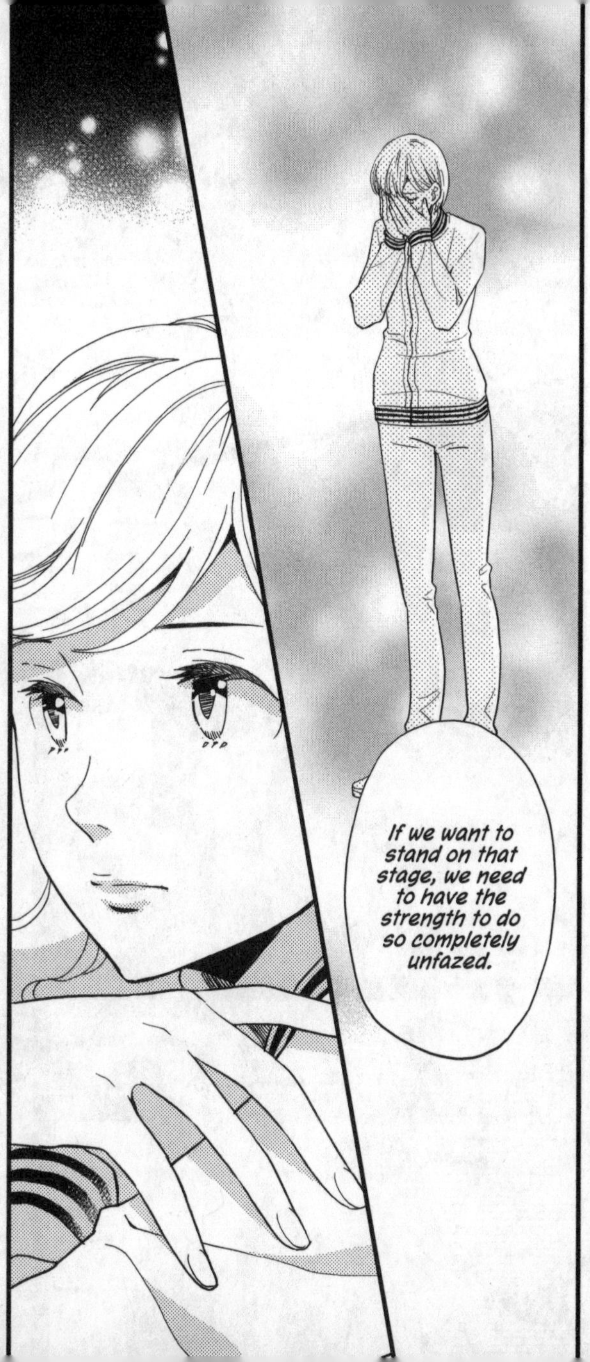
If we want to stand on that stage, we need to have the strength to do so completely unfazed.

Special Thanks

Asai-san
Kazami-san
Takisawa-san
Kuroki-san
Kumatani-san
Nono Jill
&
all of
♡my readers♡

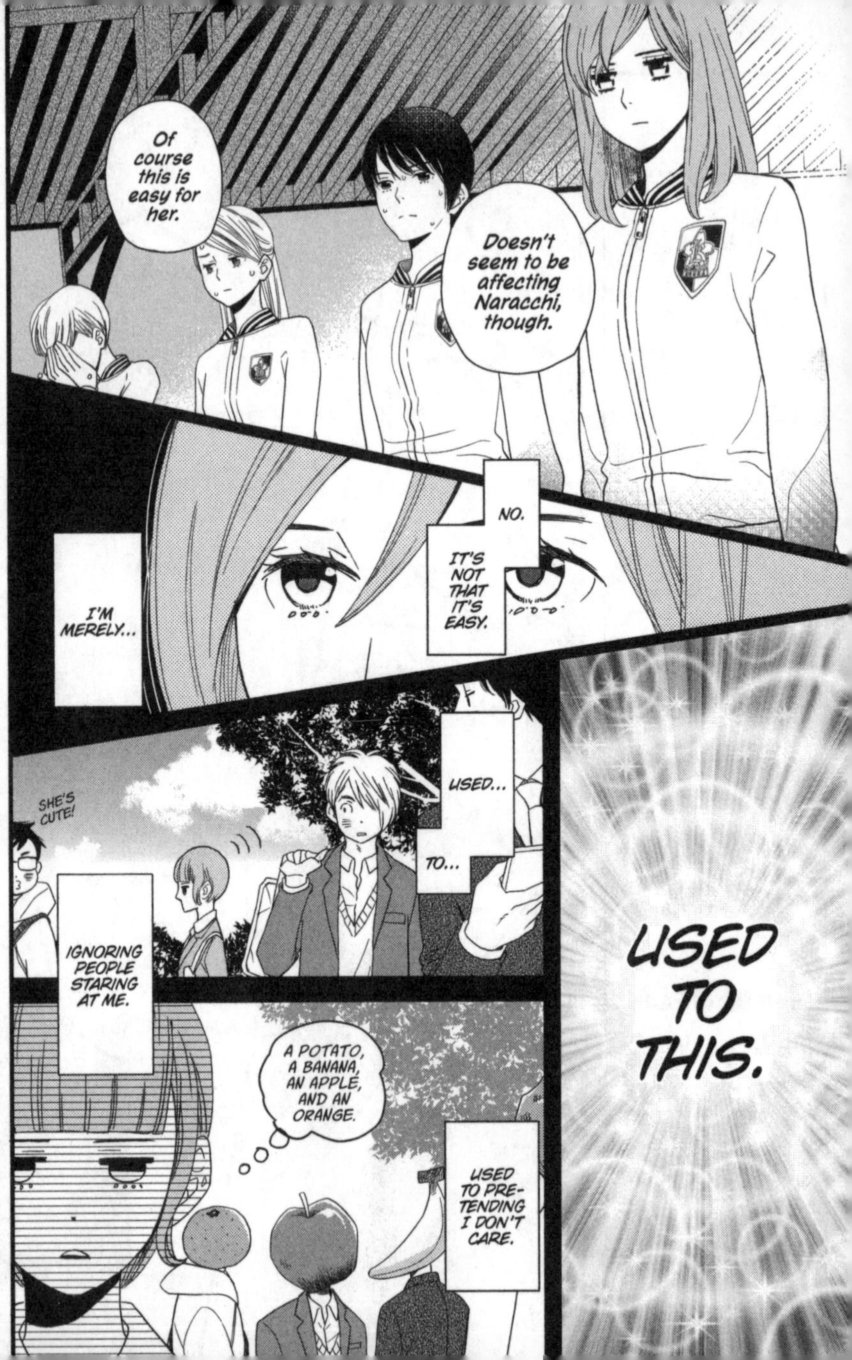
Doesn't seem to be affecting Naracchi, though.
Of course this is easy for her.
NO.
IT'S NOT THAT IT'S EASY.
I'M MERELY...
USED TO THIS.
USED...
TO...
SHE'S CUTE!
IGNORING PEOPLE STARING AT ME.
USED TO PRE-TENDING I DON'T CARE.
A POTATO, A BANANA, AN APPLE, AND AN ORANGE.

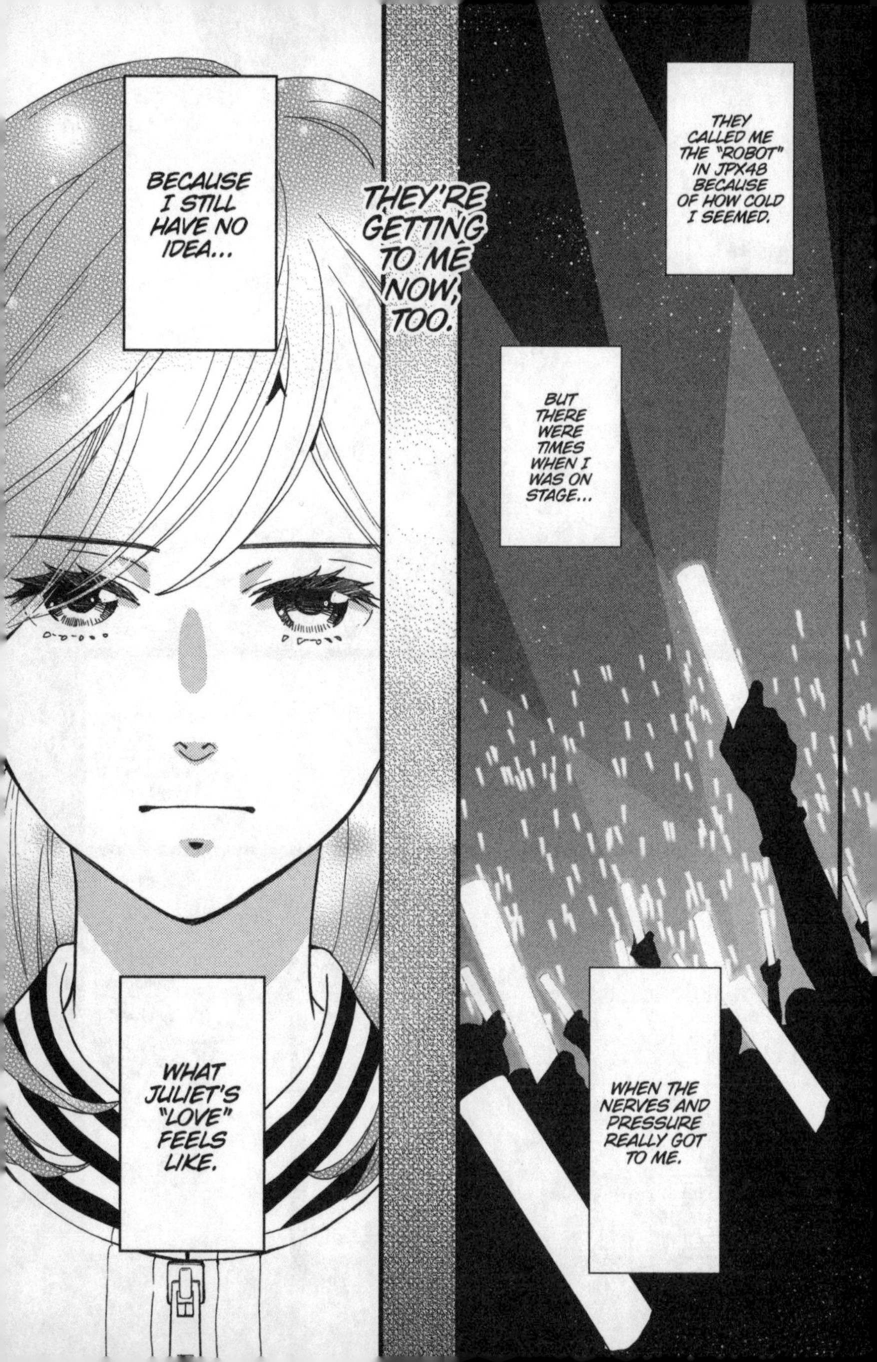
THEY CALLED ME THE "ROBOT" IN JPX48 BECAUSE OF HOW COLD I SEEMED.
BUT THERE WERE TIMES WHEN I WAS ON STAGE...
WHEN THE NERVES AND PRESSURE REALLY GOT TO ME.
THEY'RE GETTING TO ME NOW, TOO.
BECAUSE I STILL HAVE NO IDEA...
WHAT JULIET'S "LOVE" FEELS LIKE.

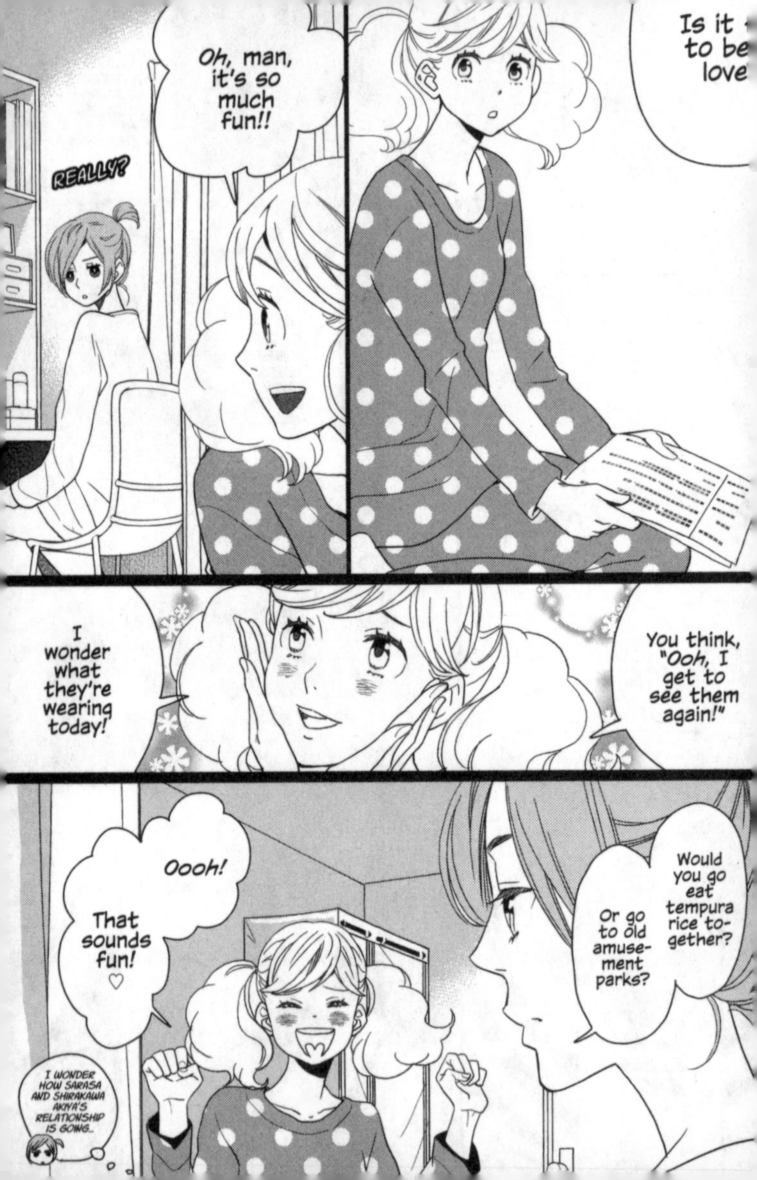
Is it
to be
love
Oh, man, it's so much fun!!
REALLY?
You think, "Ooh, I get to see them again!"
I wonder what they're wearing today!
Would you go eat tempura rice to-gether?
Or go to old amuse-ment parks?
Oooh!
That sounds fun! ♡
I WONDER HOW SARASA AND SHIRAKAWA AKIYA'S RELATIONSHIP IS GOING...

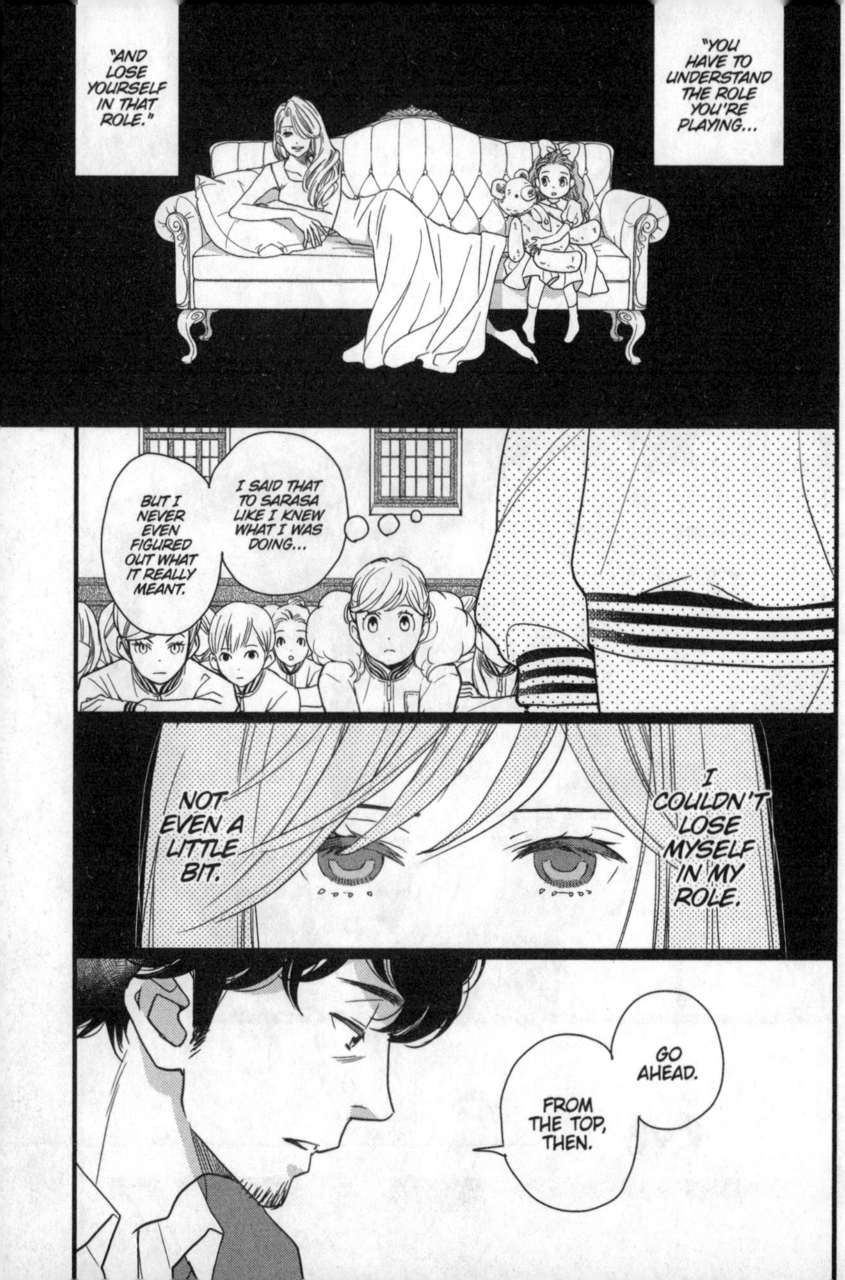
"YOU HAVE TO UNDERSTAND THE ROLE YOU'RE PLAYING...
"AND LOSE YOURSELF IN THAT ROLE."
I SAID THAT TO SARASA LIKE I KNEW WHAT I WAS DOING...
BUT I NEVER EVEN FIGURED OUT WHAT IT REALLY MEANT.
I COULDN'T LOSE MYSELF IN MY ROLE.
NOT EVEN A LITTLE BIT.
GO AHEAD.
FROM THE TOP, THEN.

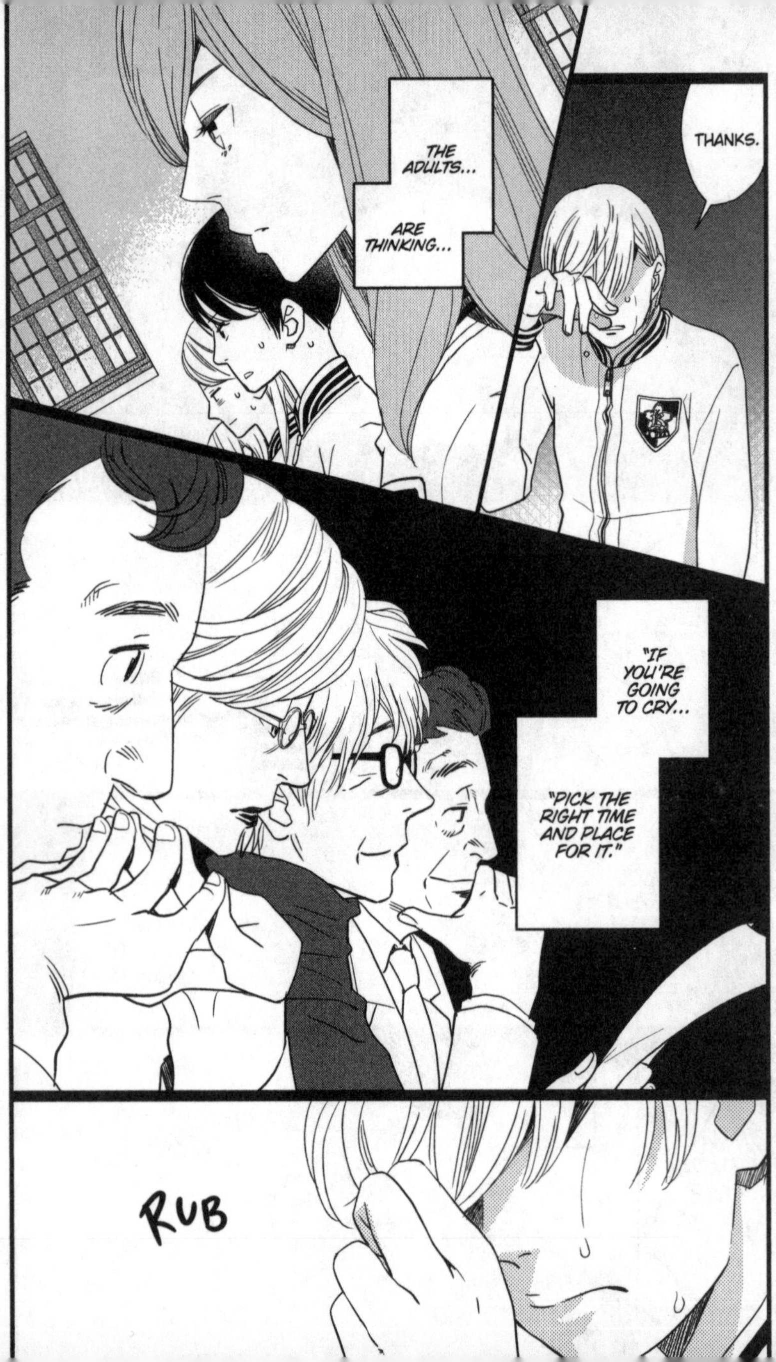
THANKS.
THE ADULTS...
ARE THINKING...
"IF YOU'RE GOING TO CRY...
"PICK THE RIGHT TIME AND PLACE FOR IT."
RUB

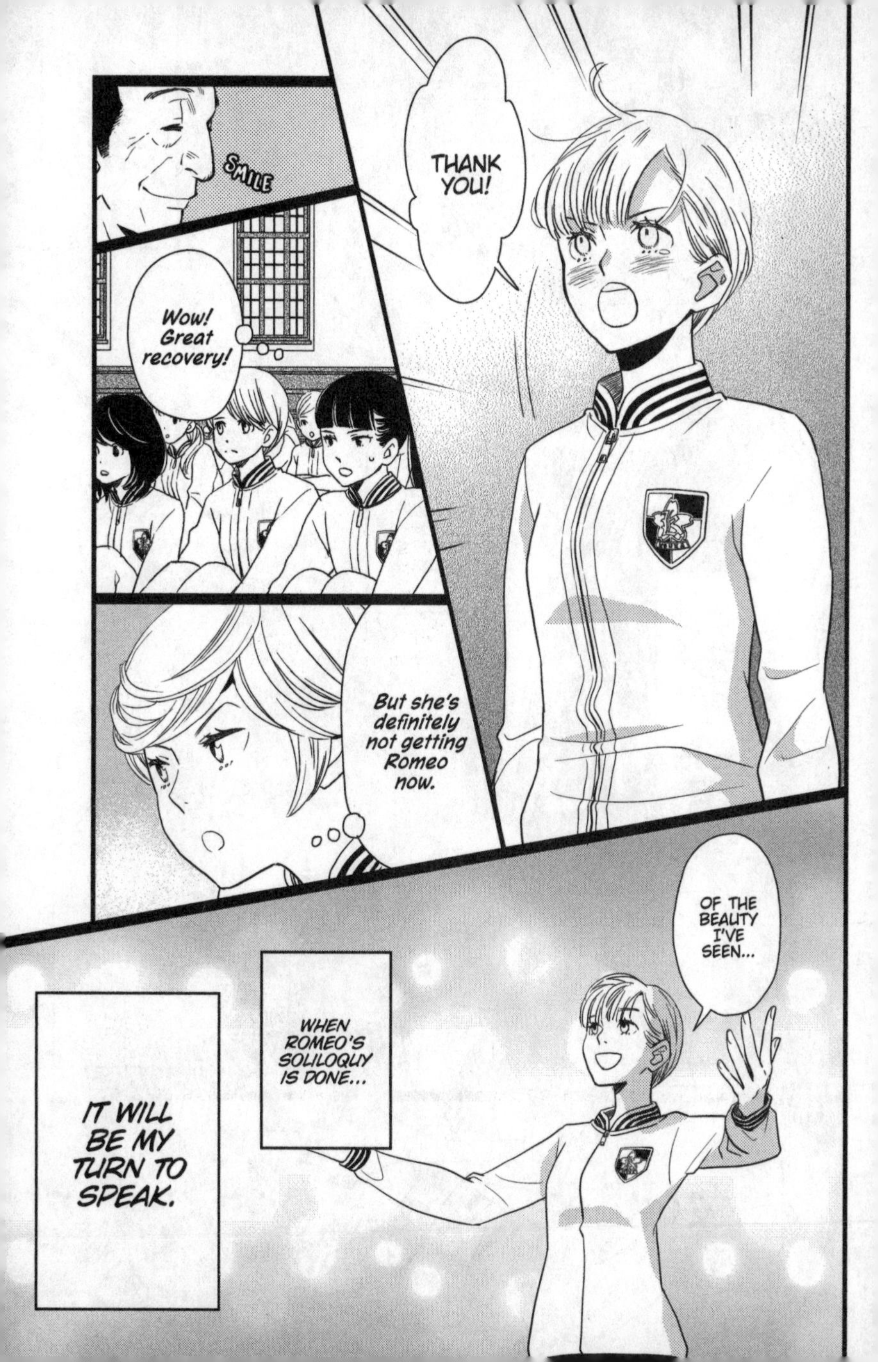
THANK YOU!
SMILE
Wow! Great recovery!
But she's definitely not getting Romeo now.
OF THE BEAUTY I'VE SEEN...
WHEN ROMEO'S SOLILOQUY IS DONE...
IT WILL BE MY TURN TO SPEAK.

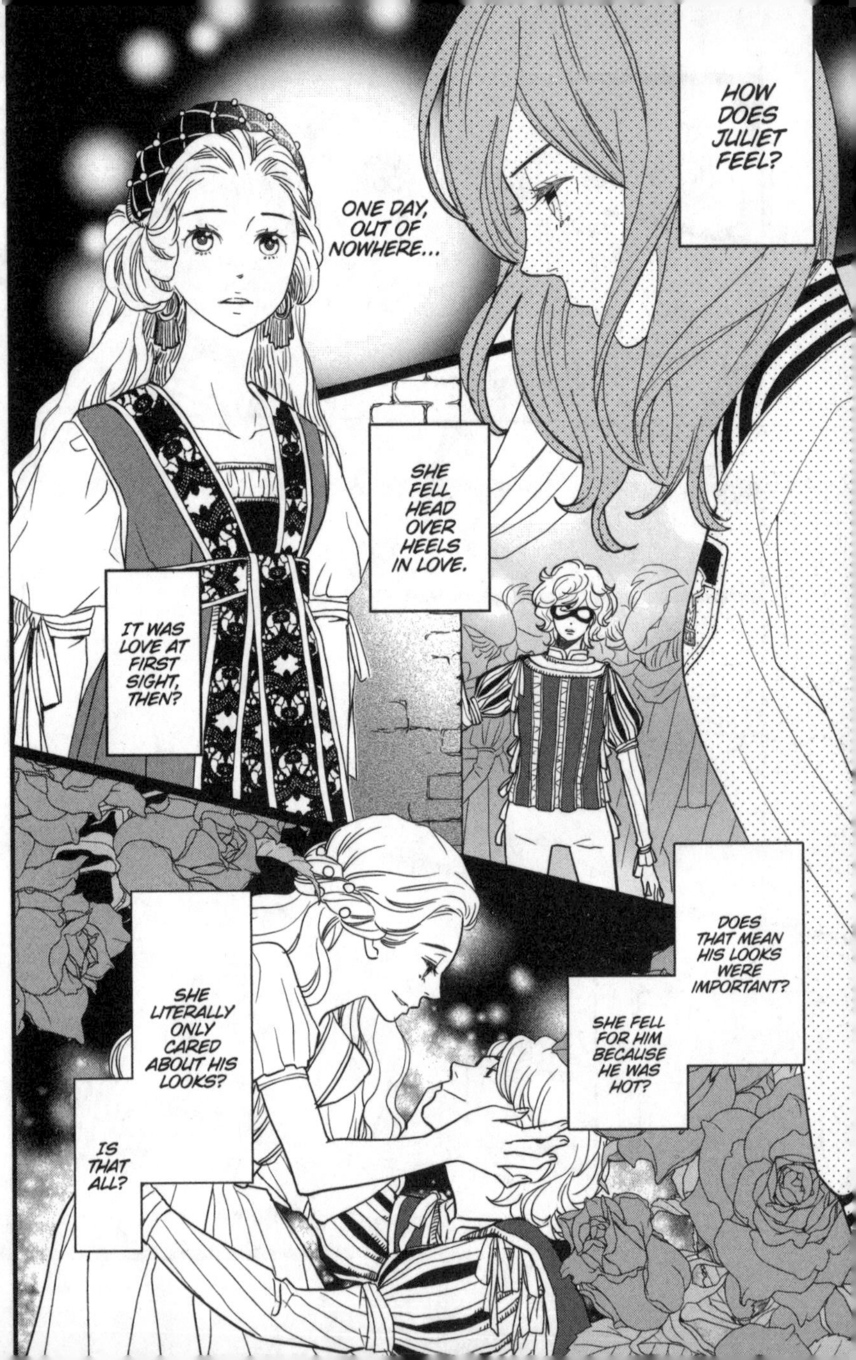
HOW DOES JULIET FEEL?
ONE DAY, OUT OF NOWHERE...
SHE FELL HEAD OVER HEELS IN LOVE.
IT WAS LOVE AT FIRST SIGHT, THEN?
DOES THAT MEAN HIS LOOKS WERE IMPORTANT?
SHE FELL FOR HIM BECAUSE HE WAS HOT?
SHE LITERALLY ONLY CARED ABOUT HIS LOOKS?
IS THAT ALL?

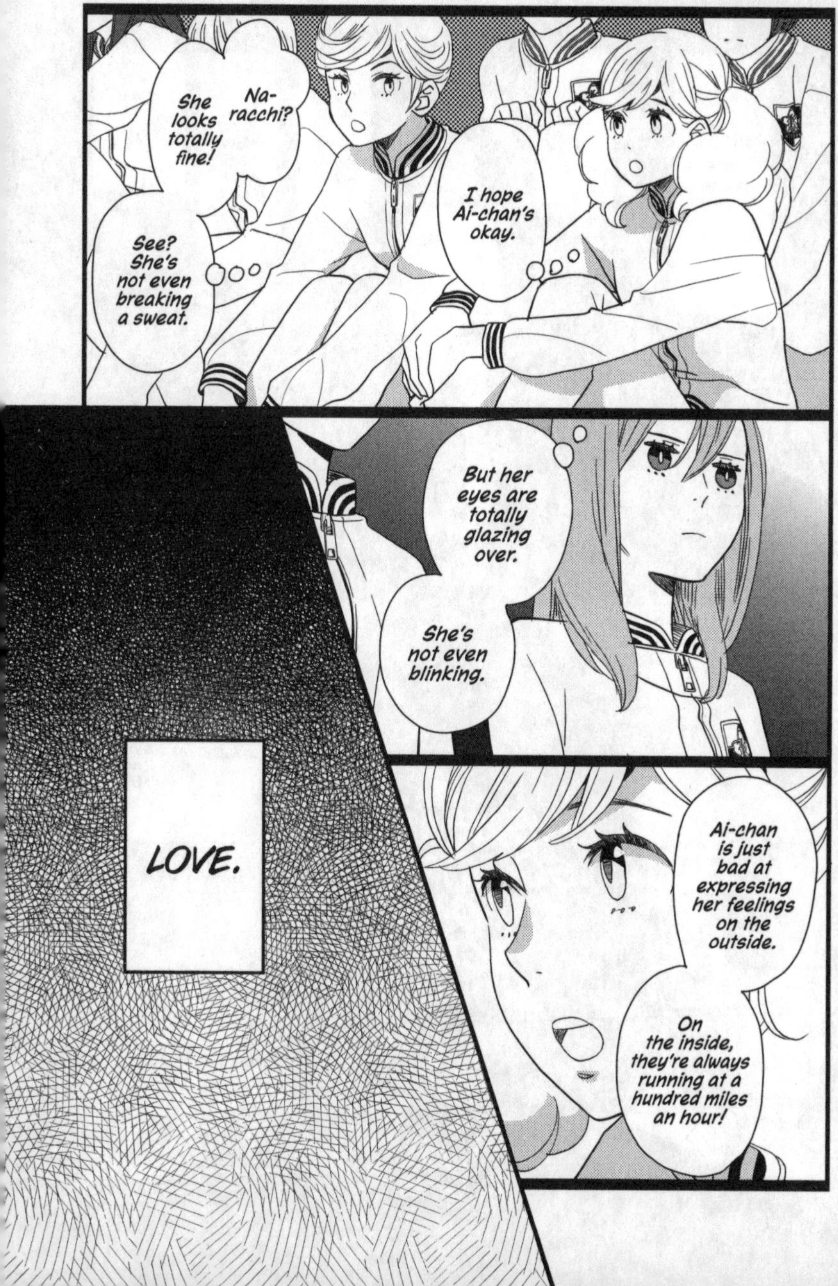
I hope Ai-chan's okay.
Na-racchi? She looks totally fine!
See? She's not even breaking a sweat.
But her eyes are totally glazing over.
She's not even blinking.
Ai-chan is just bad at expressing her feelings on the outside.
On the inside, they're always running at a hundred miles an hour!
LOVE.

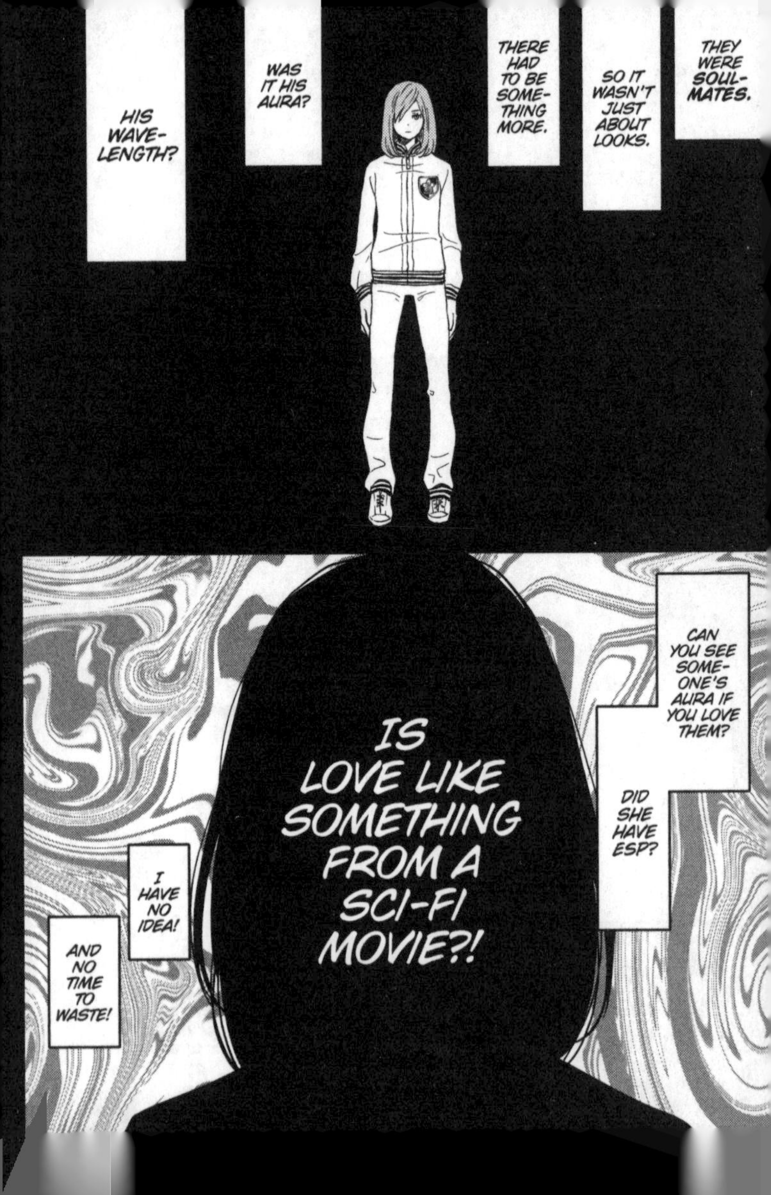
THEY WERE SOUL-MATES.
SO IT WASN'T JUST ABOUT LOOKS.
THERE HAD TO BE SOME-THING MORE.
WAS IT HIS AURA?
HIS WAVE-LENGTH?
CAN YOU SEE SOME-ONE'S AURA IF YOU LOVE THEM?
DID SHE HAVE ESP?
IS LOVE LIKE SOMETHING FROM A SCI-FI MOVIE?!
I HAVE NO IDEA!
AND NO TIME TO WASTE!

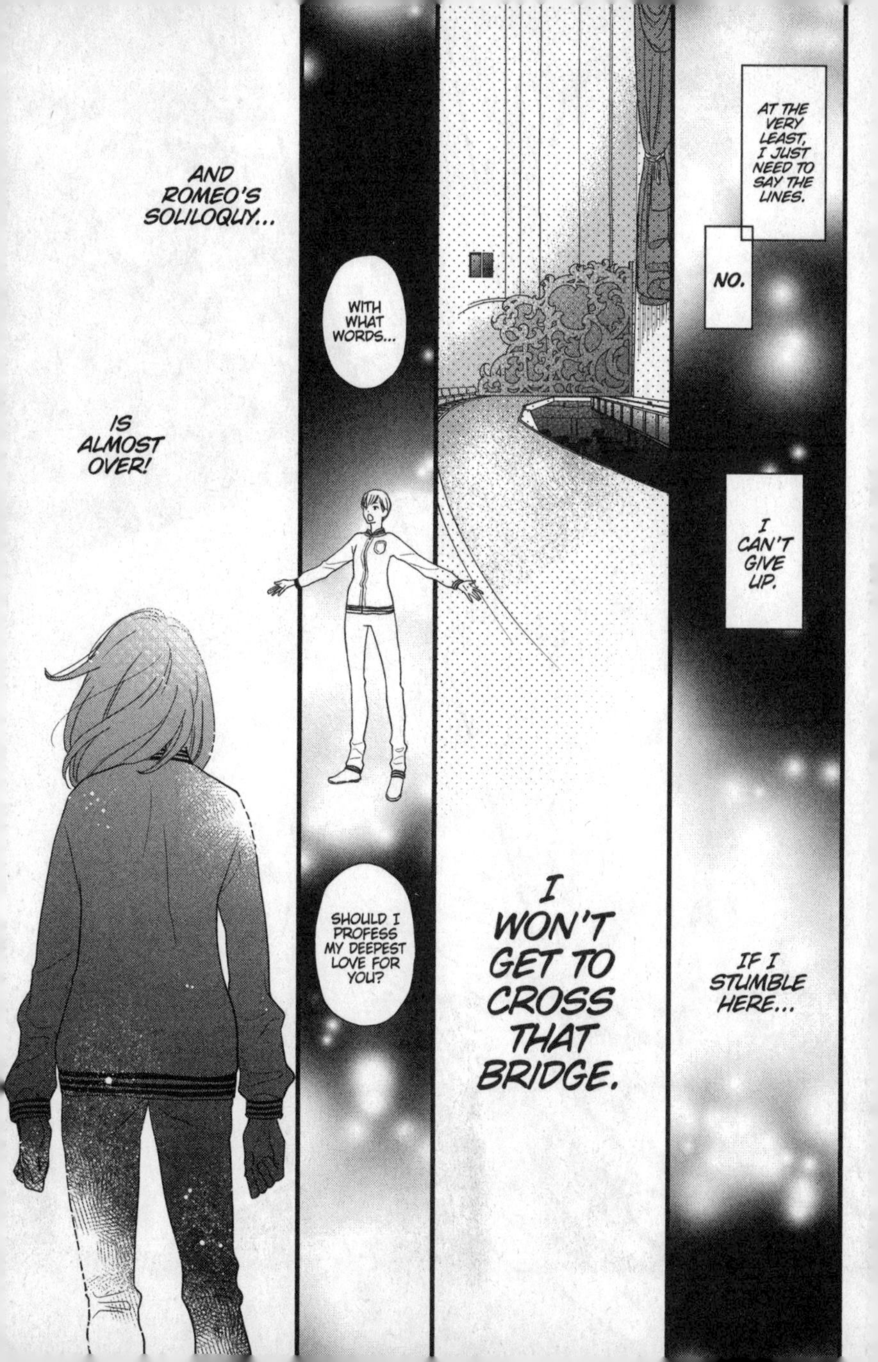
AT THE VERY LEAST, I JUST NEED TO SAY THE LINES.
NO.
I CAN'T GIVE UP.
IF I STUMBLE HERE...
I WON'T GET TO CROSS THAT BRIDGE.
WITH WHAT WORDS...
SHOULD I PROFESS MY DEEPEST LOVE FOR YOU?
AND ROMEO'S SOLILOQUY...
IS ALMOST OVER!

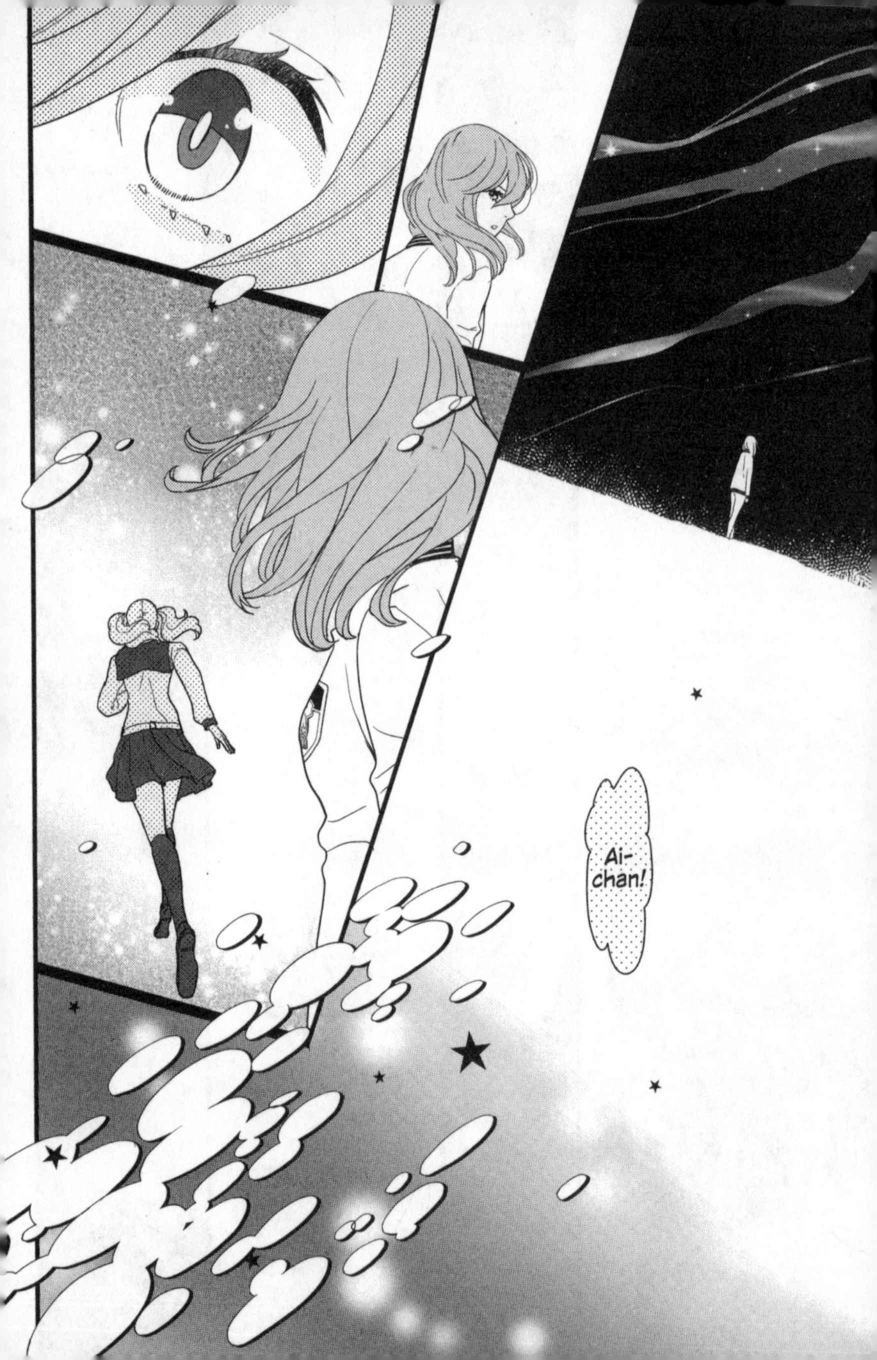
Ai-chan!

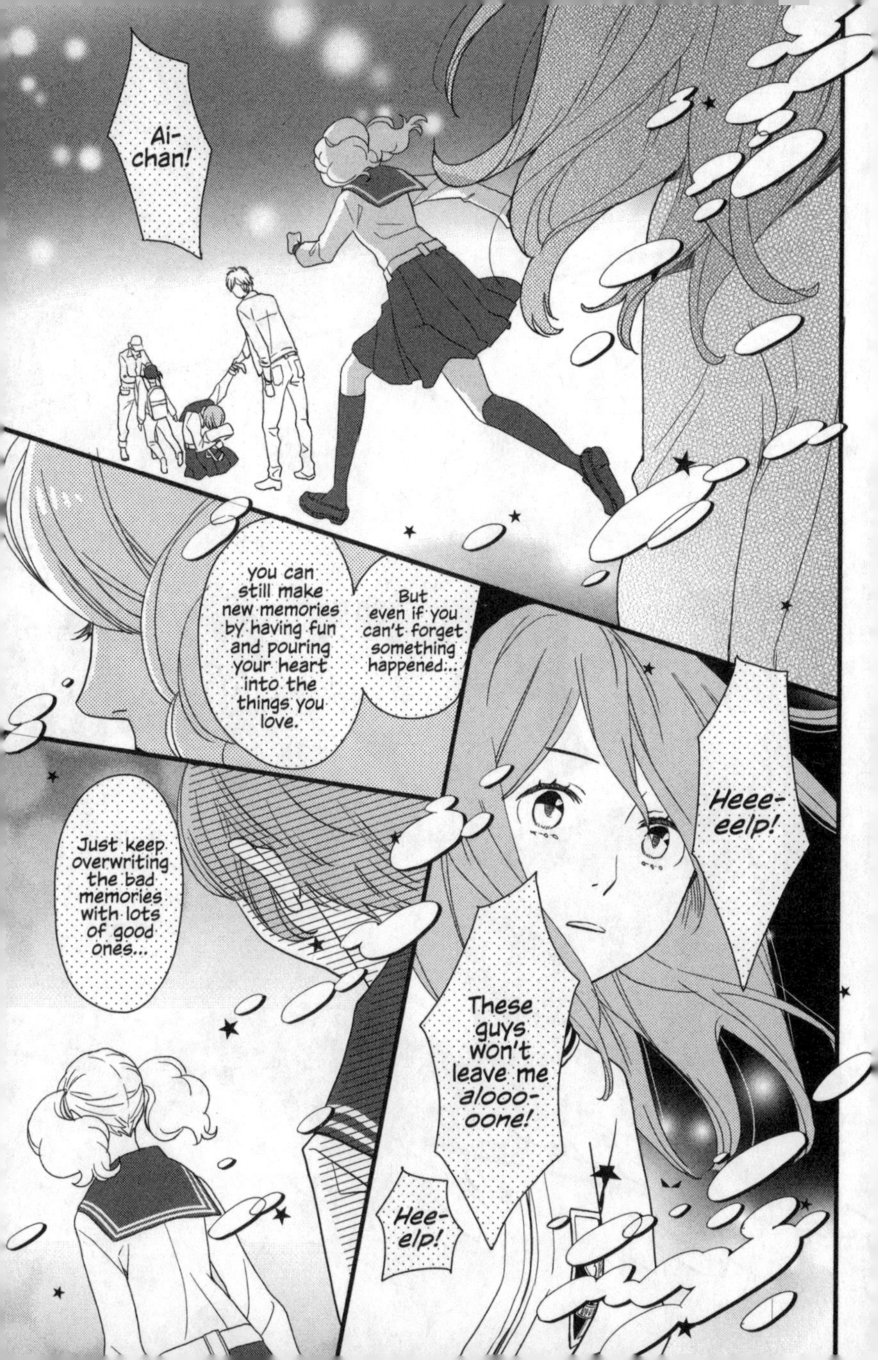
Ai-chan!
Heeee-eelp!
These guys won't leave me alooo-oone!
Hee-eelp!
But even if you can't forget something happened...
you can still make new memories by having fun and pouring your heart into the things you love.
Just keep overwriting the bad memories with lots of good ones...

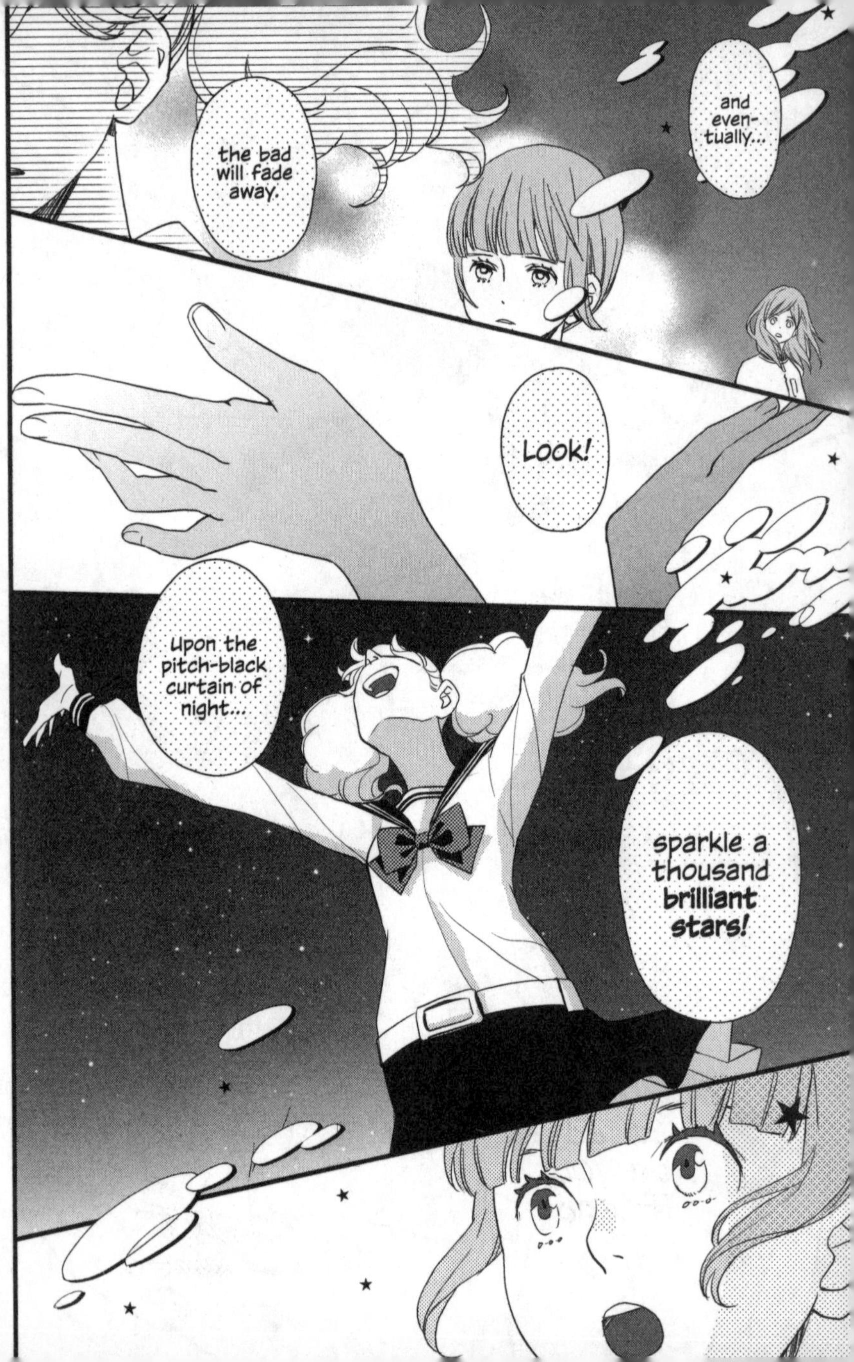
and eventually...
the bad will fade away.
Look!
Upon the pitch-black curtain of night...
sparkle a thousand brilliant stars!

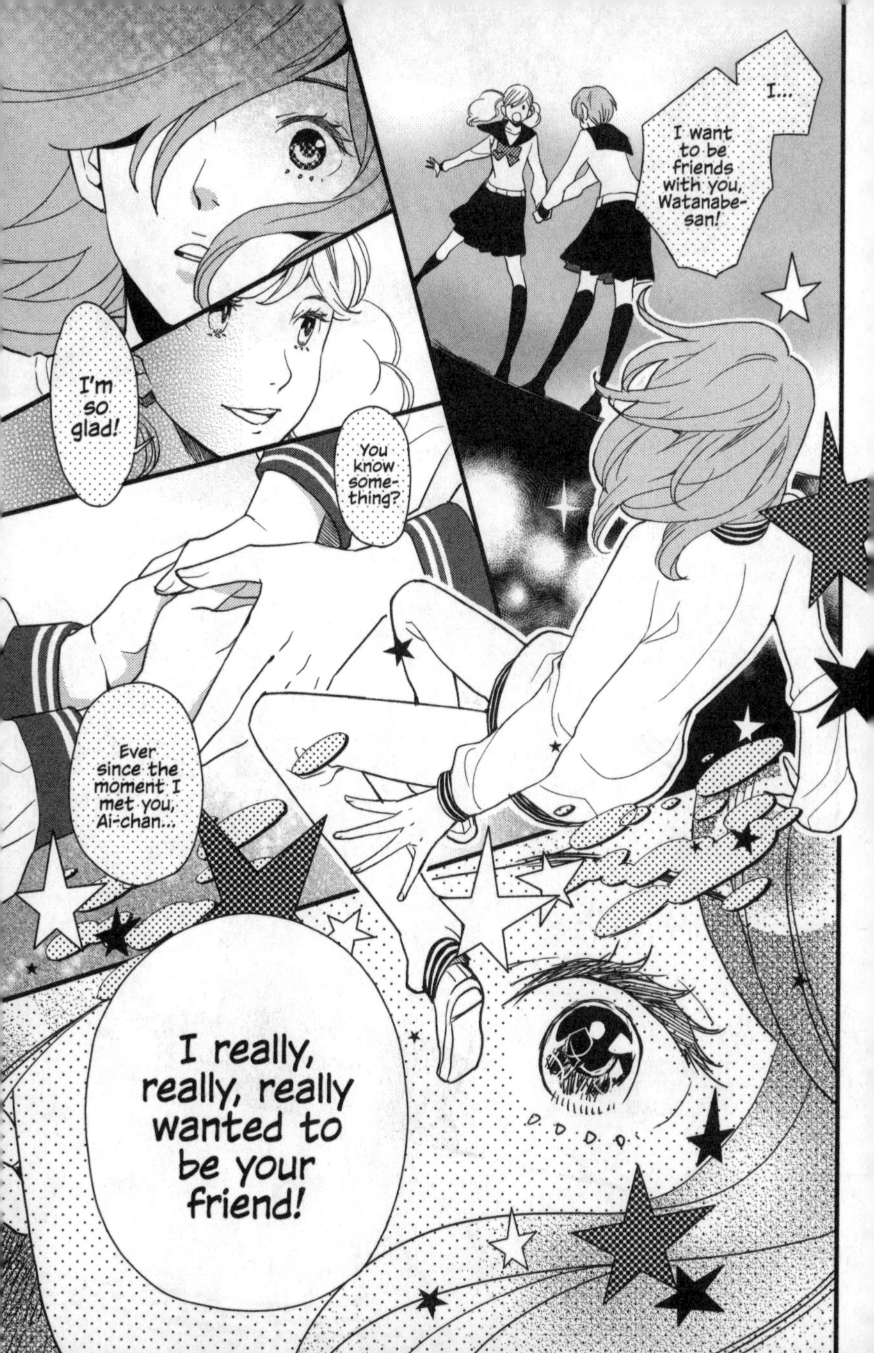
I...
I want to be friends with you, Watanabe-san!
I'm so glad!
You know something?
Ever since the moment I met you, Ai-chan...
I really, really, really wanted to be your friend!

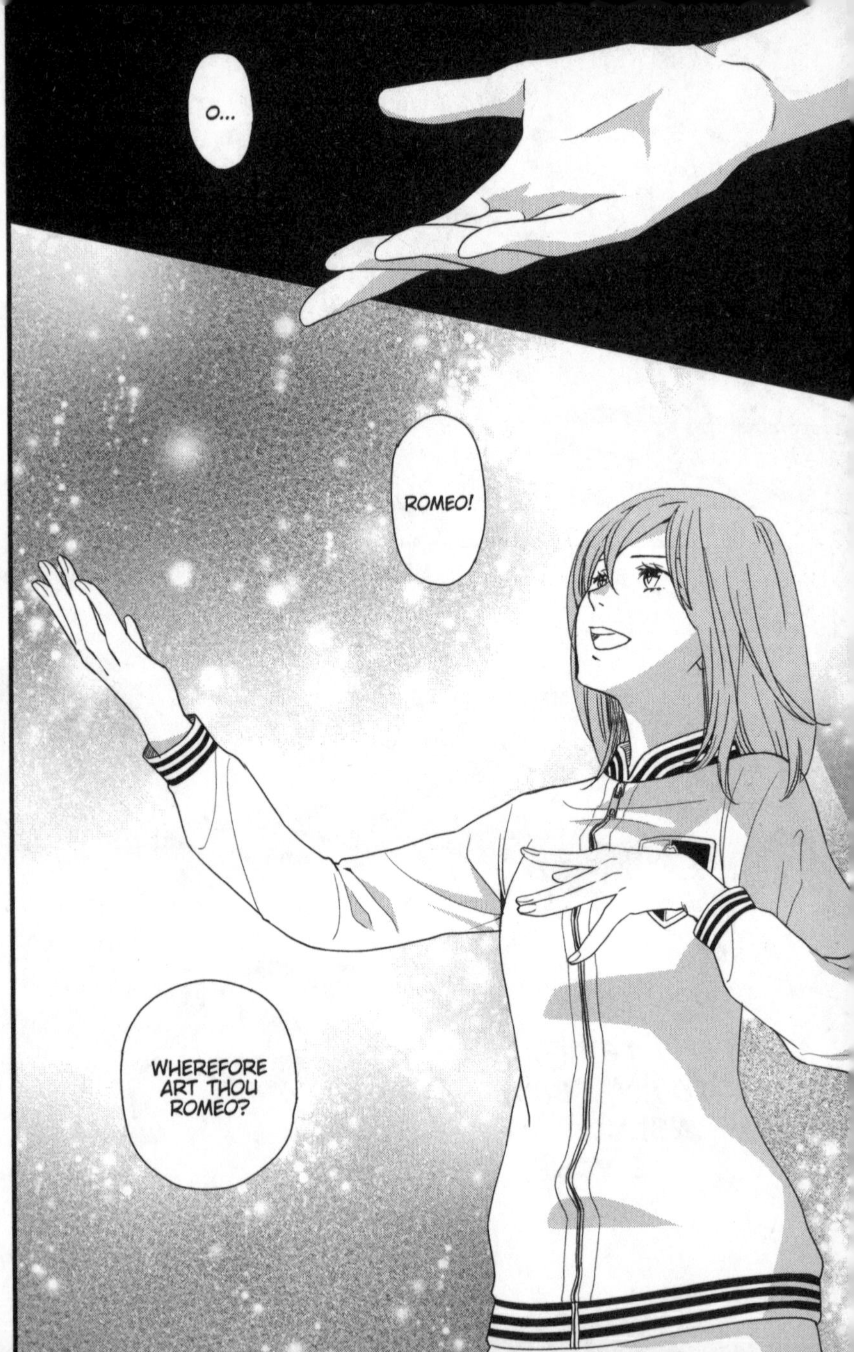
O...
ROMEO!
WHEREFORE ART THOU ROMEO?

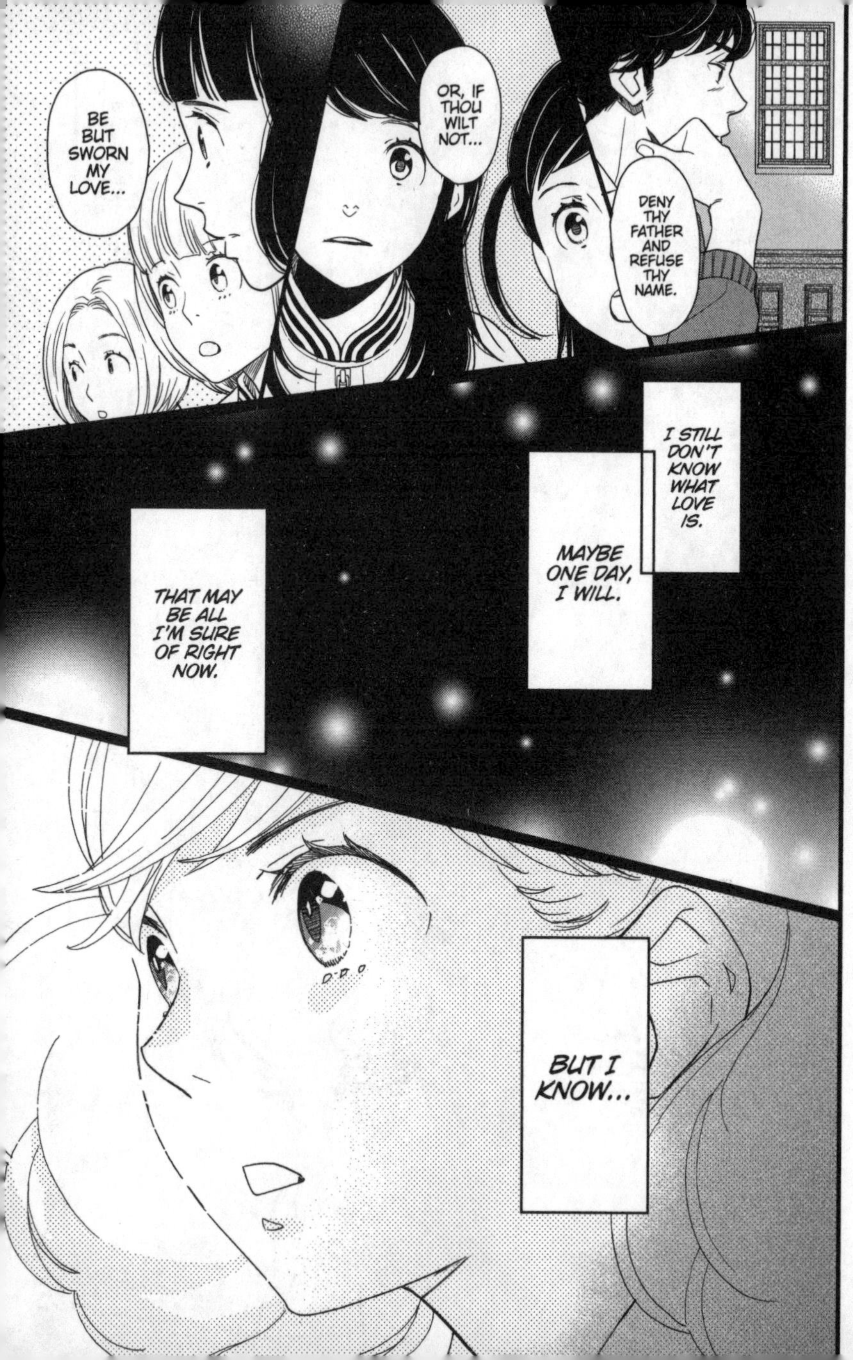
DENY THY FATHER AND REFUSE THY NAME.
OR, IF THOU WILT NOT...
BE BUT SWORN MY LOVE...
I STILL DON'T KNOW WHAT LOVE IS.
MAYBE ONE DAY, I WILL.
THAT MAY BE ALL I'M SURE OF RIGHT NOW.
BUT I KNOW...

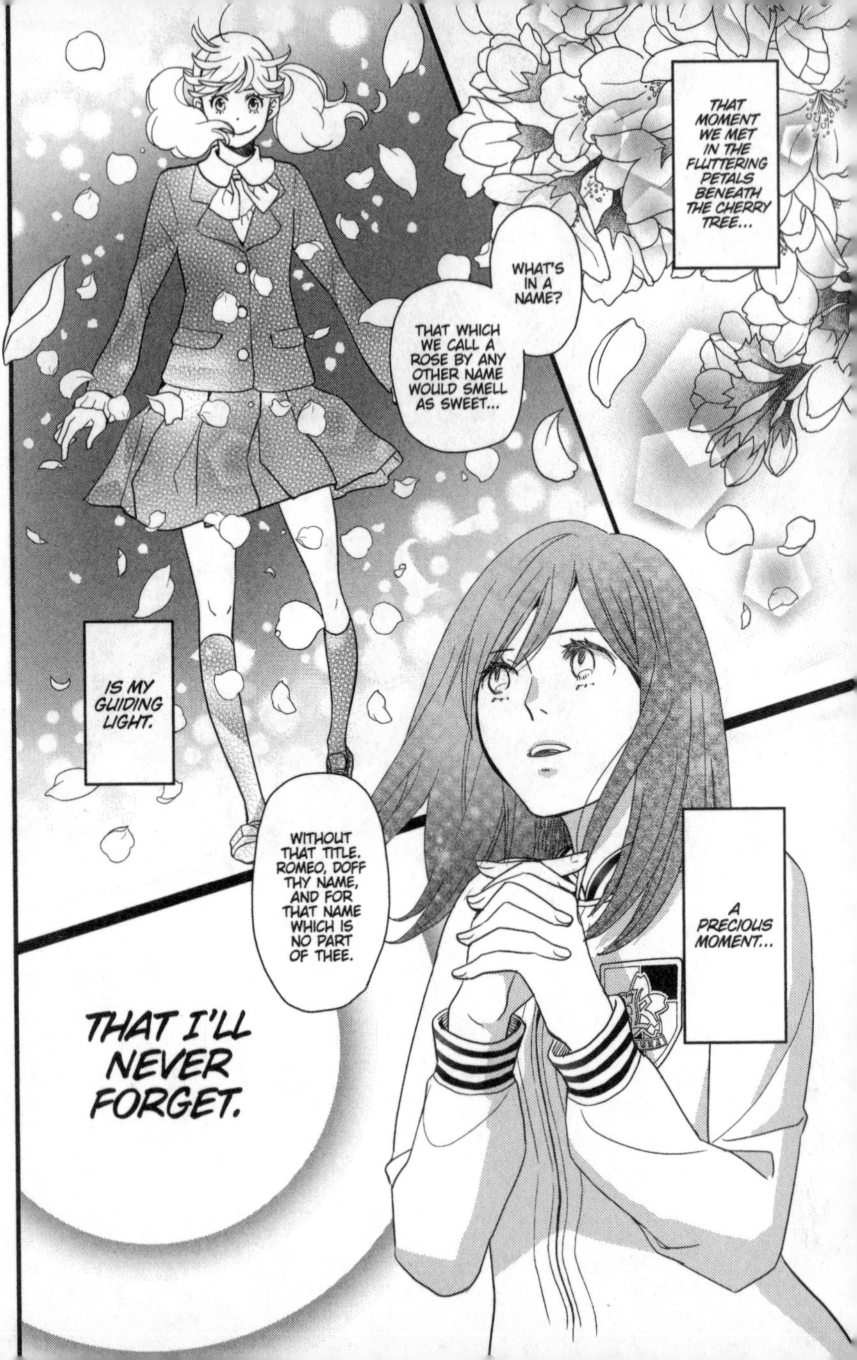
THAT MOMENT WE MET IN THE FLUTTERING PETALS BENEATH THE CHERRY TREE...
WHAT'S IN A NAME?
THAT WHICH WE CALL A ROSE BY ANY OTHER NAME WOULD SMELL AS SWEET...
IS MY GUIDING LIGHT.
A PRECIOUS MOMENT...
WITHOUT THAT TITLE. ROMEO, DOFF THY NAME, AND FOR THAT NAME WHICH IS NO PART OF THEE.
THAT I'LL NEVER FORGET.

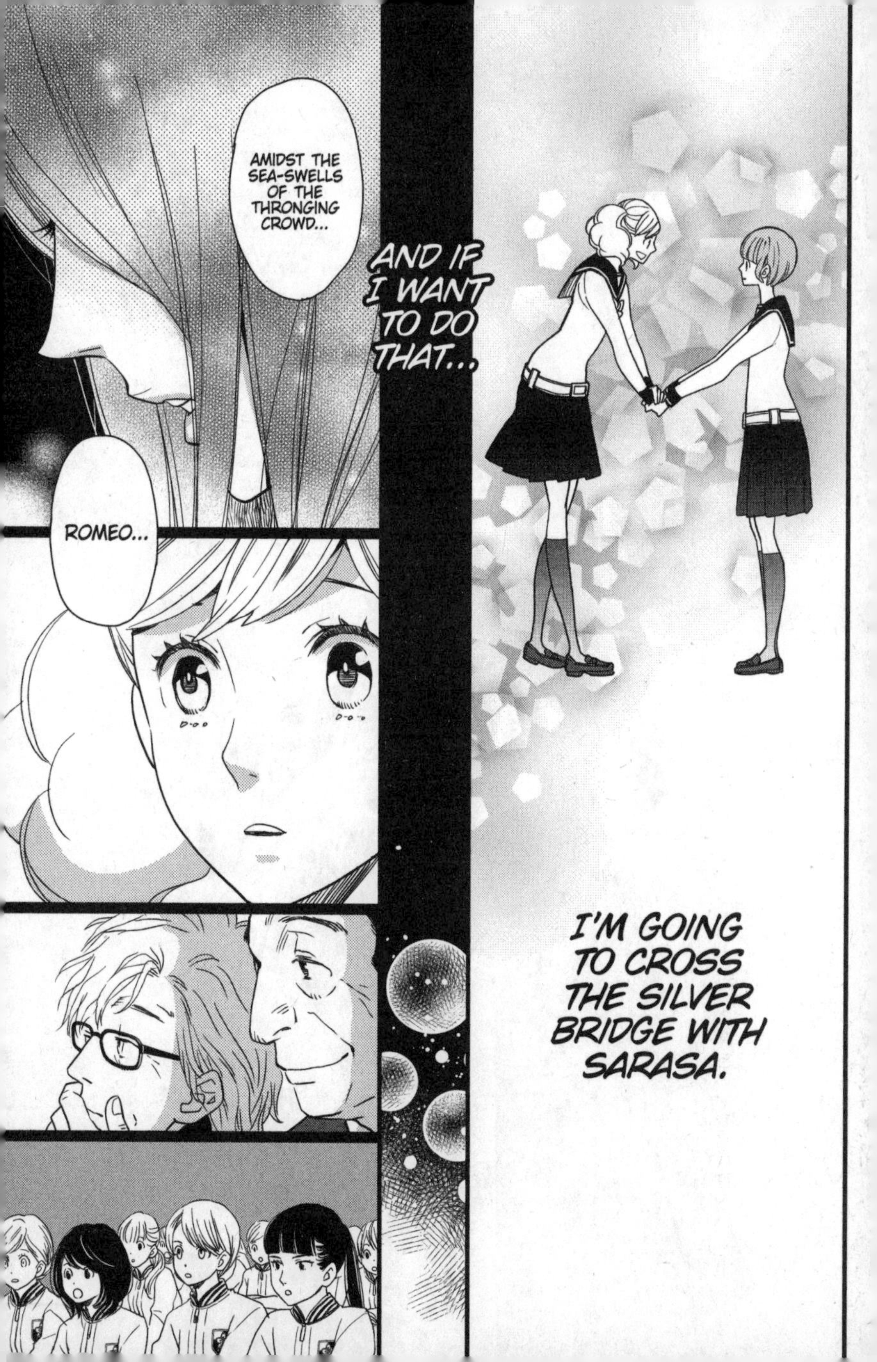
AND IF I WANT TO DO THAT...
I'M GOING TO CROSS THE SILVER BRIDGE WITH SARASA.
AMIDST THE SEA-SWELLS OF THE THRONGING CROWD...
ROMEO...

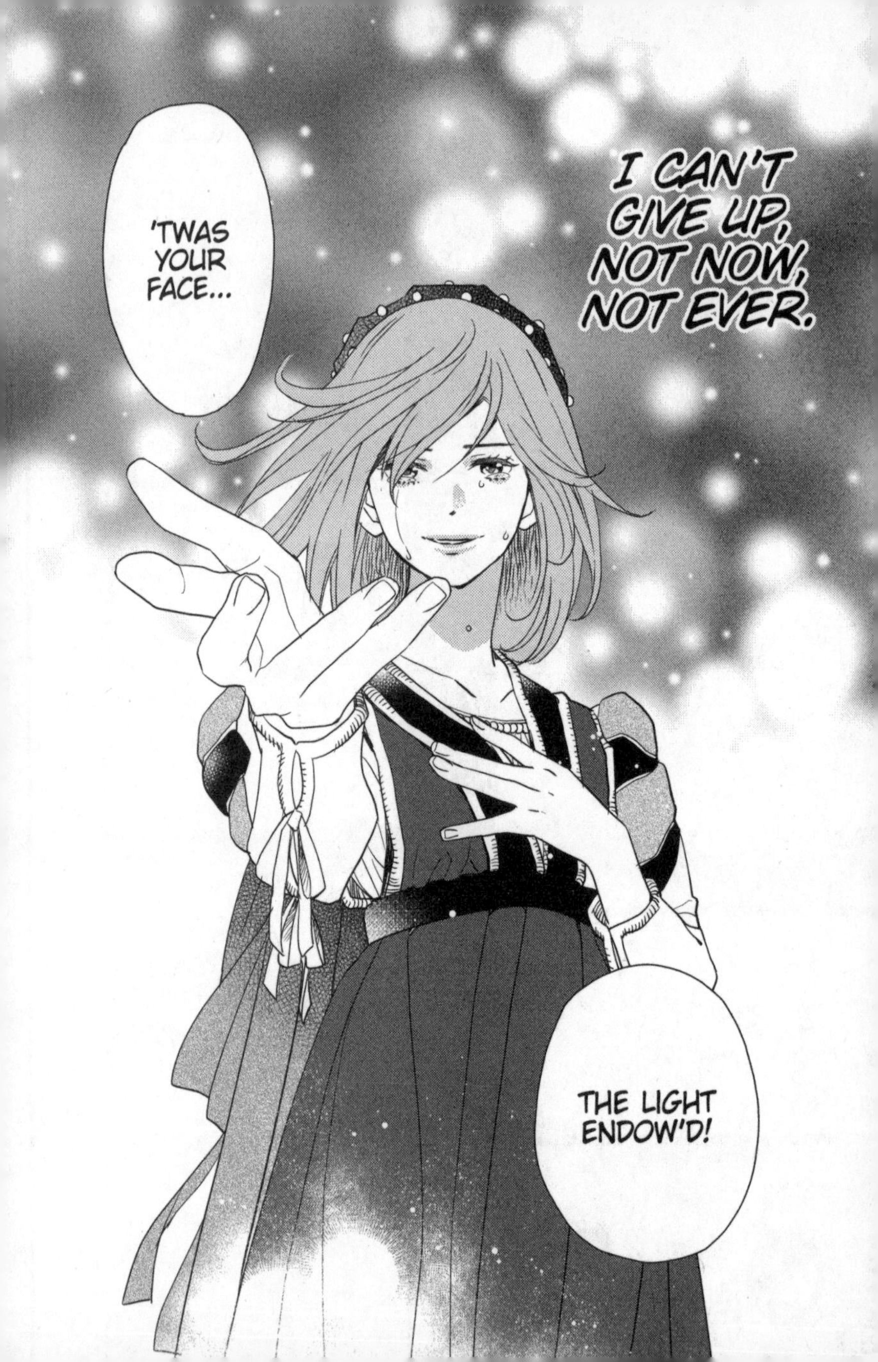
I CAN'T GIVE UP, NOT NOW, NOT EVER.
'TWAS YOUR FACE...
THE LIGHT ENDOW'D!

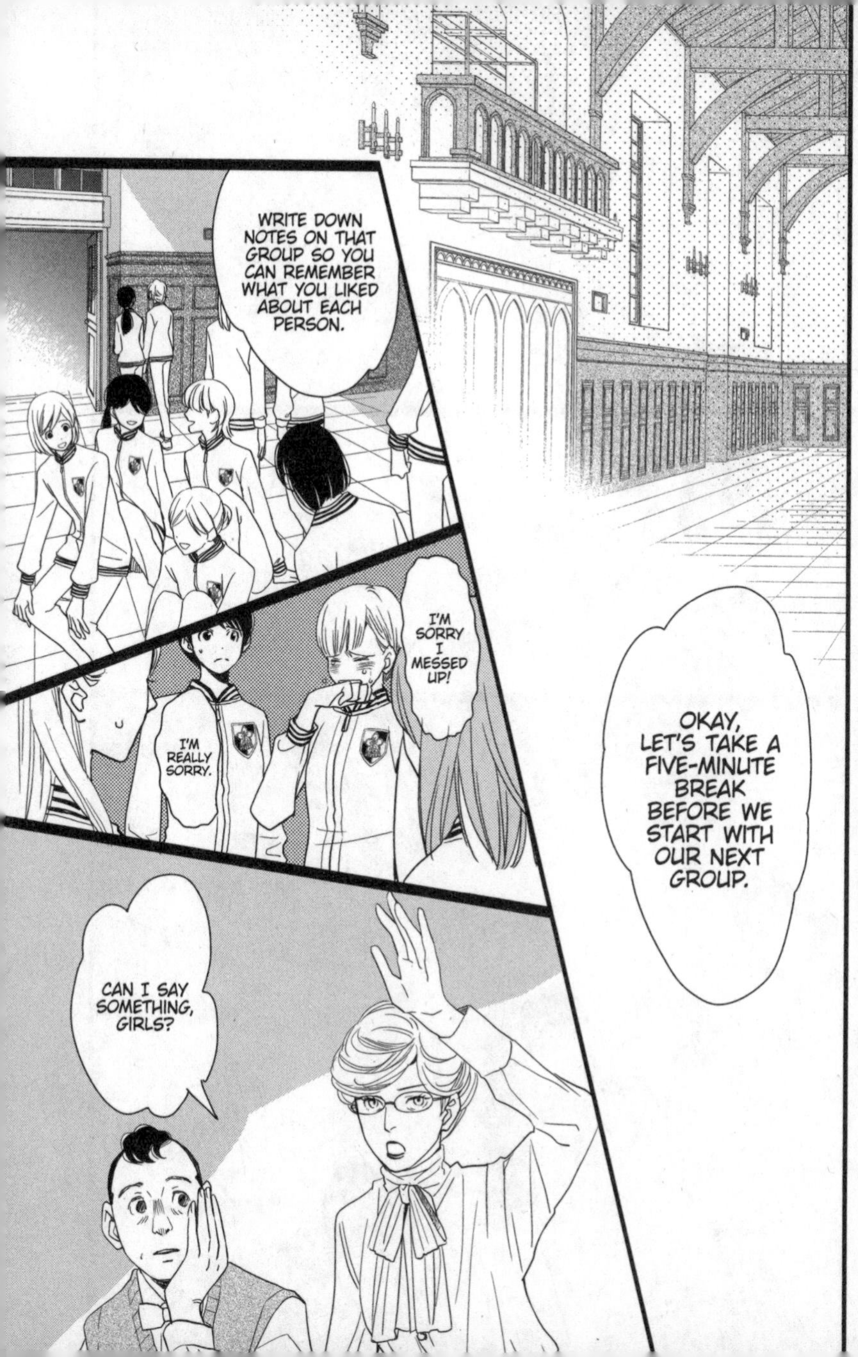
OKAY, LET'S TAKE A FIVE-MINUTE BREAK BEFORE WE START WITH OUR NEXT GROUP.
WRITE DOWN NOTES ON THAT GROUP SO YOU CAN REMEMBER WHAT YOU LIKED ABOUT EACH PERSON.
I'M SORRY I MESSED UP!
I'M REALLY SORRY.
CAN I SAY SOMETHING, GIRLS?

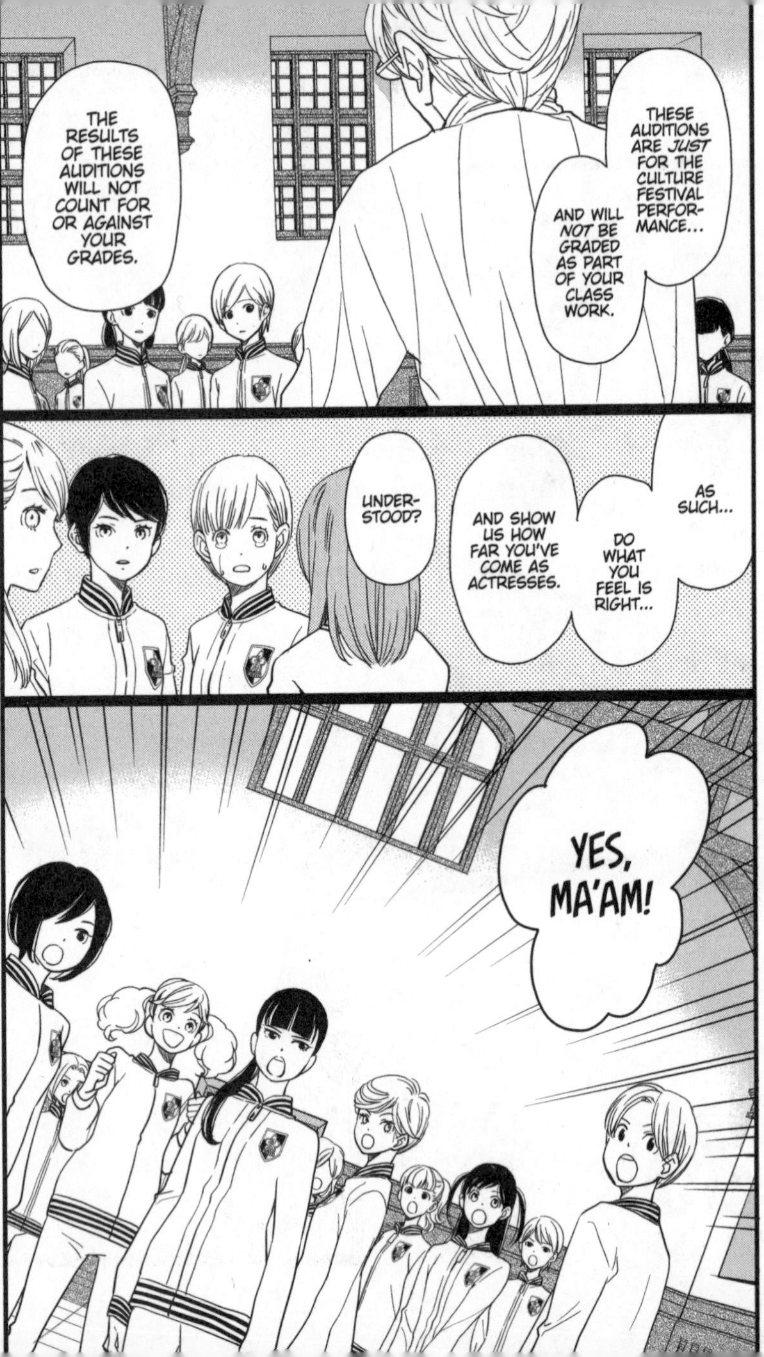
THESE AUDITIONS ARE *JUST* FOR THE CULTURE FESTIVAL PERFORMANCE...
AND WILL *NOT* BE GRADED AS PART OF YOUR CLASS WORK.
THE RESULTS OF THESE AUDITIONS WILL NOT COUNT FOR OR AGAINST YOUR GRADES.
AS SUCH...
DO WHAT YOU FEEL IS RIGHT...
AND SHOW US HOW FAR YOU'VE COME AS ACTRESSES.
UNDER-STOOD?
YES, MA'AM!

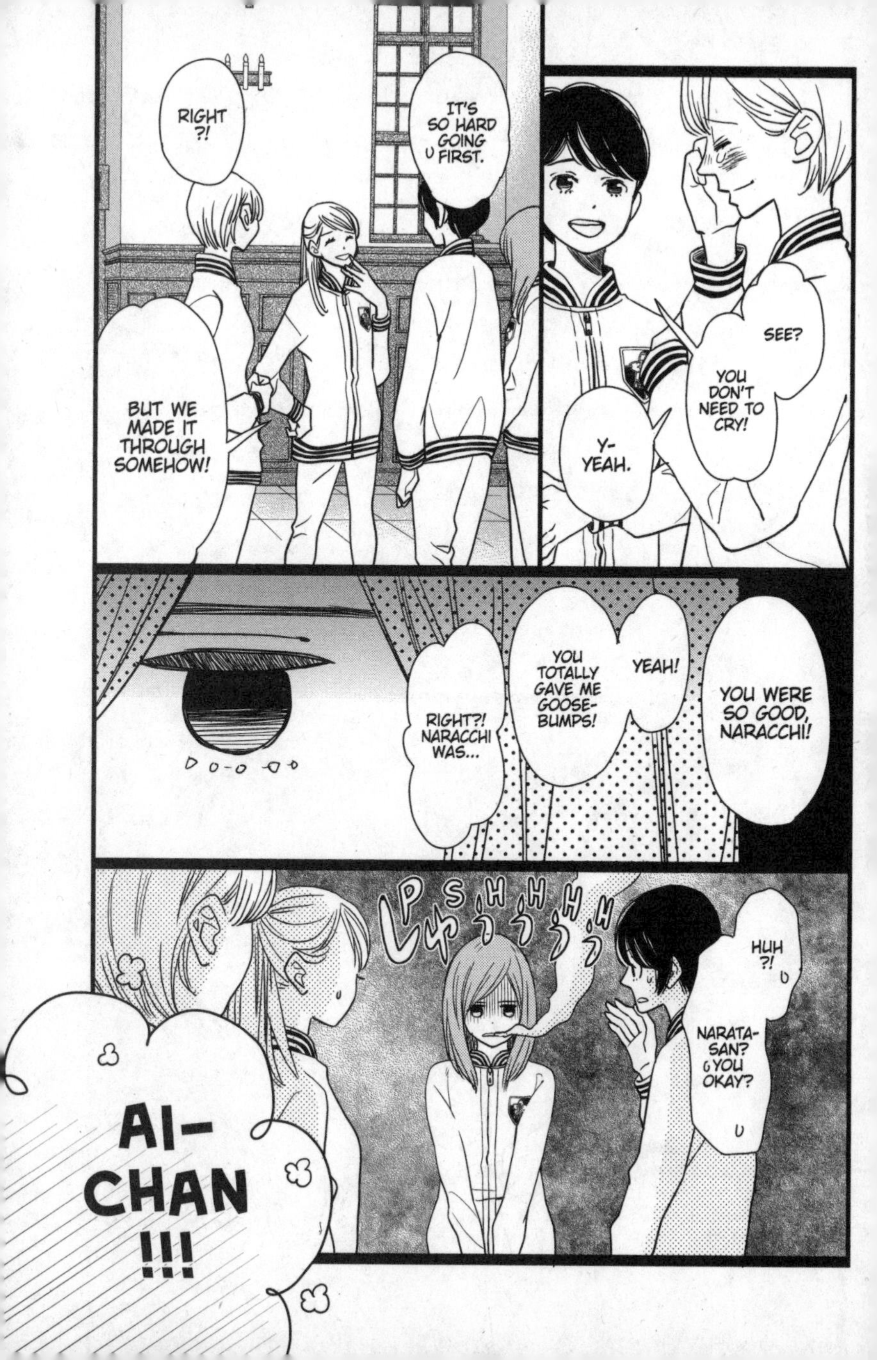
SEE?
YOU DON'T NEED TO CRY!
Y-YEAH.
IT'S SO HARD GOING FIRST.
RIGHT ?!
BUT WE MADE IT THROUGH SOMEHOW!
YOU WERE SO GOOD, NARACCHI!
YEAH!
YOU TOTALLY GAVE ME GOOSE-BUMPS!
RIGHT?! NARACCHI WAS...
HUH ?!
NARATA-SAN? YOU OKAY?
PSHHHHH
AI-CHAN !!!

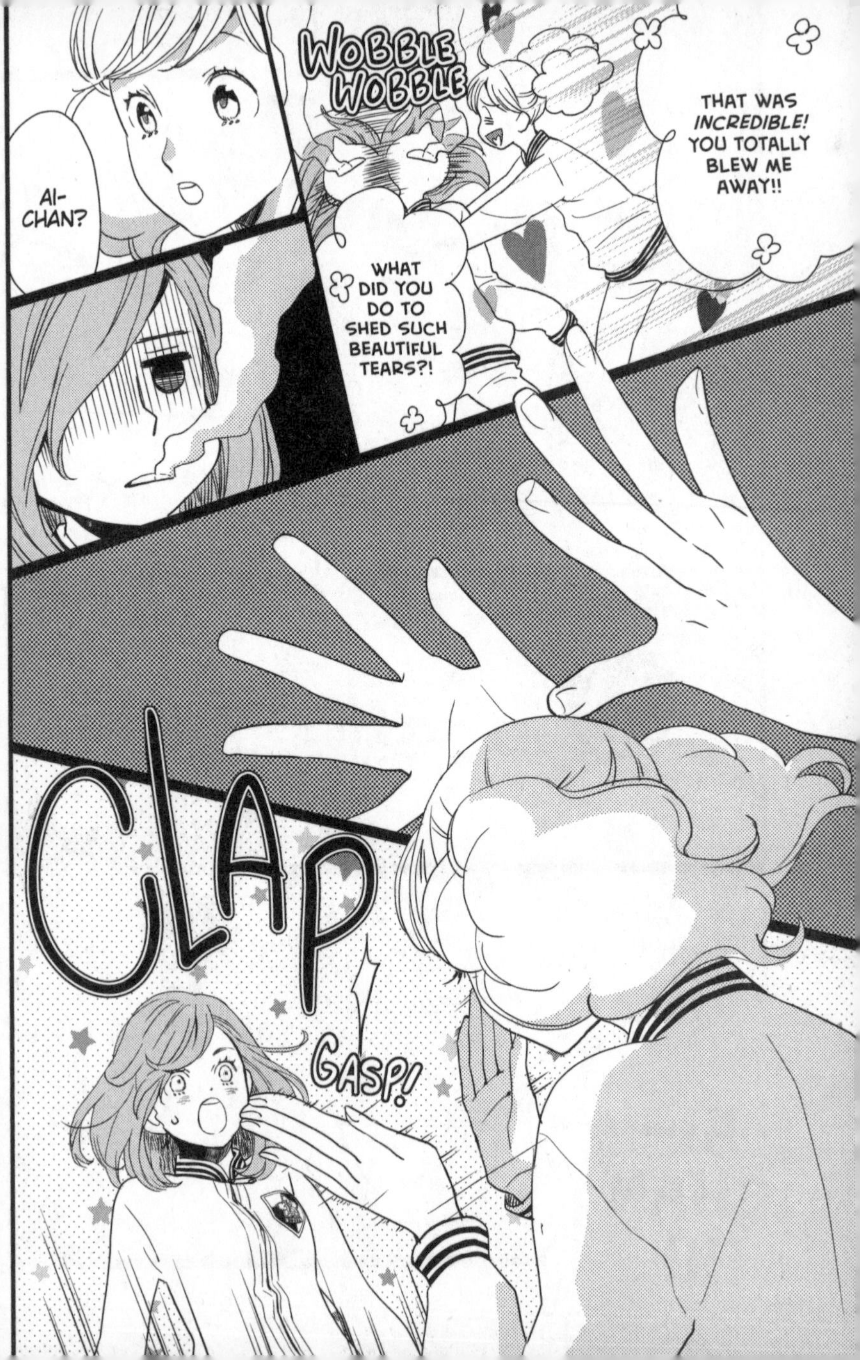
THAT WAS *INCREDIBLE!* YOU TOTALLY BLEW ME AWAY!!
WOBBLE WOBBLE
WHAT DID YOU DO TO SHED SUCH BEAUTIFUL TEARS?!
AI-CHAN?
CLAP
GASP!

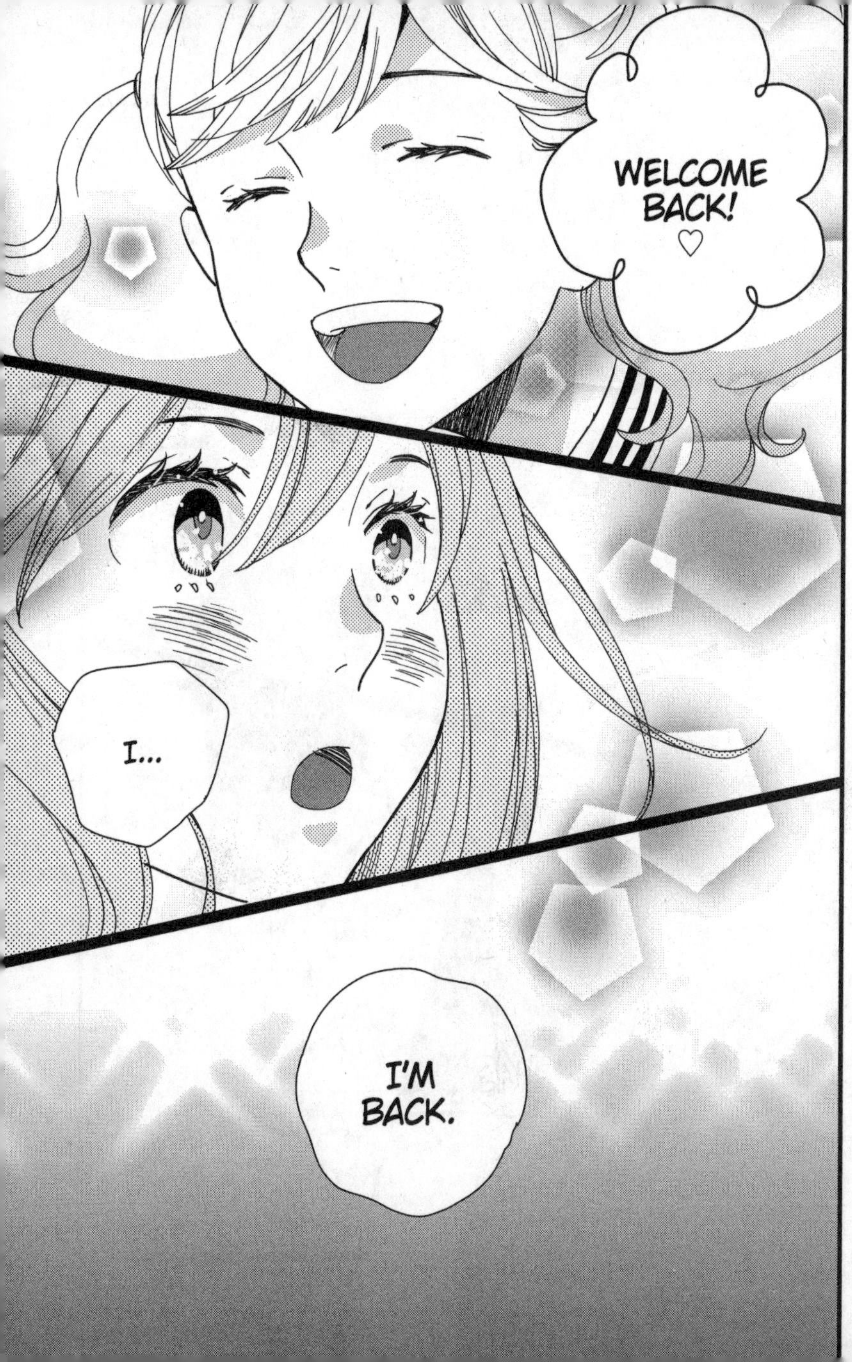
WELCOME BACK! ♡
I...
I'M BACK.

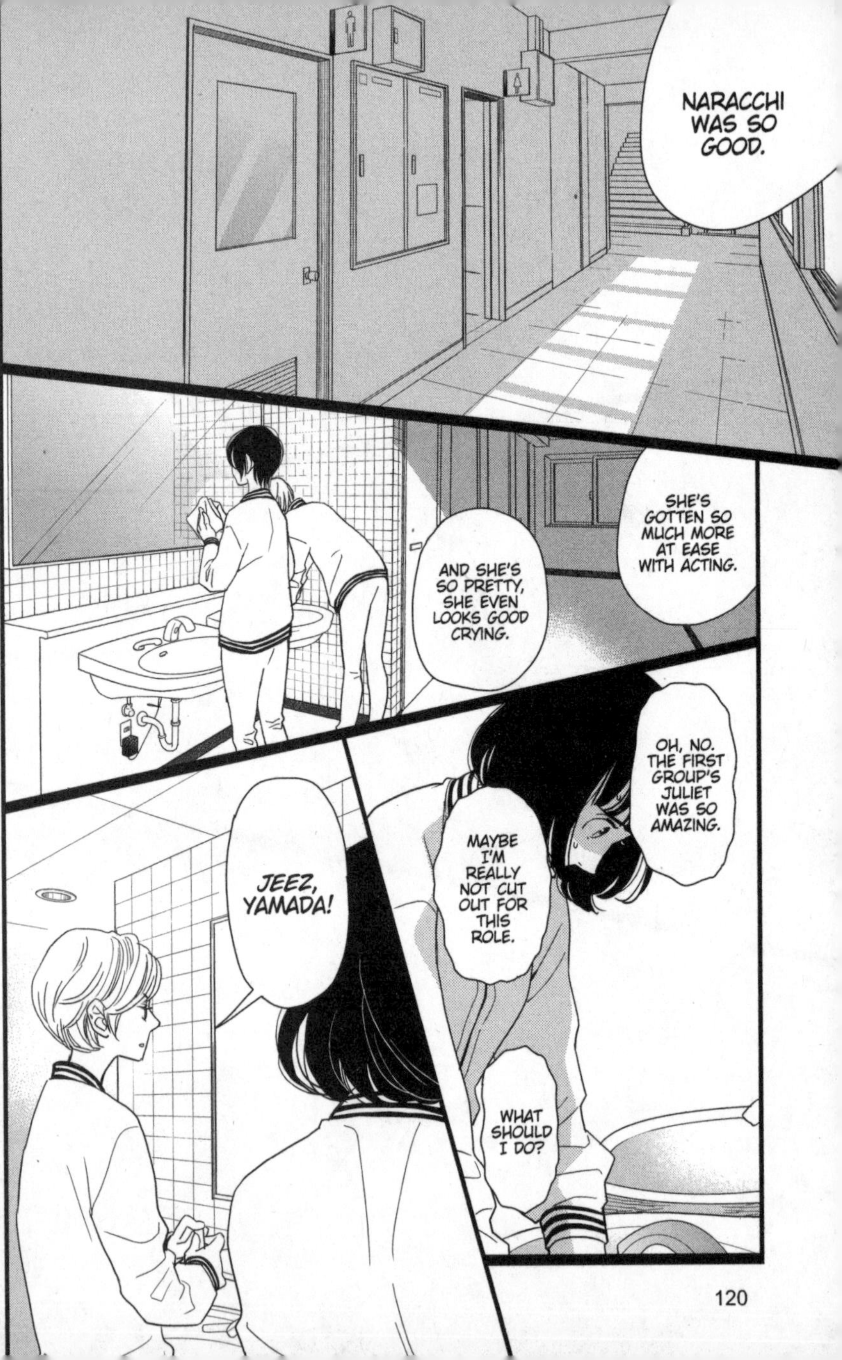
NARACCHI WAS SO GOOD.
SHE'S GOTTEN SO MUCH MORE AT EASE WITH ACTING.
AND SHE'S SO PRETTY, SHE EVEN LOOKS GOOD CRYING.
OH, NO. THE FIRST GROUP'S JULIET WAS SO AMAZING.
MAYBE I'M REALLY NOT CUT OUT FOR THIS ROLE.
WHAT SHOULD I DO?
JEEZ, YAMADA!

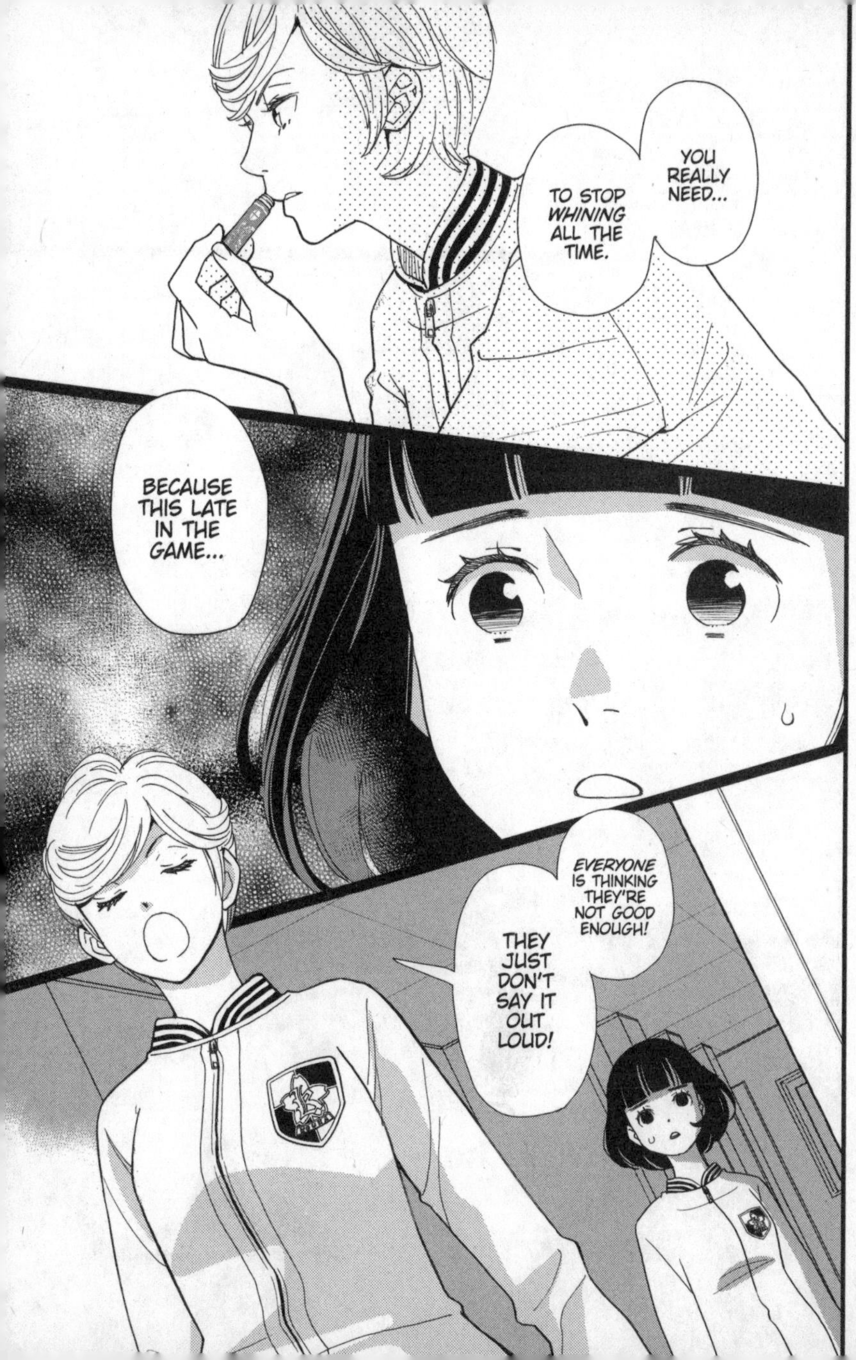
YOU REALLY NEED...
TO STOP *WHINING* ALL THE TIME.
BECAUSE THIS LATE IN THE GAME...
EVERYONE IS THINKING THEY'RE NOT GOOD ENOUGH!
THEY JUST DON'T SAY IT OUT LOUD!

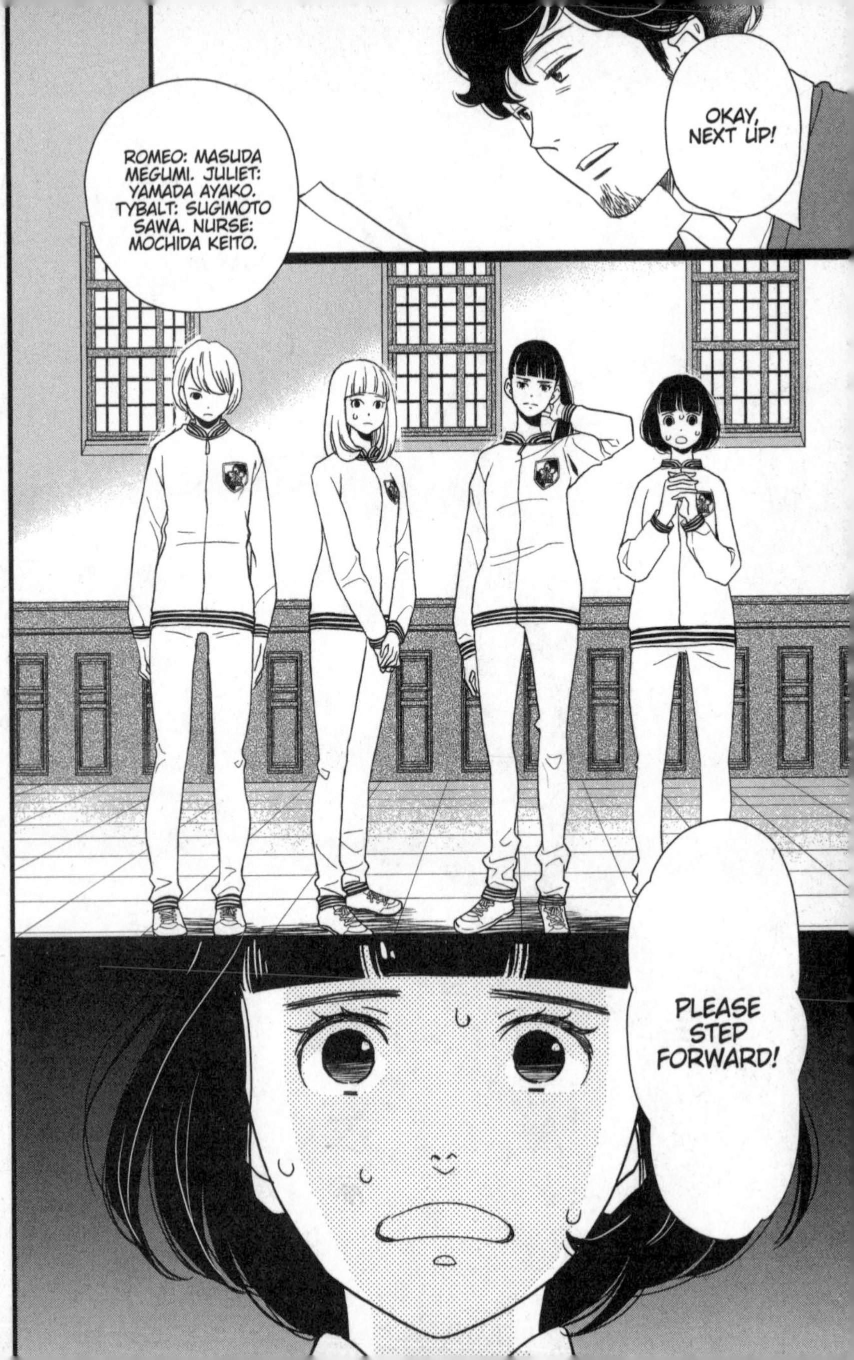
OKAY, NEXT UP!
ROMEO: MASUDA MEGUMI. JULIET: YAMADA AYAKO. TYBALT: SUGIMOTO SAWA. NURSE: MOCHIDA KEITO.
PLEASE STEP FORWARD!

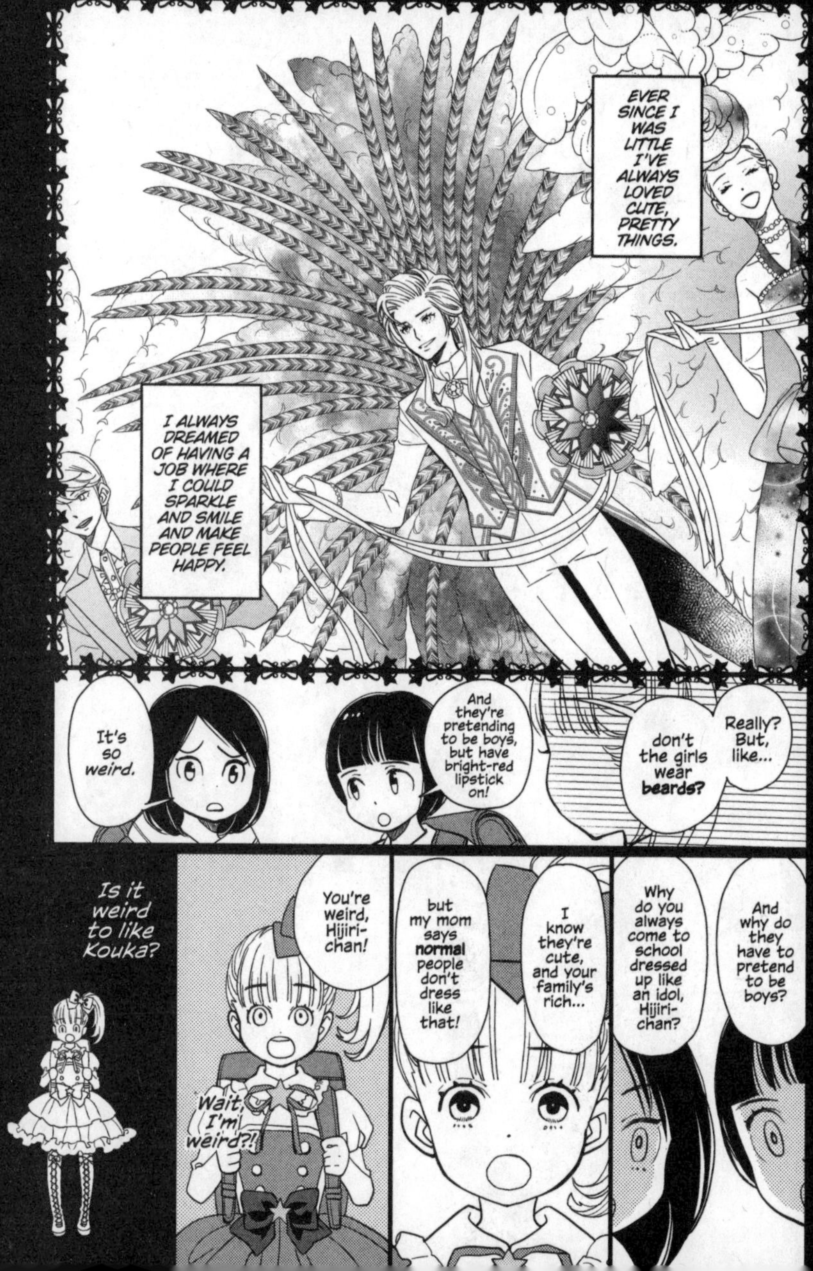
EVER SINCE I WAS LITTLE I'VE ALWAYS LOVED CUTE, PRETTY THINGS.
I ALWAYS DREAMED OF HAVING A JOB WHERE I COULD SPARKLE AND SMILE AND MAKE PEOPLE FEEL HAPPY.
Really? But, like...
don't the girls wear **beards?**
And they're pretending to be boys, but have bright-red lipstick on!
It's so weird.
And why do they have to pretend to be boys?
Why do you always come to school dressed up like an idol, Hijiri-chan?
I know they're cute, and your family's rich...
but my mom says **normal** people don't dress like that!
You're weird, Hijiri-chan!
Wait, I'm weird?!
Is it weird to like Kouka?

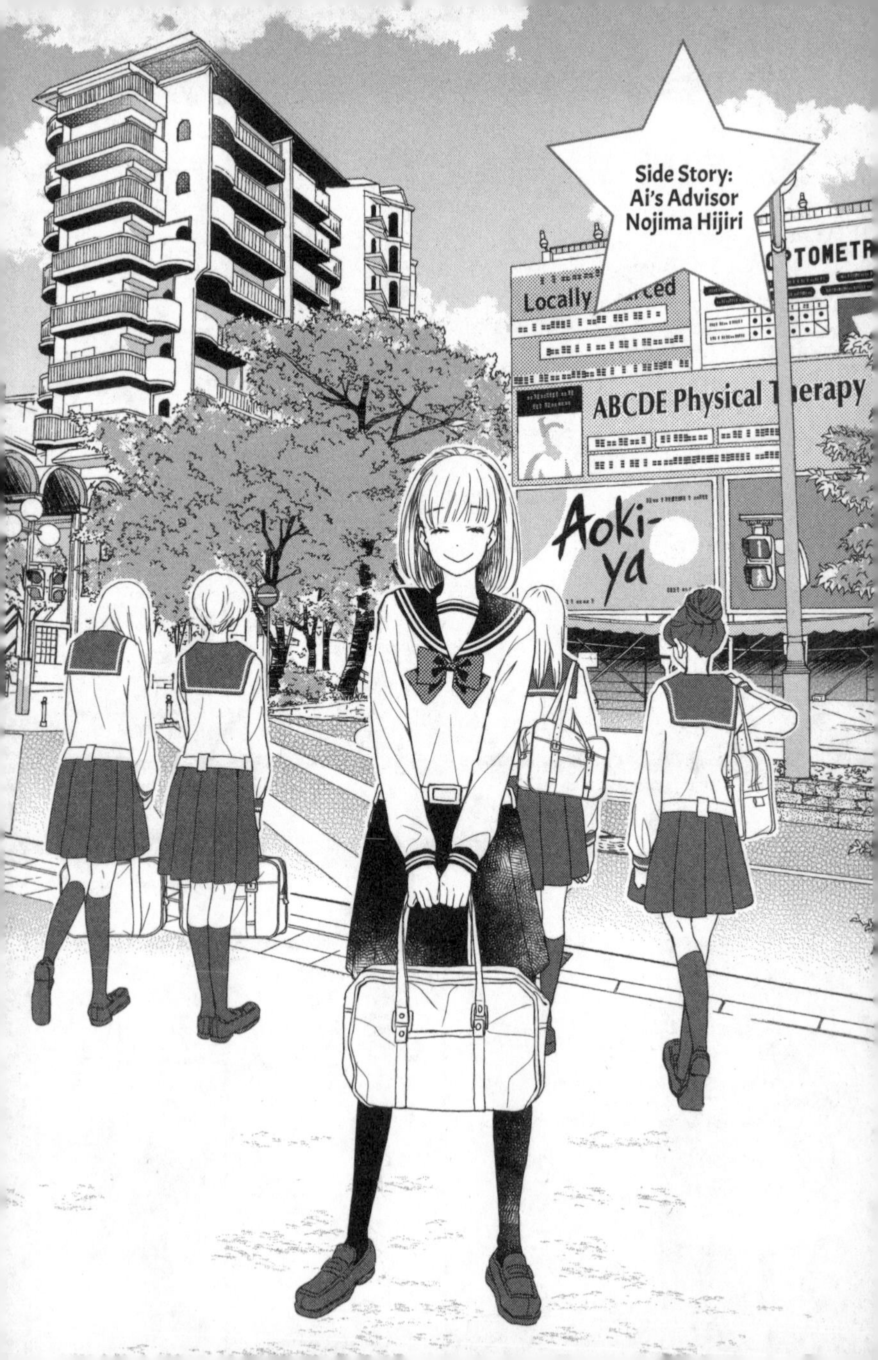
Side Story:
Ai's Advisor
Nojima Hijiri
OPTOMETR
Locally ...rced
ABCDE Physical T...erapy
Aoki-
ya

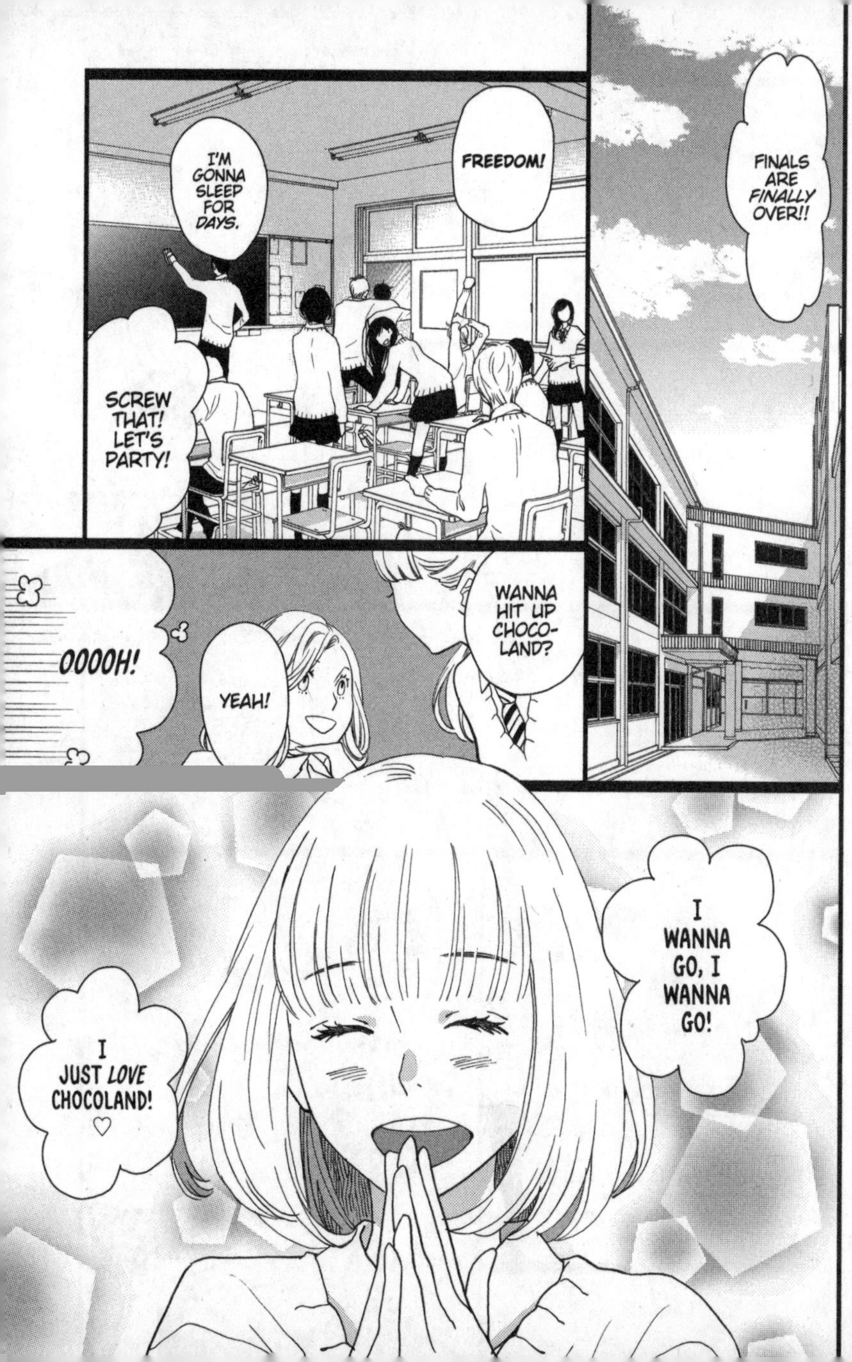
FINALS ARE FINALLY OVER!!
FREEDOM!
I'M GONNA SLEEP FOR DAYS.
SCREW THAT! LET'S PARTY!
WANNA HIT UP CHOCOLAND?
YEAH!
OOOOH!
I WANNA GO, I WANNA GO!
I JUST LOVE CHOCOLAND! ♡

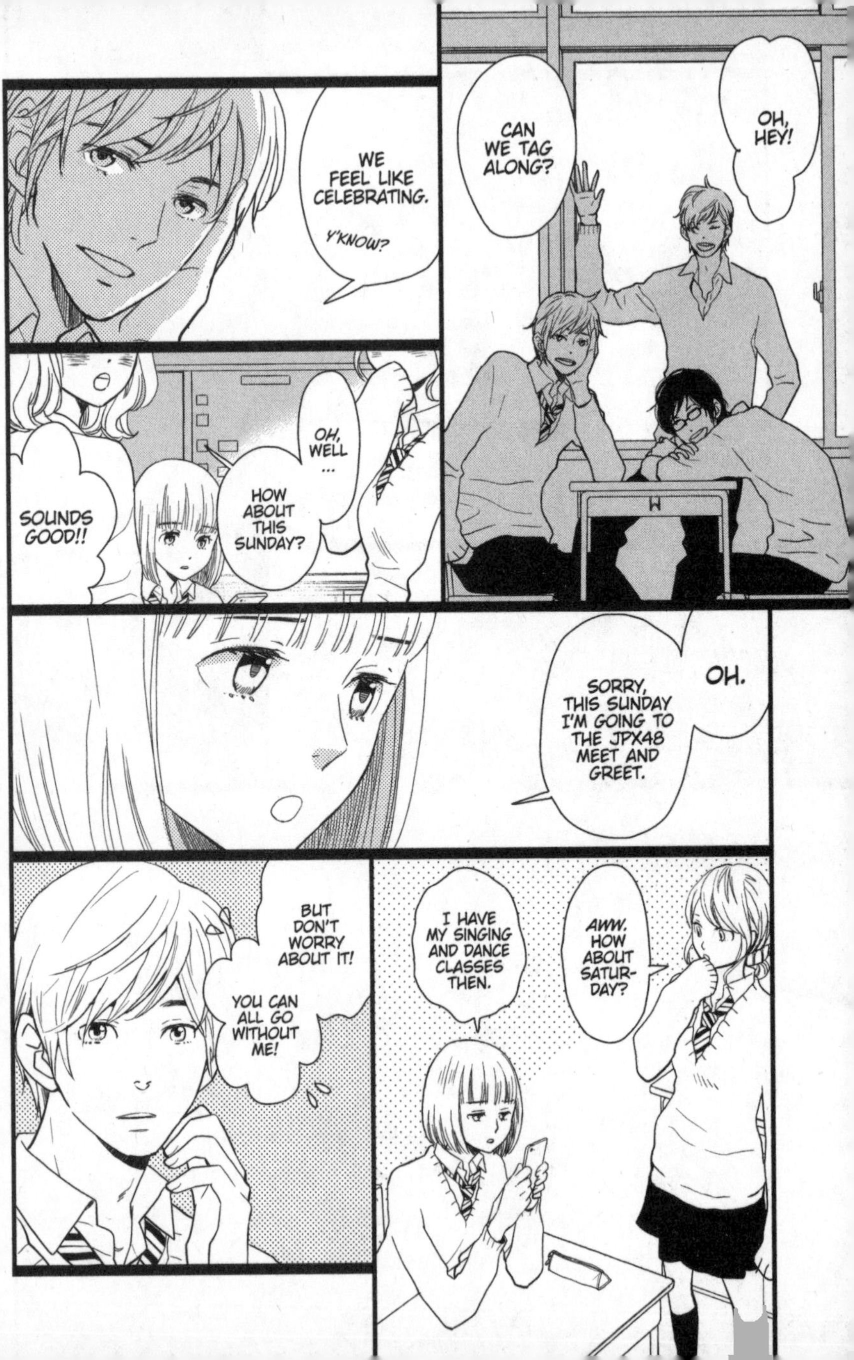
OH, HEY!
CAN WE TAG ALONG?
WE FEEL LIKE CELEBRATING. Y'KNOW?
OH, WELL ... HOW ABOUT THIS SUNDAY?
SOUNDS GOOD!!
OH.
SORRY, THIS SUNDAY I'M GOING TO THE JPX48 MEET AND GREET.
AWW. HOW ABOUT SATUR-DAY?
I HAVE MY SINGING AND DANCE CLASSES THEN.
BUT DON'T WORRY ABOUT IT! YOU CAN ALL GO WITHOUT ME!

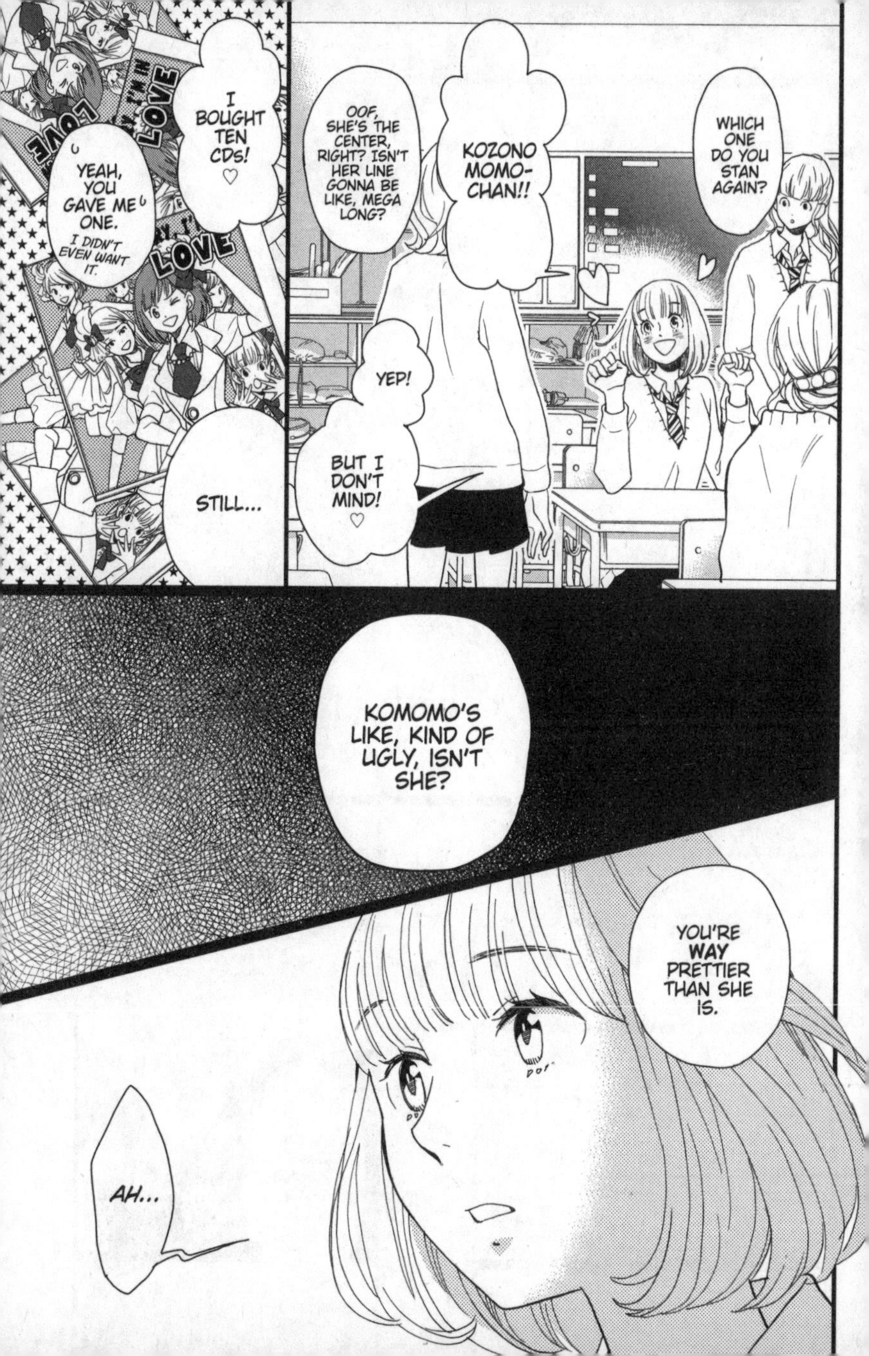

WHICH ONE DO YOU STAN AGAIN?
KOZONO MOMO-CHAN!!
OOF, SHE'S THE CENTER, RIGHT? ISN'T HER LINE GONNA BE LIKE, MEGA LONG?
YEP!
BUT I DON'T MIND! ♡
I BOUGHT TEN CDs! ♡
LOVE
YEAH, YOU GAVE ME ONE. I DIDN'T EVEN WANT IT.
STILL...
KOMOMO'S LIKE, KIND OF UGLY, ISN'T SHE?
YOU'RE WAY PRETTIER THAN SHE IS.
AH...

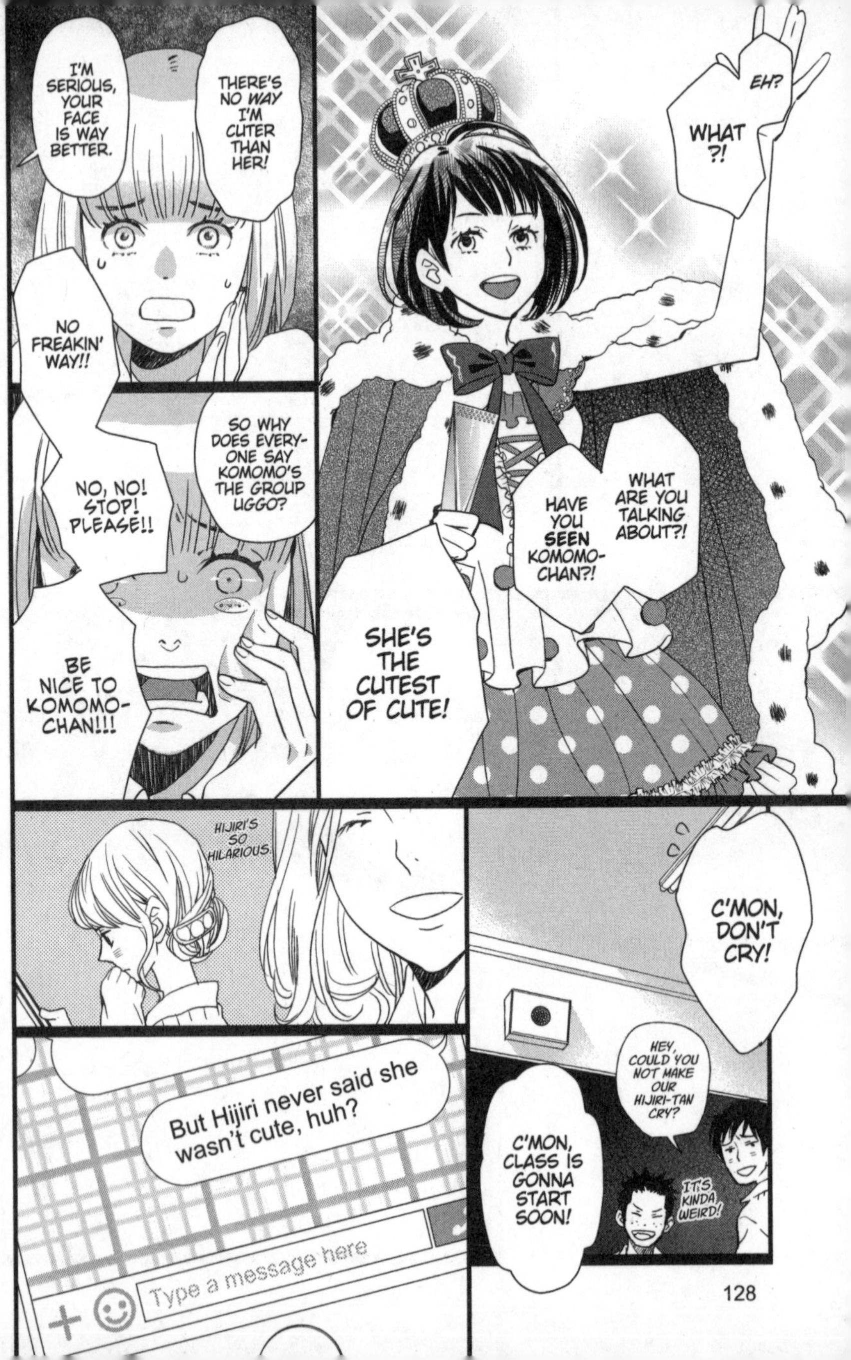
EH?
WHAT?!
WHAT ARE YOU TALKING ABOUT?!
HAVE YOU SEEN KOMOMO-CHAN?!
SHE'S THE CUTEST OF CUTE!
THERE'S NO WAY I'M CUTER THAN HER!
I'M SERIOUS, YOUR FACE IS WAY BETTER.
NO FREAKIN' WAY!!
SO WHY DOES EVERY-ONE SAY KOMOMO'S THE GROUP UGGO?
NO, NO! STOP! PLEASE!!
BE NICE TO KOMOMO-CHAN!!!
C'MON, DON'T CRY!
HEY, COULD YOU NOT MAKE OUR HIJIRI-TAN CRY?
IT'S KINDA WEIRD!
C'MON, CLASS IS GONNA START SOON!
HIJIRI'S SO HILARIOUS.
But Hijiri never said she wasn't cute, huh?
Type a message here

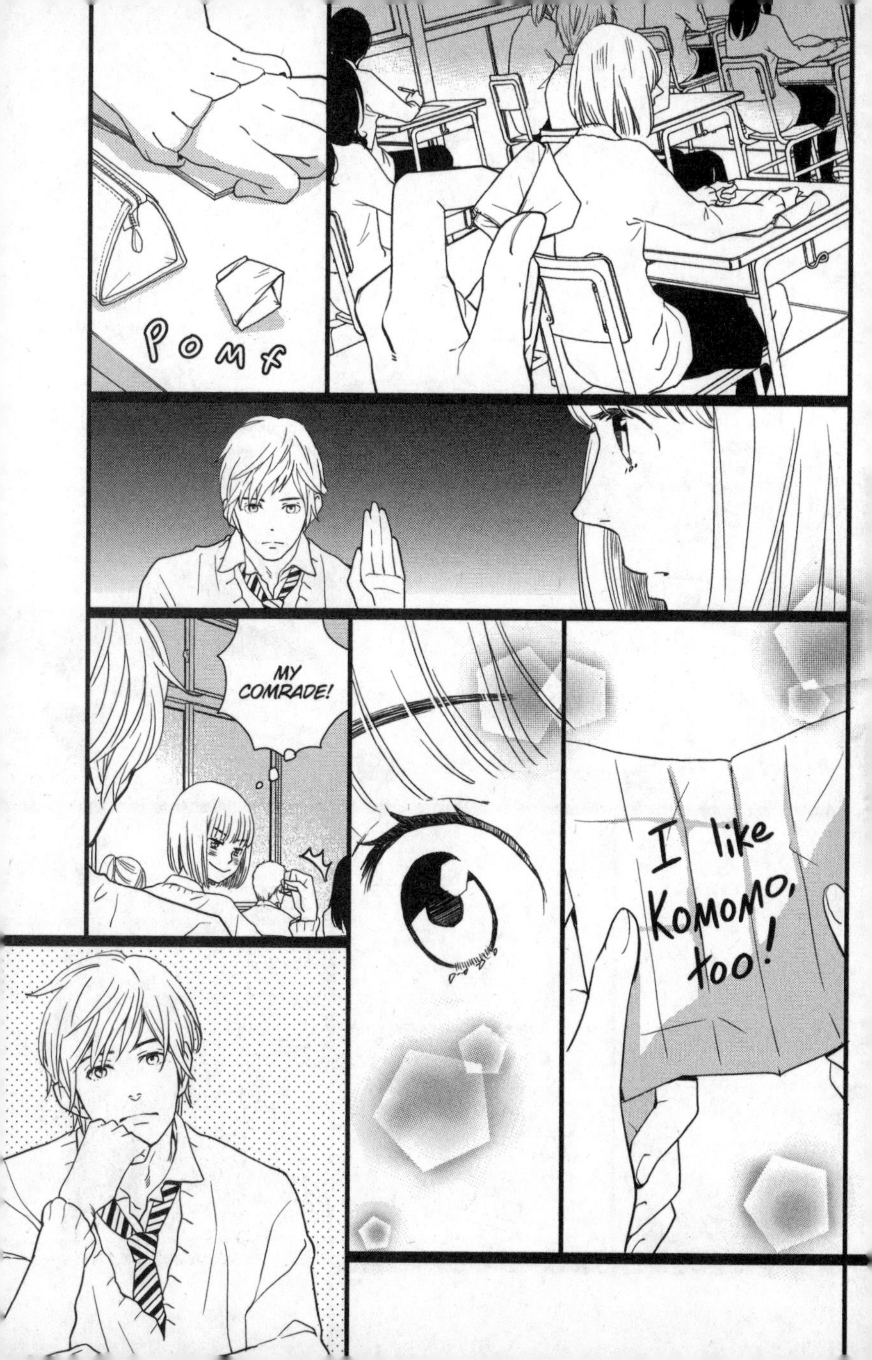
pomf
I like Komomo, too!
MY COMRADE!

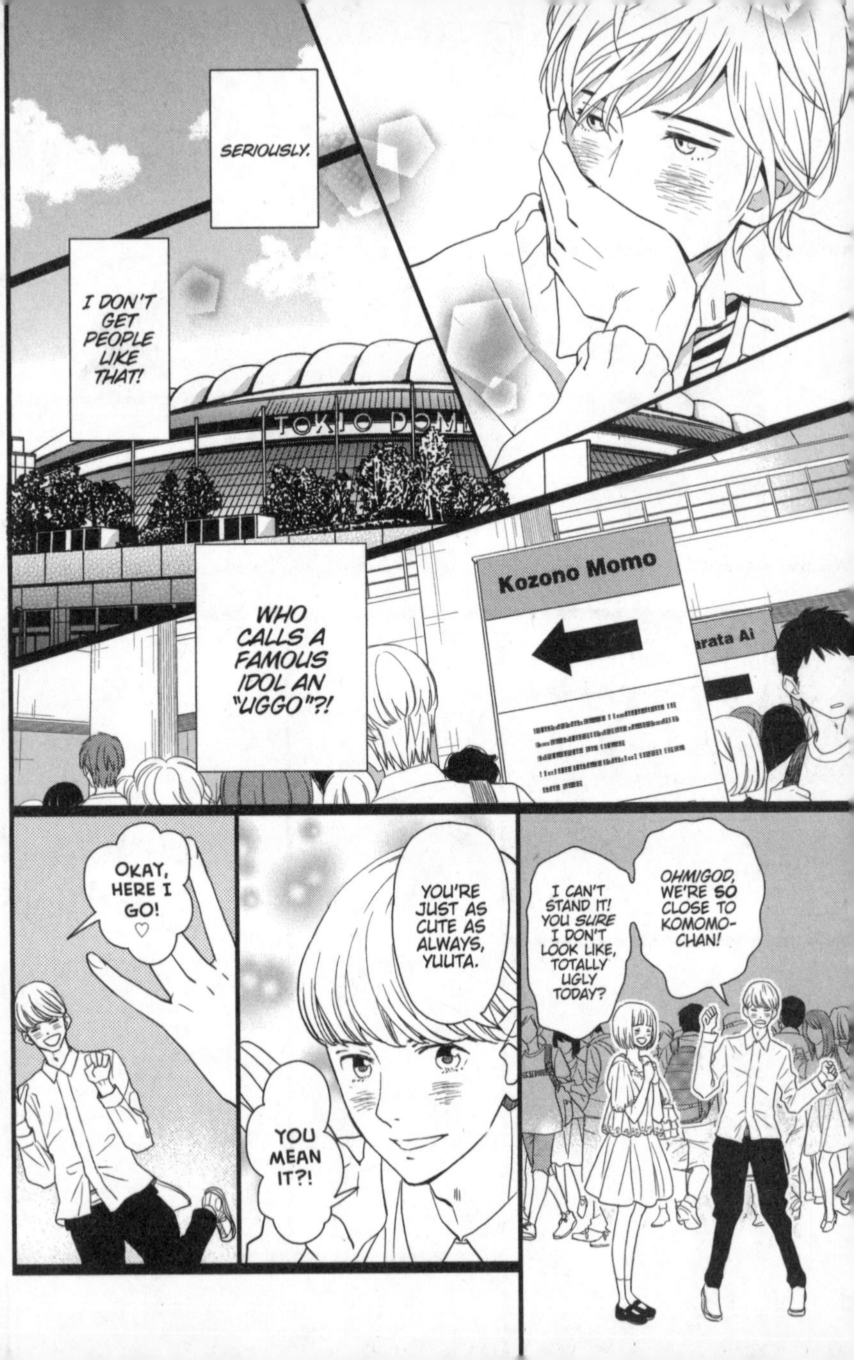
SERIOUSLY.
I DON'T GET PEOPLE LIKE THAT!
WHO CALLS A FAMOUS IDOL AN "UGGO"?!
Kozono Momo
OHMIGOD, WE'RE SO CLOSE TO KOMOMO-CHAN!
I CAN'T STAND IT! YOU *SURE* I DON'T LOOK LIKE, TOTALLY UGLY TODAY?
YOU'RE JUST AS CUTE AS ALWAYS, YUUTA.
YOU MEAN IT?!
OKAY, HERE I GO! ♡

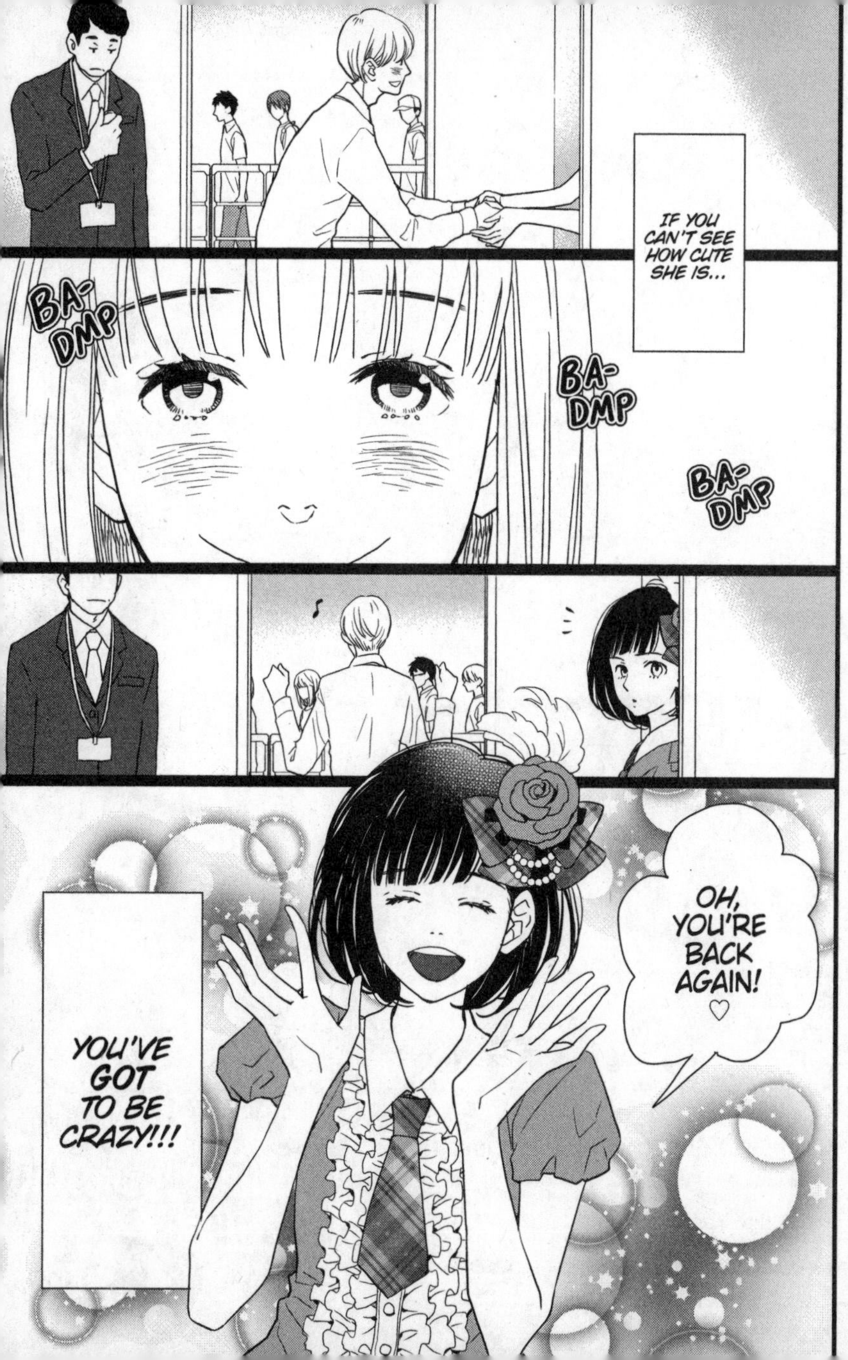
IF YOU CAN'T SEE HOW CUTE SHE IS...
BA-DMP
BA-DMP
BA-DMP
OH, YOU'RE BACK AGAIN! ♡
YOU'VE GOT TO BE CRAZY!!!

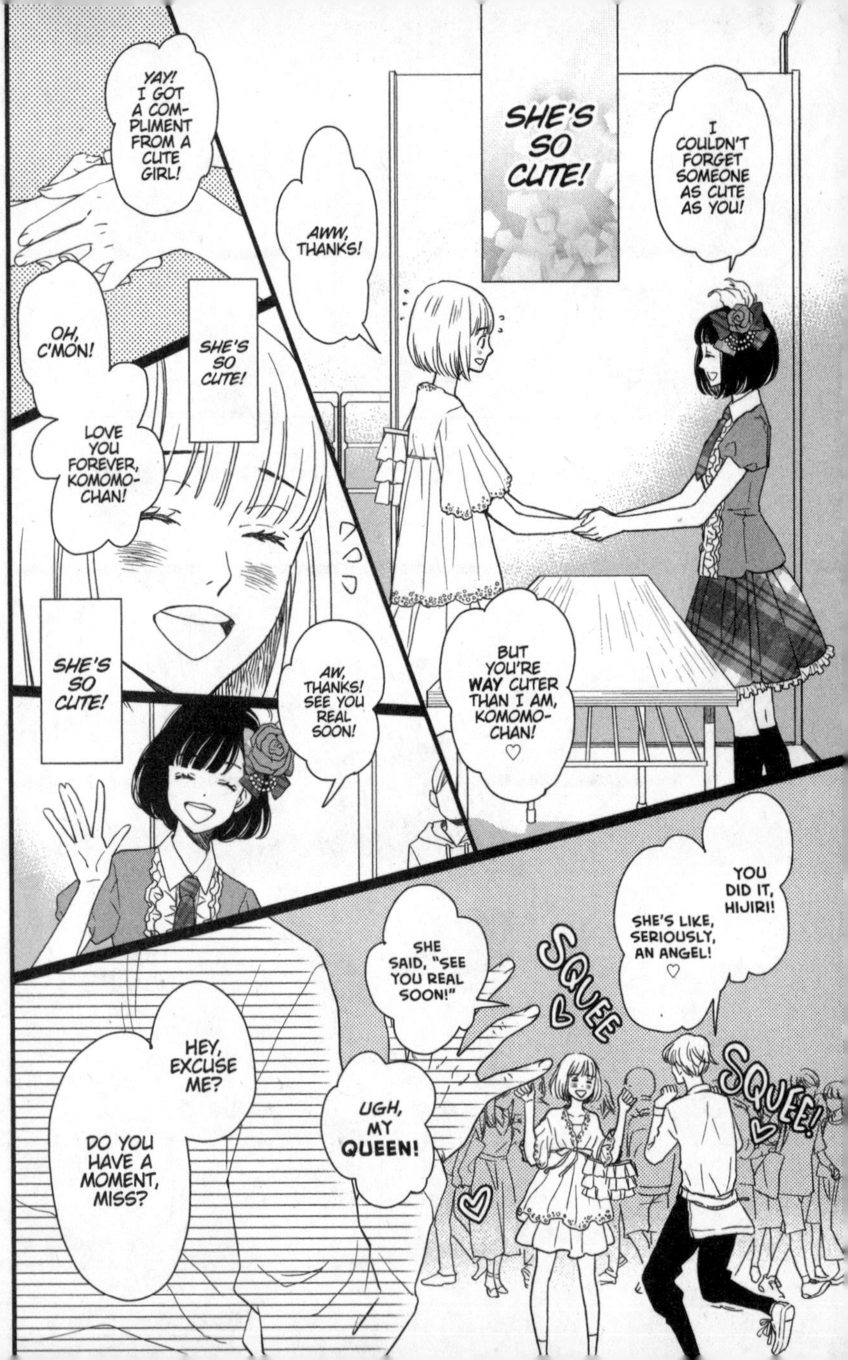
I COULDN'T FORGET SOMEONE AS CUTE AS YOU!
SHE'S SO CUTE!
AWW, THANKS!
BUT YOU'RE WAY CUTER THAN I AM, KOMOMO-CHAN! ♡
YAY! I GOT A COMPLIMENT FROM A CUTE GIRL!
SHE'S SO CUTE!
OH, C'MON!
LOVE YOU FOREVER, KOMOMO-CHAN!
AW, THANKS! SEE YOU REAL SOON!
SHE'S SO CUTE!
YOU DID IT, HIJIRI!
SHE'S LIKE, SERIOUSLY, AN ANGEL! ♡
SQUEE!
SQUEE
SHE SAID, "SEE YOU REAL SOON!"
UGH, MY QUEEN!
HEY, EXCUSE ME?
DO YOU HAVE A MOMENT, MISS?

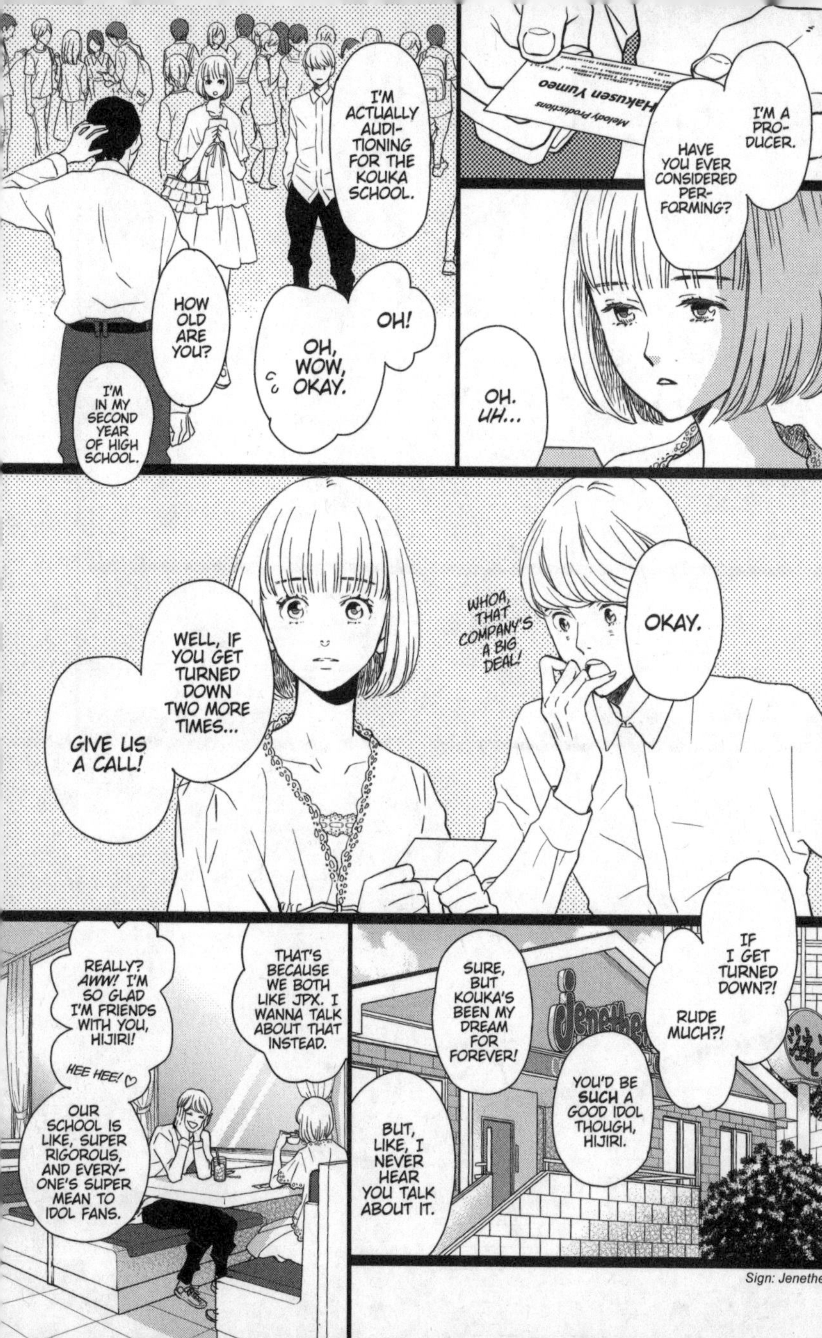
Hakusen Yumeo
Melody Productions
I'M A PRODUCER.
HAVE YOU EVER CONSIDERED PERFORMING?
OH. UH...
I'M ACTUALLY AUDITIONING FOR THE KOUKA SCHOOL.
OH!
OH, WOW, OKAY.
HOW OLD ARE YOU?
I'M IN MY SECOND YEAR OF HIGH SCHOOL.
OKAY.
WHOA, THAT COMPANY'S A BIG DEAL!
WELL, IF YOU GET TURNED DOWN TWO MORE TIMES...
GIVE US A CALL!
IF I GET TURNED DOWN?!
RUDE MUCH?!
SURE, BUT KOUKA'S BEEN MY DREAM FOR FOREVER!
YOU'D BE SUCH A GOOD IDOL THOUGH, HIJIRI.
BUT, LIKE, I NEVER HEAR YOU TALK ABOUT IT.
THAT'S BECAUSE WE BOTH LIKE JPX. I WANNA TALK ABOUT THAT INSTEAD.
REALLY? *AWW!* I'M SO GLAD I'M FRIENDS WITH YOU, HIJIRI!
HEE HEE! ♡
OUR SCHOOL IS LIKE, SUPER RIGOROUS, AND EVERYONE'S SUPER MEAN TO IDOL FANS.

Sign: Jenethen

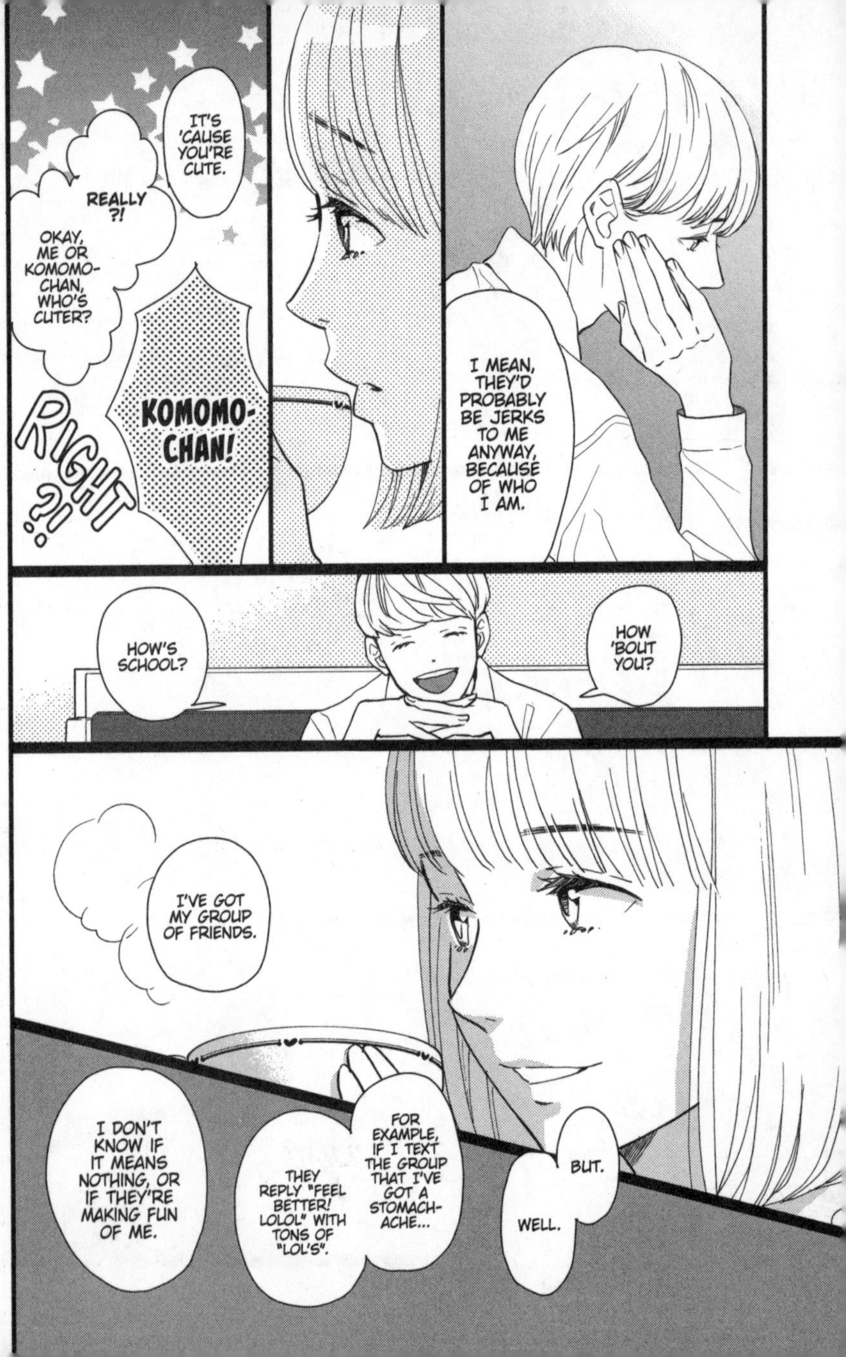
I MEAN, THEY'D PROBABLY BE JERKS TO ME ANYWAY, BECAUSE OF WHO I AM.
IT'S 'CAUSE YOU'RE CUTE.
REALLY ?!
OKAY, ME OR KOMOMO-CHAN, WHO'S CUTER?
KOMOMO-CHAN!
RIGHT ?!
HOW 'BOUT YOU?
HOW'S SCHOOL?
I'VE GOT MY GROUP OF FRIENDS.
BUT.
WELL.
FOR EXAMPLE, IF I TEXT THE GROUP THAT I'VE GOT A STOMACH-ACHE...
THEY REPLY "FEEL BETTER! LOLOL" WITH TONS OF "LOL'S".
I DON'T KNOW IF IT MEANS NOTHING, OR IF THEY'RE MAKING FUN OF ME.

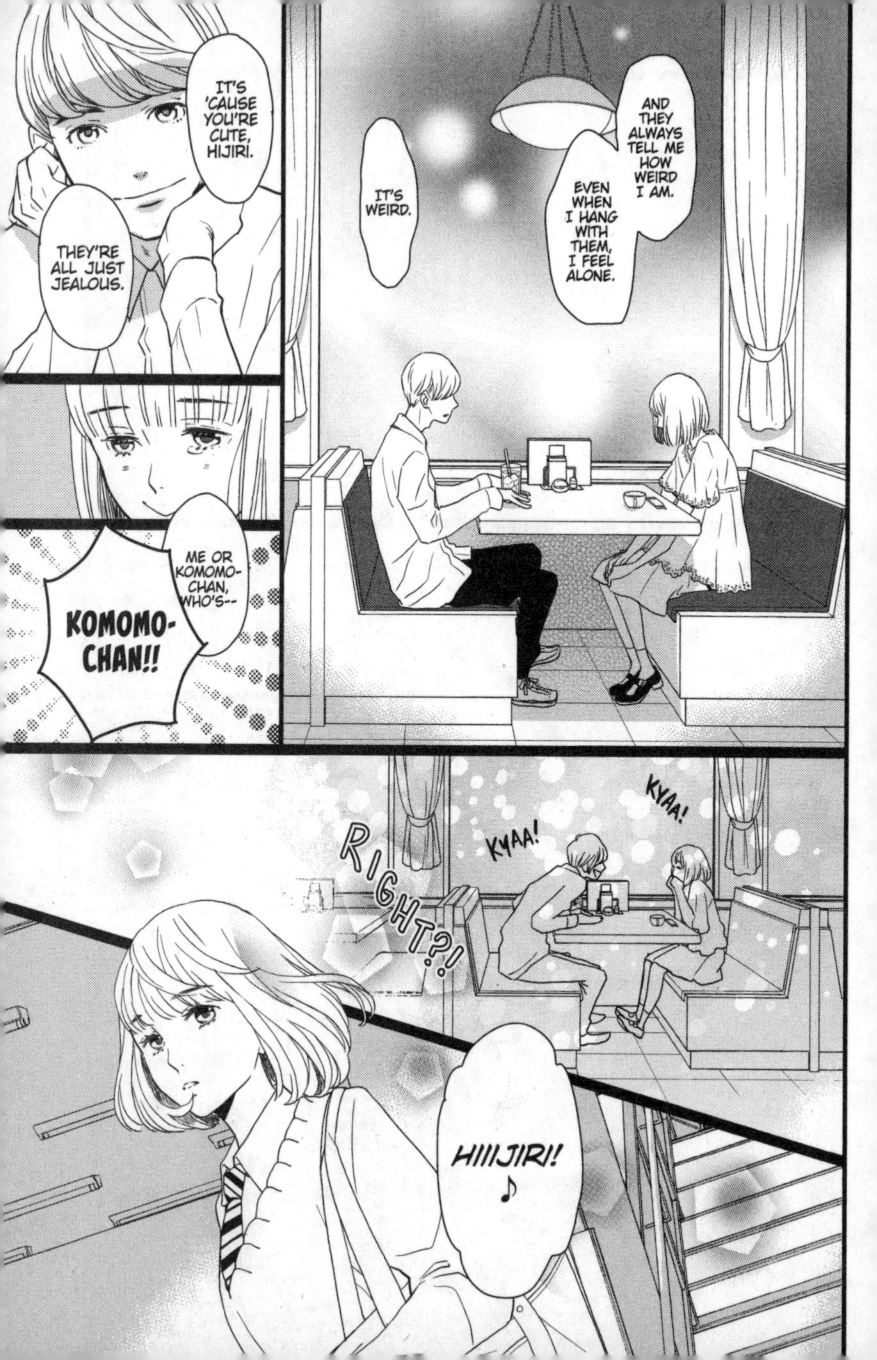
AND THEY ALWAYS TELL ME HOW WEIRD I AM.
EVEN WHEN I HANG WITH THEM, I FEEL ALONE.
IT'S WEIRD.
IT'S 'CAUSE YOU'RE CUTE, HIJIRI.
THEY'RE ALL JUST JEALOUS.
ME OR KOMOMO-CHAN, WHO'S--
KOMOMO-CHAN!!
KYAA!
KYAA!
RIGHT?!
HIIIJIRI! ♪

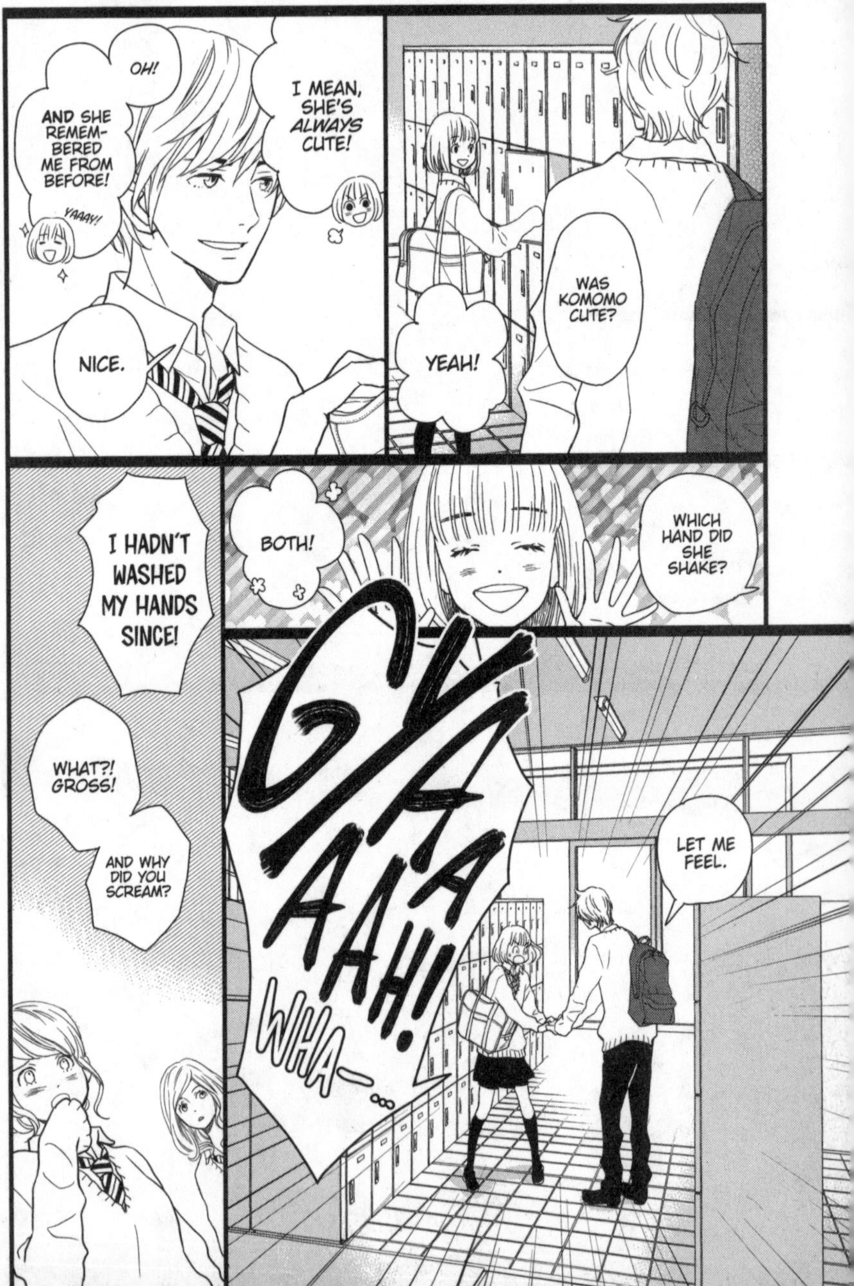
WAS KOMOMO CUTE?
YEAH!
I MEAN, SHE'S *ALWAYS* CUTE!
OH!
AND SHE REMEM-BERED ME FROM BEFORE!
YAAAY!
NICE.
WHICH HAND DID SHE SHAKE?
BOTH!
LET ME FEEL.
GYAAAAH!
WHA—...
I HADN'T WASHED MY HANDS SINCE!
WHAT?! GROSS!
AND WHY DID YOU SCREAM?

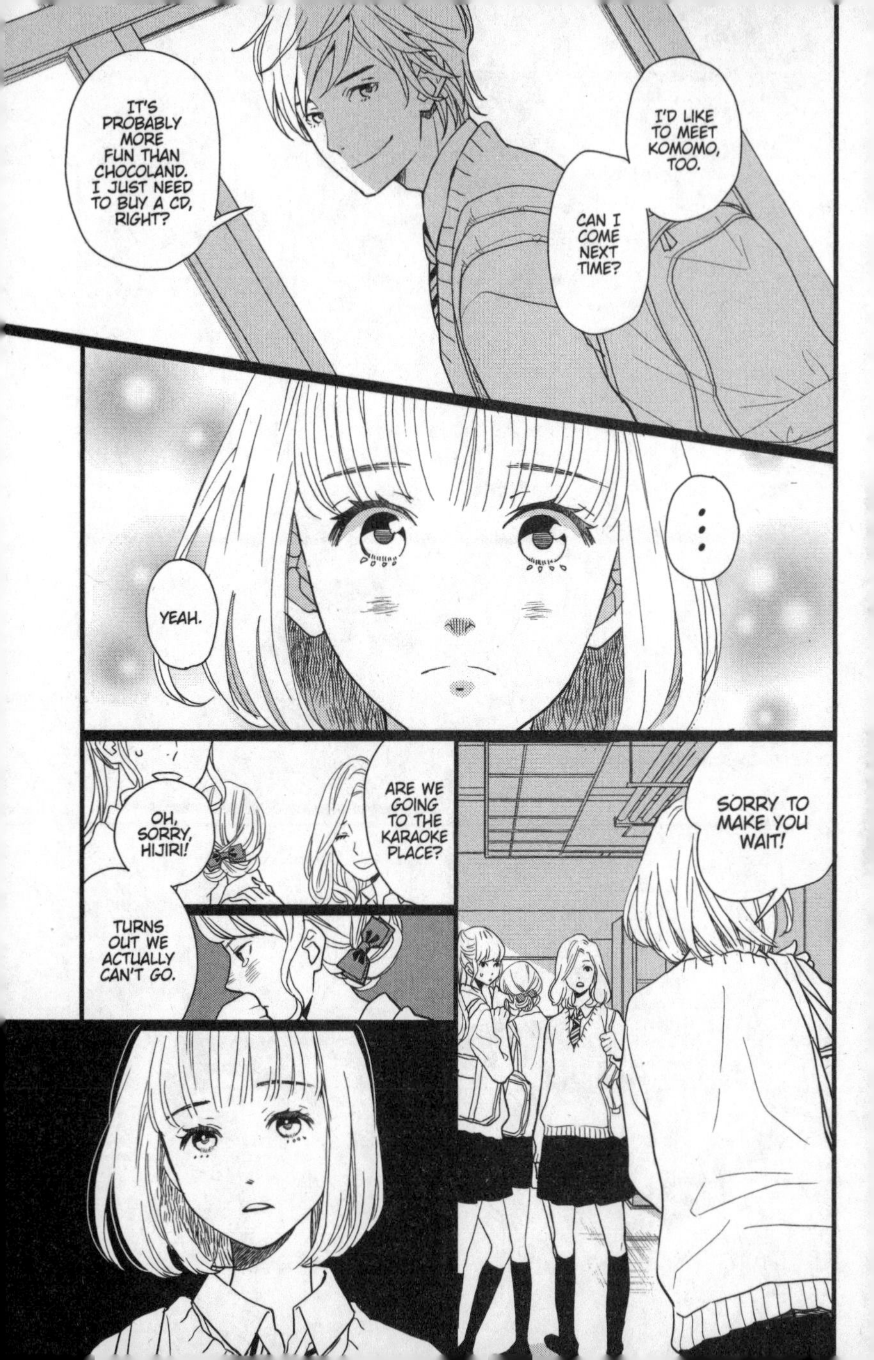
I'D LIKE TO MEET KOMOMO, TOO.
CAN I COME NEXT TIME?
IT'S PROBABLY MORE FUN THAN CHOCOLAND. I JUST NEED TO BUY A CD, RIGHT?
...
YEAH.
SORRY TO MAKE YOU WAIT!
ARE WE GOING TO THE KARAOKE PLACE?
OH, SORRY, HIJIRI!
TURNS OUT WE ACTUALLY CAN'T GO.

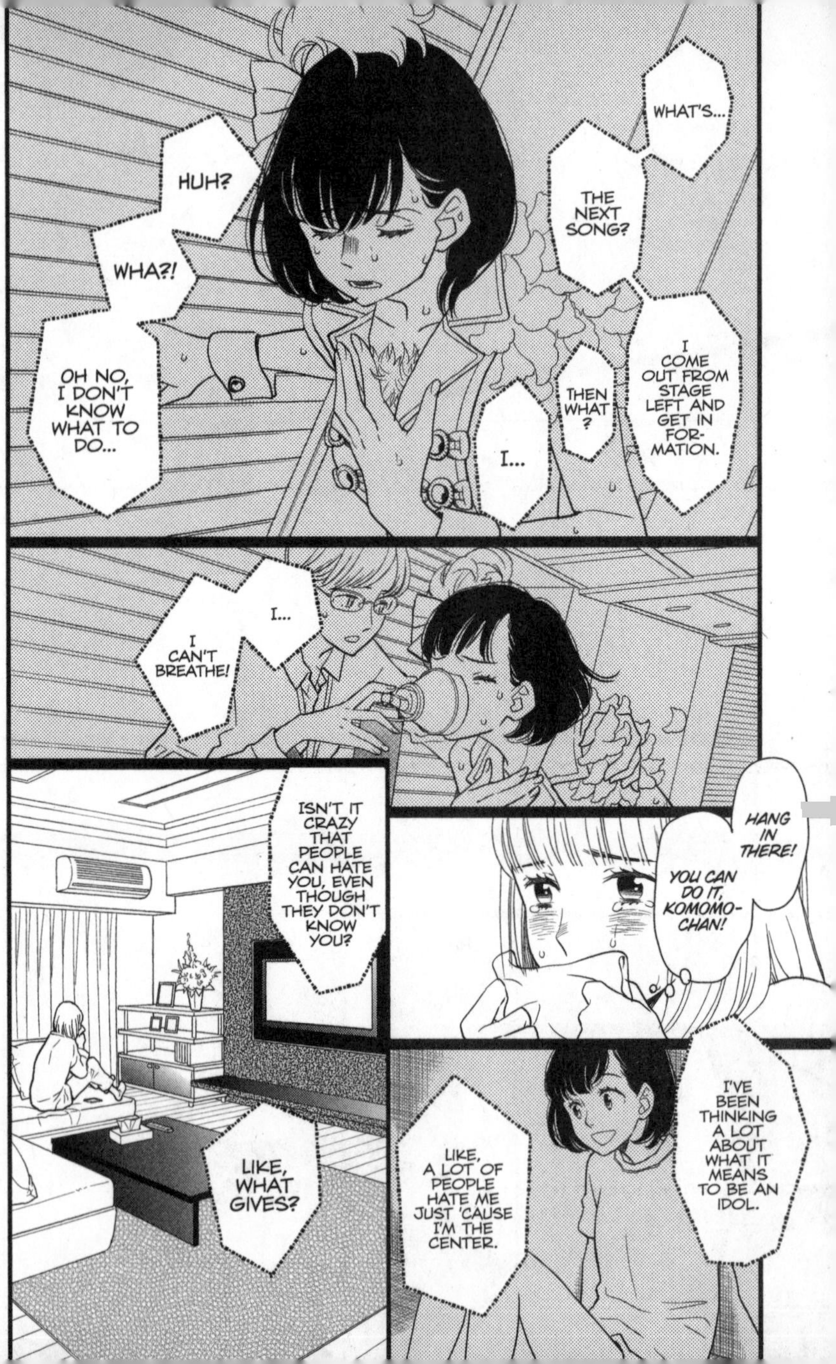
WHAT'S...
THE NEXT SONG?
I COME OUT FROM STAGE LEFT AND GET IN FORMATION.
THEN WHAT?
I...
HUH?
WHA?!
OH NO, I DON'T KNOW WHAT TO DO...
I...
I CAN'T BREATHE!
HANG IN THERE!
YOU CAN DO IT, KOMOMO-CHAN!
I'VE BEEN THINKING A LOT ABOUT WHAT IT MEANS TO BE AN IDOL.
LIKE, A LOT OF PEOPLE HATE ME JUST 'CAUSE I'M THE CENTER.
ISN'T IT CRAZY THAT PEOPLE CAN HATE YOU, EVEN THOUGH THEY DON'T KNOW YOU?
LIKE, WHAT GIVES?

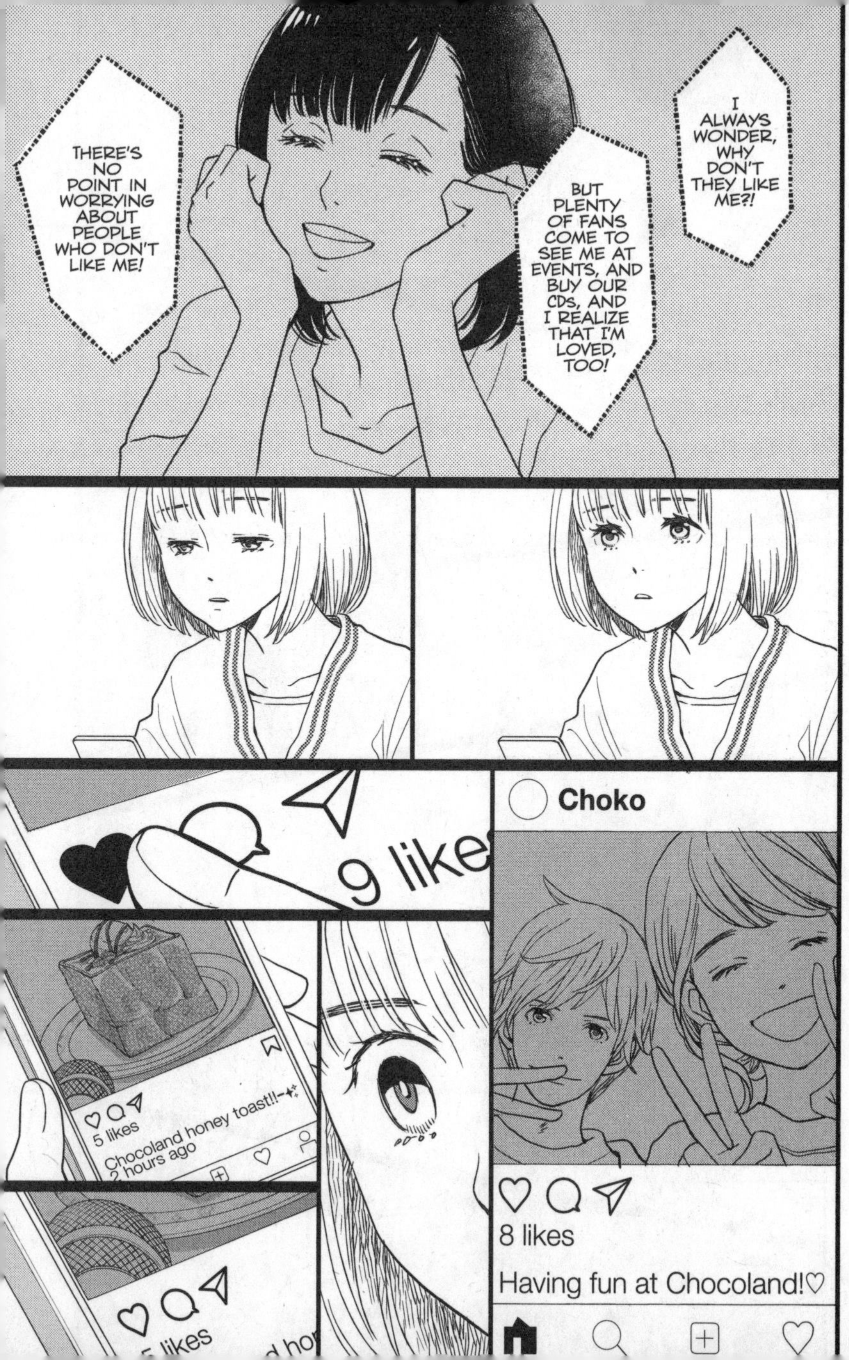
I ALWAYS WONDER, WHY DON'T THEY LIKE ME?!
BUT PLENTY OF FANS COME TO SEE ME AT EVENTS, AND BUY OUR CDs, AND I REALIZE THAT I'M LOVED, TOO!
THERE'S NO POINT IN WORRYING ABOUT PEOPLE WHO DON'T LIKE ME!
Choko
8 likes
Having fun at Chocoland!♡
9 likes
5 likes
Chocoland honey toast!!
2 hours ago

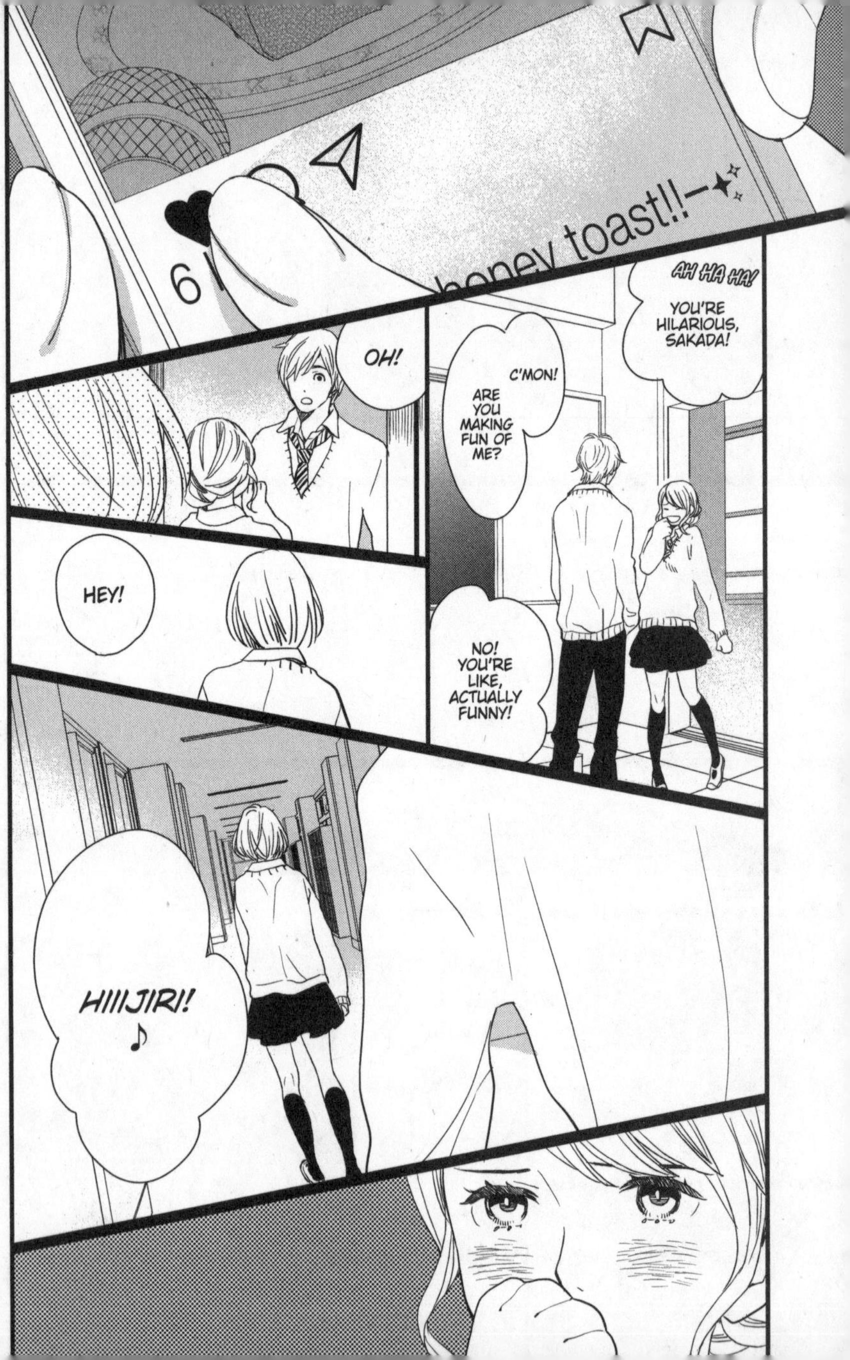

6
honey toast!!—
AH HA HA!
YOU'RE HILARIOUS, SAKADA!
C'MON!
ARE YOU MAKING FUN OF ME?
NO! YOU'RE LIKE, ACTUALLY FUNNY!
OH!
HEY!
HIIIJIRI! ♪

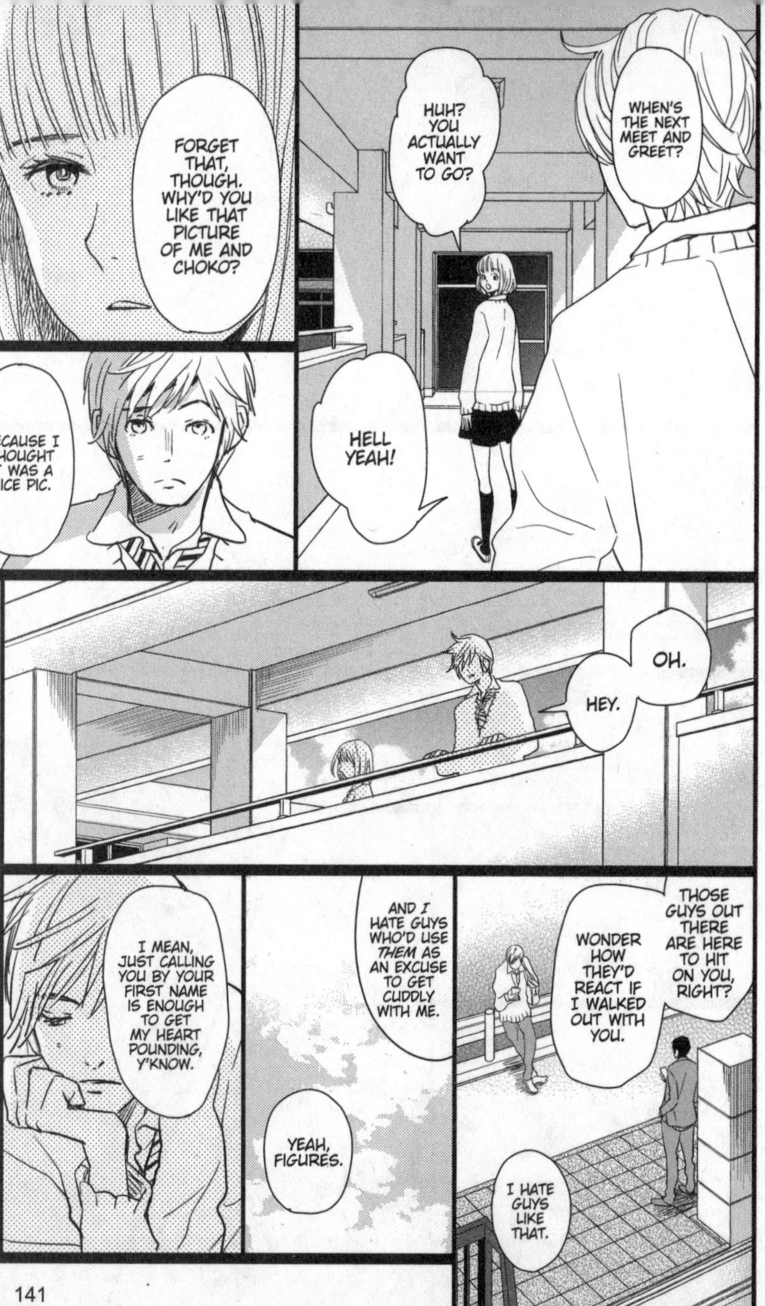
WHEN'S THE NEXT MEET AND GREET?
HUH? YOU ACTUALLY WANT TO GO?
HELL YEAH!
FORGET THAT, THOUGH. WHY'D YOU LIKE THAT PICTURE OF ME AND CHOKO?
BECAUSE I THOUGHT IT WAS A NICE PIC.
OH.
HEY.
THOSE GUYS OUT THERE ARE HERE TO HIT ON YOU, RIGHT?
WONDER HOW THEY'D REACT IF I WALKED OUT WITH YOU.
I HATE GUYS LIKE THAT.
AND *I* HATE GUYS WHO'D USE *THEM* AS AN EXCUSE TO GET CUDDLY WITH ME.
YEAH, FIGURES.
I MEAN, JUST CALLING YOU BY YOUR FIRST NAME IS ENOUGH TO GET MY HEART POUNDING, Y'KNOW.

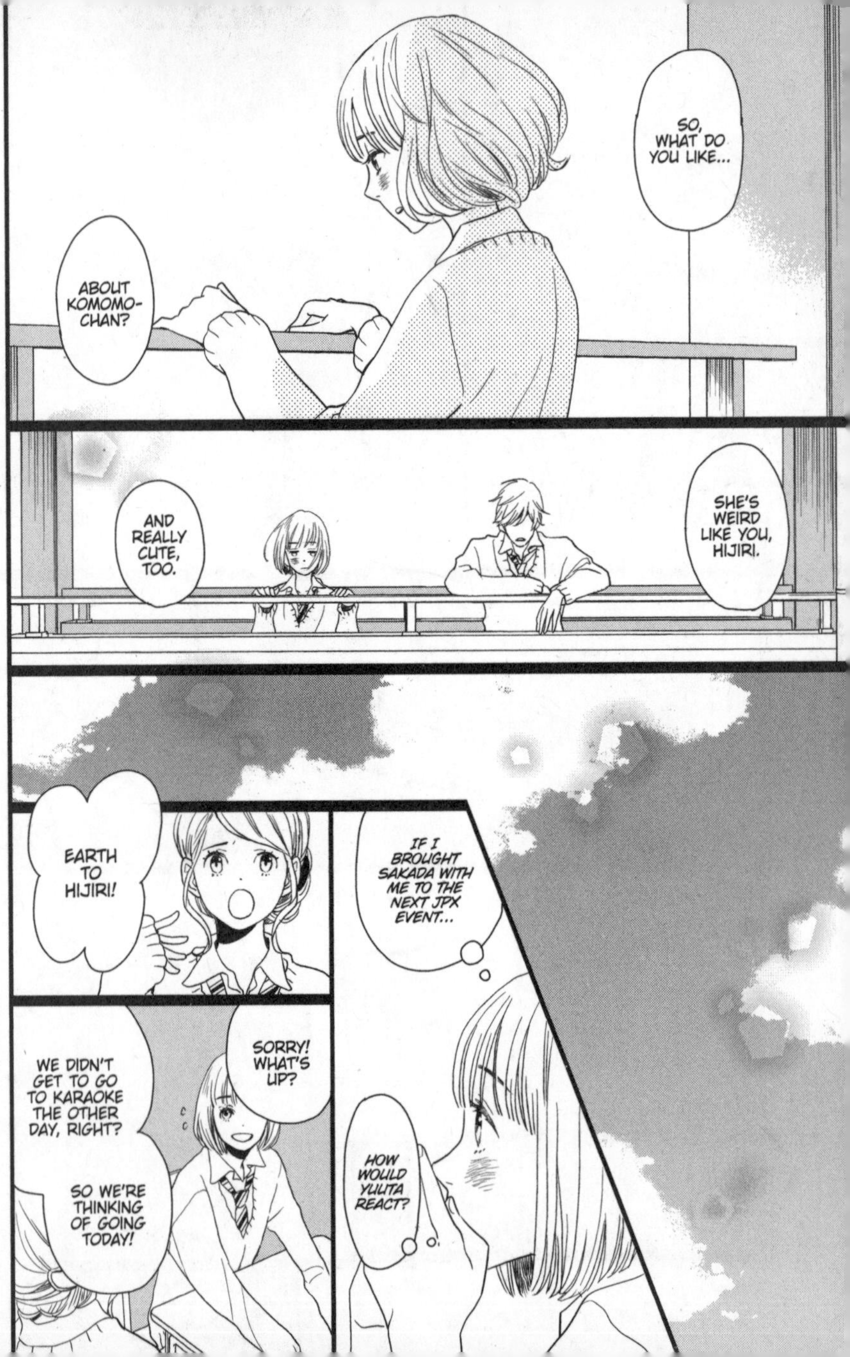
SO, WHAT DO YOU LIKE...
ABOUT KOMOMO-CHAN?
SHE'S WEIRD LIKE YOU, HIJIRI.
AND REALLY CUTE, TOO.
IF I BROUGHT SAKADA WITH ME TO THE NEXT JPX EVENT...
HOW WOULD YUUTA REACT?
EARTH TO HIJIRI!
SORRY! WHAT'S UP?
WE DIDN'T GET TO GO TO KARAOKE THE OTHER DAY, RIGHT?
SO WE'RE THINKING OF GOING TODAY!

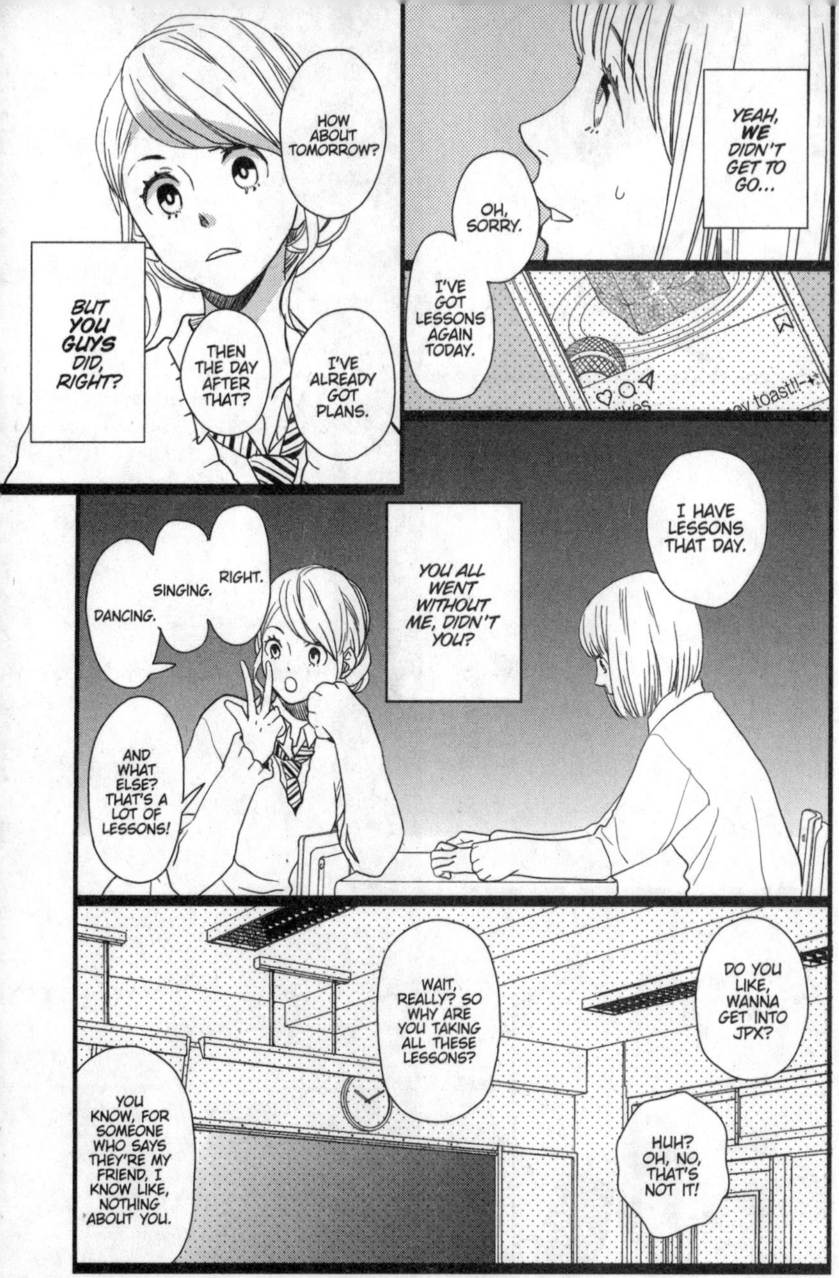
YEAH, WE DIDN'T GET TO GO...
OH, SORRY.
I'VE GOT LESSONS AGAIN TODAY.
HOW ABOUT TOMORROW?
I'VE ALREADY GOT PLANS.
THEN THE DAY AFTER THAT?
BUT YOU GUYS DID, RIGHT?
I HAVE LESSONS THAT DAY.
YOU ALL WENT WITHOUT ME, DIDN'T YOU?
RIGHT. SINGING. DANCING.
AND WHAT ELSE? THAT'S A LOT OF LESSONS!
DO YOU LIKE, WANNA GET INTO JPX?
HUH? OH, NO, THAT'S NOT IT!
WAIT, REALLY? SO WHY ARE YOU TAKING ALL THESE LESSONS?
YOU KNOW, FOR SOMEONE WHO SAYS THEY'RE MY FRIEND, I KNOW LIKE, NOTHING ABOUT YOU.

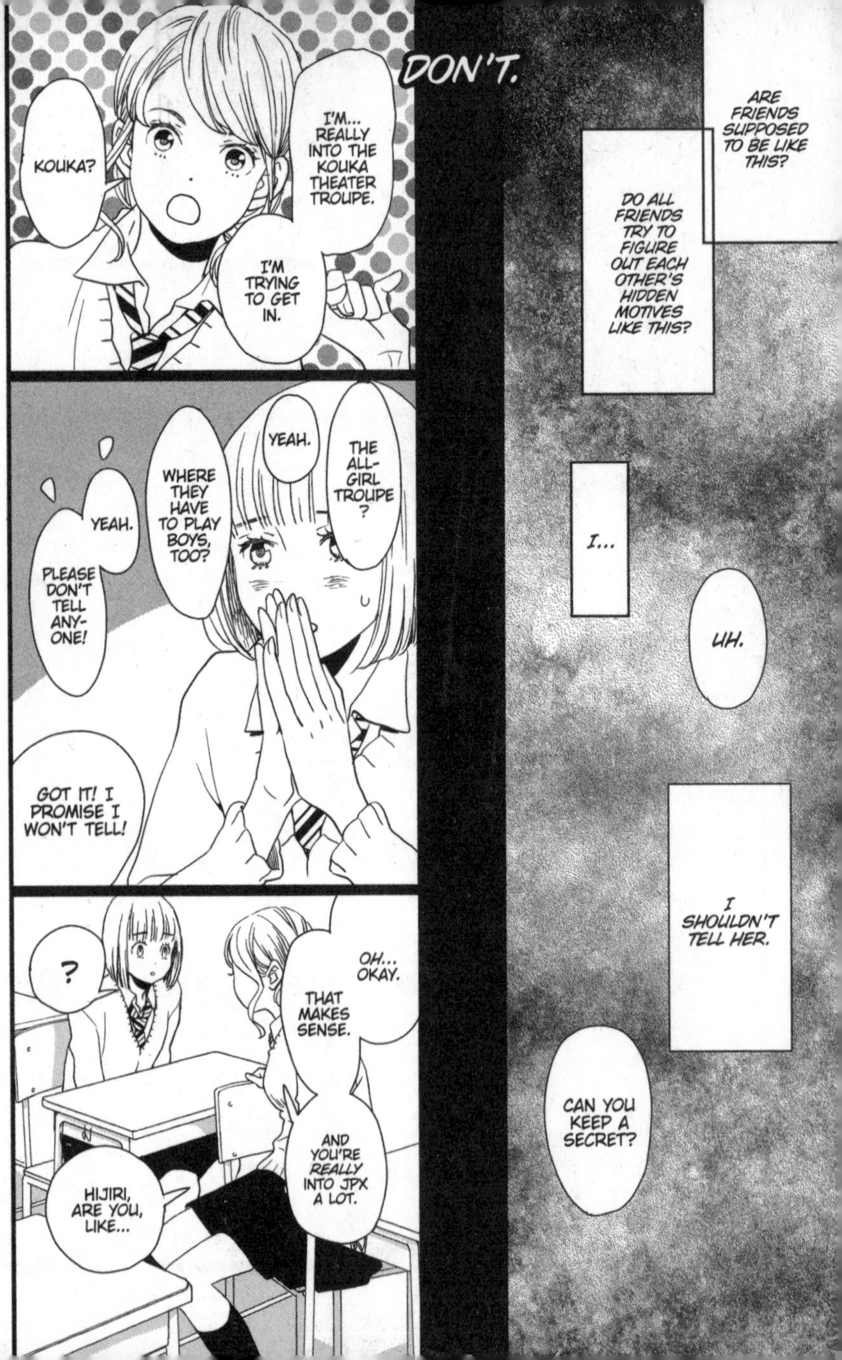
DON'T.
ARE FRIENDS SUPPOSED TO BE LIKE THIS?
DO ALL FRIENDS TRY TO FIGURE OUT EACH OTHER'S HIDDEN MOTIVES LIKE THIS?
I...
UH.
I SHOULDN'T TELL HER.
CAN YOU KEEP A SECRET?
I'M... REALLY INTO THE KOUKA THEATER TROUPE.
KOUKA?
I'M TRYING TO GET IN.
THE ALL-GIRL TROUPE?
YEAH.
WHERE THEY HAVE TO PLAY BOYS, TOO?
YEAH.
PLEASE DON'T TELL ANY-ONE!
GOT IT! I PROMISE I WON'T TELL!
OH... OKAY.
THAT MAKES SENSE.
?
AND YOU'RE REALLY INTO JPX A LOT.
HIJIRI, ARE YOU, LIKE...

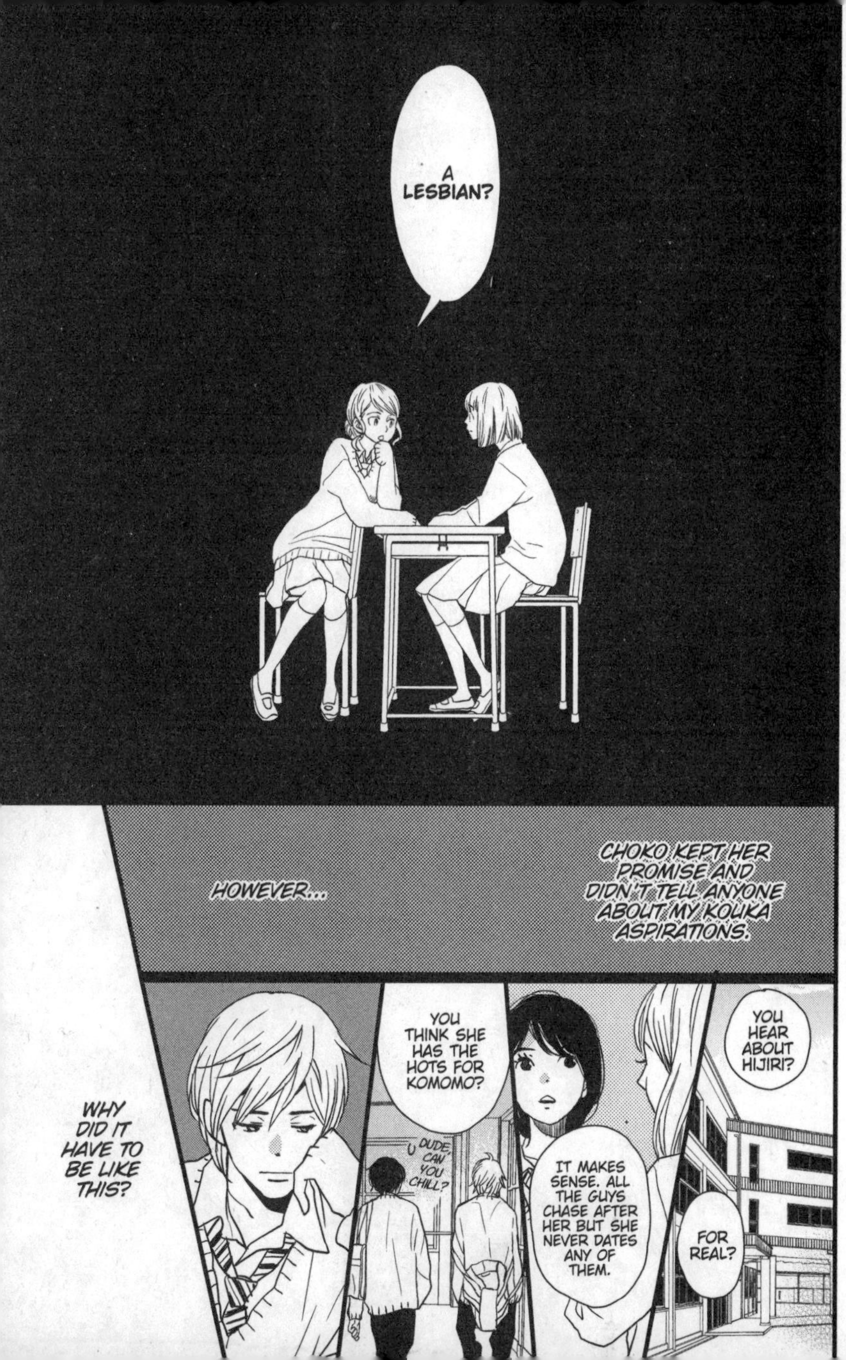
A LESBIAN?
CHOKO KEPT HER PROMISE AND DIDN'T TELL ANYONE ABOUT MY KOUKA ASPIRATIONS.
HOWEVER...
YOU HEAR ABOUT HIJIRI?
FOR REAL?
IT MAKES SENSE. ALL THE GUYS CHASE AFTER HER BUT SHE NEVER DATES ANY OF THEM.
YOU THINK SHE HAS THE HOTS FOR KOMOMO?
DUDE, CAN YOU CHILL?
WHY DID IT HAVE TO BE LIKE THIS?

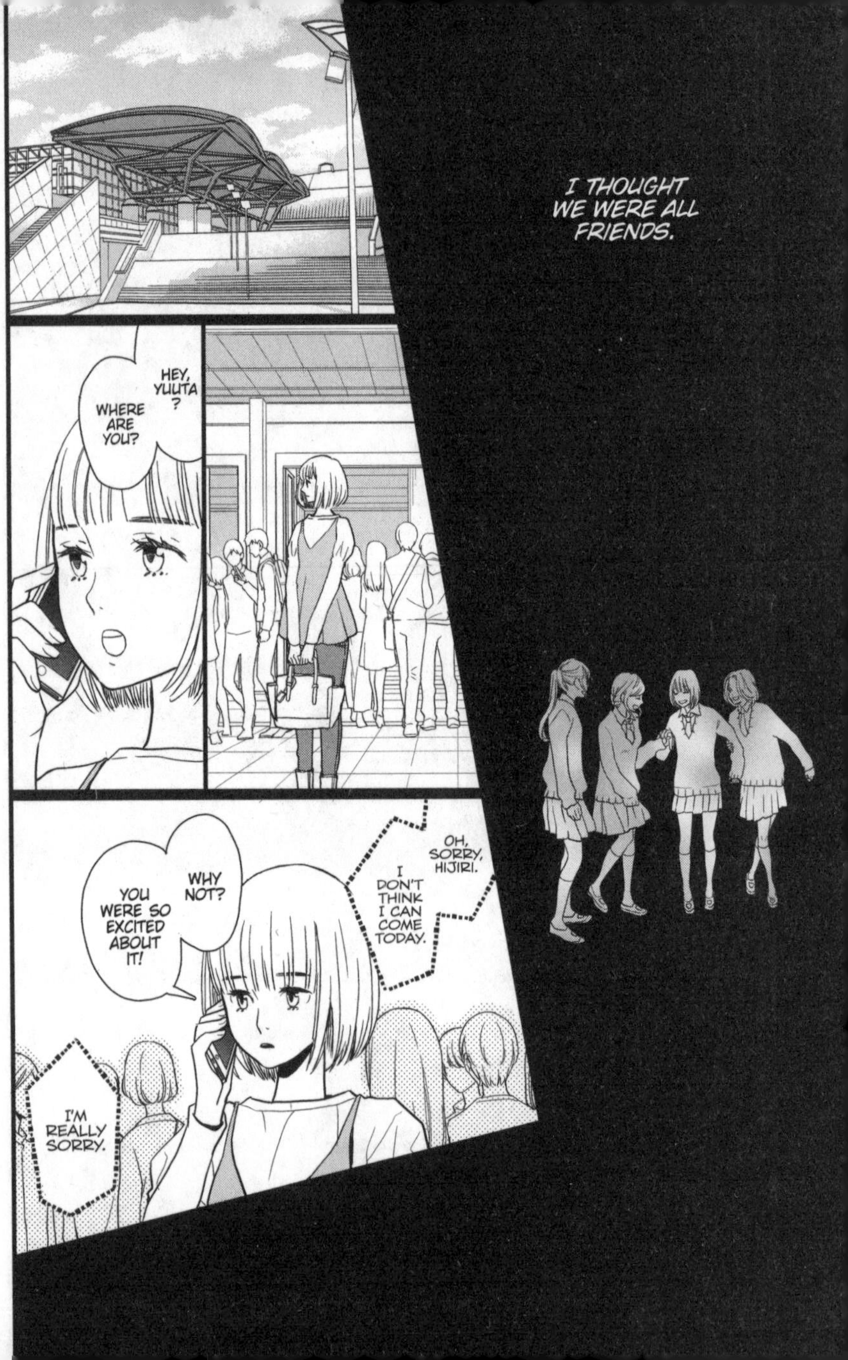
I THOUGHT WE WERE ALL FRIENDS.
HEY, YUUTA?
WHERE ARE YOU?
OH, SORRY, HIJIRI.
I DON'T THINK I CAN COME TODAY.
WHY NOT?
YOU WERE SO EXCITED ABOUT IT!
I'M REALLY SORRY.

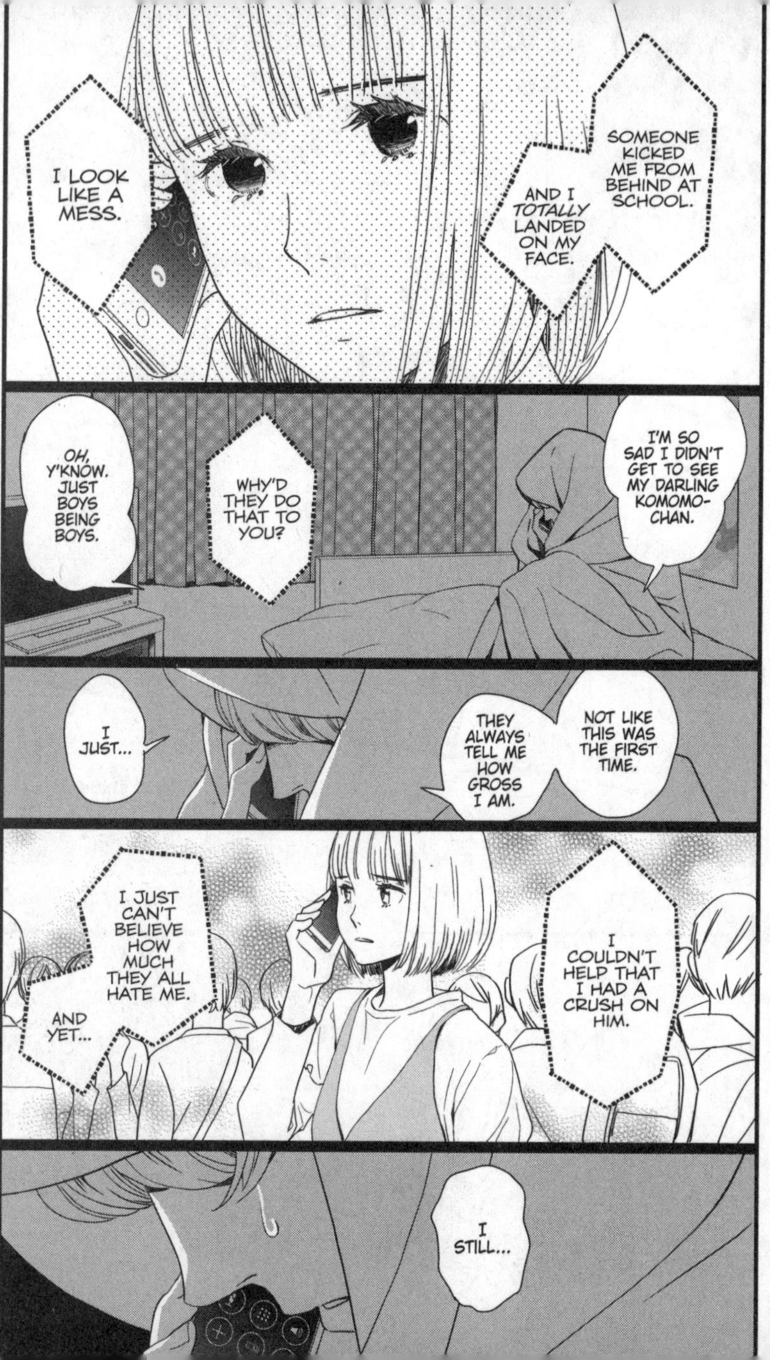
SOMEONE KICKED ME FROM BEHIND AT SCHOOL.
AND I *TOTALLY* LANDED ON MY FACE.
I LOOK LIKE A MESS.
I'M SO SAD I DIDN'T GET TO SEE MY DARLING KOMOMO-CHAN.
WHY'D THEY DO THAT TO YOU?
OH, Y'KNOW. JUST BOYS BEING BOYS.
NOT LIKE THIS WAS THE FIRST TIME.
THEY ALWAYS TELL ME HOW GROSS I AM.
I JUST...
I COULDN'T HELP THAT I HAD A CRUSH ON HIM.
I JUST CAN'T BELIEVE HOW MUCH THEY ALL HATE ME.
AND YET...
I STILL...

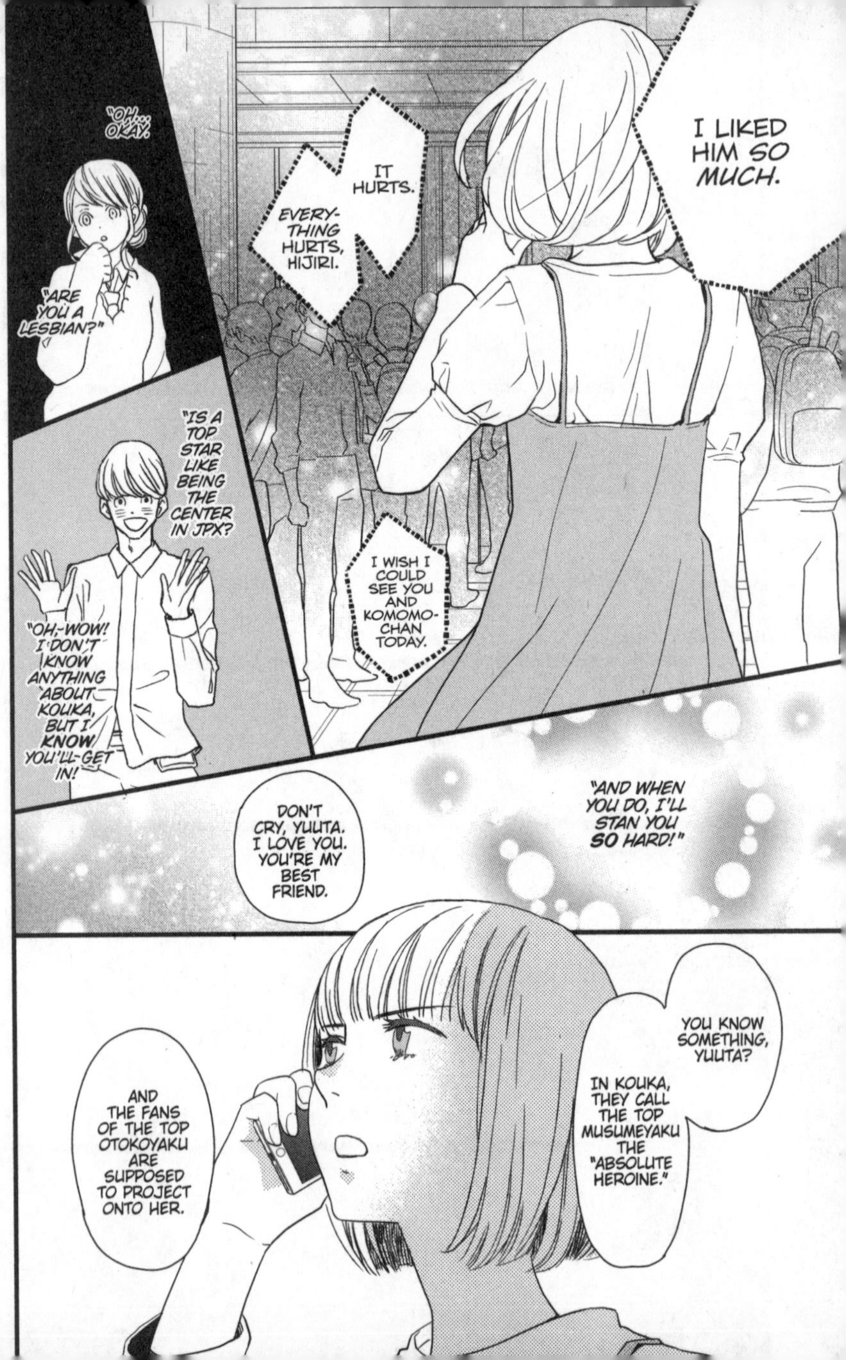
I LIKED HIM SO MUCH.
IT HURTS.
EVERYTHING HURTS, HIJIRI.
I WISH I COULD SEE YOU AND KOMOMO-CHAN TODAY.
"OH... OKAY."
"ARE YOU A LESBIAN?"
"IS A TOP STAR LIKE BEING THE CENTER IN JPX?
"OH, WOW! I DON'T KNOW ANYTHING ABOUT KOUKA, BUT I KNOW YOU'LL GET IN!
"AND WHEN YOU DO, I'LL STAN YOU SO HARD!"
DON'T CRY, YUUTA. I LOVE YOU. YOU'RE MY BEST FRIEND.
YOU KNOW SOMETHING, YUUTA?
IN KOUKA, THEY CALL THE TOP MUSUMEYAKU THE "ABSOLUTE HEROINE."
AND THE FANS OF THE TOP OTOKOYAKU ARE SUPPOSED TO PROJECT ONTO HER.

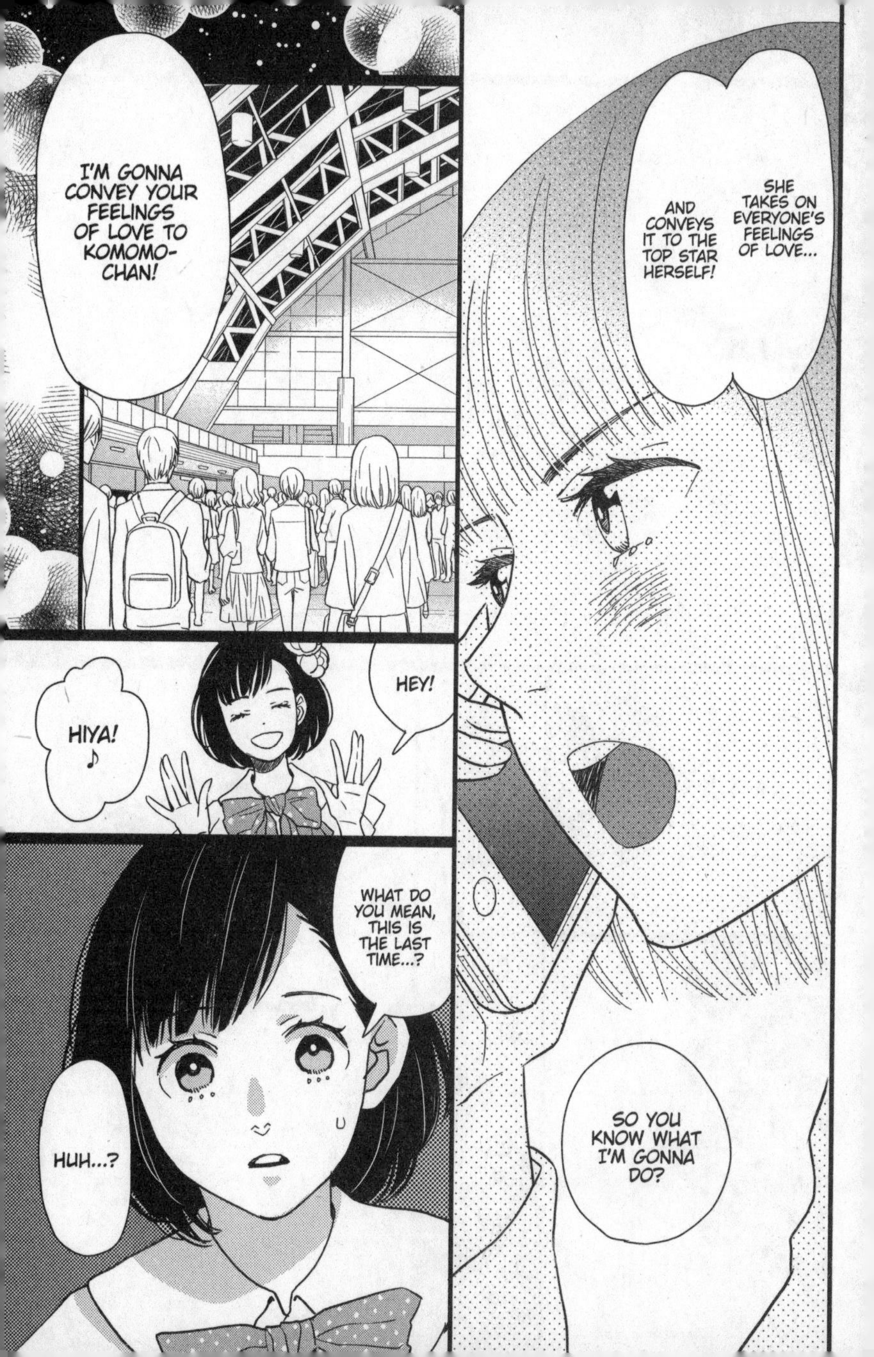
SHE TAKES ON EVERYONE'S FEELINGS OF LOVE...
AND CONVEYS IT TO THE TOP STAR HERSELF!
SO YOU KNOW WHAT I'M GONNA DO?
I'M GONNA CONVEY YOUR FEELINGS OF LOVE TO KOMOMO-CHAN!
HEY!
HIYA! ♪
WHAT DO YOU MEAN, THIS IS THE LAST TIME...?
HUH...?

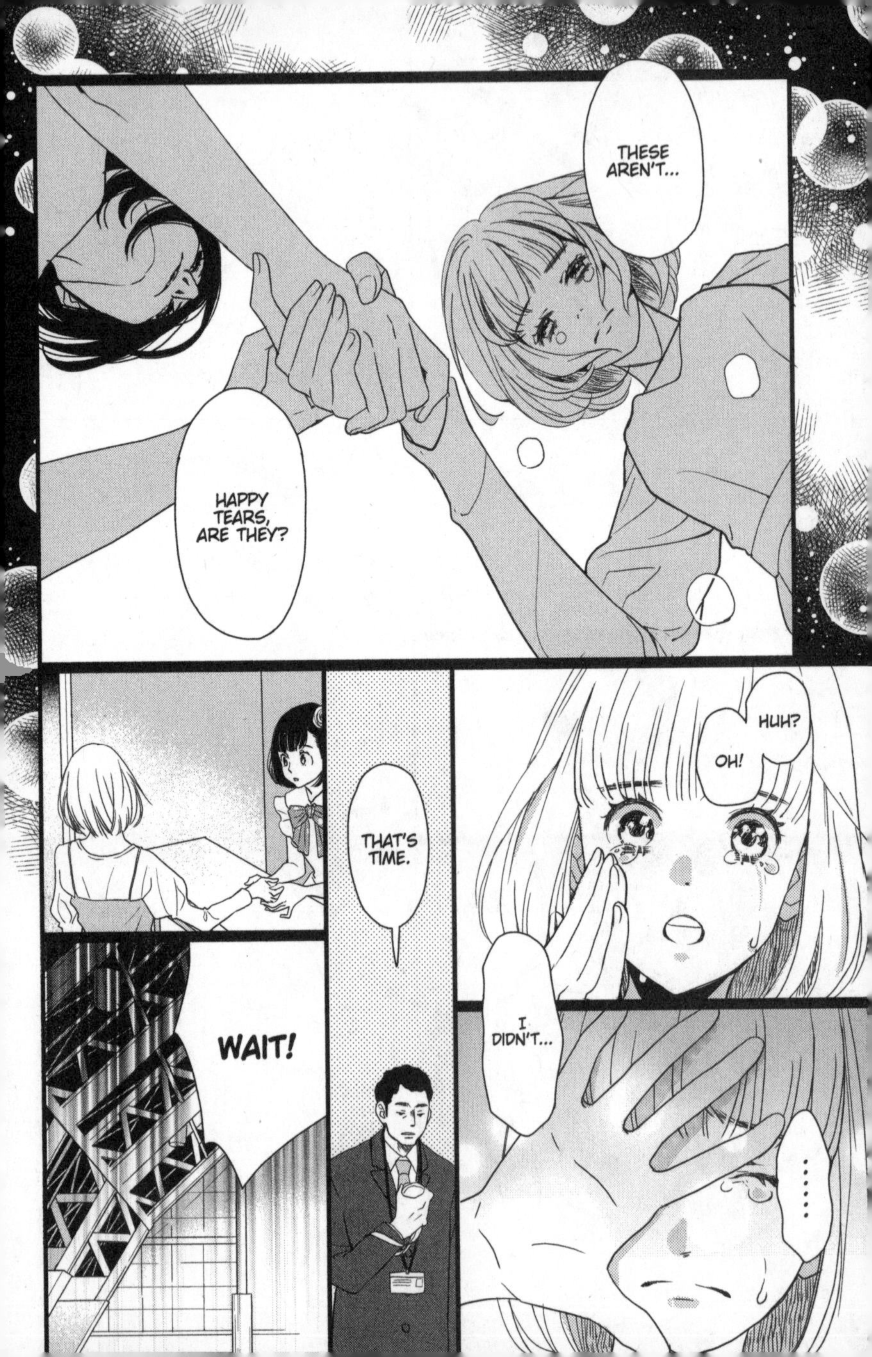
THESE AREN'T...
HAPPY TEARS, ARE THEY?
HUH? OH!
I DIDN'T...
......
THAT'S TIME.
WAIT!

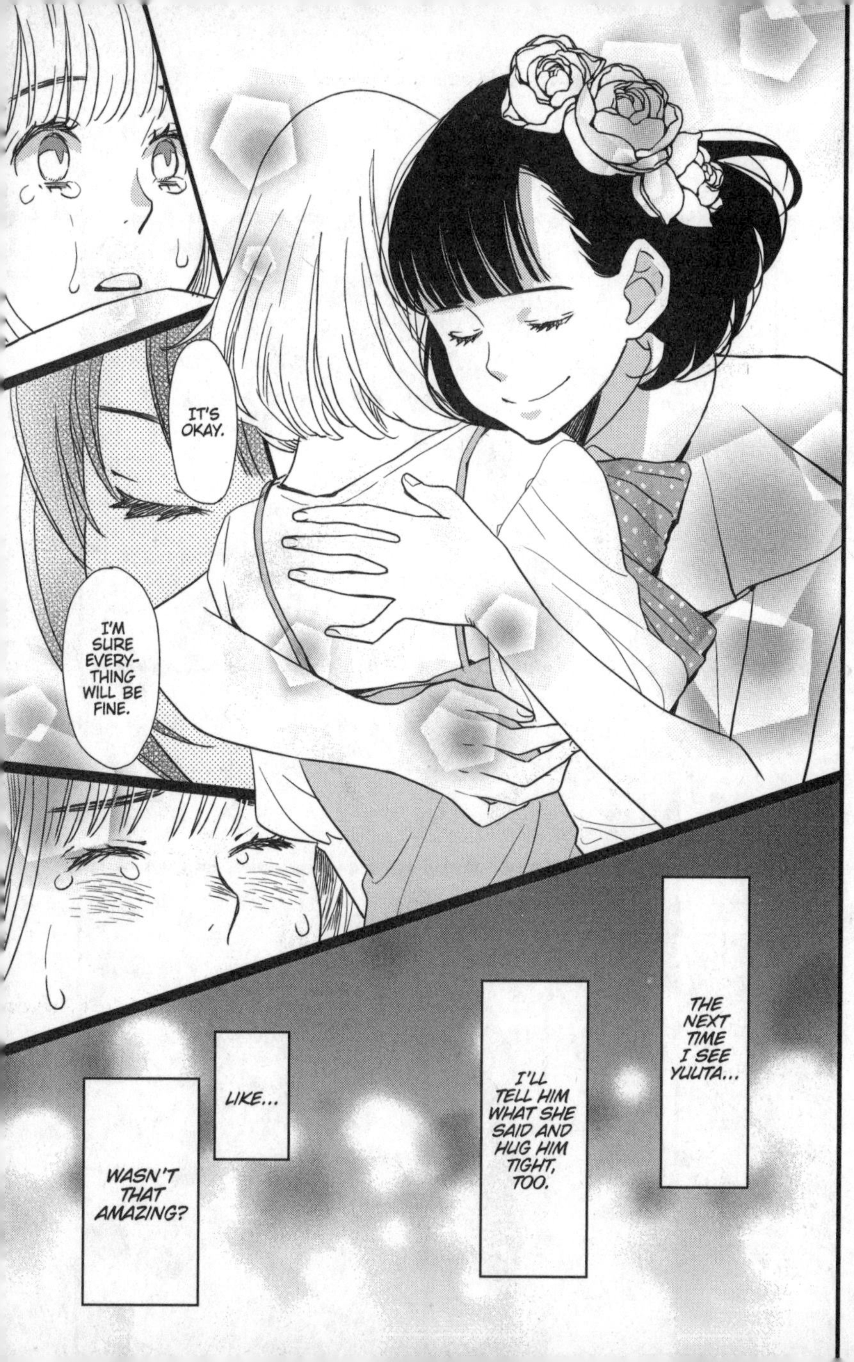
IT'S OKAY.
I'M SURE EVERYTHING WILL BE FINE.
THE NEXT TIME I SEE YUUTA...
I'LL TELL HIM WHAT SHE SAID AND HUG HIM TIGHT, TOO.
LIKE...
WASN'T THAT AMAZING?

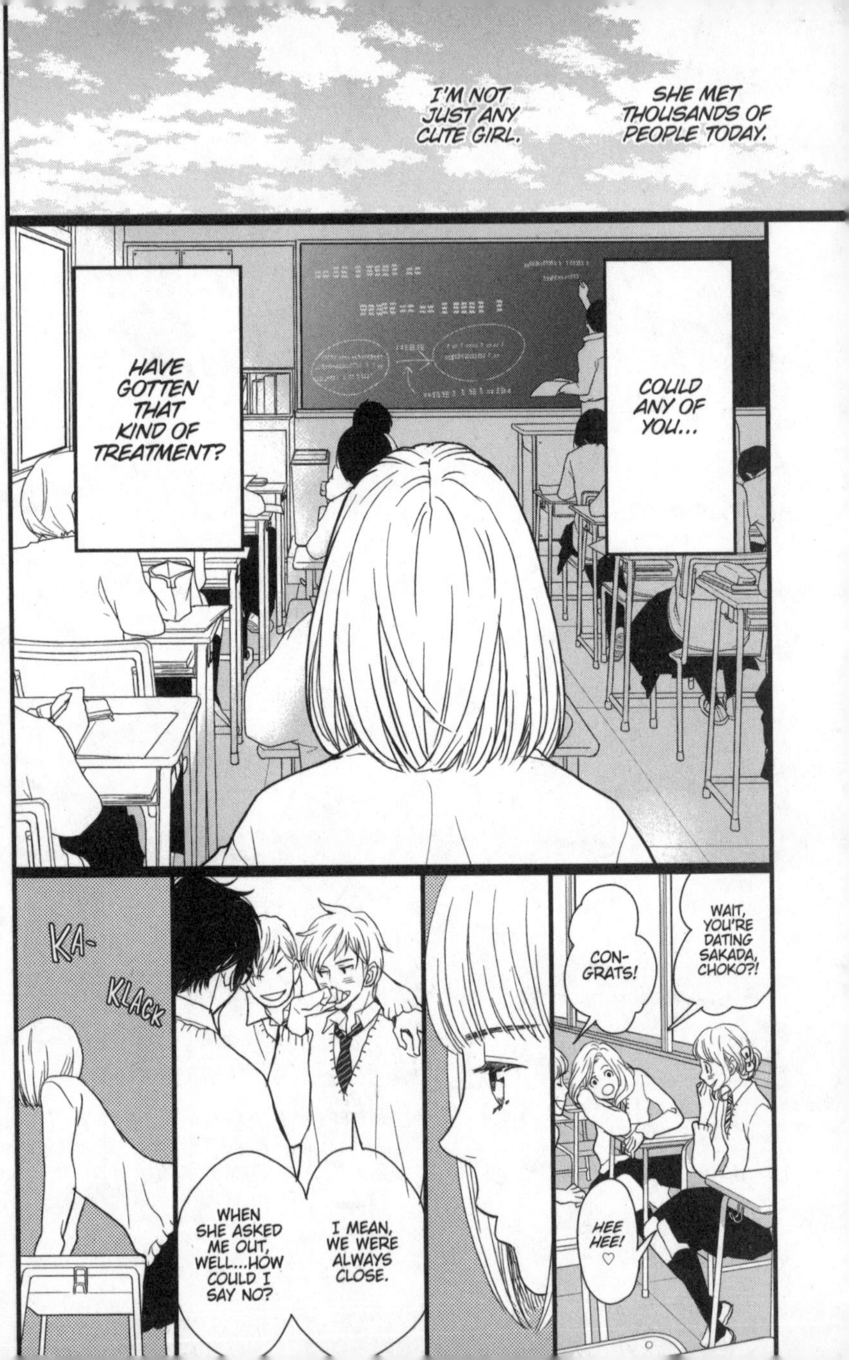
SHE MET THOUSANDS OF PEOPLE TODAY.
I'M NOT JUST ANY CUTE GIRL.
COULD ANY OF YOU...
HAVE GOTTEN THAT KIND OF TREATMENT?
WAIT, YOU'RE DATING SAKADA, CHOKO?!
CON-GRATS!
HEE HEE! ♡
I MEAN, WE WERE ALWAYS CLOSE.
WHEN SHE ASKED ME OUT, WELL...HOW COULD I SAY NO?
KA-KLACK

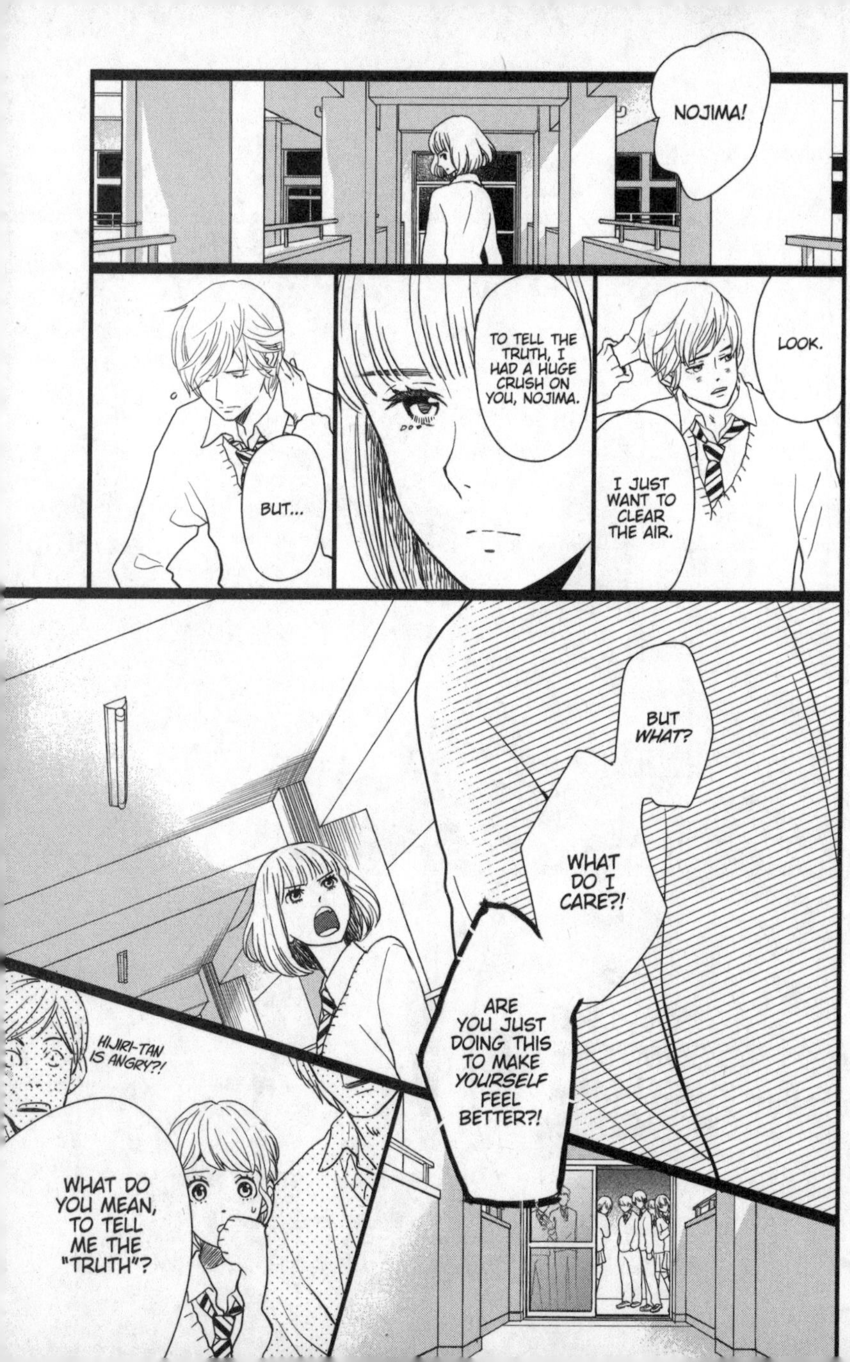
NOJIMA!
LOOK.
I JUST WANT TO CLEAR THE AIR.
TO TELL THE TRUTH, I HAD A HUGE CRUSH ON YOU, NOJIMA.
BUT...
BUT *WHAT?*
WHAT DO I CARE?!
ARE YOU JUST DOING THIS TO MAKE *YOURSELF* FEEL BETTER?!
HIJIRI-TAN IS ANGRY?!
WHAT DO YOU MEAN, TO TELL ME THE "TRUTH"?

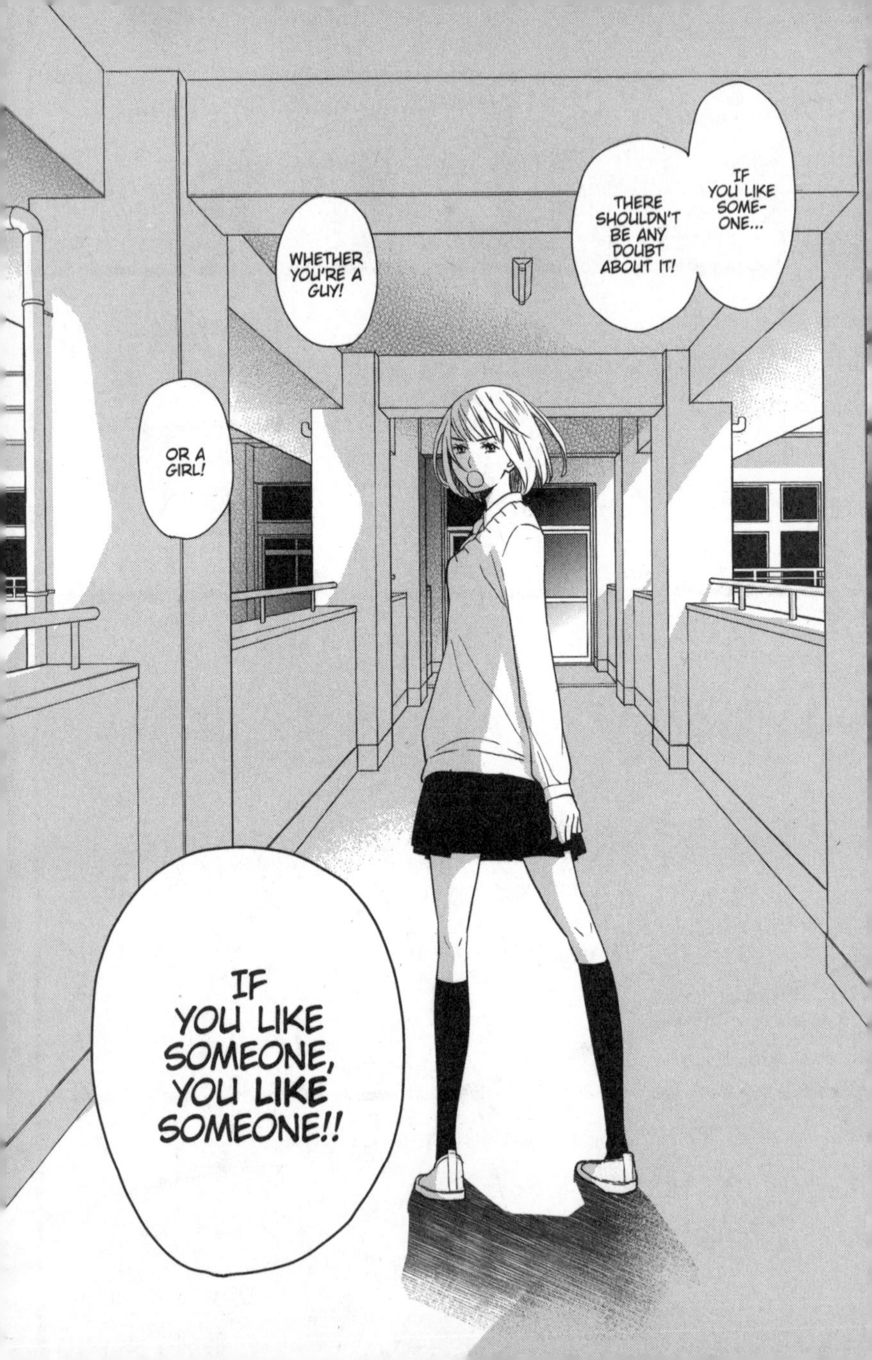
IF YOU LIKE SOME-ONE...
THERE SHOULDN'T BE ANY DOUBT ABOUT IT!
WHETHER YOU'RE A GUY!
OR A GIRL!
IF YOU LIKE SOMEONE, YOU LIKE SOMEONE!!

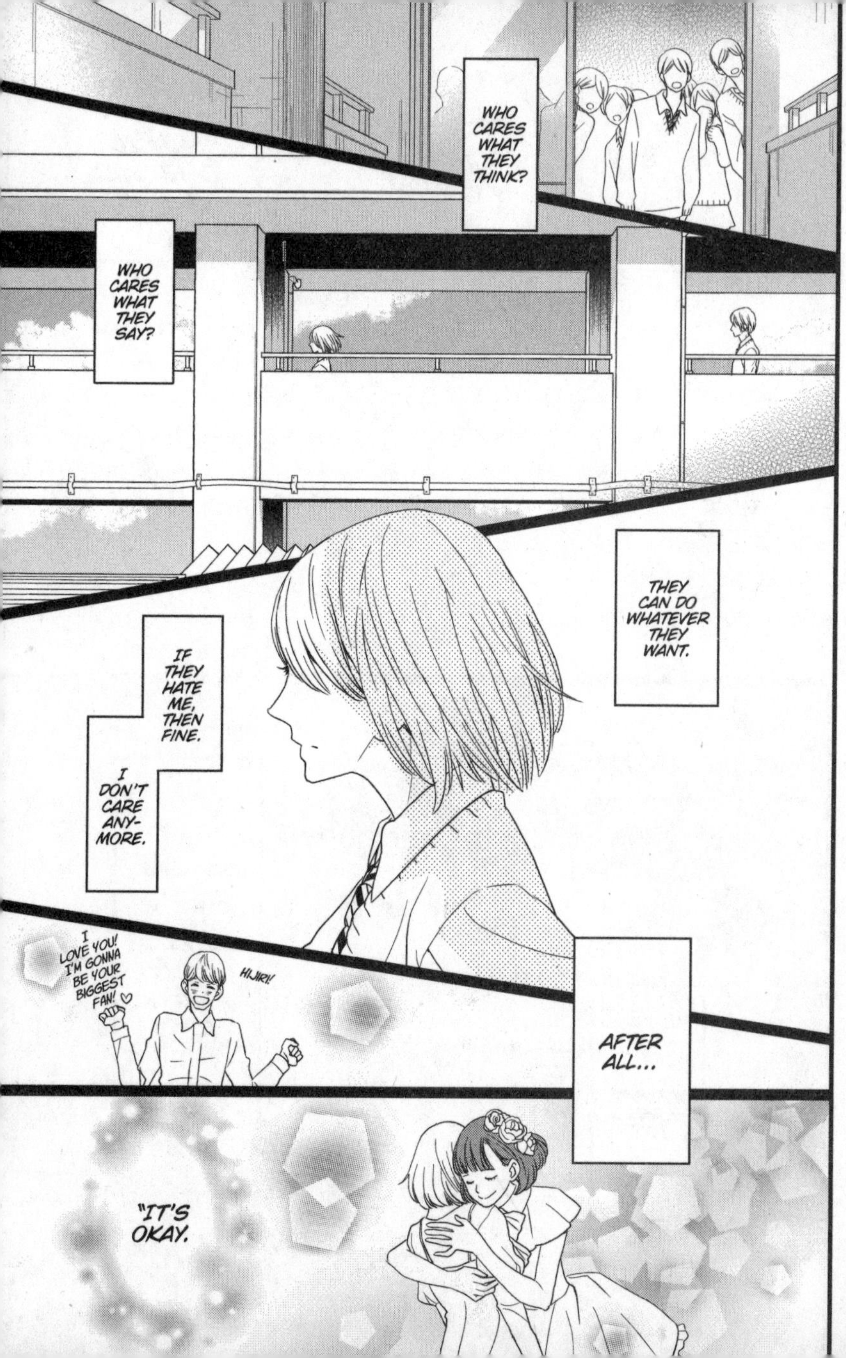
WHO CARES WHAT THEY THINK?
WHO CARES WHAT THEY SAY?
THEY CAN DO WHATEVER THEY WANT.
IF THEY HATE ME, THEN FINE.
I DON'T CARE ANY-MORE.
AFTER ALL...
HIJIRI!
I LOVE YOU! I'M GONNA BE YOUR BIGGEST FAN! ♡
"IT'S OKAY.

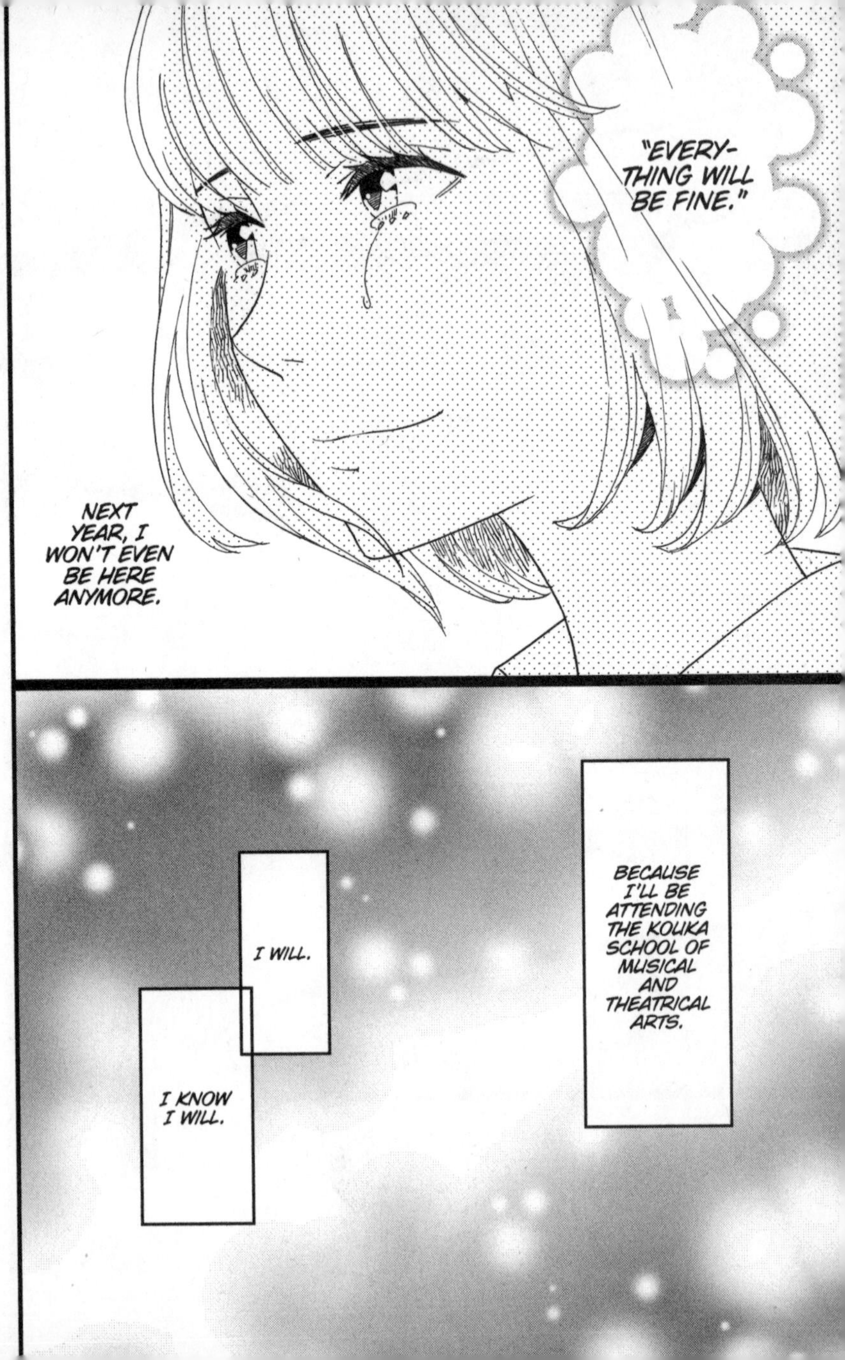
"EVERY-THING WILL BE FINE."
NEXT YEAR, I WON'T EVEN BE HERE ANYMORE.
BECAUSE I'LL BE ATTENDING THE KOUKA SCHOOL OF MUSICAL AND THEATRICAL ARTS.
I WILL.
I KNOW I WILL.

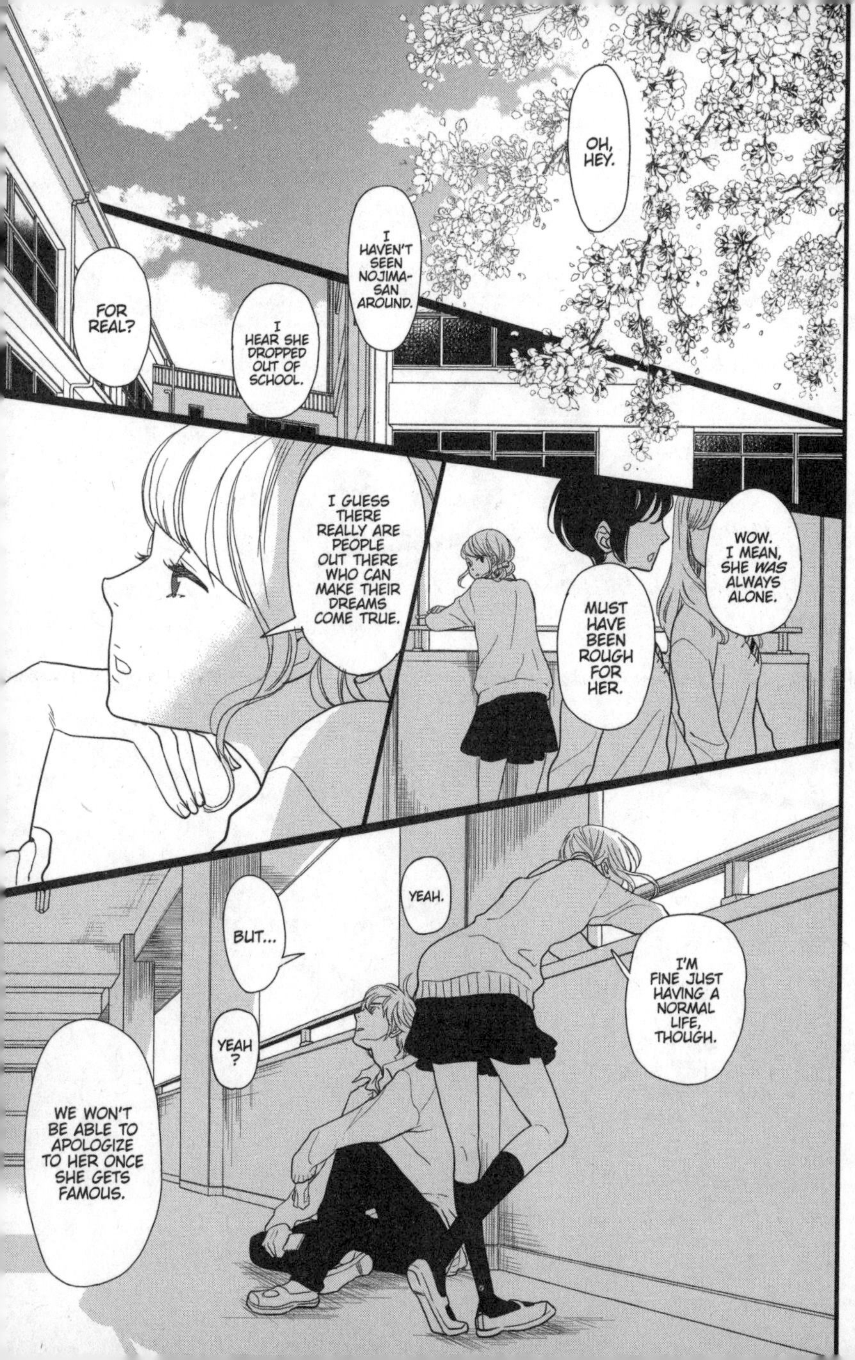
OH, HEY.
I HAVEN'T SEEN NOJIMA-SAN AROUND.
I HEAR SHE DROPPED OUT OF SCHOOL.
FOR REAL?
WOW. I MEAN, SHE WAS ALWAYS ALONE.
MUST HAVE BEEN ROUGH FOR HER.
I GUESS THERE REALLY ARE PEOPLE OUT THERE WHO CAN MAKE THEIR DREAMS COME TRUE.
I'M FINE JUST HAVING A NORMAL LIFE, THOUGH.
YEAH.
BUT...
YEAH?
WE WON'T BE ABLE TO APOLOGIZE TO HER ONCE SHE GETS FAMOUS.

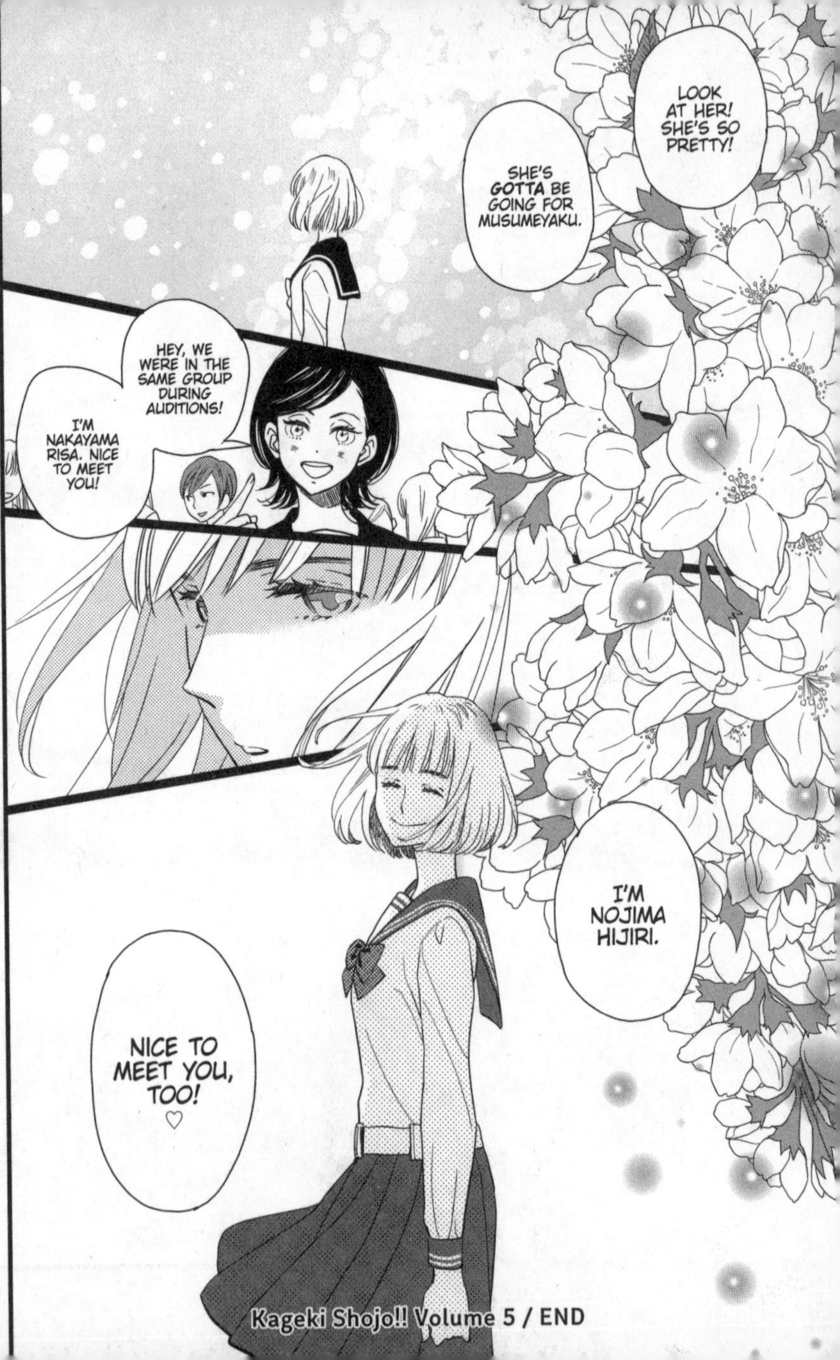
LOOK AT HER! SHE'S SO PRETTY!
SHE'S GOTTA BE GOING FOR MUSUMEYAKU.
HEY, WE WERE IN THE SAME GROUP DURING AUDITIONS!
I'M NAKAYAMA RISA. NICE TO MEET YOU!
I'M NOJIMA HIJIRI.
NICE TO MEET YOU, TOO! ♡

Kageki Shojo!! Volume 5 / END

SEVEN SEAS ENTERTAINMENT PRESENTS

KAGEKI SHOJO!!★

story and art by **KUMIKO SAIKI**   **VOLUME 5**

TRANSLATION
Katrina Leonoudakis

LETTERING
Aila Nagamine

COVER DESIGN
H. Qi

LOGO DESIGN
Courtney Williams

PROOFREADER
Rebecca Schneidereit
B. Lillian Martin

SENIOR EDITOR
Shannon Fay

PRODUCTION DESIGNER
Christina McKenzie

PRODUCTION MANAGER
Lissa Pattillo

PREPRESS TECHNICIAN
Melanie Ujimori

PRINT MANAGER
Rhiannon Rasmussen-Silverstein

EDITOR-IN-CHIEF
Julie Davis

ASSOCIATE PUBLISHER
Adam Arnold

PUBLISHER
Jason DeAngelis

ISBN: 978-1-63858-188-8
Printed in Canada
First Printing: April 2022
10 9 8 7 6 5 4 3 2 1

READING DIRECTIONS

This book reads from *right to left*,
Japanese style. If this is your first time
reading manga, you start reading from
the top right panel on each page and
take it from there. If you get lost, just
follow the numbered diagram here.
It may seem backwards at first,
but you'll get the hang of it! Have fun!!

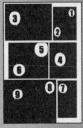

Follow us online: www.SevenSeasEntertainment.com

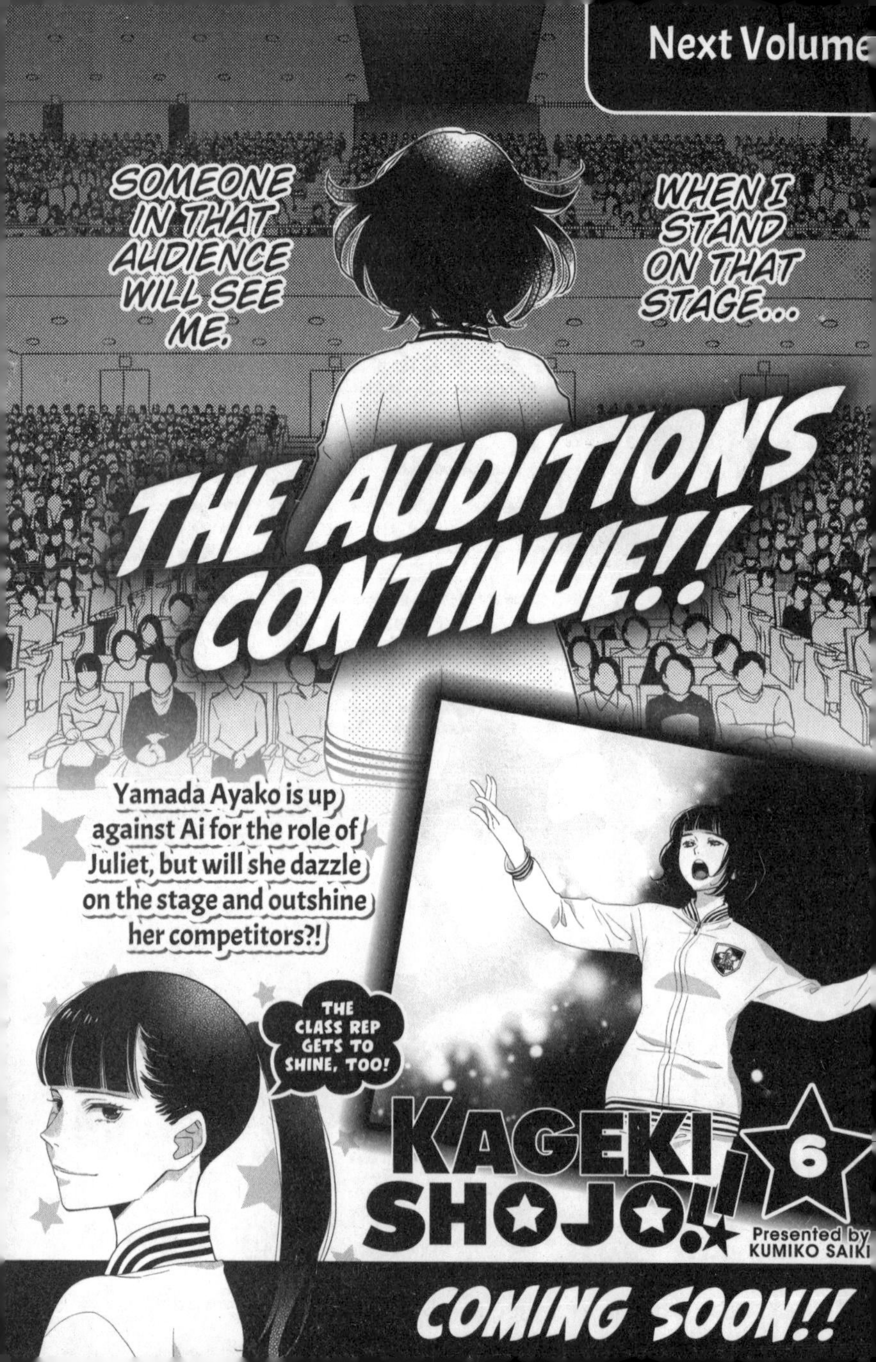

Next Volume
WHEN I STAND ON THAT STAGE...
SOMEONE IN THAT AUDIENCE WILL SEE ME.
THE AUDITIONS CONTINUE!!
Yamada Ayako is up against Ai for the role of Juliet, but will she dazzle on the stage and outshine her competitors?!
THE CLASS REP GETS TO SHINE, TOO!
KAGEKI SHOJO!! 6
Presented by KUMIKO SAIKI
COMING SOON!!